Out of the Ruins:
The Emergence of Radical
Informal Learning Spaces

Edited by Robert H. Haworth & John M. Elmore

Out of the Ruins: The Emergence of Radical Informal Learning Spaces
Edited by Robert H. Haworth & John M. Elmore
© 2017 PM Press
All rights reserved.

ISBN: 978-1-62963-239-1
Library of Congress Control Number: 2016948145

Cover: John Yates / www.stealworks.com
Interior design by briandesign

10 9 8 7 6 5 4 3 2 1

PM Press
PO Box 23912
Oakland, CA 94623
www.pmpress.org

Printed in the USA by the Employee Owners of Thomson-Shore in Dexter, Michigan.
www.thomsonshore.com

CONTENTS

INTRODUCTION   Thoughts on Radical Informal Learning Spaces   1
Robert H. Haworth

Section 1   Critiques of Education

CHAPTER 1   Miseducation and the Authoritarian Mind   16
John M. Elmore

CHAPTER 2   Don't Act, Just Think!   35
David Gabbard

Section 2   Constructing Theoretical Frameworks for Educational Praxis

CHAPTER 3   From the Unlearned Un-man to a Pedagogy without Moulding: Stirner, Consciousness-Raising, and the Production of Difference   56
Rhiannon Firth and Andrew Robinson

CHAPTER 4   Creating Transformative Anarchist-Geographic Learning Spaces   74
Farhang Rouhani

CHAPTER 5   The Wretched of the Network Society: Techno-Education and Colonization of the Digital   86
Petar Jandrić and Ana Kuzmanić

Section 3   **The Emergence of Radical Informal Learning Spaces "Using the Institutional Space without Being *of* the Institution"**

CHAPTER 6   What Do We Mean When We Say "Democracy"? Learning towards a Common Future through Popular Higher Education   106
Sarah Amsler

CHAPTER 7   The Space Project: Creating Cracks within, against, and beyond Academic-Capitalism   126
Andre Pusey

CHAPTER 8   Anarchists against (and within) the Edu-Factory: The Critical Criminology Working Group   139
Jeff Shantz

CHAPTER 9   Teaching Anarchism by Practicing Anarchy: Reflections on Facilitating the Student-Creation of a College Course   153
Dana Williams

Section 4   **Of the Streets and the Coming Educational Communities**

CHAPTER 10   Toward an Anti- and Alter-University: Thriving in the Mess of Studying, Organizing, and Relating with ExCo of the Twin Cities   174
Erin Dyke and Eli Meyerhoff

CHAPTER 11   What Is Horizontal Pedagogy? A Discussion on Dandelions   195
Authors: David I. Backer, Matthew Bissen, Jacques Laroche, Aleksandra Perisic, and Jason Wozniak.
Participants: Christopher Casuccio ("Winter"), Zane D.R. Mackin, Joe North, and Chelsea Szendi Schieder.

CHAPTER 12   Street Theory: Grassroots Activist Interventions in Regimes of Knowledge   223
Sandra Jeppesen and Joanna Adamiak

CHAPTER 13   Theory Meet Practice: Evolving Ideas and Actions in Anarchist Free Schools   245
Jeff Shantz

CONTRIBUTORS   261

INDEX   266

Thoughts on Radical Informal Learning Spaces

Robert H. Haworth

For most of my life, I have gravitated toward reading, writing, listening, and acting outside of traditional lines. Although I have been educated to operate within the confines of our current structures and cultural norms, I look at how and what I have "learned" from quite a different perspective. In other words, my learning and my education are in stark contrast.

By the time I was ten, I knew I was in deep conflict between my learning, outside of school, and my education, within public schools. At that time, the Cold War was still a dominant debate within the United States. Although I was still in elementary school, I remember some of the drills and the films we saw that were supposed to scare us into submitting to particular U.S. policies and to demonize the Soviet Union and other places around the world that were not like us. On the other hand, I was beginning to explore and learn about contemporary political issues through a different lens, punk rock.

I had been introduced to punk early on. My older brother's bedroom always intrigued me. It was filled from floor to ceiling with the artwork (flyers, album inserts, etc.) of local and international bands that were attempting to construct a very different narrative of what was going on in the world. It was in my social studies classes where I was being educated to believe that Ronald Reagan was a heroic figure and Margaret Thatcher was the important sidekick. They were our leaders in protecting the population against communism and democratic socialism, all while opening up the world to "freedom" and "democracy" and the global marketplace.

On the flip side, punk provided me with a counter narrative to my formal education. For example, my brother had a foldout poster that was included in Crass's album *The Feeding of the 5000*. The poster was a collage that included

Reagan's face placed on a bodybuilder flexing his muscles, while Thatcher was shitting hotdogs and human skulls. As someone who was young and being introduced to the music, culture, and politics of punk, I didn't understand the nuances of what the artist, Gee Vaucher, was conveying. However, it produced a much larger shift in my learning—moving me to question how, and what, we were being taught in school and ultimately, who benefits, and who does not, from traditional and formal educational processes.

Another example of learning through punk was through reading zines. Zines were a way to disseminate information about different scenes, political movements and ideas, punk ethics, interviews with bands, and music reviews. As I mentioned in another essay (Haworth, 2010), some of these political interactions became intense and, at times, divisive, but they enabled us to see the complexities of punk and the diverse ways we interpreted our experiences. From a learning standpoint, punk has its problems and contradictions, but what I feel is important are the tensions that emerged within my own learning, particularly between how I was formally educated and how punk embraced a different way of knowing and interacting with the world. It is not that I believe everyone should go out and join a punk band, shout revolutionary slogans, or create a zine (although that would be cool), but it is important to point out that there are various learning spaces that resonate more with individuals and to question whether the statist educational institutions to which many are exposed have the capacity to create a more sustainable and critically conscious future.

Formal Education: Our Current Path
In a recent keynote address at the University of Colorado, Boulder, David Stovall (2011) noted, "There are really three paths young people are being forced to take in order to survive our current economic system—service sector employment, the military and prison. It is no doubt that this is what Giroux (2013) and others have referred to as the 'zero generation'—zero jobs, zero hope, zero possibilities, zero employment."

From an educational standpoint, the move to privatize, vocationalize, and credentialize (Brown, 2003; 2013) k–12 and higher education is not surprising. The massive commercial campaigns of for-profit universities bombard cable networks and local billboards to entice young adults to return to higher education. University of Phoenix is a perfect example, as they promise that a degree from them will lead to a choice of corporate jobs. There is quite a different story that is beginning to permeate the larger social narrative, particularly through the economic realities of students accumulating enormous amounts of debt, fraudulent for-profits extracting federal dollars from the public till, and the shrinkage of jobs within the corporate sector.

This is not a new phenomenon. The development of public education, particularly in the United States, has worked primarily in conjunction with the dominant social, political, economic, and cultural institutions to create a specific type of citizen/individual. Historically, Adam Smith believed that workers would need a particular education under the state in order to protect the economic system that exploited them. Spring (2006) argues: "Smith proposed educating workers to defend a state whose role is to protect an economic system that exploits those same workers. In other words, Smith's argument is that workers should be educated to defend their own exploitation." (p. 10)

Additionally, mainstream educators in the United States continue to champion Horace Mann's fight in the early nineteenth century for compulsory, tax-based, common schools for all citizens. What we don't discuss or even recognize is the "behind the scenes" concessions Mann and other preindustrial capitalists had made during the early part of the nineteenth century to make sure that public education created a particular type of citizenry and coincided with a particular economic order. Katz's (1971) research critiques Mann's intentions and the outcomes of the development of the common schools during that time:

> The crusade for educational reform led by Horace Mann . . . was not the simple, unambiguous good it had long been taken to be; the central aim of the movement was to establish more efficient mechanisms of social control, and its chief legacy was the principle that "education was something the better part of the community did to the others to make them orderly, moral, and tractable." (p. ix–x)

Beyond Mann's ideals and eloquent speeches and writings, which advocated for a tax-supported, compulsory education for white citizens, there were enormous compromises. In order for Mann to get wealthy businessmen and landowners to pay taxes for poor people to attend the common schools, they needed a guarantee that these schools would produce students with appropriate skills and mannerisms conducive to becoming loyal and obedient workers. Bowles and Gintis (1976) elaborate: "Mann's reforms had the intent of forestalling the development of class consciousness among the working people . . . preserving the legal and economic foundations of the society in which he had been raised" (p. 173).

Over the past century and half, Mann's work of developing an education system that would level the playing field for poor and working-class students has been embraced. Unfortunately, supporters of Mann's vision of public education in general, have not examined the ways in which these institutions have preserved an extremely oppressive order. In essence, over the past two centuries, the state and emerging capitalists have worked closely to advocate for public schools that are, as Foster (2011) describes, "less about education than a kind of behavioral modification, preparing the vast majority of students for a life of routinization and standardization, in which most will end up employed in essentially unskilled, dead-end jobs" (p. 2).

During the early twentieth century, public education not only continued to play a role in teaching poor and working-class youth to become more obedient and efficient workers, but also left teachers with little autonomy over their work. For example, in 1912, Joseph S. Taylor, district superintendent of schools in New York City stated:

> (1) The state as employer must cooperate with the teacher as employee, for the latter does not always understand the science of education; (2) the state provides experts who supervise the teacher, and suggest the processes that are most efficacious and economical; (3) the task system obtains in the school as well as in the shop, each grade being a measured quantity of work to be accomplished in a given term; (4) every teacher who accomplishes the task receives a bonus, not in money, but in the form of a rating which may have money value; (5) those who are unable to do the work are eliminated. (quoted in Callahan, 1962; p. 103)

When I show this quote to pre-service educators in my classes, they usually smile and shake their heads in agreement because of its similarity to their own experiences of control and scientific management in schools and the classroom. They see that the standardized curriculum is not only assessing their students but also "measuring and rating" the quantity of work they have accomplished.

From an anarchist perspective, the harsh realities and outcomes of these institutions were not surprising. Anarchists believe that state run institutions are inherently corrupt and have historically upheld the values of bureaucratic and hierarchical institutions. Voltairine de Cleyre (1909) argued that there are also certain persons she describes as "statesmen," whose interest in education is purely for the "formation of good citizens to support the State, and directs education in such channels as he thinks will produce these" (p. 322). She concludes that the statesman "is not interested in the actual work of schools, in the children as persons, but in the producing of a certain type of character to serve certain subsequent ends" (p. 322).

A few years earlier, Emma Goldman (1906) wrote an article entitled "The Child and its enemies" that gives a scathing critique of educational practices. One of her main criticisms is that teachers and schools drive children to "become foreign to themselves and to each other." She highlights that "systems of education are being arranged into files, classified and numbered. . . . Instructors and teachers, with dead souls, operate with dead values. Quantity is forced to take the place of quality. The consequences thereof are inevitable" (p. 3).

In contemporary terms, Goldman's remarks on education are still a haunting reality. It's evident that education is still reduced to quantifiable outcomes and is governed by what Au (2011) argues is a new form of Taylorism. This new form of education controls the curriculum, teaching and ultimately, the learning that goes on in the classroom. Therefore, administrators and political authorities make decisions and manage what is happening at all levels of the educational process, thus forcing teachers to ultimately teach to the test and uphold a centralized and narrow subject matter and curriculum. Au argues, "Based upon research evidence from the modern day era of high-stakes testing in US public education, the fundamental logics guiding scientific management have resurfaced 100 years later, as teachers' classroom practices are increasingly standardized by high-stakes testing and scripted curriculum" (p. 25).

Let's not shy away from the important understanding that education has become a commodity. It is now a multi-billion-dollar industry that drives many corporations to shift their focus to the buying and selling of curriculum and assessable outcomes and thus forces public funding of public education over to the private sector. Even Diane Ravitch (2010), who once believed that school choice and standards could "co-exist," has become a sharp critic of the move to privatize education. Of course, state and corporate driven educational institutions have created extremely unhealthy environments for students and teachers. I say this not because of the quality of teachers, but more the institutions, curricula, and forced pedagogical practices that have been so destructive of any possibility of nurturing critical minds.

As I have highlighted above, I don't believe state driven education has ever been particularly open to developing free and creative imaginations. In fact, over the past three decades the social, political, economic, and cultural toxicity of public schools has increased. In the United States, we have seen a clear evolution from the publication of *A Nation at Risk* leading to the current Common Core State Standards Initiative across the country which has perpetuated hyper-standardization, testing, and accountability measures. This has led to teacher-, student-, and community-proofing educational practices and policies as well as cutting away any autonomy teachers may have had in the past, thus depriving students of opportunities to learn from critical and thoughtful individuals. Some have gone so far as to call this "a war on kids." Moreover, within this war on public institutions, the outcomes have been quite substantial, particularly regarding people imagining a world beyond our current mess. Graeber (2011) has described these systemic movements and relationships as a "war on the imagination." He states,

> In the terms I've been developing, what "the public," "the workforce," "consumers," "population" all have in common is that they are brought

into being by institutionalized frames of action that are inherently bureaucratic, and therefore, profoundly alienating. Voting booths, television screens, office cubicles, hospitals, the ritual that surrounds them—one might say these are the very machinery of alienation. They are the instruments through which the human imagination is smashed and shattered. (p. 115)

Graeber is not alone in articulating how our structures, in part, are destructive and diminish imagining a world outside these powerful systems and everyday practices. Haiven (2014) also describes the warped realities and normalizing nature of living under these conditions,

capitalism relies not only on the brutal repression of workers in factories and fields; it also relies on conscripting our imaginations. On a basic level, it relies on each of us imagining ourselves as essentially isolated, lonely, competitive economic agents. It relies on us imagining that the system is the natural expression of human nature, or that it is too powerful to be changed, or that no other systems could ever be desirable. (p. 7)

Graeber and Haiven make important arguments in that our institutions (I would add educational practices) uphold and reinforce a particular imagination: one that is restricted to thinking about particular political, economic, social, and cultural ideas and practices in society as stagnant and, yes, extremely lonely. In most cases, these institutions have no desire to support imagination outside of profiteering and consumerism. Our ability to imagine possibilities beyond the confines of market values, especially those thoughts and ideas based in possible futures outside our current practices is minimized or squashed.

Informal Learning: A Different Path?

Of course, it is a difficult task to create spaces where individuals can imagine different educational paths and processes. Does it need to take place within an institution or can it be informal? As I mentioned earlier, there are spaces that embrace more informal learning, but how are these spaces being discussed or reflected upon?

In much of the literature, informal learning is seen as a broad and multifaceted subject (Livingstone, 2006). It encompasses many areas within popular education, adult education, life-long learning, experiential learning, workplace learning, and others. However, it has been unfortunate to see that most of the research over the past few decades has focused its energies on workplace efficiency and reproducing dominant global capitalist structures (Birden, 2004; Brookfield & Holst, 2011). As Choudry points out, workplace learning has been linked to "domesticat[ing] learners, focus[ing] on strategies for self-improvement, and adjust[ing] minds to conform to a capitalist society" (Choudry, 2015, p. 82). Under these conditions, informal learning adheres to the changes in the workforce, to the individual becoming a "casualized and contractualized flex-worker" (Vandenberghe, 2008, p. 880). Because informal learning, in many cases, has become co-opted and embedded within the logic of a capitalistic economic system, it should be viewed with a critical lens. Using informal learning as a means to enhance worker productivity creates another support mechanism for the bosses, managers, and workplace overseers, not for the everyday lives and well-being of the learners (Overwien, 2000). From learning new technological innovations with colleagues or other flexi-workers, to "learning by doing" with other associates within corporate life, the dominant research on informal learning has been incorporated into restructuring labor and to build more efficient models of productivity. As Brookfield and Holst (2011) point out, the emphasis on adult learning is not on democracy and socialism (I would add anarchism)—it is "focused on 'skilling' or 'retooling' America's workforce to compete in the global market place" (p. 2). Ultimately, this operates to produce more hierarchical, authoritarian, and profitable structures all while making it seem that the bewildered worker is happier under a new specialized knowledge base and assessed through individualized performances and productivity (Haeger & Halliday, 2006, p. 18). It is not that informal learning has potential to support different communities, but there are larger political and ideological challenges that need further critique and dialogue.

Radical Informal Learning

Radical informal learning takes a significantly different approach to learning than what was stated above. For one, radical informal learning would be an ongoing process and geared toward freedom, autonomy, critical reflection, and liberation rather than supporting hierarchical, authoritarian, and economically corrupt institutions and relationships. I would argue that it coincides with Freire's (1970) notion of *radical love* or what bell hooks (2004) describes as having *radical openness*. This would mean that we begin to develop spaces that are critically reflective, dialogical, horizontal and mutual, as opposed to anti-dialogical, vertical and hyper-individualistic. Of course, this is not a simple process, particularly within the dominant and unsustainable educational practices and institutions we inhabit.

Additionally, in developing a basis for radical informal learning, it is important to question our particular desires. Similar to our lack of imagining a world outside these oppressive circumstances, our misplaced desires also need serious considerations. According to Smith (2007) desires are "constructed, assembled, and arranged in such a manner that your desire is positively invested in the system that allows you to have this particular interest" (p. 74). Part of our struggle is questioning those processes and ideas that uphold particular systems of dominance. In other words, our internal motivations and constructs that drive us to gravitate, and in many cases, embrace particular ideologies and systems of control (micro and macro) must be recognized. There are many examples of people embracing oppressive systems happening in the U.S. ranging from working-class people voting against universal health care to supporting corporate control of public institutions. Our desires become embedded and "invested" in the choices that are already pre-packaged and digested internally.

From an educational standpoint, our desires to transform teaching and learning could take on quite a different approach. For many, transforming education more radically becomes an internal shock to an individual's beliefs and desires. I've encountered this working with pre-service teachers. Most of my students have been educated under the effects of No Child Left Behind (NCLB), inundating them with standardized curricula and high-stakes testing. Most have never experienced education outside of these norms. Although they desire another type of education, it is usually a reform or a slight tweaking of the system. Rarely do they steer outside of the confines of what has been discussed through binary mainstream media (conservative/liberal). It is when we move the conversation in class to talk about free schools and more democratic educational experiences, that most students become uncomfortable. Having young people be a part of the decision-making on what is learned, and equally important, how it is learned, becomes discomfiting. In many cases, my students ask, how do students learn to read if they are able to make their own choices on when and what they learn, how do they get into college if they are not tested, and maybe there is just too much democracy and too much freedom? In other words, it is completely foreign to my students because of their fixed beliefs of what teaching and learning should be. It contests their worldview and assumptions regarding the purpose of education in our society, challenges the educational system to which students are accustomed, and provokes questions about their particular desires. For many students, this discomfort brings about resistance and a defensiveness about their educational desires. Their comments repeat the conventional assumptions: students should only have limited choices, testing is necessary for successful learning, and democracy and freedom should be minimized. So, within radical informal learning spaces it is important to understand these educational desires, and how they permeate our lived realities and worldviews in the hope of transforming those desires and develop new subjectivities. At times, this can be painful. It is not an easy process because it takes into consideration the *radical openness* I mentioned earlier, which bell hooks (1989; 2004) describes as a struggling process: "Radical openness is a margin—a profound edge. Locating oneself there is difficult yet necessary. It is not a 'safe' place. One is always at risk. One needs a community of resistance" (1989, p. 206). She not only highlights that radical openness places our learning on the "margins" and within struggle, but emphasizes that it should be done with others who are also working through these processes.

An important part of understanding these radical learning experiences is that they are not homogenous spaces, but situated in different locales. This gets back to my earlier discussion of the cultural aspects of punk. Many of us knew that the different "scenes" across the country were not all the same. Some were bigger and urban, while others were located in more suburban or even rural areas. This meant that negotiating these spaces was experientially different. Of course, there was cultural affinity but there were differences in experiences and understandings. Radical informal learning, within this context emphasizes situated knowledge of the material, cultural, and learning environments. From a pedagogical view Kitchens (2009) points out these important connections:

> A situated pedagogy attends to specific places and localities, but not merely as places for discursive analysis and academic study, but as the spaces for action, intervention, and perhaps transformation. As such, it means that education is meant to move beyond the schools and out into the world in an active, performative participation in the study and reconstruction of material spaces in and outside of their schools as well as the curricular landscapes of their education. (p. 259)

Utopianism and Education

Of course, when I discuss the potential of these radical informal learning spaces with others, a barrage of criticisms comes with it. Criticism mostly comes from the idea that they are utopian, isolated, and small experiences that can't build larger capacities or broader movements for social change. Another question I hear is, "Where is the blueprint?" The assumption is that we need a handbook for educational experiences in a post-capitalist society. I would argue that there is some validity to some of the criticisms, but they are not as realistic as one would think, considering some of the current social movements and learning spaces that have been created.

From an anarchist view, education has always been an important part of transforming society (Suissa, 2009). In fact, there has been a long history of such alternative educational practices that have not been isolated in contemporary experiences. Anywhere from the social gatherings on weekends and the development of the modernist schools during the early twentieth century to the skill sharing and free schools in contemporary movements, anarchists have continued to believe in alternative forms of educational experiences. Suissa underlines the historical importance of education within anarchist theory and practice, stating:

> Behind these radical experimentations lay a faith in the anarchist vision—some would say utopia—of a society without injustice, without oppressive hierarchical social structures, where individual freedom and mutual aid would flourish ... even within the authoritarian structures of the capitalist state, an alternative was possible; thus that the anarchist society, while utopian in the sense of transcending current social and political reality, was not unattainable. (p. 243)

Additionally, in Ferguson's (2011) book on Emma Goldman's political philosophy, she highlights the "sprawling" and vibrant anarchist communities emerging in New York City prior to and during the early years of the twentieth century. Ferguson recounts: "The anarchist social imaginary flourished in these micro worlds, where a few dozen, a few hundred, or a few thousand participants assembled in places they create to share or contest anarchist ideas, invent or participate in anarchist actions, and confirm or dispute anarchist identities" (p. 80).

These informal gatherings give insight into early twentieth-century radical informal learning spaces, where participants engaged in educational practices outside the confines of the state. Goldman and others understood the importance of these gathering places. From the anarchist-leaning beer halls and cafés to the Ferrer Center in New York City and other modernist schools across the country, anarchists recognized the transformative potential of these learning spaces. Ferguson points out that these spaces created a challenging atmosphere filled with ambiguity and, sometimes, ideological tensions.

Even today, we see these types of educational experiences emerging. The Occupy movement and some of the new creative free schools and mutual learning spaces have all continued along paths of radical informal learning.

So, as we move deeper into the ruin of our communities and the destruction of our planet, the questions that need further discussion are these: Is it possible to create educational alternatives within the exponential growth and expansion of capitalism into our everyday lives? Is it within our capacity to do what Holloway (2010) describes as "opening up cracks" to create non-hierarchical, voluntary, non-authoritarian, and mutual learning experiences for our communities in spite of a world that functions to alienate one another and reinforce corrupt hierarchical relationships? I believe Deleuze and Guattari (1987) make an important point that, as much as these ways of being are dominant, overwhelming, and in many cases reproduced, these systems are neither totalizing nor universal. There are holes in the capitalist system where collective efforts are happening in different locales throughout the world. Not only are radical educational experiments emerging, but these efforts actively oppose and denounce the liberal authoritative state that has failed us. These movements challenge us to think about learning in unique ways, focusing on experiences and processes that are what Shor (1992) describes as "desocializing," thus providing us opportunities to move our sense of being beyond the driving forces of the marketplace. Moreover, it is evident from some of the current research on the dynamic learning processes within these social movements (see Hall et al., 2012) that new relationships are being forged, and that these experiments in horizontal and mutual learning environments have had important influences within different communities. Therefore, "transformative possibilities" emerge as people within these spaces attempt to meet the needs of a particular community (including anything from developing a deeper economic and political analysis to learning bicycle repair) while working to disrupt the flow and the intrusions of oppressive structures into everyday life. Moreover, education becomes more dynamic, active, and in many cases, informal.

So, how can radical informal learning spaces inform us and expand our understandings of current social movements and communities resisting neoliberal capitalism? Of equal importance, what knowledge is created/produced within those spaces? It is under these distorted and oppressive conditions that this volume was created. In no way is it all encompassing. Rather, what we envisioned with the contributors are ways to reconceptualize the purpose of education outside of the boundaries and limitations of authoritarian practices or institutional goals, particularly those that are guided by institutional and statist structures. This highlights some important questions. Is it feasible to construct learning spaces and larger movements that do not adopt the goals of the institution while simultaneously using the institution for other, more liberating purposes? Can we struggle within these spaces to transform the hierarchical and authoritarian institutions where we work, live, and learn or should we abandon these efforts and focus our energies elsewhere? From the recent actions of individuals and collectives around the world, in our universities and in the streets, the answer does not seem definitive. From my viewpoint, the struggle is much more complex than dismantling state and authoritarian structures.

There are other factors involved that are important when creating challenging learning environments with a culture of resistance in mind—one that "wages permanent struggle on our movements" (Deleuze & Guattari, 1987). Consistently, the bombardments and cooptation of state, corporate, and other fascist (micro and macro) entities have been relentless in disrupting unique and potentially transformative experiments and projects. This means that local and global movements attempting to transcend their conditions need to critically reflect upon their actions. This includes their own internal democratic decision-making processes where authoritarian mindsets and practices can emerge. In many cases, these difficult interactions and struggles are where the fragments of radical informal learning occur. To a certain degree, these narratives give us a much more complex picture of what is occurring within these learning environments. According to Hall, Clover, Crowther & Scandrett (2012) these spaces "give visibility to rich and varied stories of how ordinary people in literally every part of the world are resisting, organizing and learning to overcome a world that we do not like but have no recipe to change" (p. x). In part, this is where imagination and the "spontaneity of character" materialize into what Coté, Day, and de Peuter (2007) describe as "myriad teaching and learning contexts—from university classrooms to media literacy programs to community-based education to co-research—such radical pedagogy strives to draw out and examine links between the practices of everyday life and the wider structures of domination" (p. 7).

From the autonomous community education programs in the streets of Argentina (Sitrin, 2007), to the student and working-class movements in the United Kingdom, Canada, Chile, Greece, Turkey, and other parts of the world (included in this volume), the emergence of radical informal learning spaces are, in part, a response to the efforts of global capitalism and other dominant forces that are used to undermine our autonomy and reinforce a world we reject. Due to these conditions, Chatterton (2002) argues it has become a necessity for communities to "intervene in the corporate city" (p. 1). Collective spaces have emerged to "denounce" the oppressive structures that are so pervasive under capitalism, while at the same time, they are "imagining" and "announcing" new ways of becoming (Foley, 1999; Freire, 1970). Therefore, it is important to note that such learning spaces are not fixed or permanent—they are examples that emerge out of situated spaces and, at times, spontaneous circumstances (Conway, 2006; Kitchens, 2009). To learn from these experiences, we rely on the theoretical frameworks, narratives, testimonies, and dialogical encounters of individuals and collectives who inhabit those radical learning environments. Again, by no means is this volume all-encompassing, but we hope it will foster more discussion and further actions in creating more meaningful and radical learning spaces. We hope you enjoy this collection and we thank all the amazing contributors for their support of this project.

References

Au, W. (2011). Teaching under the new Taylorism: High-stakes testing and the standardization of the 21st century curriculum. *Journal of Curriculum Studies*, 43(1), 25–45.

Birden, S. (2004). Theorizing a coalition-engendered education: The case of the Boston women's health book collective's body education. *Adult Education Quarterly, 54*(4), 257–272.

Bowles, S., & Gintis, H. (1976). *Schooling in capitalist America: Educational reform and the contradictions of economic life.* New York, NY: Routledge & Kegan Paul.

Brookfield, S., & Holst, J. (2011). *Radicalizing learning: Adult education for a just world.* San Francisco, CA: Jossey-Bass.

Brown, P. (2003). The opportunity trap: Education and employment in a global economy. *European Educational Research Journal, 2*(1), 141–177.

Brown, P. (2013) Education, opportunity and the prospects for social mobility. *British Journal of Sociology of Education, 34*(5–6), 678–700.

Callahan, R.E. (1962). *Education and the cult of efficiency: A study of the social forces that has shaped the administration of public schools.* Chicago, IL: University of Chicago Press.

Chatterton, P. (2002). Squatting is still legal, necessary and free: A brief intervention in the corporate city. *Antipode, 34*(1), 1–7.

Choudry, A. (2015). *Learning activism: The intellectual life of contemporary social movements.* Toronto, ON: University of Toronto Press.

Conway, J. (2006). *Praxis and politics: Knowledge production in social movements.* New York, NY: Routledge.

Coté, M., Day, R., & de Peuter, G. (2007). *Utopian pedagogy: Radical experiments against neoliberal globalization.* Toronto, ON: University of Toronto Press.

de Cleyre, V. (1909). Modern education reform. In S. Presley & C. Sartwell (Eds.), *Exquisite rebel: The essays of Voltairine de Cleyre—Anarchist, feminist, genius.* Albany, NY: SUNY Press.

Deleuze, G., & Guattari, F. (1987). *A thousand plateaus: Capitalism and schizophrenia.* (B. Massumi, Trans.). Minneapolis, MN: University of Minnesota Press.

Ferguson, K. (2011). *Emma Goldman: Political thinking in the streets.* Lanham, MD: Rowman & Littlefield.

Foley, G. (1999). *Learning in social action: A contribution to understanding informal education.* London, UK: Zed Books.

Foster, J.B. (2011). Education and the structural crisis of capital: A case study. *Monthly Review, 63*(3), 6–37. Retrieved from http://monthlyreview.org/2011/07/01/education-and-the-structural-crisis-of-capital/.

Freire, P. (1970). *Pedagogy of the oppressed.* New York, NY: Continuum.

Giroux, H.A. (2013). The politics of disimagination and the pathologies of power. Retrieved from http://www.truth-out.org/news/item/14814-the-politics-of-disimagination-and-the-pathologies-of-power.

Goldman, E. (1906). The child and its enemies. *Mother Earth, 1*(2), 7–14.

Graeber, D. (2011). *Revolutions in reverse: Essays on politics, violence, art, and imagination.* London, UK: Minor Compositions.

Haeger, P., & Halliday, J. (2006). *Recovering informal learning: Wisdom, judgement and community.* Dordrecht: Springer.

Haiven, M. (2014). *Crisis of imagination, crisis of power: Capitalism, creativity and the commons.* London, UK: Zed Books.

Hall, B., Clover, D., Crowther, J., & Scandrett, E. (2012). Introduction. In B. Hall et al. (Eds.), *Learning and education for a better world: The role of social movements.* Rotterdam: Sense Publishers.

Haworth, R. (2010). Anarcho-punk: Radical experiments in informal learning spaces. In B.J. Porfilio & P.R. Carr (Eds.), *Youth culture, education and resistance: Subverting the commercial ordering of life*. Rotterdam: Sense Publishers.

Holloway, J. (2010). *Crack capitalism*. New York, NY: Pluto Press.

hooks, b. (1989). *Yearning: Race, gender and cultural politics*. Boston, MA: South End Press.

hooks, b. (2004). *Teaching community: A pedagogy of hope*. New York, NY: Routledge.

Katz, M. (1971). *Class, bureaucracy, and schools*. New York, NY: Praeger.

Kitchens, J. (2009). Situated pedagogy and the Situationist International: Countering a pedagogy of placelessness. *Educational Studies, 45*, 240-261.

Livingstone, D.W. (2006). Informal learning: Conceptual distinctions and preliminary findings. In Z. Bekerman, N. Burbules & D. Silberman-Keller (Eds.), *Learning in places: The informal education reader*. New York, NY: Peter Lang.

Overwien, B. (2000). Informal learning and the role of social movements. *International Review of Education, 46*(6), 621-640.

Ravitch, D. (2010, March 9). Why I changed my mind about school reform. *Wall Street Journal*. Retrieved from http://www.wsj.com/articles/SB10001424052748704869 304575109443305343962.

Shor, I. (1992). *Empowering education: Critical teaching for social change*. Chicago, IL: University of Chicago Press.

Sitrin, M. (2007, Autumn). Ruptures in imagination: Horizontalism, autogestion and affective politics in Argentina. *Policy & Practice: A Development Education Review, 5*, 43-53.

Smith, D.W. (2007). Deleuze and the question of desire: Toward an immanent theory of ethics. *Parrhesia: A Journal of Critical Philosophy, 2*, 66-78.

Spring, J. (2006). *Wheels in the head: Educational philosophies of authority, freedom, and culture from Socrates to human rights*. Mahwah, NJ: L. Erlbaum Associates, Publishers.

Stovall, D. (2011). *Reframing the gap: Educational debt and the responsibility of socially conscious educators in troubling times* [video]. Retrieved from https://youtu.be/VOMcj7naxdg.

Suissa, J. (2009). "The space now possible": Anarchist education as utopian hope. In L. Davis & R. Kinna (Eds.) *Anarchism and utopianism*. Manchester, UK: Manchester University Press.

Vandenberghe, F. (2008). Deleuzian capitalism. *Philosophy & Social Criticism, 34*(8) 877-903.

Critiques of Education

CHAPTER 1

Miseducation and the Authoritarian Mind

John M. Elmore

Historical examples of education—and more specifically, compulsory schooling that is defined and controlled by dominant political, theological, or plutocratic groups—being employed as a tool of hegemony, are numerous and well documented. As I tell my students regularly when discussing and comparing systems of education throughout history and around the globe, it can feel like identifying exemplars of liberatory education requires dedicated and detailed examination, while spotting systems of authoritarian education requires only the casual opening of one's eyes. Education has clearly proven to be an invaluable instrument in the production of despotic systems and institutions. The obvious reason for this fact is that the more rigid and domineering a social system becomes, the greater the perceived need to produce minds and personalities that are compatible, if not welcoming of control and domination. This chapter will consider this concept of authoritarianism and the ways that authoritarian personalities are reflected and fostered in traditional, compulsory schooling via traditional teaching methods, curricular materials and school structure. While I will acknowledge the other cultural institutions and socializing forces which account for a population's levels of authoritarianism (such as the existence of particular political, economic, and theological systems, and traditional family structures and parenting practices), I contend that mass schooling is in the unique social position of assembling the overwhelming majority of a society's young and influencing their development via an extended, and increasingly specific, common experience. In short, even in today's world where the young are continuously bombarded with the messaging of mass media throughout their formative years, compulsory schooling maintains a very powerful influence over the development and validation of conscious-ness. Changing the nature of consciousness serves as a critical prerequisite to achieving the type of society that we, as individuals and collectively, wish to construct and support. If we seek a more just society, where freedom is sought, protected, and valued—the development of critically conscious, biophilic citizens is fundamental. Therefore, within a volume dedicated to considering alternatives to traditional forms of popular schooling, for the purpose of advancing freedom, an examination of those traditional aspects of school life and structure, which are reflective of authoritarian practices and orientations and can be tied to the development of authoritarian dispo-sitions, seems especially pertinent. In other words, as we attempt to move *out of the ruins* of traditional schooling, it is important that we first clearly define those ruins and diagnose their failures in fostering freedom in order to produce genuine and affective alternatives.

The Tradition of Miseducation as Control

Critical educators have long challenged the structures, practices, and pur-poses of traditional schooling. In fact, it is fair to describe critical pedagogy itself as originating first and foremost as a rejection of popular and tradi-tional education methods and the domineering structures and practices they demand. Declaring much of traditional education as anti-democratic, if not outright anti-human, critical educators labor to transform educational spaces into seedbeds for freedom and independent thought. In seeking to manipulate, if not outright commandeer, the role that education plays within the superstructure, we acknowledge that the maintenance of a society's base always demands the development of a specific human character and, in turn, a specific "form of social conscience"—informed by what Marx and Engels (1996) described as the "ruling ideas" that represent the "ideal expression of the dominant material relationships" (p. 61). As Erich Fromm (1941) indicated, there is a dynamic correlation between the structure of human character within a given society and the economic base of that society. In other words, the maintenance of any particular "way of life" requires a compatible, if not mirrored, version of human consciousness and character. Fromm (1941) argued that even intellectuality itself "aside from the purely logical ele-ments that are involved in the act of thinking, [is] greatly determined by the personality structure of the person who thinks" (p. 305). This, Fromm (1941) continued, "holds true for the whole of a doctrine or of a theoretical system, as well as for a single concept, like love, justice, equality, sacrifice" (p. 306).

What Fromm (1956) suggests is that an overt structure, dedicated to the task of shaping the thoughts and beliefs of a populace, is a fundamen-tal apparatus within authoritarian societies. This apparatus allows for an official means of indoctrinating a citizenry—shaping consciousness and human character for the purpose of adaptation. In short, authoritarian social systems do not generate oppressive settings out of thin air but instead are slowly validated in the context of authoritarian nurturing in various social and cultural institutions and practices; they ultimately reflect the dispositions of the people. While one can point to multiple agencies well positioned to nurture the transition to authoritarian political systems, such as dogmatic and faith-based institutions, popular compulsory schooling has historically offered much potential in this regard.

Education therefore, when carefully shaped and crafted, can serve the pernicious goal of providing those in power with an invaluable tool for nurturing and shaping a particular human character, consciousness, and epistemology that is tuned to the specific needs of a respective base. Should one require further convincing, one need look no further than the desperate efforts to control education by some of the most authoritarian regimes in history, from Hitler to Stalin to Kim Jung-un. As Anton Makarenko (1955), architect of Stalin's educational system, wrote, "It was clear to me that many details of human personality and behavior could be made from dies, simply stamped out en masse . . . although of course the dies themselves had to be of the finest description, demanding scrupulous care . . . by the communist party" (pp. 267–268). Conversely, when education is conceived as an act of liberation, illuminating systems of oppression, it becomes an equally powerful threat to the dominant. For such liberatory education, as Marx (1843) contended, "our motto must be: reform of consciousness not through dogmas, but by analysing the mystical consciousness that is unintelligible to itself, whether it manifests itself in a religious or a political form" (para. 12). In short, a liberated mind has never been the outcome of dogmatic training— regardless of its source.

When there exists a deprivation in the development of criticality within a given society, in concert with other forms of socio-psychological manipulation, a "cultural hegemony" is produced that "manufactures consent," which Antonio Gramsci (1971) argued is maintained at:

> two major superstructural "levels": the one that can be called "civil society', that is, the ensemble of organisms commonly called "private", and that of "political society" or "the State". These two levels correspond on the one hand to the functions of "hegemony" which the dominant group exercises throughout society and on the other hand to that of "direct domination" or command exercised through the State and "juridical" government. The functions in question are precisely organizational and connective. The intellectuals are the dominant group's "deputies" exercising the subaltern functions of social hegemony and political government. They comprise:

1. The "spontaneous" consent given by the great masses of the population to the general direction imposed on social life by the dominant fundamental group [and] . . .
2. The apparatus of state coercive power which "legally" enforces discipline on those groups who do not "consent" either actively or passively. (p. 12)

As superstructural institutions fail to inspire such "spontaneous consent," the consciousness attuned to domination is disrupted. As a result, the imposed definitions of social, political, and economic life come to be viewed as mere social constructions, perspectives that can be challenged rather than merely consumed. In such a transformative period it is often the superstructure itself, rather than the base that is first brought into question. In the 1960s, for example, the political unrest in the U.S. was not due to a rebellion of the working class against bourgeois domination, but an intellectual and youth revolt against what Engels (1893) labeled "false consciousness" and a "new spirit of the age" where endless consumerism was to define the human experience (Chomsky, 2000, p. 39). From the perspective of the '60s youth movement, society was to be transformed not by directly attacking the capitalistic base, but by deconstructing the superstructural institutions producing its ideological hegemony. It can be reasonably predicted that had the youth movement been sustained it would have eventually expanded its critique from superstructure to base—and some elements within the broader movement had already begun to do so by the time of the Kent State shootings (Clancy, 2007). More recently, the Occupy movement demonstrated the potential of liberated consciousness; the taken-for-granted assumptions about the way the world has to work were replaced with the clear contradiction between democracy and capitalism. As in the case of the '60s youth movement, and of many revolutionary movements, the first gasp for freedom demands the critique and destruction, or radical transformation, of the socio-political institutions that malform the collective social conscience, via the planting of what Stirner (1842/1967) described as "wheels in the head," which produce the illusion of free choice. It is this transformation of human consciousness that is always at the core of the renovation of social, economic, or political structures. As Godwin claimed in 1783, "Let the most oppressed people under heaven once change their mode of thinking, and they are free."

The transmission model of education, or what Freire (1974) termed the "banking model," has defined education within the U.S. from the outset and it continues to the present day. This authoritarian, top-down approach to education has pervaded our society and culture, and come to be taken for granted, suppressing alternative perspectives, values, interests, and discussion about what Guttman (1987) termed "the good life." This actuality has only been exasperated in recent years with the rise of so-called core curriculum and the essentialist standardization movement. There has long been a view of traditional education, like John Stuart Mill (1951) argued, functioning as:

> a mere contrivance for moulding people to be exactly like one another; and as the mould in which it casts them is that which pleases the dominant power in the government, whether this be a monarch, an aristocracy, or a majority of the existing generation; in proportion as it is efficient and successful, it establishes a despotism over the mind, leading by a natural tendency to one over the body. (p. 88)

This tradition was clearly carried over from the "old world" in establishing mass schooling in the U.S.—and its influence reverberates to the present day. To this point, Zhao (2014) issues a warning to U.S. education policymakers about continuing to function under what he calls "the spell of authoritarianism." As Zhao (2014) argues:

> high-stakes testing is one of the many symptoms of a virus threatening America's future. That virus is the rising tide of authoritarianism in the United States. In exchange for the comfort of knowing how their children are doing academically and that their schools are being held accountable, Americans welcomed high-stakes testing into public education. Without the benefit of historical experience with these kinds of high-stakes tests, however, Americans failed to recognize those benign-looking tests as a Trojan horse—with a dangerous ghost inside. That ghost, authoritarianism, sees education as a way to instill in all students the same knowledge and skills deemed valuable by the authority. (p. 3)

The centerpiece of authoritarian education—and any societal march toward systems and structures of hegemony—is the development of a specific form of consciousness. Although sometimes lacking pre-meditated intent, traditional schooling environments have consistently fostered the development of structures, perspectives, and dispositions that are aligned with hierarchal social arrangements.

Introduction to Authoritarianism & the Authoritarian Personality

In spite of how they are often portrayed within popular culture, totalitarian societies rarely arise from the mere existence of a single despot. To the contrary, any serious analysis of the myriad of authoritarian examples throughout human history demonstrates a gradual amassing of circumstances, which eventually overwhelm any resistance or alternative narrative. Historians, sociologists, and psychologists have deliberated at length in attempting to understand and diagnose the political and social occurrences that produce authoritarian cultures. While the question of what social forces and phenomena produce a Hitler or a Kim Jong-il are relevant, most researchers have acknowledged that comprehending what circumstances produced populations desirous of and supportive of such political dictatorships is far more critical. At the core of this issue has been the question of what has been termed "the authoritarian personality," which has been seen as resulting from factors such as particular family influences, dogmatic and absolutist training (religious or otherwise), economic systems and structures, and jingoistic nationalism.

In *The Authoritarian Personality*, Adorno, Frenkel-Brunswik, Levinson, and Sanford (1950) described authoritarians as individuals who were rigid thinkers, obeyed authority, and demanded strict adherence to social rules and hierarchies. Additionally, as they reported, the authoritarian personality maintained an inflexible and fixed worldview, a strong desire to be directed by the superior, an equally strong desire to direct the inferior, and a strong tendency to view everything in absolutist, black-or-white terms. As such, authoritarian people are more likely than others to harbor prejudices against low-status groups. Adorno et al. (1950) also discovered a connection between racism/fascism and the authoritarian parenting style. His studies led him to propose a personality framework that may be described as follows:

> While finding comfort in the identification of submissive behavior towards authority, the authoritarian person directs his/her aggression towards other groups, often racial minorities. This is an attempt to relieve the feeling of personal weakness with a search for absolute answers and strengths in the outside world. (p. 12)

It is this consistent exclusion of others that has proven to be one of the most poisonous exports of the authoritarian personality. According to Fromm (1957), "What they have in common, what defines the essence of the authoritarian personality is an inability: the inability to rely on one's self, to be independent, to put it in other words: to endure freedom" (p. 3). From the lack of confidence in oneself a lack of confidence in others naturally follows, which serves as fertile ground for condemning anyone who is different from what has been deemed ideal by those in power. Such a negative view of others leads to the conclusion that harsh laws and a strong police or army are necessary. Also, it leads people to the pessimistic certainty that humans would devolve into narcissistic debauchery and be totally immoral if they were left to govern themselves free of external control. Ultimately, because they lack the confidence for self-governance, authoritarian personalities believe it is important to have a powerful leader and to be part of a powerful group.

To declare the incompatibility of such personalities with freedom broadly
and social democracy specifically, is both obvious and accurate. Adorno et
al. (1950) made a special effort to explain that the authoritarian personality
is not a singular personality type. There are different, even contradictory,
aspects of authoritarianism.

Two Types of Authoritarianism

According to Fromm (1957), there are two clear aspects of the authoritarian
personality type, which can be viewed as both distinct and interconnected.
The "sadistic" authoritarian is one who gauges life in degrees of domination
and control. Freire (1974), using the language of Fromm, argued that such
a "necrophilic" disposition ultimately manifests as a "love of death, not life"
(p. 64). This aspect of the authoritarian personality, while the most common
identified, is not exclusive. Fromm (1957) describes the other half of the
equation:

> The passive-authoritarian, or in other words, the masochistic and sub-
> missive character aims—at least subconsciously—to become a part of
> a larger unit, a pendant, a particle, at least a small one, of this "great"
> person, this "great" institution, or this "great" idea. The person, insti-
> tution, or idea may actually be significant, powerful, or just incredibly
> inflated by the individual believing in them. What is necessary, is that—
> in a subjective manner—the individual is convinced that "his" leader,
> party, state, or idea is all-powerful and supreme, that he himself is
> strong and great, that he is a part of something "greater." The paradox
> of this passive form of the authoritarian character is: the individual
> belittles himself so that he can—as part of something greater—become
> great himself. The individual wants to receive commands, so that he
> does not have the necessity to make decisions and carry responsibil-
> ity. This masochistic individual looking for dependency is in his depth
> frightened—often only subconsciously—a feeling of inferiority, pow-
> erlessness, aloneness. Because of this, he is looking for the "leader,"
> the great power, to feel safe and protected through participation and
> to overcome his own inferiority. Subconsciously, he feels his own pow-
> erlessness and needs the leader to control this feeling. This masochistic
> and submissive individual, who fears freedom and escapes into idola-
> try, is the person on which the authoritarian systems—Nazism and
> Stalinism—rest. (pp. 3-4)

The fact that both forms of the authoritarian personality can be tied to
one final common point—the regimented inclination—demonstrates why
one can find both the sadistic and masochistic component even within the
same individual. The two idiosyncratic behavior patterns are submissive-

ness and aggressiveness—these two patterns seem to be at odds, but in fact their coexistence within the authoritarian personality is a hallmark. The authoritarian personality wants to fit into a chain of command and to be told what to do (being submissive to a superior), and by the same token, enjoys greatly the prospect of giving orders to those below them. It is always the system itself that demands allegiance—the authoritarian may climb its ranks, but shudders at the thought of climbing beyond and out of the safety certitude. In short, authoritarians like to be herded like sheep even as they enjoy commanding. So, while she or he is aggressive towards others, especially those considered to be lesser in some way (e.g., of a different faith or ethnicity, sexual orientation or socio-economic class), they are also aggressive in maintaining a pious and politically correct sense of self. Kirscht and Dillehay (1967) contend that such an individual's "judgments are governed by a punitive conventional moralism, reflecting external standards towards which he remains insecure since he has failed to make them really his own. His relations with others depend on considerations of power, success, and adjustment, in which people figure as means rather than ends, and achievement is valued competitively rather than for its own sake" (p. vii).

Unsurprisingly, given this description, bigotry and intolerance are common in the authoritarian personality type. The Hitler Youth were prime examples of this, as are children raised in dogmatic religious institutions or white supremacist organizations. While this mind-set exists across all political, economic, and religious spectra, and afflicts both genders, it is found most frequently within what Altemeyer (1988) referred to as "right-wing conservatives."

While the original F (fascism) scale, offered by Adorno et al. (1950), focused on the fascist personality in Hitler's Germany, the more recent work of Bob Altemeyer (1988) connects authoritarianism to rightist ideologies more broadly. Altemeyer introduces the term "Right-Wing Authoritarianism" in seeking to classify common connections between particular political attitudes and authoritarian dispositions. In reducing Adorno's original nine characteristics of the F-scale to three, Altemeyer establishes his RWA (right-wing authoritarianism) scale. While Altemeyer explains that "right-wing" means a "psychological sense of submitting to perceived authorities in one's life," and is not identified with a specific political ideology, the parallels are easily drawn between RWAs and contemporary social conservatives within the U.S. In his investigations, Altemeyer (1988) developed an inventory, which reliably assesses individual levels of authoritarianism and, in agreement with Adorno, concluded that authoritarians consistently favor absolute obedience and tend to stand against the value of individual freedom.

According to Altemeyer (1988), to achieve unquestioning obedience, the authoritarian "is prepared to implant fear and to punish severely in

order to produce it" and they advocate physical punishment in childhood
(p. 7). In the same vein for adults, RWAs deplore leniency in the criminal
justice system and believe that anything less than the harshest punishments
simply encourages criminals—as such, they are strong advocates of capital
punishment. The dramatic increase in incarceration within the U.S. evinces
the immense RWA influence among contemporary policymakers. Because
these "necrophilics" equate freedom with chaos, there is a commonality to
every solution proposed to every perceived problem: more control and less
freedom. What is primarily offered in exchange for submission to domination is pacification of fear: the authoritarian system relies heavily on irrational fears as a means of control. Under such Orwellian conditions doublespeak at work and in the public square is common—citizens are encouraged
to see every military venture as a "defense of freedom" and any criticism of
the power elite as "unpatriotic" heresy. Citizens are regularly bathed in the
language of freedom, yet consistently argue on behalf of restricting political
freedoms rather than expanding them. In such circumstances, as stated by
Romanish (1995),

> Since true freedom is taken to be a synonym for chaos and since
> chaos has few defenders, the net effect is that freedom has few as
> well. Democracy is seen as patriotism, and patriotism can become a
> synonym for militarism. Freedom is restricted to abstract references
> during political debates and otherwise meets resistance in its libera-
> tory form such as empowering the young or assuring equal rights for
> women. (p. 19)

Traditional schooling and its "banking model" of education have consistently
operated in such a way that students become comfortable with such authoritarian conditions. As Bowles and Gintis (1976) point out, the domination that
students learn to endure from their teachers and principals prepares them
perfectly for the domination they will endure in adult life, where the workplace replaces the school and the boss replaces the teacher. Of course, such
schooling is not alone in this process; organized religion has been a powerful
purveyor of authoritarian dispositions and attitudes as well (Harris, 2004).
In challenging authoritarianism, it is critical to consider these sites where
the development of the authoritarian personality takes place.

The Development of the Authoritarian Personality

What is made clear by an even cursory examination of totalitarian systems is
that education is almost always perceived as critical and a process that is best
engaged as early in life as possible. This training is not only begun early, it
tends to be all-encompassing, compulsory, standardized, and inflexible—the
child is expected to "fit" the system and not the other way around. It is often

this early indoctrination that carries the greatest long-term effect. Paul Nash (1966) reiterates this opinion by stating that "children brought up under authoritarian influences are liable to suffer from many of the defects of the authoritarian personality, to which can be attributed some of the world's most serious ills" (p. 107). Nash's description of the authoritarian personality matches with the previously shared perspectives of Adorno and Altemeyer: one plagued by fear of life's ambiguities and uncertainties. As such, Nash (1966) continues, authoritarians favor conformity, dogmatic beliefs, and absolute doctrines, making them ideal candidates for institutions steeped in absolutist, dogmatic beliefs. The authoritarian admires strength, power, and aggressiveness and is willing to impose the rigidities of orthodoxy on others through the use of manipulation, coercion, and malice. There is a tendency to prefer concrete and fixed perspectives, favoring sharp absolutism over the doubt, uncertainty, and paradox that life often suggests. Instead of coping with ambiguities, there is an inclination to suppress them below a conscious level where they fester and cause inner chaos and fear. The result of such alienating experiences is a deep-seated need to find mechanisms that will generate a feeling completeness—effectively healing the overwhelming sense of alienation. God delusions are one such mechanism that has served this purpose within societies throughout human history.

Religion has, in fact, served as a primary source of relief for authoritarians in this regard—providing the illusion of order wherever chaos is perceived. The ideal parishioner fostered within the vast majority of religious institutions maintains characteristics compatible with authoritarianism; characteristics that are not only exclusionary and counterproductive to democratic participation, but that actually undermine the institution of democracy itself. This fact is especially vivid in the dogmatic training of children, which is fundamental within most religions, so to foster the maintenance of magical and fanatical consciousness. This is, in reality, what has proven religious dogma so dangerous to democracy: it encourages, and ultimately requires, the development and maintenance of the authoritarian personality. As Dean (2006) so accurately put it, "the vehicle despotism rides is authoritarianism" and the authoritarian personality is, and always has been, the centerpiece of every movement towards totalitarianism, both today and throughout history (p. 45). Unfortunately, rather than traditional education in the U.S. functioning as a rational, logical, and secular antidote to the dogmatic training of the mind, as Paine and Ingersoll might have imagined, it has become a co-conspirator.

It is certainly worth noting that the price we pay as a species for this absolutist-inspired "cessation of doubt and fear" is immense and goes well beyond being an impediment to liberty. In fact, as noted by Harris (2004), it is quite simply, "our most cherished beliefs about the world . . . leading us, inexorably, to kill one another" (p. 12). If human history has proven anything conclusive, it is that through offering pacification of fear, single-minded answers for the ambiguities of life, and a sense of order where the perception of chaos persists, absolutism fashions a mind that serves as fertile ground for the weeds of intolerance, hatred, and destruction. When education is perverted for such purposes it must be challenged and destroyed.

As negative as the result of such authoritarian training is, perhaps more important for critical educators is the fact that the resulting consciousness does not operate in isolation. The central question as such is: does the development and maintenance of absolutist ideologies in one aspect of a person's mind "infect" other aspects of a person's mind? In terms of religion, for example, as Winell and Tarico (2014) stated, "over time some religious beliefs can create habitual thought patterns that actually alter brain function, making it difficult for people to heal or grow" (para. 3). Dawkins (1976) coined the term "meme" to describe these thought patterns on a macro level:

> Just as genes propagate themselves in the gene pool by leaping from body to body via sperms or eggs, so memes propagate themselves in the meme pool by leaping from brain to brain via a process which, in the broad sense, can be called imitation. (p. 192)

On a micro level, however, such patterns can take on the characteristics of what has been termed a "viral meme," which is less concerned with an idea spreading from person to person, or generation to generation, than it is about ideas that spread within and throughout the individual mind, infecting every aspect of consciousness. The most dangerous viral memes, as Benscoter (2013) argues, are those that function as "a viral memetic infection," which are essentially ideas that generate circular logic and loop through the mind, providing a singular and all-encompassing answer to all possible questions. At their worst, such viral memes foster a form of consciousness where the most absolutist definitions of "us" and "them" can take root and almost any act can be justified in their defense and advancement. Unfortunately, these viral memetic infections do not simply stay partitioned, safely tucked away in the part of a person's consciousness where she or he convenes with a god. Such viral memes, and the sectarian perspectives they spawn, spread and can have a grave impact on the prospect of developing criticality in other aspects of one's life. Stated directly, it is not a coincidence that those we encounter in our lives who are the most fundamentalist and rigid in their religiosity tend to be equally as such in their views on politics, power structures, and socio-cultural norms.

What we see in examining the multiple sources that foster the development of the authoritarian personality is that such individuals do not merely exist within formalized totalitarian states. As stated by Romanish (1995),

A common misconception in democratic societies is that conformity and social control are features of non-democratic systems when in fact the differences can better be described in degree rather than kind. Unless a concerted effort is made to educate a population in the ways of democratic living, almost as a counter balance to the forces of authoritarianism inherent in a range of social activities and enterprises, there exists the danger of a natural drift towards anti-democratic conditions. Such inertia, if assisted by social calamity or economic dislocation, can ignite political extremism and pose an ultimate threat to democratic and constitutional freedoms. (p. 20).

It is simply not enough to recalibrate schooling to biophilic aims, when other social institutions are so clearly dedicated to generating individuals bent on submission to "higher powers." In other words, to oppose one system of domination while supporting—or turning a blind eye to—another, is to engage in intellectual hypocrisy of the highest level. We cannot condemn the corporation who exploits and controls the worker's body, while giving a wink and a nod to the clergy who exploits that same workers capacity for empathy and perverts and vilifies their capacity for logic and reason. Conformity is highly valued in authoritarian systems and social norms, which rely upon broad conformity to assist the system's control. To this end, it is critical to determine how individuals arrive at authoritarian orientations and what role social institutions, including schools, may play in that development.

Without the development of the critically conscious personality, society is left with citizens that are authoritarian, conforming, uncritical of cultural values, conservative, and intolerant of ambiguity. This, of course, is the result of psychological predispositions as well as the experiences provided by one's environment—hence the critical role of education in the development of individual and collective consciousness. When schooling is driven by fear, full human faculties are prevented from developing or made to develop in perverse and malformed ways. The use of fear, found regularly in behaviorist school environments, reduces these capacities to desires for pleasure and the avoidance of pain. Preventing learners from thinking and acting freely means to arbitrarily restrain them from organic development, which in turn equally restrains their choices and decisions. Arnstine (1971) states:

The longer action is restrained in this way, the less likely it is that people will even think about choices or decisions. From this point it is but a short stop to the cessation of thinking altogether. People who cannot act freely may busy themselves doing efficiently the tasks they have been assigned, and they may also engage in fantasies over the entertainments they have been given. In this way entire societies can acquire the mentality of slaves. (p. 5)

Finding alternatives to traditional schooling, as this volume seeks to highlight, is paramount if we are to achieve a society that lives up to its most profound creeds. Education as such must be engaged for the primary purpose of fostering the development of critically conscious citizens with biophilic dispositions.

Freire and the Development of Consciousness

The power and pervasiveness of authoritarianism highlights the ways in which it is universal and intertwined with the development of human consciousness. Individuals did not simply come to these belief structures spontaneously. These institutions, while growing directly out of human feeling, imagination and will, as noted by Feuerbach (1841), simultaneously inform, shape and control them. Along with other superstructural institutions, traditional schooling contributes to the development of a type of consciousness detailed by Paulo Freire in his works *Education for Critical Consciousness* (1974) and *The Politics of Education: Culture, Power and Liberation* (1985).

Throughout much of his work Freire (1974/1985) calls for specific attention to be paid to the conditioning of the human mind. Yet this conditioning is not merely the socialization that many sociological works use to describe a seemingly natural evolution, free of conscious human direction. For Freire, this conditioning, what he calls education, is shaped by social, political, and historical contexts yet also shapes social, political, and historical contexts. It is in this potential for education as a source of reflective agency that Freire's account of the development of consciousness is grounded.

Freire (1974) argued that human beings move through specific stages in the development of consciousness. We are born into what he termed "intransitive" consciousness, in which we lack the necessary skills and experience to comprehend or dialogue with our world. Over time this intransitivity gives way to the construction of very limited connections within our world, mostly in terms of rudimentary cause and effect, although within such "semi-intransitivity" we still "cannot apprehend problems outside their biological sphere of necessity. . . . [our] interests center almost totally around survival, and they lack a sense of life on a more historical plane" (Freire, 1974, p. 14). The semi-intransitive stage of consciousness, Freire (1985) contends, "is a kind of obliteration imposed by objective conditions . . . the only data the dominated consciousness grasps are the data that lie within its lived experience," and individuals in this immobile state of consciousness "lack what we call structural perception, which shapes and reshapes itself from concrete reality in the apprehension of facts and problematical situations" (p. 75).

As these rudimentary connections in the semi-intransitive stage expand, and we begin to develop simple schema from which we can enter into dialogue with our world, we develop "naive consciousness," which Freire (1974) described as the "very limited consciousness," of "men who are still almost part of a mass, in whom the developing capacity for dialogue is still fragile and capable of distortion" (p. 15). As stated by Freire (1974), this naive stage of consciousness is characterized by:

> An oversimplification of problems; by a nostalgia for the past; by underestimation of the common man . . . by a lack of interest in investigation, accompanied by an accentuated taste for fanciful explanations; by fragility of argument; by a strongly emotional style; by the practice of polemics rather than dialogue; by magical explanations. (p. 14)

Naive consciousness ultimately constricts the openness and "permeability" of the individual, which was beginning to develop. Without such openness, human beings will not be historical agents capable of reflective action, and are thus alienated from their own consciousness and humanity. Those of naive consciousness survive on circumscribed conclusions about the world and their place in it; they are dependent on definitions of the world that are not of their own determination. This is neither about the intelligence of the person nor the correctness or incorrectness of the positions such a person might take; the defining circumstance of naive consciousness is in an undeveloped capacity for rational dialogue with their world and a resulting dependency on external definitions.

From this position of naiveté, according to Freire (1974), consciousness can move in two very distinct directions depending upon the educative experiences of the individual. In one case, the "distorted," incomplete, and inaccurate interpretations of the world go unchallenged or they may even be reinforced. This leads to the development of "magical consciousness" and, as Freire (1974) described, as a stunted state of consciousness in which "the possibility of dialogue diminishes markedly. Men are defeated and dominated, though they do not know it; they fear freedom, though they believe themselves to be free. They follow general prescriptions and formulas as if by their own choice. They are directed; they do not direct themselves" (p. 17).

Again, Freire (1974), via the work of Fromm (1941), argued that this is not a matter of intelligence or lack thereof, but simply the recognition that when the opportunity for the development of a consciousness born of dialogue with one's world is withheld and, instead, replaced by a consciousness born of monologue, the resulting person is deprived of the capacity to ever truly understand their conditions free of the cultural invasion of the dominant. Accurate or inaccurate, the only source of truth that is perceived as reliable becomes one that is generated externally—truth is established "magically."

As the individual becomes ever more dependent on these magical definitions of their world, the ideas cease to be viewed as separate from, or owned by, the individual—the ideas come to define the individual, they are merged into one. As Stirner (1842/1967) contended, the freeman owns his ideas, the educated-man is owned by them:

> If one awakens in men the idea of freedom, then the freemen will incessantly go on to free themselves; if, on the contrary, one only educates them, then they will at all times accommodate themselves to circumstances in the most highly educated and elegant manner and degenerate into subservient cringing souls. (p. 23)

When the person can no longer separate themselves from the ideas that have come to define them—which are not of their own creation—they devolve into a state of what Freire (1974) termed "fanaticized consciousness." The transition to fanaticized consciousness leads the person to "become even more disengaged from reality than in the semi-intransitive state," and the person now "acts more on the basis of emotionality than of reason" (p. 29). In terms of the development of full human consciousness, they devolve. In the state of fanaticized consciousness, the magical explanations and ideas become so central and necessary to the core of the person's relationship with the world, they no longer see themselves separate from them. Therefore, an attack on these ideas is, in effect, an attack on the person themselves. They no longer own the ideas; the ideas own them. They defend them passionately, often violently. "The idea is my own," Stirner (1845/1963) contended, "only when I have no misgiving about bringing it in danger of death every moment, when I do not have to fear its loss as a loss for me, a loss of me" (p. 342). Those of fanaticized consciousness are effectively puppets whose strings only await a master—they and the institutions that shape their minds exist as an impediment to individual and collective freedom alike.

Yet "whatever his state, man is an open being" and, because of this, capable of a continuous rather than predetermined development of consciousness (Freire, 1974, p. 13). In contrast to the progression from naive to magical and fanatical consciousness, when naive consciousness is encouraged to continuously question interpretations one can "amplify their power to perceive and respond to suggestions and questions arising in their context, and increase their capacity to enter into dialogue ... they become transitive" (Freire, 1974, p. 13). Transitive-conscious persons are moving beyond merely being "in the world"; they are becoming "of the world"—they are integrating, not adapting and transforming from an "object of history" into a "subject of history." Leaving the previously stagnant state of semi-intransitivity, individuals of a transitive consciousness begin to seek answers outside of their immediate experience, ultimately opening up the possibility for the joining of agency and a critical structural perception of social, political, and historical realities or what Freire termed "critical consciousness." The critically conscious person, Freire (1974) argued, is "characterized by a depth in the interpretation of problems; by the substitution of causal principles for magical explanations; by the testing of one's 'findings' and the openness to revision; by the attempt to avoid distortion when perceiving problems and to avoid preconceived notions when analyzing them" (p. 29). This fully humanized state of critical consciousness, however, can only be developed if the individual (and society in general) engages in dialogue-centered educative practice, which, in essence, is an encounter between individuals "mediated by the world, in order to name the world" (Freire, 1972, p. 88). Without a collective capacity for critical consciousness, the societies inevitably slide into polarized sectarian camps.

Out of the Ruins: Education as an Act of Freedom

Freedom in a particular society is not assured as a result of birth. True liberation—overcoming despotism of mind and body—is an acquired status not easily achieved. If the education of youth does not prove to be consciously and actively engaged on behalf of the kind of education required for active democratic citizenship, then by default it contributes to its demise. A basic assumption of this chapter is that if the education of youth is to be in some sense a seedbed for genuine participatory democracy it should in turn exhibit characteristics and behaviors that evince this aim. Education must go beyond platitudes about "lifelong learning" and "no child left behind" and be situated within a truly democratic context. In bearing witness that education can be employed for the purpose of liberation and acknowledging the conscious political implications of the way it is organized, the way power is exercised within it, and the ways in which the young are classified, balkanized, and controlled, the authors of this volume provide hope.

As Proudhon (1851) suggested, capitalism, statism and religion represent a "trinity of absolutism [that] is as baneful in practice as it is in philosophy" (p. 44). Each of these purveyors and benefactors of the authoritarian mind must be contested as the interconnected, co-conspirators that they are, no matter how disconnected, or even opposed, they may seem. Until the institutions that generate and exploit such dehumanized consciousness are exposed, challenged, and eventually destroyed, humanity will never rid itself of their divisive and destructive impact. A critical education, aimed at the development of full and independent human consciousness, can and must play a critical and concerted role in attacking dogmatic institutions and ideologies. When education is constructed for the purpose of promoting what Freire (1974) termed "critical consciousness," and the capacities for logic and reason are made paramount, institutions that promote exclusionary, egocentric ideologies will wither and fade from human society. In short, as Persinger (1987) states,

> These insights require education, and this is lethal to egocentrism. As a person becomes more educated, particularly in the behavioral sciences, he begins to realize that he is not unique. Education forces the ego-centric child in each of us as equal to others in human experience. The sacred and profoundly personal experiences that once were proofs of our individual uniqueness are seen for what they are, predictable and necessary behaviors that allow us to deal with the existential terror of personal death and the horror of realizing that we are as vulnerable as everyone else. (p. 116)

It is the development of critical consciousness that serves as the universal cure for human-created systems of domination and exploitation—whether religious, economic, or statist. As Harris (2003) contended, there appears nowhere in history a case where a civilization destroyed itself through an overdependence on rationality, logic, and reasonableness. Systems of injustice are maintained, above all else, by way of the miseducation of the people who suffer within them.

The fertile soil within which every exclusionary ideology and institution takes root—whether theological, economic, statist, or otherwise—is the authoritarian personality, born of a fanatical consciousness and a fear-induced need of absolute control. As Freire (1974) explained, "sectarianism is predominantly emotional and uncritical. It is arrogant, antidialogical and thus anticommunicative" (p. 9). Lacking a reflective element—and seeing no need for one—the sectarian mind eliminates the potential for dialogue, questioning and agency, ultimately alienating individuals not only from others,but also first from themselves as historical and autonomous beings. From their absolutist position, the sectarian consistently views the "other" as an adversary because, from such a viewpoint, there can be only one truth, and that is their own. However, because the sectarian is typically formed from an anti-dialogical and authoritarian process, the absolute truth that they vehemently profess is rarely, if ever, actually their own; rather it is a truth that has been instilled by some perceived source of authority. Such a reactionary position is inherently exclusionary, and such disengagement from humanity is a necessary precondition to the development and perpetuation of discriminatory systems.

History clearly evinces that making visible the circumstances and power relations undergirding any form of hegemony, by way of the development of a critical and dialectic lens within the people, has always been the most fundamental ingredient for counter-hegemonic struggle. Authoritarians recognize this threat inherent to liberatory education and, in maintenance of its agenda, seek to nullify and obliterate any such form of democratic resistance to the expansion of hegemonic control. In response, critical educators must revisit our missions, recommit ourselves to the ideals of democracy, citizenship, and social justice, and find ways to dedicate our pedagogical spaces to liberation. We must each find ways to turn our classrooms into laboratories of critical consciousness, to encourage the development of critical agency, to promote engagement by activist citizens and teachers, and nourish a new generation of transformative intellectuals for a participatory democracy. In short, educators must lead the way *out of the ruins*.

References

Adorno, T.W., Frenkel-Brunswik, E., Levinson, D.J., & Sanford, R.N. (1950). *The authoritarian personality*. New York, NY: Harper and Row.

Altemeyer, R. (1988). *The enemies of freedom*. San Francisco, CA: Jossey-Bass.

Arnstine, D. (1971). Freedom and bureaucracy in the schools. In V.F. Haubrich (Ed.), *Freedom, bureaucracy, and schooling*. Washington, DC: ASCD, 1971, 3–28.

Benscoter, D. (2013). *Shoes of a servant: My unconditional devotion to a lie*. New York, NY: Lucky Bat Books.

Bowles, S., & Gintis, H. (1976). *Schooling in capitalist America: Educational reform and the contradictions of economic life*. New York, NY: Basic Books, Inc.

Chomsky, N., (2000). *Chomsky on miseducation*. Lanham, MD: Rowman & Littlefield Publishers.

Clancy, E. (2007). Youth, students and revolution. Democratic Socialist Perspective. Retrieved from http://www.dsp.org.au/node/168.

Dawkins, R. (1976). *The selfish gene*. New York, NY: Oxford University Press.

Dean, J. (2005). *Conservatives without consciousness*. New York, NY: Viking Publishing.

Engels, F. (1893). Engels to Franz Mehring: London, July 14, 1893. Retrieved at: https://www.marxists.org/archive/marx/works/1893/letters/93_07_14.htm

Feuerbach, L.A. (1841). The distinction between Christianity and heathenism. Retrieved from http://www.marxists.org/reference/archive/feuerbach/works/essence/index.htm.

Freire, P. (1974). *Education for critical consciousness*. London, UK: Continuum Press.

Freire, P. (1985). *The politics of education: culture, power and liberation*. Westport, CT: Greenwood Publishing Group.

Fromm, E. (1941). *Escape from freedom*. New York, NY: Farrar & Rinehart.

Fromm, E. (1956). *The art of loving*. New York, NY: Bantam Books.

Godwin, W. (1783). *An account of the seminary that will be opened*. London: T. Cadell.

Gramsci, A. (1971). *Selections from the prison notebooks of Antonio Gramsci*. New York, NY: International Publishers.

Gutmann, A. (1987). *Democratic education*. Princeton, NJ: Princeton University Press.

Harris, S. (2006). *The end of faith*. New York, NY: W.W. Norton & Co.

Kirscht, J., & Dillehay, R. (1967). *Dimensions of authoritarianism: A review of research and theory*. Lexington, KY: University of Kentucky Press.

Makarenko, A. (1955). *The road to life*. Moscow, USSR: Foreign Language Press.

Marx, K., (1843). Marx to Ruge: Kreuznach, September 1843. Retrieved at: https://www.marxists.org/archive/marx/works/1843/letters/43_09.htm

Marx, K., & Engels, F. (1996). *The German ideology*. New York, NY: International Publishers.

Mill, J.S. (1951). *Utilitarianism, liberty, and representative government*. New York, NY: Dutton.

Nash, P. (1966). *Authority and freedom in education*. New York, NY: John Wiley & Sons.

Persinger, M. (1987). *Neurological bases of god beliefs*. New York, NY: Praeger Publishers.

Proudhon, J. (1851). *The general idea of revolution in the nineteenth century*. New York, NY: Cosimo Books (reprinted 2007).

Romanish, B. (1995, fall). Authority, authoritarianism, and education. *Education and Culture, XII*, 2, 17–25.

Spring, J. (1999). *Wheels in the head: Educational philosophies of authority, freedom, and culture from Socrates to human rights*. 2nd ed. New York, NY: McGraw Hill College.

Stirner, M. (1842/1967). *The false principle of our education*. Colorado Springs, CO: Ralph Myles.

Winell, M., & Tarico, V. (2014). The crazy-making in Christianity. In J. Luftus (Ed.), *Christianity is not great: How faith fails*. New York, NY: Prometheus Books, 376–401.

Zhao, Y. (2014). *Who's afraid of the big bad dragon?* San Francisco, CA: Jossey-Bass.

CHAPTER 2

Don't Act, Just Think!

David Gabbard

Introduction

Just because I am a critical educational theorist does not mean I am not an idiot. At least, I am not a moron. I don't use these terms lightly, but neither do I use them in their everyday derogatory sense. I do not intend to offend, only to illuminate through provocation. I borrow the specific meanings of these words from Slavoj Žižek's book, *Less Than Nothing* (2012a) in an effort to shed light, primarily, on the predicament of critical educational theorists, and also on how I view my own predicament and the trajectory of my thought on schools over the years.

When I entered graduate school immediately upon completing my enlistment contract with the U.S. Army in 1987, I was seeking a cure to the stupidity that led me to sign that contract in the first place. During the course of my enlistment, I entered into the very early stages of my evolution as a critical educational theorist, believing that my teachers had lied to me about the nature of our government and the uses to which it puts its military. They led me to believe that our military serves to defend the same democratic principles that they purported as characterizing our form of government. Once in the military and from various sources, I learned this to be horrifically untrue. Had I known that the military and the government itself both function to serve corporate interests rather than democratic ones, I would have never agreed to sign that contract. Again, I believed the problem to have rested with my own teachers, as if the institutional context of the schools in which they worked existed independent from government.

On the first night of my very first graduate class, I learned that I was wrong. The problem did not lie with my teachers, but was far more systemic. The state created schools, I learned, precisely in order to impose ignorance. I continue to view education as I always have, as a value intimately tied to the pursuit of an even higher value, namely, truth. Viewed from this perspective, I could only view the mission of schools as highly antithetical to the value of education. In this, I found myself allied with Ivan Illich, whose *Deschooling Society* (1971) left a deep impression on me, but evidently not deep enough. While I was busy studying Illich and connecting his works to those of Michel Foucault, Paulo Freire's *Pedagogy of the Oppressed* (1970)—first published in English only a year before the appearance of Illich's *Deschooling Society*—was registering far more influence over the larger arena of critical educational studies. Though Freire did not work in a U.S. school, his ideas inspired many to believe that schools should and could serve liberatory and democratic purposes, that teachers could function as Gramscian organic intellectuals, and that schools could become instruments for leveraging massive social and political change. This faith in, or hope for, schools has come to function as a kind of orthodoxy among critical educational theorists, leading many to describe neoliberalism's effects on schools in heavily militaristic terms as an assault on public schools, suggesting that schools operate to serve the public and not target it. While neoliberal reforms have undoubtedly intensified the traditional patterns of schooling described below, we delude ourselves if we frame those reforms as somehow undermining the democratic foundations of those institutions, for such foundations have never existed.

However reluctantly, I have at times, and to varying degrees, succumbed to the "will to believe" in the redemptive power of schools that is characteristic of critical educational theorists. After twenty years of reading and writing critical educational theory, I see things as having only deteriorated, leading me to feel a little bit stupid, but no less stupid than I felt when I realized what I'd done when I voluntarily joined the military.

Morons and Idiots

In his introduction to *Less Than Nothing*, Žižek distinguishes idiots from morons, and he describes them as two opposing forms of stupidity (Žižek, 2012a, pp. 1–2). Within the framework of Žižek's Lacanian understanding of the human psyche, we can understand the moron as someone who identifies with, that is, draws their identity from, the "big Other." For Lacan, the big Other is the symbolic order—the rules and norms of society (Lacan, 1991a; Lacan, 1991b; Žižek, 2007). As the big Other constitutes part of the human psyche, each of us internalizes the symbolic order as it is manifested in language. While those rules and norms guide our actions and our interactions, informing what we come to know as "common sense," not everyone derives their identity from them, only—by Žižek's definition—morons.

Though Žižek does not make this connection, I think it is worth our time here to consider the pathology of the moron. What distinguishes the moron most from non-morons? In my view, if I understand Žižek and Lacan properly, the issue rests with the object of the moron's identification—the big Other—that shapes his or her subjectivity (Lacan, 1991b). We must contrast that with the object of the non-moron's identification. Identity and identification, for Lacan, lie in a domain of the psyche that is separate from but closely intertwined with the symbolic order, namely the imaginary order. In his theory of psychosexual development, he asserts that human beings exist in a state of nature from birth to six months; a period marked exclusively by our primal needs and our internal drives to satisfy those needs. In this stage of our development, we experience the full materiality of our existence in the world (the Real), and we have no sense of being separate from it. We have yet to form an identity outside of the world. There is no "I." As the "I" germinates, the Real begins to dissipate (Lacan, 1991a).

The formation of an "I"-dentity occurs during what Lacan (1991a) terms the "mirror stage." Around the age of six months, we develop the capacity to recognize and identify with our image in a mirror. At the same time, this recognition of our self generates an awareness of our separateness from the world, leading to great anxiety and an impossible demand to recover our lost sense of holism, our original feeling of oneness with, and attachment to, the Real. Typically, as we pass through our psychosocial development, we falsely recognize our image in the mirror as a stable, coherent self that can substitute for the self that is lost. The image becomes what Lacan refers to as our "Ideal-I" or our "ideal ego." As an idyllic construct, however, it serves only as a fantasy to be filled in later in life by some other object/mirror image with which we come to identify. For non-morons, that object of identification from the imaginary order exists in constant interaction with, but remains separate from, the big Other of the symbolic order. For morons, however, there is no separation of the imaginary from the symbolic as the big Other becomes the object of identification through which they structure their subjectivity.

Idiots, on the other hand, manifest an altogether different and opposite form of stupidity. Rather than deriving their sense of reality and their sense of identity from the big Other of the symbolic order, idiots act in a manner that is oblivious to the big Other taken by others to be the dictates of common sense. Žižek is not suggesting that anyone behaves as an idiot at all times. Typically, idiocy is confined to discrete situations, he provides as an example a story from his first visit to New York when a waiter asked him: "'How was your day?' Mistaking the phrase for a genuine question," Žižek says, "I answered him truthfully ('I am dead tired, jet-lagged, stressed out . . .'), and he looked at me as if I were a complete idiot . . . and he was right: this kind of stupidity is precisely that of an idiot" (Žižek, 2012a, p. 1).

What I want to argue here is that critical educational theorists, including myself at times, have made a habit of this kind of idiocy. Even so, idiocy is not symptomatic of the critical condition, meaning that we all aren't idiots all of the time. When we are, I believe we can trace our idiocy back to the prompting of a certain subset of morons constituted by a certain subset of teachers and teacher educators. So, I'm not calling all teachers and teacher educators morons; however, a certain subset, even probably, based on some of the data presented below, a majority of them, demonstrate the character-istics of morons as described above. And I have nearly fifty years of research to support this claim (e.g., Meyers & Torrance, 1961; Getzels & Jackson, 1962; Torrance, 1963; Urick & Frymier, 1963; Bachtold, 1974; and Westby & Dawson, 1995).

The Big Other in the Classroom

If a majority of teachers and teacher educators, "schooled" people in general—especially administrators—weren't morons, our schools wouldn't be so hostile toward creative teachers and creative students. As Westby and Dawson (1995) explain, "One of the most consistent findings in educational studies of creativity has been that teachers dislike personality traits asso-ciated with creativity" (ibid., p. 1). They particularly don't like one of the three inner traits of creative persons identified by Harvard professor Teresa Amabile in her componential theory of creativity (2012). Namely, they don't like what she recognizes within creative people as *creativity-relevant processes*.

Some of these processes, she explains, give expression to elements of a person's cognitive qualities, while others relate more directly to their per-sonality. Cognitively, creative persons demonstrate "the ability to use wide, flexible categories for synthesizing information and the ability to break out of perceptual and performance 'scripts'" (Amabile, 2012, p. 4). Such a capac-ity would certainly pose a threat to the identity and subjective leanings of any moron. What, after all, is the symbolic order, if not a perceptual and performance script? Equally as threatening to the self-image of the moron, creative persons also demonstrate, according to Amabile's findings, a person-ality that tolerates ambiguity. For morons, the very purpose of the symbolic order—with its rules and norms—is to eliminate and repress ambiguity, and their purpose for seeking their identify in image of the big Other is to maxi-mize their feelings of stability within that order. In combination, these two dimensions of creativity-relevant processes allow people to work indepen-dently, to take risks, and to bring fresh perspectives on problems that allow them to create new ideas. This places them at odds with the big Other and the self-image/personality of those teachers who identify with it and who, in so doing, define the culture of their classroom through the enforcement of the rules and norms of the symbolic order.

Instead, "teachers prefer traits that seem to run counter to creativity, such as conformity and unquestioning acceptance of authority" (Westby and

Dawson, 1995, p. 1). These are precisely the types of character traits that we would associate with the big Other that supports our society's and, increasingly, the world's dominant institutions, namely the market institutions that gave rise to the modern nation-state as an instrument for policing the world, in the sense of serving and protecting market interests. Part of this policing required the reproduction of the values and beliefs supporting those market institutions. Takis Fotopoulos (2003) refers to those values and beliefs as the "dominant social paradigm," which I view as roughly analogous to Lacan's idea of the symbolic order—the big Other that morons identify with and draw upon in forming their identities/self-images. The basic organizing principles of market institutions include heteronomy and individualism, and, according to Fotopoulos, "involve the values of inequity and effective oligarchy (even if the system calls itself a democracy), competition and aggressiveness." We clearly see these principles and values, particularly the principle of heteronomy—submission to external authority—in the character traits of students most preferred by teachers as cited by Westby and Dawson.

In forming their conclusion regarding teacher's attitudes toward creative students, whose own traits would lean more in the direction of preferring autonomy, Westby and Dawson cite a rich tradition of research dating back to the early 1960s. Among the studies they cite, we find works by Robert E. Meyers and E. Paul Torrance (1961), Jacob W. Getzels and Phillip W. Jackson (1962), Louise M. Bachtold (1974), Peggy Dettmer (1981), and Arthur J. Copley (1992). In addition to citing Westby and Dawson, Kyung Hee Kim (2008) draws upon an equally impressive body of literature to support her conclusion that "research has shown that teachers are apt to prefer students who are achievers and teacher pleasers rather than disruptive or unconventional creative students" (p. 236) As she elaborates,

> Scott reported that teachers see creative children as a source of interference and disruption. Westby and Dawson found that teachers' judgment of their favorite students was negatively correlated with creativity. Teachers prefer students to exhibit traits such as unquestioning acceptance of authority, conformity, logical thinking, and responsibility that make students easy to manage in the classroom. Teachers' images of the ideal student emphasize traits that were conformist and socially acceptable. (Ibid.)

Drawing upon the work of Everett E. Hagen (1962), as well as that of Myers and Torrance (1962), Ronald Urick and Jack R. Frymier (1963) help us extend beyond recognizing how teachers' attitudes have historically contributed to the creation of classroom norms that are hostile toward creativity. Their work helps us understand why those same attitudes work to ensure that the learning environments in the U.S. school system will likely never change. The majority of teachers deplore and resist change as much as they deplore and punish creativity.

With regard to people's attitudes toward change, Hagen (1962) distinguished between two different personality types: innovational and authoritarian. The innovational personality, he claimed, demonstrates "an openness to experience, a confidence in one's own evaluations, a satisfaction in facing and resolving confusion or ambiguity, and a feeling that the world is orderly, and that the phenomenon of life can be understood and explained" (cited in Urick & Frymier, 1963, p. 109). Conversely, Urick and Frymier explain, Hagen viewed the authoritarian personality as "characterized by a fear of using his initiative, an uncertainty concerning the quality of his own judgment, and tendency to avoid frustration and anxiety, an uneasiness in facing unresolved situations, and a tendency to see the world as arbitrary and capricious," and therefore in dire need of management (ibid.).

Studies by Myers and Torrance (1962) reveal that teachers who resist change demonstrated the characteristics of "authoritarianism, defensiveness, insensitivity to pupil needs, preoccupation with information-giving functions, intellectual inertness, disinterest in promoting initiative in pupils, and preoccupation with discipline" (cited in Urick & Frymier, 1963, p. 109). This latter authoritarian preoccupation with discipline reveals itself in the feedback received by teacher education programs on surveys of their graduates in response to the question, "If you could have had more instruction in one area during your years spent in teacher training, what would that area have been?" Invariably, in my twenty years of experience in teacher education, across four different institutions in four different states, the most frequent response to that question has always been "classroom management."

This tells me, in light of all the research revealing their authoritarian personality that most teachers must view the work they demand of students as being a kind of necessary drudgery. They also view it as immutable. The nature of the work is not up for questioning or challenge. It's a given. It's not going to change, but why should it? It worked well enough for them.

Here we witness how the principle of individualism differs from the notion of autonomy. Far from contradicting the principle of heteronomy already shown to be at work in the schooled psyche of teachers, identifying with the big Other worked for them while they were students and continues working for them as teachers. While they were students in schools, while they were learning to identify with the big Other of the symbolic order being manifested through the behavior of their teachers, they demonstrated the same traits that they would later come to prefer in their own students. And they continue demonstrating this identification with the big Other through their behavior as students throughout undergraduate as well as graduate school.

In Melissa Engleman's study (2007) of 213 graduate students in education with a median of four years of classroom teaching experience, she found that more than half of her respondents fell into either the ISFJ (25 percent) or ESFJ (28 percent) personality type on the Humanetrics "Jung Typology" Test. Another 6 percent fell into the ESTJ type and 10 percent fell into the ISTJ type, making a total of 69 percent of the teachers fit the SJ temperament profile. While we do find differences among the various "SJ-Types," (e.g., they can be either introverted or extroverted, thinking or feeling in their personality orientation, they share the traits of being "sensors" rather than "intuitives" and "judgers"rather than "perceivers" (Wikibooks, 2006). While perceivers lean toward leaving "their options open to perceive new possibilities and processes as long as possible," judgers "prefer to come to decisions and move on. They can feel betrayed if a decision is "'reopened.'" In their focus on *getting things done*, judgers are often prone to hastiness. Intuitives use logic and metaphors in considering options, while sensors pride themselves in what they perceive to be their pragmatism and their focus on *the real world* (Wikibooks, 2006). In combination, the traits of sensing and judging forge a personality type that is "conservative and hardworking, values responsibility and service to others, is serious, trustworthy, and diligent, focused on duty and getting the job done, adheres to traditional values and dress, and is slow to accept new ideas. The SJ has a strict idea of how things should be done and frowns on deviation from it" (Wikibooks, 2006). Their tendency to demonstrate great attention to detail and quick decision-making suits their vocational calling to pursue careers in the management of institutions/organizations.

In his *Learning Patterns and Temperament Styles* (1982), Keith Golay characterizes SJs as "Actual Routine Learners" (ARLs). These people feel a need to establish and preserve social units, which fits with their demand for clear expectations and specific, clearly defined procedures for accomplishing a task. These traits align with their tendency to be meticulous as well as highly industrious. As students, ARLs also display a very strong need to please and receive approval from authority figures, including and especially their teachers. In turn, they hold authority figures in reverence, deferring to that authority through obedience and conformity (Golay, 1982).

If we can accept Engleman's numbers as fairly representative of the broader population of those people who chose to enter teaching as a career, we can hypothesize that 70 percent of the classroom learning environments in America's system of compulsory schooling are created and maintained by *Actual Routine Teachers*. We can further hypothesize that those environments most heavily reward children who learn to revere the authority of teachers and who work diligently at their assigned tasks to win their approval through their obedience to and their conformity with the teachers' values and expectations. Because they experience these rewards from their teach-

ers in these environments, ARLs/SJs might be more disposed toward choosing teaching as a career, but the *cycle of compliance* does not begin or end here.
Actual Routine Teachers beget Actual Routine Learners, many of whom grow
up to become Actual Routine Teachers, Actual Routine Administrators, and
Actual Routine Teacher Educators, all of whom demonstrate the traits of
stupidity that Žižek attributes to morons—those who derive their identities
from the big Other of the symbolic order supporting the dominant institutions of a market society. All of this leaves us to wonder why many critical
educational theorists so ardently express such a deep commitment to the
defense of schools from institutions whose symbolic order is already being
reproduced by those same schools? They must be idiots!

Origins of an Illusion

It bears repeating at this point that Žižek distinguishes idiots from morons,
describing them as two opposing forms of stupidity. If they are opposites,
and if morons become stupid by taking the symbolic order as their imaginary, deriving their self-image from the big Other, then idiots must do the
opposite. Idiots must become stupid by mistaking some imaginary order to
be the symbolic order. Again, Žižek describes the idiot as "the (occasionally
hyper-intelligent subject who just doesn't 'get it,' who understands a situation logically, but simply misses its hidden contextual rules" (Žižek, 2012a,
p. 1). Those of us who count ourselves as critical educational theorists do not
lack for intelligence. So, what situation do we understand logically, but at the
same time wrongly? What hidden contextual rules do we miss? What leads
us toward the idiocy of mistaking the imaginary order for the symbolic order,
and what imaginary order am I even referring to here?

As I have already discussed, the symbolic order that so many teachers
subconsciously participate in reproducing through their work in schools
reflects the values and beliefs of our society's dominant institutions, namely,
market institutions. I would submit that the level of dominance enjoyed by
those institutions and the symbolic order upon which they rest defines our
society as a market society. It is the degree of this dominance, however, that
is lost on many critical educational theorists. Most of my colleagues, especially my American ones, I believe, would stop short of describing society in
these terms for the reason already given, or at least implied. Namely, they
do not recognize the actually existing symbolic order as the actually existing
symbolic order. For them, the character of society and its institutions (or at
least those of the state) are defined by some imaginary order, and it is in the
mirror of this imaginary order that they see themselves reflected.

In *The Great Transformation*, Karl Polanyi (1944) describes the marketization of European societies, the process by which traditional societies
come to be market societies. All traditional societies, Polanyi argues, have

markets, but those markets remain embedded within social relations. Food, for example, is grown and harvested by people on ground that is held in common for the purpose of sustaining the community. It is not a commodity. The land is not property. And the people who grow and harvest the food are not commodified as labor. In market societies, the market becomes disembedded from social relations, operating outside of those social relations for the benefit of profit-seekers. Social relations become subordinate to the market. (See Polanyi, 1944; Gabbard, 2007, 2008c.)

In Western Europe and, even more dramatically in what would become the United States—a former colonial possession of European powers—the modern state originated as a consequence of this marketization of society. The financial power of the new merchant class translated into political power, allowing this class to rival and, ultimately, triumph over the feudal aristocracy. In the United States, the successful revolution and consequent independence of the former colonies meant that merchants, bankers, and other "men of property," unlike their European contemporaries, would no longer be impeded in their economic pursuits by monarchical authority as vested in the remnants of the feudal state. In effect, independence meant that they could create their own state that would "serve and protect" their liberty to pursue their economic interests—the essence of economic liberalism (Gabbard, 2007).

In their ascendancy, they forged a state apparatus to serve two fundamental purposes. First, at an individual level, the state would play an active role in advancing their freedom to pursue profit. Second, at a more communal level, the state would also assist in the enforcement and expansion of the market regime as a whole and for the benefit of "all." This, for them, was democracy. (See Gabbard, 2004a, 2004b, 2004c.)

Organizing the state as a nation-state was critical to the success of the market regime. On the one hand, it defined the territorial boundaries of the market regime's reach in relation to that of other emergent market regimes in other nations, though all of them sought to expand their respective reach and the size of their territory to gain access to more resources. This led, of course, to inevitable conflicts, necessitating the creation and maintenance of a military force large enough and powerful enough to secure the interests of the market regime. The military requirements themselves created a market for weaponry, transport, and other accoutrements of war. Those requirements also intensified the need to mobilize the population behind the interests of the market regime. Not only were their energies needed to fuel the productive capacities of the market, but they were also needed to fuel the military capacities of the state to expand and enforce the market regime across greater territory. The formation of the nation-state would play a tremendous role in this as well.

Not only did the idea of the nation define the territorial limits of the market regime, it tied its identity and the identity of the state to that territory. Mobilizing the population to serve the interests of the regime, lending their energies to the pursuit of profit, meant working to attach their own identity to that territory, state, and regime as well. From this came the need to formulate an imaginary order that would contribute to the individual's docility so that the already existing symbolic order of the market regime that demanded her/his utility could be imposed. The idea of nationhood provided a partial basis for this imaginary order, cultivating people's sense of loyalty and commitment to *their* country, for they had to be made to feel part of something larger than themselves. But this imaginary order required something more concrete against which they could measure their loyalty and commitment. Their loyalty and commitment to "their" country had to measure up against the loyalty and commitment of the state and their "public servants." Thus, this symbolic order included the conception of a benevolent state, dedicated to serving and leading the country and its people to ever-greater glory and abundance. The state inscribed itself, then, with what Michel Foucault referred to as *pastoral power* (Foucault, 1988, pp. 57–85). (See also Gabbard, 1993, 1994.)

Particularly in the United States, much of the contents of this pastoral imaginary order that sought to ensure the docility of the population in order to better secure its utility expressed itself through the language of democracy. After all, elites of the market regime had, in fact, established a democratic state for themselves that would enhance their individual autonomy as well as their collective interests. Such democratic values found little substantive expression in the lives of the majority of the population. Initially, we must remember, the property-owning elite who designed the state granted the franchise solely to themselves. For the rest of the population, this democratic imaginary served as little more than an empty gesture, designed to increase their docility by reducing any potential resistance they might mount against the imperatives of the state/market regime, including the imperative to increase their utility through the cultivation and channeling of the population's energies in the service of the market regime more directly.

In this sense, the imaginary order of the political sphere was only authentically meaningful for the elites of the market regime who served as the architects and directors of the state. For the majority of the population, it was an illusion created only to make them feel part of something in which they had never been fully enfranchised. On the other hand, they experienced the symbolic order of the market regime that sought to increase their utility as something far more real. While the pastoral imagery of the state emphasized the values of autonomy and community, the disciplinary language of the market regime privileged the values of heteronomy (submitting to external authority) and individualism. In other words, one advances one's own economic self-interest by doing what one is told and doing it to maximal efficiency (Gabbard, 1995, 2003, 2008a, 2008b, 2008c). Many critical educational theorists, then, have staked their identities to an illusion or, better, layers of illusion.

The Pastoral Imaginary Order of School and State

In *How to Read Lacan* (2007), Žižek elaborates on the analogy drawn by Lacan between language and "gifts of the Danaoi," the Trojan horse. Hidden within language, which forms a major portion of the larger symbolic order, lies the big Other. "When we speak (or listen, for that matter), we never merely interact with others; our speech activity is grounded in our accepting and relying on a complex network of rules and other kinds of presuppositions" (Žižek, 2006, p. 9). Whenever we read, speak, write, and listen, we activate and sustain those rules. Through these communicative interactions, we interact with more than just each other; we interact with those rules. We must refer to them as a guide to direct us as we act and interact. In this way, they act as the big Other.

In what was my doctoral dissertation at the University of Cincinnati and became the book *Silencing Ivan Illich: A Foucauldian Analysis of Discursive Exclusion*, I examined those rules as they govern educational discourse. Had I read Žižek and Lacan during that period, I would have had a much different career. I mean this in the sense that I would have written much differently than I have written. I would have had a much different perspective, for it would have allowed me to have taken the next logical step from the conclusions that I reached in that dissertation. Instead, I chose a different path and, in the process, became a little bit of an idiot myself. I shall return to those matters later.

What is important for me to address now are the conclusions I was able to draw in *Silencing Ivan Illich*. Having read Foucault (1988) extensively during my doctoral studies, I wanted to unpack the rules governing educational discourse (Gabbard, 1993, 1994). More specifically, in Lacanian terms, I wanted to reveal the big Other that governs what we can and cannot say about schools. From studying how and why those rules led to the eventual exclusion of Ivan Illich from educational discourse, I determined that his exclusion resulted from his violation of what I termed the messianic rule of discursive inclusion.

This rule stipulates that in order to speak or write about education, we must present the school as either an inherently benevolent institution—or at the very least, with the proper reforms, a potentially benevolent institution—capable of delivering the individual and/or society into some condition of secular salvation. The vision of what that condition looks like can take an infinite number of forms, as can the vision of the means by which schools can reach their full pastoral potential. In *Deschooling Society*, Illich denounced what Foucault called the "pastoral power" of the school, just as he had in his earlier writings denounced the "pastoral power" of the institutional church to deliver people's souls to salvation in the afterlife. As a consequence, interest in Illich's ideas (1970) waned very rapidly during the 1970s, though they have received a small degree of renewed interest over the past decade.

The pastoral image of the school as a benevolent institution functions as perhaps the most pervasive big Other in the educational discourse. It asks or demands us to take its benevolence as an article of faith. As such, while it permits us to exercise our critical faculties in judging the efficacy or the desirability of its outcomes, we cannot direct those faculties toward questioning the benevolence of its intentions or potential. Once we internalize this benevolent image, maintaining the big Other of the imaginary order becomes a matter of conscience.

The pastoral image functions on the exterior of the school. In this sense, we can view it as being somewhat superficial, operating as what Noam Chomsky might call a "necessary illusion" or an "emotionally potent oversimplification" intended largely for public consumption in order to manufacture consent for what is otherwise compulsory (Achbar, 1994, p. 42). Here we can best witness how the notion of "public education" functions analogously to Lacan's view of language as a Trojan horse. As Žižek explains, "For Lacan, language is a gift as dangerous to humanity as the horse was to the Trojans: it offers itself to our usage free of charge, but once we accept it, it colonizes us. The symbolic order emerges from a gift, an offering that marks its content as neutral in order to pose as a gift: when a gift is offered, what matters is not its content but the link between the giver and receiver established when the receiver accepts the gift." (Žižek, 2007, pp. 11–12)

As just stated, the pastoral image of the school enforced by the messianic rule of discursive inclusion, functions as part of a symbolic order that is largely exterior to the school, though it can be invoked within the interior as well, typically, to goad the conscience of noncompliant students and critical educational theorists who might lack sufficient appreciation for the gift of what is otherwise compulsory. To the general population, the institutional school is to be recognized as part of a larger system of public education. Though the state collects local, state, and federal taxes to operate the school, the school is to be experienced as a gift from the state. It serves as a gift to the public from the state, symbolizing a transfer of the benevolence of the state to the school. The benevolence of the school, then, originates from the benevolence of the state, making the pastoral power of the school an element of the larger imaginary order that fuels and sustains the pastoral power and the benevolence of the state. The state serves the public through the gift of schools, which, in turn, serve the value of education. But Žižek helps us recognize something paradoxical in this idea of public education as a gift.

The most elementary act of symbolic exchange is a so-called empty gesture, an offer made that is meant to be rejected. Brecht gave a poignant expression to this feature in his play *Lasager*, in which a young boy is asked to comply freely with what will in any case be his fate (to be thrown into the valley); as his teacher explains, it is customary to ask the victim if he agrees with his fate, but it is also customary for the victim to say yes. Belonging to a society involves a paradoxical point at which each of us is ordered to embrace freely, as the result of our choice, what is anyway imposed on us (we all *must* love our country, our parents, our religion). This paradox of willing (choosing freely) what is in any case compulsory, or pretending (maintaining the appearance) that there is a free choice although effectively there isn't one, is strictly co-dependent with the notion of a symbolic gesture, a gesture—an offer—that is meant to be rejected (Žižek, 2006, pp. 12–13).

The pastoral image of the school as a benevolent institution, whether inherently or potentially, presents the school to the public as a gift. Again, that big Other of the imaginary order operates on the exterior to cloak the compulsory nature of schooling and the big Other of the symbolic order functioning on the interior of the school. This cloaking has been so successful that most people, including many critical educational theorists (e.g., De Lissovoy, Means & Saltman, 2013; Giroux, 1998; Saltman, 2007; Spring, 2000), fail to recognize the compulsory nature of schooling while understanding it as a fundamental human need to which people have a right. Not only have they accepted the gift of the Trojan Horse, they have learned to demand it. What could be more Orwellian than to learn to love and long for the big Other? But is this not precisely the essence of Žižek's definition of a moron, or is it something even more stupid?

The School Is the State, and Neither Is Benevolent

If the pastoral image of the gift is an illusion, what is the big Other that is compulsory? If we "buy into" (an ominous phrase) the illusion, we might ask ourselves: what entity is benevolent enough to offer us this gift of public education? Otherwise, we should ask ourselves what entity has the authority to compel us to subject ourselves—and our children—to this institutional process of schooling? The answer to each question, of course, is the same: the state (see Gabbard, 2013, 2012; 2010, 2008a.)

Schools do not exist independently from the state; they *are* the state. The notion that they are public is, perhaps, the grandest part of the illusion. Yes, the public pays for schools, but the public also pays for private corporations such as Halliburton, Northrup Grumman, and Bechtel. Are they public?

Yes, the public elects people to serve on local school boards, but those local school boards serve chiefly to administer the policies adopted by federal and state-level officials. Aren't they elected as well? Some of them are, but elected state legislators depend on corporate donors for their campaigns. In turn, they appoint representatives from the corporate sector to sit on state school boards and other state-level, educational policy entities. The connections between the corporate sector and national educational policy-making bodies are even stronger.

At this point, I must clarify further the relation between the symbolic order and the imaginary order. This is important because they apply as much to the state as they do to the schools, and understanding this relation is crucial for grasping why we cannot view schools as anything other than the state. On one hand, it may be tempting to view these two orders as competing ideologies, with one of these ideologies framing the public as the recipient of education as a gift bestowed by a democratic government committed to serving the public interests, and the other framing the population as the target of compulsory schooling and other social technologies aimed at a different set of interests. Adopting this view, however, would mark an early step toward the idiocy previously addressed.

Again, I believe that the Trojan Horse provides the best metaphor for understanding the relations between these two orders. And it applies to our understanding of the state as much as it does to our understanding of the school because the two are the same. And, again, the school is the state. Just as there is a pastoral imaginary order of a benevolent school, there also exists a pastoral imaginary order of a benevolent state, and each feeds into the other, reciprocally. Within this order, we find images and empty symbols (words as well as objects such as flags and monuments) of patriotism, nationalism, and American exceptionalism. The character of the state becomes equated with the character of the country and the character of "the people." Part of the function of the school, of course, entails initiating the young into this imaginary order, socializing them toward feelings of sentimentality about the state—irrational feelings of pride, as if they had achieved something through the accident of having been born within the boundaries of territory to which the state claims ownership and legal jurisdiction. Moreover, one of the principle aims of this ritual of schooling is the formation of the individual's American identity founded upon the benevolent image of the state. As Benjamin Rush, known as the father of American psychiatry and signatory to the Declaration of Independence, wrote in his "Thoughts upon the Mode of Education Proper in a Republic" (1786): "Let our pupil be taught that he does not belong to himself, but that he is public property. Let him be taught to love his family, but let him be taught at the same time that he must forsake and even forget them when the welfare of his country requires it"

(Rush, 1786). In other words, through the rituals of compulsory schooling, the state aims to produce idiots as well as morons.

Of all of the rituals supporting the pastoral symbolic order of the state, none holds as much importance as elections in terms of affirming one's identity as an American. Video of British actor and comedian Russell Brand's exchange with BBC *Newsnight*'s Jeremy Paxman went viral soon after it was aired on October 23, 2013. It was the day before the publication of a special edition of *The New Statesman* guest edited by Brand. As soon as the interview began, Paxman challenged Brand's qualifications to edit a political magazine. Upon learning that Brand had never participated in any elections in the UK, he challenged his authority to even talk about politics. While Brand demonstrated great brilliance, both comic and political, in defending himself on *Newsnight*, his article in *The New Statesman* merits even greater appreciation:

> I have never voted. Like most people I am utterly disenchanted by politics. Like most people I regard politicians as frauds and liars and the current political system as nothing more than a bureaucratic means for furthering the augmentation and advantages of economic elites.

Brand went on to quote Billy Connolly:

> "Don't vote, it encourages them," and, "The desire to be a politician should bar you for life from ever being one." I don't vote because to me it seems like a tacit act of compliance; I know, I know my grandparents fought in two world wars (and one World Cup) so that I'd have the right to vote. Well, they were conned. As far as I'm concerned there is nothing to vote for. I feel it is a far more potent political act to completely renounce the current paradigm than to participate in even the most trivial and tokenistic manner, by obediently X-ing a little box. (Brand, 2013)

Brand's comments here come very close to the point I'm trying to make. What I believe he is saying is that voting only legitimates the "current paradigm," that it represents its own kind of "empty gesture" in an act of symbolic exchange. Just as the notion of "public education" frames compulsory schooling as a gift, the ritual of "democratic elections" serves to convince the electoral majority, at the very least, that the results of the election represent a gift, one of the many gifts of living in a free and democratic society. As a gift, the results of the election affirm for them, and the voting public at large, that "the people" will receive the government that they want. So, the state, itself, takes on the qualities of a gift for the majority who voted.

By the same token, aren't many critical educational theorists subconsciously legitimating a historic status quo in schools that has always functioned to reproduce and enforce the symbolic order of a market society when they posture as defenders of state-mandated compulsory schooling? What are they defending, and from what?

By now, many critical educational theorists might be asking me the same kind of question that school people have traditionally asked them over the years. "Well, I hear a lot of criticisms, but what solutions do you have to offer?" To my ears, such questions sound like efforts to goad my conscience into acknowledging at least the potential of compulsory schooling to deliver on the promise of its pastoral imaginary. On numerous occasions after submitting chapters and articles for publication, editors have asked me if I couldn't close my offering with "a little hope or optimism." Reluctantly, I've usually agreed, but it always felt like I was writing a speech for a beauty pageant. But at no time have I felt the tension between my thought and the norms of critical educational theory more than when I was co-editing a volume with Ken Saltman. It was his idea to title that book *Education as Enforcement*, and it was no accident that I chose to title my chapter "Education IS Enforcement," because it is (Gabbard, 2003)!

Conclusion: Spanking Our Pedagogy?

None of this should be taken to suggest that I am not still stupid, but my stupidity has never fit Žižek's definition of a moron, and it hasn't fit his definition of an idiot for a very long time now. In addition to the "original stupidity" that I described earlier, I suffer from a form of stupidity that comes much closer to what he describes as proper to an imbecile. That is, I am aware of the layers of symbolic order that surround me, but I don't trust it. More significantly, I'm too stupid to know what to do about it, aligning me perfectly with Žižek's position in a video he did for Big Think in 2012 which inspired the title of this chapter. "My advice," he begins,

> would be—because I don't have simple answers—two things: (a) precisely to start thinking. Don't get caught into this pseudo-activist pressure. Do something. Let's do it, and so on. So, no, the time is to think. I even provoked some of the leftist friends when I told them that if the famous Marxist formula was, "Philosophers have only interpreted the world; the time is to change it" . . . thesis 11 . . . maybe today we should say, "In the twentieth century, we maybe tried to change the world too quickly. The time is to interpret it again, to start thinking." (Žižek, 2012b)

His second recommendation entails making a demand that touches the fundamentals of our ideology (he uses the ongoing issue of universal health care as an example) but that cannot be accused of promoting an impossible agenda—like abolishing all private property. No, it's something that can be done relatively successfully. So that would be my idea, to carefully select issues like this where we do stir up public debate without being accused of being utopians in the bad sense of the term.

His advice here comes close to the advice given by the administration at Brigham Young University–Idaho (Thomas, 2014) to those students suffering from chronic masturbation stemming from their addiction to internet pornography. Though I would argue that BYU–Idaho's advice is much more pragmatic. This advice was given via an internet video that went relatively viral here in Idaho, and I am assuming also in Utah. It opens with a college-age male sitting at this laptop. The camera is positioned so that we only see his face and torso, not the computer screen. As the president of the university narrates the scene, we see the silhouette of this student's roommate enter and stand in the doorway. Obviously, the roommate is embarrassed over having caught this fellow surfing internet porn, because he quickly retreats down the hallway. The scene then shifts to a battlefield, where we see the same porn-addicted student as a soldier, wounded and writhing in pain. Across the battlefield, we see his roommate with the rest of the military squad. The roommate sees his friend lying in pain and begins moving in his direction to help him. Another squad member, however, pulls him back, telling him that it's not his concern, that the porn-addict is a goner. All the while, the university president is telling us that we have an obligation to reach out to those we know who are porn-addicted masturbators. We need to let them know our concern for them, and the harm that their acts bring to their souls.

In the final scene, we see that the roommate has taken his friend to a party. We see the former (?) porn addict mingling and chatting with a group of young women. And therein, I think, is a message for us. Many critical educational theorists have been fantasizing about transforming schools and transforming society for more than forty years. In a sense, our addiction to our fantasy has been quite lucrative in terms of helping us build our vitae. It lays a formula for us to follow in our writing. We can portray the schools as benevolent institutions and then report on the latest corporate reforms and the threat they pose to our democratic society, over and over again. On the other hand, however good it felt to write them, all of our books, articles, chapters, and keynote addresses have proven impotent in terms of effecting any significant change. If anything, neoliberal school reforms have only intensified the long-standing routines for reproducing the symbolic order of our market society. Critical educational theorists who ignore those historic patterns and routines and their ties to economic liberalism and the modern nation-state that it birthed betray their own criticality for the sake of the illusion that compulsory schooling was ever or will ever be otherwise. As I have argued elsewhere, there really is nothing "neo" (new) about neoliberalism (Gabbard, 2007). As long as market institutions maintain their dominance over society, the state will function as one of the principal means for enforcing that dominance, and compulsory schooling will function as one of the primary instruments through which the security state fulfills that mission.

Maybe critical educational theorists should heed the message of the video from BYU–Idaho by stopping with our grandiose fantasies of some large-scale transformation of the entire system of compulsory schooling and focusing our attention on the body of available partners in hope of finding willing partners: creative teachers who share our interests and concerns and who might be open to partnering with us in creating more meaningful learning experiences for children in schools.

References

Achbar, M. (Ed.). (1994). *Manufacturing consent: Noam Chomsky and the media.* Cheektowaga, NY: Black Rose Books.

Amabile, T.M. (2012). Componential theory of creativity. (HBS Working Paper Number: 12-096.) Retrieved from http://www.hbs.edu/faculty/Publication%20Files/12-096.pdf

Bachtold, L.M. (1974). The creative personality and the ideal pupil revisited. *Journal of Creative Behavior, 8,* 47–54.

Brand, R. (2013, October 24). Russell Brand on revolution: "We no longer have the luxury of tradition." *The New Statesman.* Retrieved from http://www.newstatesman.com/politics/2013/10/russell-brand-on-revolution

Copley, A.J. (1992). *More ways than one: Fostering creativity.* Norwood, NJ: Ablex.

De Lissovoy, N., Means, A.J., & Saltman, K.J. (2013). *Toward a new common school movement.* Dulles, VA: Paradigm Publishers.

Dettmer, P. (1981). Improving teacher attitudes toward characteristics of the creatively gifted. *Gifted Child Quarterly, 25,* 11–16.

Engleman, M. (2007). Applying learning styles and personality preference information to online teaching pedagogy. *Journal of Interactive Instruction and Development, 19* (3), 3–10.

Fotopoulos, T. (2003). From (mis)education to paideia. *Democracy in Nature, 9*(1). Retrieved from http://www.inclusivedemocracy.org/dn/vol9/takis_paideia.htm

Foucault, M. (1988). Politics and reason. In L.D. Krtizman (Ed.), *Michel Foucault: Politics, philosophy, culture* (pp. 57–85). New York, NY: Routledge.

Freire, P. (1970). *Pedagogy of the oppressed.* New York, NY: Herder and Herder.

Gabbard, D. (1993). *Silencing Ivan Illich: A Foucauldian analysis of intellectual exclusion.* San Francisco, CA: Austin & Winfield.

Gabbard, D. (1994). Ivan Illich, postmodernism, and the eco-crisis: Reintroducing a wild discourse. *Educational Theory, 44*(2), 173–187.

Gabbard, D. (1995). NAFTA, GATT & Goals 2000: Reading the political culture of post-industrial America. *Taboo: A Journal of Culture and Education, 26*(3), 184–205.

Gabbard, D. (2003). Education IS enforcement! In K.J. Saltman & D. Gabbard (Eds.), *Education as enforcement: The militarization and corporatization of schools* (pp. 61–80). New York, NY: Routledge.

Gabbard, D. (2004a). Introduction: Defending public education from the public. In D.A. Gabbard & E.W. Ross (Eds.), *Defending public schools: Education under the security state* (pp. xxv–xxxv). Westport, CT: Praeger.

Gabbard, D. (2004b). What is the matrix? What is the republic?: Understanding the crisis of democracy. In D.A. Gabbard & E.W. Ross (Eds.), *Defending public schools: Education under the security state* (pp. 31–42). Westport, CT: Praeger.

Gabbard, D. (2004c). Welcome to the desert of the real: A brief history of what makes schooling compulsory. In D.A. Gabbard & E.W. Ross (Eds.), *Defending public schools: Education under the security state* (pp. 1–13). Westport, CT: Praeger.

Gabbard, D. (2007). Militarizing class warfare: The historical foundations of the neoliberal/neoconservative nexus. *Education Policy Futures, 5*(2), 119–136. Retrieved from http://www.wwwords.co.uk/rss/abstract.asp?j=pfie&aid=2993

Gabbard, D. (2008a). Compulsory schooling. In S. Mathison & E.W. Ross (Eds.), *Battleground schools: An encyclopedia of conflict and controversy* (pp. 136–147). Westport, CT: Greenwood.

Gabbard, D. (2008b). Accountability. In D. Gabbard (Ed.), *Knowledge and power in the global economy: The effects of school reform in a neoliberal/neoconservative age* (2nd ed., pp. 191–198). New York, NY: Routledge.

Gabbard, D. (2008c). Global economy. In D. Gabbard (Ed.), *Knowledge and power in the global economy: The effects of school reform in a neoliberal/neoconservative age* (2nd ed., pp. 91–100). New York, NY: Routledge.

Gabbard, D. (2010). The outlook for social justice in our compulsory schools: An anarchist forecast. *Peace Studies Journal, 3*(1), 191–126. Retrieved from http://ejournal.narotama.ac.id/files/An%20anarchist%20forecast.pdf.

Gabbard, D. (2012). Updating the anarchist forecast for social justice in our compulsory schools, In R.H. Haworth (Ed.), *Anarchist Pedagogies: Collective Actions, Theories, and Critical Reflections on Education* (pp. 105–118). Oakland, CA: PM Press.

Gabbard, D. (2013). Educational leadership or followership? A response to Vital Miller. *Democracy&Education,20*(2),1–4.Retrievedfromhttp://democracyeducationjournal.org/cgi/viewcontent.cgi?article=1081&context=home

Gabbard, D., & Flint, L. (2013). Not too big to fail: How teacher education killed the foundations. *Critical Questions in Education, 4*(2), 181–191. Retrieved from http://files.eric.ed.gov/fulltext/EJ1046721.pdf.

Getzels, J.W., & Jackson, P.W. (1962).*Creativity and intelligence* (New York, NY: Wiley.

Giroux, H.A. (1998). Education incorporated? *Educational Leadership.* 56(2), 12–17,

Golay, K. (1982). *Learning patterns and temperament styles.* Newport Beach, CA: Manas Systems.

Hagen, E.E. (1962). *On the theory of social change: How economic growth begins.* Belmont, CA: Dorsey Press.

Illich, I. (1971). *Deschooling society.* New York, NY: Harper and Row.

Kim, K.H. (2008). Underachievement and creativity: Are gifted underachievers highly creative? *Creativity Research Journal,* 20(2), 235–242.

Lacan, J. (1991a). *The seminar of Jacques Lacan, Book I, Freud's papers on technique: 1953-1954.* (J. Forrester, Trans.). New York, NY: W.W. Norton & Company.

Lacan, J. (1991b). *The seminar of Jacques Lacan, Book II, The ego in Freud's theory and the technique of psychoanalysis: 1954-1955.* (S. Tomaselli, Trans.). New York, NY: W.W. Norton & Company.

Lacan, J. (2006). The mirror stage as formative of the function of the I as revealed in psychoanalytic experience. In Écrits. (B. Fink, Trans.). New York, NY: W.W. Norton & Company, 75–81.

Myers, R.E., & Torrance, E.P. (1961). Can teachers encourage creative thinking? *Educational Leadership,* 19, 156–159.

Polanyi, K. (1944). *The great transformation.* New York, NY: Farrar and Rinehart.

Rush, B. (1786). Thoughts upon the mode of education proper in a republic. Retrieved from http://www.schoolchoices.org/roo/rush.htm.

Saltman, K.J. (2007). Schooling in disaster capitalism: How the political right is using disaster to privatize public schooling. *Teacher Education Quarterly, 34*(2), 131–156. Retrieved from http://www.teqjournal.org/Back%20Issues/Volume%2034/VOL34%20PDFS/34_2/14saltman-34_2.pdf

Spring, J. (2000). *The universal right to education: Justification, definition, and guidelines.* New York, NY: Taylor and Francis.

Thomas, E. (2014, February, 5). BYU-Idaho video depicts porn addiction as war. *Huffington Post.* Retrieved from http://www.huffingtonpost.com/2014/02/03/byu-idaho-anti-masturbation-video-war_n_4719599.html

Torrance, E. (1963). The creative personality and the ideal pupil. *Teachers College Record, 65,* 220–226.

Urick, R., & Frymier, J.R. (1963). Personalities, teachers and curriculum change. *Educational Leadership, 21*(2). 107–111. Retrieved from http://www.ascd.org/ASCD/pdf/journals/ed_lead/el_196311_urick.pdf

Westby, E., & Dawson, V. (1995). Creativity: Asset or burden in the classroom? *Creativity Research Journal, 8*(1), 1–10.

Wikibooks. (2006). Myers-Briggs Type Indicator. Retrieved from http://en.wikibooks.org/wiki/Myers-Briggs_Type_Indicator

Žižek, S. (2007). *How to read Lacan.* New York, NY: W.W. Norton & Company.

Žižek, S. (2012a). *Less than nothing: Hegel and the shadow of dialectical materialism.* London, UK: Verso.

Žižek, S. (2012b, July 8). Don't act. Just think. Big think. Retrieved from http://bigthink.com/videos/dont-act-just-think

Constructing Theoretical Frameworks for Educational Praxis

From the Unlearned Un-man to a Pedagogy without Moulding: Stirner, Consciousness-Raising, and the Production of Difference

Rhiannon Firth and Andrew Robinson

Using the theories of Max Stirner and the jointly authored works of Gilles Deleuze and Félix Guattari, this chapter seeks to critique pedagogies of moulding and to map and theorize alternatives. We begin by summarizing "moulding,"—why it is incompatible with post-representational politics, and the ways in which it persists in contemporary pedagogical theory. We then explore Stirner's anarchism, demonstrating the complicity of moulding pedagogies with political representation. We draw on further sources of inspiration including Deleuze and Guattari's (2004) three stages of schizoanalysis as well as practices of feminist consciousness-raising in the 1970s. Using these diverse sources, we seek to provide a working model of pedagogy without moulding, which can give rise to autonomous, self-valorizing subjects of becoming.

Post-representational politics and autonomous social movements are growing fields of study in radical political theory. Growing trends within poststructuralism, anarchism, and liberation theories reject essentialist accounts of true and false representations, and the Cartesian "knowing subject." Instead, the ontology of existence is taken to be a non-hierarchical, chaotic field of becoming. This ontology gives rise to ethical positions, which valorize this process of becoming and the resultant difference and uniqueness. So far, the pedagogical implications of postrepresentational politics are underexplored and inadequately theorized. Even radical approaches frequently embrace institutional schooling as a means of producing competencies and literacies deemed desirable by the knowing subject. One reason for this is the prevalence of what we call *pedagogies of moulding*, which we argue are incompatible with political radicalism, and prevalent in existing (even critical) forms of pedagogy.

Education as Moulding

Mainstream education assumes a process in which an empowered "knowing subject" (a teacher, institution, parent, etc.) imparts skills, beliefs or personality attributes to a learner. This process transforms the learner in a direction desired by the knowing subject. The goal is usually either *social* or *moral*: conceived as necessary to meet social goals, to produce a particular kind of ethical subject, or to help the learner "succeed" relative to social criteria. Moulding is sometimes portrayed as socialization—the adaptation of individuals to an existing social system. To various degrees, a vertical command relationship is built into the pedagogical situation, generated by the assumption that the ascribed ideal goal is more valuable than the actual existing subject. As Stirner (1845) puts it, "A person of good breeding is one into whom 'good maxims' have been instilled and impressed, poured in through a funnel, thrashed in and preached in" (p. 70). For historical reasons, this is unsurprising. The institution of the school has its origins in nationalist projects, which explicitly aimed for moulding. As Spring (2004) argues, "traditional forms of nationalist education attempt to mold loyal and patriotic citizens" (p. ix). Modern schooling emerged as a fundamental part of this process, connected to the eras of integrated national economies and inclusive Fordist/corporatist social infrastructures in order to "Separat[e] children from the community and plac[e] them in a controlled environment [that] provides the opportunity to mold entire generations to serve political and economic interests" (p. 2).

The emergence of neoliberalism at a global level has not undermined the form of moulding institutions, which have been retooled for capitalist goals and connected to new modes of social control. For instance, neoliberal approaches emphasize "key competencies," which are "needed by everyone across a variety of different life contexts" and must be moulded into everyone through schooling (Brewerton, 2004, p. 3; c.f. Barth, Godemann, Rieckmann & Stoltenberg, 2007). It is common for universities to advertise "graduate attributes"—the characteristics into which students will be moulded, providing a reliable "product" for employers. Hence, neoliberal models offer a general code of moulding, providing theories of pedagogical best practice which ignore the institutional context of learning and leave disciplinary institutions in place, "sweeping under the carpet the limitations of obligatory mass schooling" (Simola, 1998, p. 339).

Critical theorists generally reject the cruder forms of moulding that assume students are passive and docile, for instance, consider Freire's critique of "banking education" (Freire, 1972, p. 58). However, it is our contention that *few writers on critical and alternative pedagogies reject the moulding approach entirely*. Instead, they either reject the dominant *methods* of moulding or the desirable *model* into which students are to be moulded. In short, most critical approaches assume the framework of modern schooling—

mass-scale compulsory institutions in which children are segregated, so as to be exposed to content or activities selected by others, and higher education institutions building on schooling in similarly segregated spaces—but seek to modify either the content of these institutions (e.g., more social critique, media awareness, ecology, ethics, challenging privilege) or the methods used once students are in place (e.g., holistic, dialogical, participatory, or student-centered methods).

Let us examine a few examples. Jonathan Arendt (2008), using Frankfurt School critical theory, argues that the education system is an effective place to instill "deconstructive and analytical abilities" to offset media influence (p. 41). Similarly, Kellner (2008) wants schooling, which "develops skills that will help create good citizens and that will make them more motivated and competent participants in social life" (p. 55). Ecological educator Martin (1996), writing for the World Wildlife Fund, argues that "the education system must . . . prepare all people for their role as well-informed, skilled and experienced participators in determining the quality and structure of the world" (p. 51). Feminist ethicist Nel Noddings (2010), a fierce opponent of character education, nevertheless observes that, "a major responsibility of parents has long been to shape children so that they will be acceptable to the community in which they will live" (p. 390). This is not something she wants to change, but to simply inflect with care ethics instead of traditional moralism. For Henry Giroux (2008), a central figure in contemporary critical pedagogy, "in order for freedom to flourish in the worldly space of the public realm, citizens have to be formed, educated, and socialized" (p. 207).

Major traditions of critical pedagogy do not escape this critique. The Deweyan tradition does not reject moulding. For instance, Rorty (1991) observes that "it never occurred to Dewey that there was something inherently 'repressive' about society. . . . He took over . . . the idea that you have to be socialized to be human" (p. 213). Freirean pedagogy is often framed as an alternative to moulding approaches and indeed provides many useful resources. Nevertheless, Marxist scholars have convincingly argued that Freire's model retains aspects of a directed process of development in which the teacher directs a process of development towards a particular teleological horizon (Au, 2007). Poststructuralists, similarly, tend to pursue transgressions *within* dominant institutions, rather than against them. Despite the anti-authoritarian tendencies of Foucault, Deleuze, and others, many who draw on their theories in the field of education fail to draw distinctions between moulding and other approaches. For instance, Stephen J. Ball's policy-relevant Foucauldianism focuses on different regimes *within* the education system, without any apparent objection to the disciplinary effects of schooling itself (see Ball, 2012). Other, particularly Deleuzian, approaches often talk about general conditions of learning in ways which apply as much to schools and other spaces (e.g., St. Pierre, 2004; Zembylas, 2002), which emphasize education as affective and bodily self-transformation, with little emphasis on power. Their key task is to show that education (in schools or out) is partly networked, affective, embodied and so on, rather than to challenge the repressive affective regime of moulding. This often leads to a kind of flattening of thought onto reality, when, in the absence of structural contestation, micro-level resistances (which keep authoritarianism in place) constitute the whole of opposition. For example, in an explicitly political story aimed at education students, critical race scholars Green and Dantley (2013) explore a fictional case of a white principal sent into a mainly black inner-city school. After exposing epistemological privilege and structural racism, the modeled solution is simply to facilitate black leadership and better results *within* this skewed system.

The lack of critical attention to the question of moulding is in some respects, surprising. There is a growing trend towards the critique of current patterns of epistemic privilege and power. For instance, decolonial scholars have called for the rejection of colonial epistemological politics and the resultant ideas of a unified thinking subject, the privileging of mind over body, and the disciplining of subjectivity (Motta & Cole, 2014, p. 14). However, the extent to which this requires revolutionizing or overcoming formal educational institutions—rather than simply changing their methods, contents or curricula—has been neglected. In many respects, a critique of moulding is coextensive with a critique of modern epistemic power. Moulding is fundamentally connected to sovereignty in Agamben's sense, the split between valueless bare life and politically valued life (Agamben, 1998). If people lack the "key competencies" or "personality traits" (Barth et al., 2007, p. 420) to "live and work successfully in our globalised world" (Clifford & Montgomery, 2011, p. 13), or the "competencies to participate in a democratic culture" (Kellner, 2008:63), or any of the other formulations of political ideas, they are excluded from participation in society. The structure here is fundamentally a structure of abyssal thinking (Santos, 2007), in which certain ways of being are devalued and suppressed—the same style of thinking which is typically criticized in decolonial accounts (Mignolo, 2009; Ndlovu-Gatshemi, 2012). The unlearned and unschooled (or unsuccessfully schooled, or unschoolable) person, including most of the global poor (c.f. Reimer, 1971, pp. 15, 39, 74), is defined, as Stirner would put it, as an *un-man*—a valueless being to be excluded from the order of recognition, and therefore, quite possibly, from a "life worth living." This abyssal effect—and the epistemic hierarchy and epistemicide it necessarily implies—is the ineliminable remainder of pedagogies of moulding.

We contend that the rejection of moulding is a necessary part of a comprehensive project of dis-alienation. Critical pedagogues, Marxists, ecological educators, poststructuralists, and human rights educators are in their own ways, seeking dis-alienation. The difficulty is that they usually seek it by alienated means, using structures designed for moulding an alienated subject so as to instead mould a dis-alienated subject. This performative contradiction draws them back into reproducing modernist pedagogical power. In the next section, we explore Stirner's critique of moulding as necessarily alienating, before outlining a potentially dis-alienating pedagogical approach.

Stirner, Spooks, and Moulding

Stirner, who worked as a teacher for much of his life, was intimately concerned with questions of education from a post-Hegelian point of view. He was working in an educational context, dominated by the Humboldtian model of self-development through schooling, which was elaborated from theories such as Schiller's (2006 [1794]), in which education is seen as a means to self-actualization. Stirner rejected the prior Hegelian theories of self-actualization on epistemological grounds, because of their reliance on belief that one's ideas are objective and substantive aside from the knowing self (Stepelevitch, 1985, p. 613). Instead, Stirner argues that self-actualization emerges from an 'egoist' perspective unique to each of us. Like Hegel and Marx, Stirner is concerned with the question of dis-alienation: the achievement of "man's proper home, in which nothing alien regulates and rules him any longer" (1845, p. 60). Also, in common with his Hegelian heritage, Stirner formulates a series of stages through which societies or individuals are believed to pass, in order to arrive at the desired end-state, effectively, a theory of maturation into autonomous subjectivity. This model continues from Stirner's earliest, untranslated works in which he treated education as a process of self-development and humanization (de Ridder, 2008, p. 289).

First Stage: Hedonism

In Stirner's (1845) model, children exercise will from their earliest days; they "have no sacred interest and know nothing of a 'good cause'. They know all the more accurately what they have a fancy for" (p. 265). However, their hedonistic orientation to material objects of desire renders them vulnerable to control strategies based on rewards and punishments (p. 18). Hence, Stirner considers behaviorist strategies of reward and punishment—so central in "control society" in relation to adults as well as children—to be marks of the lowest, least mature phase of will.

Second Stage: Spook-Ridden

At a certain point, "the rod is too weak against our obduracy, and 'courage' replaces fear" (Stirner, 1845, p. 18). This leads to the second stage, where *geist* (mind/spirit) allows us to defy physical domination and incentive structures.

While this is progressive in relation to hedonism, it also leads to our being controlled or mastered by particular ideas (p. 55). People have in themselves a "wheel in the head," a reactive affect, such as fear of a spook, which gives fixed ideas and external hierarchies power over them (p. 163). These wheels function like clockwork, making people follow the "spook's" will (p. 75). This causes an inner split, as the real self has to be exiled, a "banishment" or "ostracism" of the ego or will (p. 177). Contemporary social forms and moulding pedagogies arise at this level: since the state activates the clockwork of wheels in the head, it destroys the egos it subsumes, alienating them to itself: "for as long as the State is the ego, the individual ego must remain a poor devil, a non-ego" (p. 194); it "does not let me come to my value" and requires "my valuelessness" to exist (p. 195).

As an approach to pedagogy, this reproduces alienation from oneself. Spooks always lead to an exclusion, which produces a sovereign split. For instance, "man" leads to the "un-man," a man who does not correspond to the concept and therefore is jailed, labeled insane, and so on. Such a split is possible only if "the concept of man can be separated from the existence, the essence from the appearance" (p. 139), i.e., by means of alienation.

Third Stage: Egoism

At the third stage, one discovers oneself as a "corporeal self," a "living flesh-and-blood person," escaping possession by objects and spooks (Stirner, 1845, p. 21). The second-stage realization that I "need not be the slave of my appetites" is retained in the third stage, "but I want still more" (p. 254). The third-stage egoist is to be immune not only to coercion and bribery, but also to control by spooks and wheels in the head.

The egoist self is self-valorizing: "I give my own self value" (p. 196), by a standard which is not that of a spook. A self-valorizing will seizes, rather than demands, rights (p. 50–51), and uses thoughts and things in *bricolage* (p. 255–256, 260). Language is to be subordinated to the flow of becoming, with Stirner even advocating a state of "thoughtlessness" so as to be free from dominance by ideas (p. 263). In many respects, Stirner's is a standpoint theory, arguing for a viewpoint on any matter "starting from me," precluding moral and legal criteria of judgment (p. 185). Every unique self has its own partial philosophical view, and there are no universal theories that apply to all selves. Each person is a "repository of unique experiences and ideas," which should not be reduced to any representation (Koch, 1997, p. 97). The egoist self is driven by an expressive pursuit of intensity and uniqueness, the imperative to *live life to the fullest* (Stirner, 1845, p. 231) in order to achieve dis-alienation. In effect, this is a theory of self-actualization: "'egoism' calls you to joy over yourselves, to self-enjoyment" (p. 130). Alienation is overcome in a rejection of the "foolish mania to be something else than you are" (p. 131).

Stirnerian selves are constantly changing and learning: "If you are bound to your past hour, if you must babble today because you babbled yesterday, if you cannot transform yourself each instant, you feel yourself fettered in slavery and benumbed" (Stirner, 1845, p. 39). However, this process of self-transformation is a process of *becoming* and *differenciation* (difference production), not a process of moulding. Life is not a means to an external calling or destiny; rather, one is to "make any use he likes of his life" (p. 245). Instead of an external calling, one has an imminent becoming: "forces that manifest themselves where they are because their being consists solely in their manifestation" (p. 249). Moulding is condemned as interference with becoming. "No sheep, no dog, exerts itself to become a 'proper sheep, a proper dog'. . . . It realizes itself in living itself out, in dissolving itself, passing away" (p. 252). A trained dog "is no better for itself than a natural one," though perhaps more useful for humans (1845, p. 253). As de Acosta (2007) puts it, Stirner sees the state as an "insult," which makes him "less than what he imagines he could be" (p. 36).

Stirner's idea of the "ego" needs to be clarified. "Ego" in the Cartesian, psychoanalytic, and decolonial senses is closer to what Stirner refers to as *geist* (mind or spirit). In fact, a Stirnerian ego seems to be closer to a Jungian or existentialist "authentic self" than to the socially optimizing personas or rational instrumentalists most often designated by the term. The egoist self is expressive and passionate—not a being of rational interests. It is ultimately something, which cannot be thought or conceptualized, since any fixed definition turns it into a representation or spook. As Stirner writes in his reply to critics: "What Stirner says is a word, a thought, a concept; what he means is no word, no thought, no concept. What he says is not what is meant and what he means is unsayable" (Stirner, 1977, p. 67). Egoists resist the use of normativity and social mediation in defining their relations. Instead, a kind of direct connection ("intercourse") or enmity arises. In essence, the relation to another is not mediated by a "third party," or a normative regime of rightness (1845, p. 162). Others are to be recognized as "unique beings who bear their law in themselves and live according to it," and are not subjected to normative judgments which would make them "criminals" instead of "opponents" (1845, p. 158). Each must assert his or her "distinctness or peculiarity" against others: "you need not give way or renounce yourself" (1845, p. 161). Abyssal thought is thus entirely rejected. In a sense, this is a dis-alienated recognition, a subject-subject relation, even the terminology echoes Buber and Levinas (Firth, 2012, p. 144). This I-you relation, however, is possible only between two subjects who reject spooks, which then creates conditions of possibility for the kinds of horizontal relationships that will later be discussed under the rubric of "consciousness-raising." This relation, however, is possible only between two subjects who reject spooks and have reached the third level of consciousness (Stirner, 1845, pp. 175, 207).

Stirner and Critical Pedagogy

Stirner's (1845) ideas have much in common with contemporary theories of critical pedagogy. For example, consider the themes of embodiment (e.g., p. 21), anti-essentialism (p. 36), self-transformation (p. 39), a relational or pragmatic view of science ("what is science for but to be consumed?") (p. 133), and the processual nature of knowledge and subjectivity (p. 249). However, Stirner (1845) goes further in rejecting moulding as a product of spook-ridden moral thought (p. 64). Education as moulding produces only "rigid" characters, and not creative egoists (Stirner, 2009, p. 9), It trains people to dance to another's tune, rather than to self-actualize and *become* (p. 248). It provides training suited to the state or spook, not the self (p. 173). Furthermore, even successful moulding never reaches the ideal, but simply professes it with the mouth (p. 253). Formal education singularly fails to produce egoists. "Such thoroughly true men are not supplied by school; if they are nevertheless there, they are there in spite of school" (2009, p. 8).

Hence, Stirner seeks some kind of pedagogy, but rejects the dominant structure of pedagogy as moulding. People are not already Stirnerian egoists. Maturation from the second to the third stage is desirable. For this, some kind of pedagogical process seems necessary. Modern-day Stirnerian Wolfi Landstreicher (2005), argues that

> The anarchist recognition of the primacy of the actual, living individual (as opposed to the collectivized cog and to the abstract concept of the individual) is the recognition that we need to become a certain sort of being, a being capable of acting on our own terms to realize our own desires and dreams in the face of the most fierce and powerful enemy: this entire civilization . . . the transformation of oneself into a spirited, willful being. (pp. 3–4).

In other words, he frames the Stirnerian process of reaching the third stage of an autonomous ego as inherently pedagogical. Yet existing pedagogical institutions are rejected as necessarily entangled with the second stage—the domain of spooks. We need ways to pass from the second (or first) stage to the third stage of *self-realization of value*, to come to see ourselves as unique, non-representable *wills* and not as particular attributes, spooks, or abstractions.

Deleuze and Pedagogy without Moulding

While Stirner theorizes a process of maturation through which an autonomous, disalienated "ego" emerges, Koch (1997) argues, "Stirner never developed the language to go into greater depth on the construction, functioning, and consequences of the fixed idea" (p. 102). Part of this gap can be filled by cross-reading Stirner with Deleuze and Guattari, who theorize the transition from second to third stage. While Deleuze (1986) follows the conventional (and unhelpful) analysis of Stirner as a nihilist, he also recognizes him as the ultimate theorist of dis-alienation (pp. 159–161). Despite this apparent lack of direct influence, Stirner and Deleuze are united in their "rejection of the tyranny of 'labels,' essential identities, abstractions and 'fixed ideas' . . . [i.e.] authoritarian concepts which limit thought" (Newman, 2001, p. 4).

Deleuze and Guattari's three stages of schizoanalysis offer a practical typology of the tasks of pedagogical transformation from a spook-ridden to a free subjectivity, thus providing an alternative to moulding approaches. Their approach is posited as a way of liberating energies so they can flow freely. In any territorial regime, including the neoliberal "society of control" (Deleuze, 1992), desire becomes caught-up in traps and knots, broadly analogous to the Stirnerian account of *wheels in the head*, from which it needs to free itself. The process of remaining trapped within (for example) a micro-family drama and its neurotic psychological expressions is a means by which desire is mapped onto rigid schemas and prevented from becoming. As in Stirner, so in Deleuze, this process is linked to fixed ideas such as the naturalization of the family (Deleuze & Guattari, 2004, pp. 365–368).

The first task of schizoanalysis or pedagogy is negative and consists of breaking down the traps, knots, or *wheels in the head*. Hence there is a task of destruction, a "scouring" or "curettage" of the unconscious to clear out Oedipus and its correlates (Deleuze & Guattari, 2004, p. 417). The purpose of this process is not to mould the student/analysand into a form already known to the teacher/therapist but rather to create the space for the emergence of flows beyond representation. This requires breaking down the underpinnings of ideas, which, in Stirner's terms, possess or "own" us, including subjectivities arising from them, and it frees flows at a sub-individual level (Deleuze & Guattari, 2004, p. 396). We would argue that the ego, which is deconstructed, is the psychoanalytic, not the Stirnerian ego, and it is largely coextensive with what Stirner terms *geist* (mind or spirit). Deleuze and Guattari's "prepersonal singularities" are elements of a unique subject, which is not subordinate to spooks.

Deleuze and Guattari's first stage loosely corresponds to overcoming the first and second stages of self-becoming in Stirner's theory—the first stage, purely sensory and hedonistic, and the second stage, representational or spook-ridden. Both theorists begin from the disalienated level of the sensing, experiencing self in order to challenge the closure imposed by spooks. Beginning from identification *with* spooks and repressive social structures, one progresses to an identification *of* spooks, an ability to see and to distance oneself from dominant social constructions which entails decolonization of one's self-knowledge or sense of self. As Choi and Black (2008) argue, "we can be free from ideologies. We can be without them if we become aware of them" (p. 74).

Along with this negative function, there are two positive functions of analysis/education. The first is to discover the "desiring-machines" within a subject (Deleuze & Guattari, 2004, p. 354). This process of reconstruction forms chains of connections, thus performing a process of dis-alienation between the subject and his or her environment or milieu. The second positive function is to reinvest the flows socially, in revolutionary ways (p. 373). This involves reintroducing the "outside" and relating flows of desire to emotional investments in the broader socio-political field; on an experiential level, this is termed a "body without organs"—a difficult concept to interpret, being structurally similar to Buddhist, Gnostic, and New Age models of bodily/spiritual experience, beyond the identity as "self" or "ego." In many ways, this is similar to Stirner's third-stage self. When Deleuze and Guattari (2004) argue that "the product of analysis should be a free and joyous person, a carrier of the life flows" (p. 364), they echo Stirner's language of passion, creativity, and living to the limit. Even more crucially, the process varies with the *desiring-machines* of each student/analysand, which are always-already differentiated. The resulting subject is not moulded into a fixed image, but instead, he/she is radically unique. These stages involve self-valorization as an autonomous subject, structured through desire and becoming.

In previous sections, we argued for the possibility and indeed, necessity of a pedagogy without moulding, and we have outlined some of the theoretical conditions that might underpin such a pedagogy. But how might such pedagogy, without moulding, culminating in an autonomous, joyful subject of becoming, happen in practice? We feel it is useful to look to feminist consciousness-raising (CR) from the 1970s as a non-exhaustive example of such a process. Like Stirnerian and Deleuzian pedagogies, CR is structured to break down submersion in a dominant regime of spooks, in particular, women's submersion in and acceptance of patriarchy. While it is aimed mainly for the emergence of autonomous subjectivity on a collective rather than individual level, and it has a stronger emphasis than Stirner or Deleuze on structurally situating oneself (and thus differs somewhat from the Stirnerian/Deleuzian unique standpoint model), it is sufficiently similar to exemplify what a pedagogy without moulding might involve.

Consciousness-Raising

Consciousness-raising (CR) groups were a fundamental aspect of the second-wave feminist movement, arising in the late 1960s and becoming popular during the 1970s. They have been interpreted as a pedagogical tool for social

transformation (Henderson-King & Stewart, 1999). CR groups were voluntary, usually women-only, regular discussion groups focused on recounting
and interpreting the experiences of participants, generally by presenting
members' experiences around a defined topic and then drawing out similarities and structural relations to the oppression of women. We would describe
CR as a variant of pedagogy without moulding. It is pedagogical insofar as
it seeks to transform existing consciousness so as to escape dominance by
(patriarchal) spooks, and it is non-moulding in that there is no transcendent
vision towards which participants are transformed. We argue that CR should
be revived as a form of anarchist pedagogy, compatible with Deleuzian and
Stirnerian approaches. Theorizing CR using Stirnerian-Deleuzian concepts
offers the beginnings of a transferable model of pedagogy without moulding. This is an exercise in transversal, horizontal, intellectual, translation
between contexts, rather than a vanguardist claim to know the true method.
We do not claim that CR is the only possible approach to pedagogy without
moulding; practices such as militant inquiry, Theatre of the Oppressed,
deschooling, and the more horizontalist varieties of Freirean approaches
would be other possible lines of inquiry.

Identifying and Overcoming Spooks

It was suggested above that the first task of transformation is the *negative task*—decolonizing thought or unlearning spooks. In feminist CR, the
main spooks, which acted as barriers to self-actualization, were those that
tied women to patriarchy. CR was able to challenge these spooks through a
practice of speaking from personal experiences among women, without the
mediation of men or dominant institutions. By removing the main medi-
ating spooks, CR created a possibility of subject-subject communication.
The process would "emphasize our own feelings and experiences as women"
(Sarachild, 1975, p. 145), on the assumption that women's "own true individual awareness is somehow not really operative" within patriarchy, being
"blocked or stymied or repressed or just overloaded with so much shit" (Forer,
1975, p. 151). In addition to the testifying function, there is a function of validation: "that the pain is pain, that it is also one's own, that women are real"
(MacKinnon, 1989, p. 91). This process is taken to break down what Levine
(1979) refers to as a "cop in the head" (a moralizing force within each person),
analogous to Stirner's *wheels in the head* (p. 7).

While CR did not simply leave existing narratives unchanged, it validated the reality of otherwise disavowed experiences of oppression, thus creating a standpoint from outside the dominant regime of spooks from which
the unthinkable could be thought. In discovering that the "personal narrative is political," participants "transform the dominant meaning of experience by bringing a different set of assumptions to bear on it" (Langellier,

1989, p. 269). It changed the criteria of verification, from criteria focused on dominant spooks to criteria focused on one's own experience (MacKinnon, 1989, p. 87). By assessing experiences from their embodied and affective significance for oneself—rather than their meaning in the regime of spooks, or for dominant others (in this case, men)—the representational power of spooks to overwrite and judge desire is stripped away, and the *wheels in the head* are broken down, or at least suspended for long enough for other ways of seeing to become possible.

Forming Autonomous Desires

The autonomous standpoint associated with Deleuze's second task, and with Stirner's project of self-valorization, entails beginning from one's own standpoint—a disalienated level of sensing, experiencing, and living as an embodied subject, as well as a standpoint of opposition to oppression. This is echoed in CR. A primary purpose of CR is to "develop ideology and learn to think autonomously" (Allen, 1970, p. 8). The process of forming an autonomous standpoint generally occurred through the "summing-up" process, which followed the accounts of experiences. This process constructed a distinctly feminist point of view in which everyday experiences are seen differently, as political, structurally situated experiences (Shreve, 1989, p. 45, 220; Bartky, 1977, p. 26; Brownmiller, 1970, p. 146; Allen, 1970, p. 28). A process of structural derivation consists of relating formerly personalized problems such as individual malaise, to sexism and other structural causes, so the problems appear as a political pattern rather than as diffuse bad luck or individual dysfunction (Shreve, 1989, p. 59; Dreifus, 1973, p. 5; Bruley, 1976, p. 21).

Prior to the process, participants' lives are in turmoil, but few understood why (Shreve, 1989, p. 40). The CR process provided particular ways to articulate experiences in new, feminist ways (Shreve, 1989, p. 30). The process moves from personal experience towards developing a more general view of social conditions broader than one's own position (Shreve, 1989, p. 198). This gives a "vantage point" perspective on daily life (Allen, 1970, pp. 20-21), and bridges politics and one's own life (Bruley, 1976, p. 21; c.f. Allen, 1970, p. 15), or objectifies consciousness at a given time (Forer, 1975, p. 151). The construction of an autonomous voice, expressing authentic desires, is a difficult and time-consuming task as it requires recognizing and overcoming existing habits of superficial communication (Bruley, 1976, p. 8). This aspect of CR is based on the premise that women "had been glued to our men and separated from each other all our lives" (Arnold, 1970, p. 160). CR enables women to relate directly, instead of through men as a mediator (Bruley, 1976, p. 21), whilst problematizing and overcoming feelings of hatred for the self and other women imbued by patriarchal culture (Allen, 1970, p. 11). In feminist terminology, the moment of attaining autonomy is termed the "click" (Reger, 2004, p. 211; Allen, 1970, p. 27), a term for the "eye-popping realization" of how patriarchy structures life experiences (Shreve, 1989, p. 53).

From a Stirnerian-Deleuzian perspective, the reconstruction of affective autonomy is particularly important. In CR, this process was focused on the patriarchal repression of women's anger. Bruley (1976, p. 13) suggests that consciousness-raising directly challenges the guilt one may feel about the suppression of anger. The group gives each participant "permission" to feel anger, allowing it to become an "energizing force for change, increasing confidence, and enhancing relationships" (Randolph & Ross-Valliere, 1979, p. 924), and to turn anger into "constructive energy" (Levine, 1979, p. 6). This process is not a kind of moulding through which emotions are repressed and forced into new paths. Rather, emotions are channeled *expressively* into a process of becoming and interacting creatively with the world. Anger is not channeled into resentful feelings of inferiority, but vented in a projectile, affirmative way. Crucially, emotions were expressed, not programmed in the groups (Brownmiller, 1970, p. 152). This parallels Stirner's and Deleuze's concerns with pedagogy as a process of becoming, rather than an attempt to mould participants' subjectivity to some assumed notion of human nature or moral good. There is no knowing subject who tells participants what they are to become, but rather, there is a type of self-transformation.

Forming Connections

The third task discussed above is the social recreation of new existential territories from the autonomous standpoint. Levine (n.d.) draws the conclusions of CR in this direction: the small group is not a precursor to large formal organizations but rather an alternative revolutionary approach to political organization and social life. The process of reconceptualizing experiences through a framework that acknowledges and opposes structural oppression creates a transformation in alignments, which sometimes (though not always) leads to politicization. Personal experiences and affects are rearticulated into political connections by being taken as instances of larger, structural issues (Bond & Lieberman, 1980, p. 289). This creates a worldview, an *ideology* (Allen, 1970, p. 8) or a "theoretical horizon" (Malo, 2004), which rearranges social connections, conceptualizing "where we are in light of where we are not yet" (Bartky, 1977, p. 26).

The emergence of self-expression within the group can have wider social influence, insofar as women may choose to identify and reject roles that are repressive rather than expressive (Randolph & Ross-Valliere, 1979, p. 923). For example, an interviewee in Reger's (2004) paper stated, "You know, even if it is as one woman said . . . something about nailing her husband's socks to the floor or something or not picking up his socks. Even if it is a small act in your life . . . those things can build" (Reger, 2004, p. 216). Another interviewee refers to sexism in the workplace, suggesting that CR encouraged her to respond with anger, instead of becoming depressed (Shreve, 1989, p. 102). While some groups evolved into political affinity or mutual aid groups (Shreve 1989, p. 199; Allen, 1970, p. 19), or fed into activism in wider networks, "some [participants] were not interested in larger societal change, while others worked to maintain an alternative culture" (Reger, 2004, p. 218). However, we would argue that creating an alternative space and environment for the transformation of consciousness is a form of political change. Forming dis-alienated unions, independent of society is always-already a political act. As MacKinnon (1989) states, "By providing room for women to be close, these groups demonstrated how far women were separated" (p. 87). Reconnection occurs through a sense of closeness derived from intimate communication and similarities of experience (Dreifus, 1973, p. 52). Furthermore, participation in CR helped women to relate within wider politics as it taught women a different way of relating than the dominant style within patriarchal and capitalist structures, which often encourage controlling, manipulative, and competitive communication styles (Arnold, 1970, p. 161). CR provided a new model based on co-operation, non-hierarchy and sharing, which could then be carried out into wider environments (Randolph & Ross-Valliere, 1979, p. 924). From a Stirnerian perspective, the crucial political change is the actualization of an autonomous standpoint. What is most important is that this emergent being is true to its own becoming, not that this becoming takes one or another form.

Given the continuing interest in subaltern standpoints and epistemologies, we would argue that processes of this kind are vitally necessary and need to be revived. Today there are many attempts (by poststructuralists, feminists, autonomists, decolonial scholars, etc.) to elaborate perspectives based on standpoints of marginalized groups or individuals. Yet there is a significant problem with perspectives reconstructed by academics, often based on their own experiences and/or established theories, but which are not coextensive with existing narratives of those for whom they claim to speak (Reynolds, 2002). This creates a dilemma in which one must either accept the (often conservative or conformist) everyday narratives of the oppressed, folding reality onto neoliberalism, or else one must champion intellectual versions of liberationist politics which have lost their grassroots derivation, either adopting a vanguard stance or simply speaking from one's own (typically privileged) standpoint. Processes such as CR, by creating a standpoint-based perspective, which did not pre-exist them and which is not simply imported by educators, provide a basis for an emancipatory politics which does not succumb to these positions.

Conclusion

This chapter began with the question of whether a pedagogy without mould-ing—a pedagogy compatible with horizontal relations and the rejection of command—is possible. It has woven an account, from Stirner, Deleuze, and feminist consciousness-raising, which suggests that such a pedagogy is possible as well as necessary. From a Stirnerian position, the pedagogical process of emergence as a unique "ego," a standpoint of desire in a constant process of becoming and living, is incompatible with pedagogies of moulding. Yet dominant models of education, and even those prevalent in critical peda-gogy, retain moulding as a basic assumption. We suggested that Deleuze's three stages of schizoanalysis provide a structural matrix for a pedagogy without moulding, and further demonstrated that this structural matrix was actualized in the historical practice of consciousness-raising in the feminist movement. We suggest that this provides a way forward for the development of pedagogies without moulding.

We would suggest, therefore, that there is promise in developing con-sciousness-raising as a specifically anarchist pedagogy. While feminist CR focused mainly on gender oppression—and CR focused on structural oppres-sions (still a valuable project today)—it would also be possible to develop forms of CR which focus on the self-destroying impact of spooks and the hierarchies they generate. In this way, the "click" is arrival at a Stirnerian unique standpoint, and the structural matrix one comes to see is expanded from a particular type of structural oppression to the entire field of aliena-tion and possession by spooks. Of course, this leaves unanswered the ques-tion of how to create such groups in a society of control, in which the act of coming together regularly without mediation is itself a difficult struggle (Bey, 1994, pp. 20-22). We believe, however, that we have established that a pedagogy without moulding is both *possible* and *desirable*. The remaining question is how to realize it.

References

Agamben, G. (1998). *Homo sacer: Sovereign power and bare life*. Stanford, CA: Stanford University Press.

Allen, P. (1970). *Free space*. New York, NY: Times Change Press.

Arendt, J. (2008). The "them" and the "I" of a hurricane: Broadcast news influences on the reality and attitudes of its listeners. In P.P. Trifonas (Ed.), *Worlds of difference: Rethinking the ethics of global education for the 21st century* (pp. 29–44). Boulder, CO: Paradigm.

Arnold, J. (1970), Consciousness-raising. In S. Stambler (Ed.), Women's liberation: Blueprint for the future (pp. 155-161). New York, NY: Ace Books,.

Au, W. (2007), Epistemology of the oppressed: The dialectics of Paulo Freire's theory of knowledge. *Journal for Critical Education Policy Studies*, 5(2). Retrieved from http://www.jceps.com/print.php?articleID=100

Ball, S.J. (2012). The "reluctant" state and the beginning of the end of state education. *Journal of Educational Administration and History*, 44(2), 89–103.

Barth, M., Godemann, J., Rieckmann, M., & Stoltenberg, U. (2007). Developing key competencies for sustainable development in higher education. *International Journal of Sustainability in Higher Education*, 8(4), 416–430.

Bartky, S.L. (1975). Toward a Phenomenology of Feminist Consciousness. *Social Theory and Practice*, 3(4), 425–439.

Bey, H. (1994). *Immediatism*. Edinburgh, Scotland: AK Press.

Bond, G.R., & Lieberman, M.A. (1980). The role and function of women's consciousness raising: Self-help, psychotherapy, or political activation? In C. Landau Heckerman (Ed.), *The evolving female: Women in psychosocial context* (pp. 268–306). New York, NY: Human Sciences Press.

Brewerton, M. (2004). Reframing the essential skills: Implications of the OECD defining and selecting key competencies project. Background Paper for the New Zealand Ministry of Education. Retrieved from http://nzcurriculum.tki.org.nz/content/download/504/3819/file/key-competencies.doc

Brownmiller, S. (1970). Sisterhood is powerful. In S. Stambler (Ed.). *Women's liberation: Blueprint for the future* (pp. 141–155). New York, NY: Ace Books.

Bruley, S. (1976). *Women awake: The experience of consciousness-raising*. London, UK: S. Bruley.

Choi, S.J., & Black, M. (2008). Ideology and manas. *Human Architecture: Journal of the Sociology of Self-Knowledge*, 6(3), 73–80.

Clifford, V., & Montgomery, C. (2011). Introduction: Internationalising the curriculum for global citizenship in higher education. In V. Clifford & C. Montgomery (Eds.), *Moving towards internationalisation of the curriculum for global citizenship in higher education* (pp. 13–24). Oxford, UK: Oxford Centre for Staff and Learning Development.

de Acosta, A. (2007). Two styles of anti-statist subjectivity. *International Studies in Philosophy*, 39(2), pp. 35–47.

de Ridder, W. (2008). Max Stirner, Hegel and the Young Hegelians: A reassessment. *History of European Ideas 34*, 285–297.

Deleuze, G. (1986). *Nietsche and philosophy*. London, UK: Continuum.

Deleuze, G. (1992). Postscript on societies of control. *October, 59*, 3–7.

Deleuze, G., & Guattari, F. (2004). *Anti-Oedipus*. London, UK: Continuum.

Dreifus, C. (1973). *Woman's fate: Raps from a feminist consciousness-raising group*. New York, NY: Bantam.

Firth, R. (2012). *Utopian politics: Citizenship and practice*. London, UK: Routledge.

Forer, A. (1975). Thoughts on consciousness-raising. In Redstockings (Eds.), *Feminist Revolution* (p. 151). New York, NY: Random House,.

Freire, P. (1972) *Pedagogy of the oppressed*. Harmondsworth, UK: Penguin.

Giroux, H.A. (2008). Youth and the politics of education in dark times. In P.P. Trifonas (Ed.), *Worlds of difference: Rethinking the ethics of global education for the 21st century* (pp. 199–216). Boulder, CO: Paradigm.

Green, T.L., & Dantley, M.E. (2013). The great white hope? Examining the white privilege and epistemology of an urban high school principal. *Journal of Cases in Educational Leadership*, 16(2), 82–92.

Henderson-King, D., & Stewart, A. J. (1999). Educational experiences and shifts in group consciousness: Studying women. *PSPB, 25*(3), 390–399.

Kellner, D. (2008). Technological transformation: Multiple literacies, and the re-visioning of education. In P.P. Trifonas (Ed.), *Worlds of difference: Rethinking the ethics of global education for the 21st century* (pp. 45–72). Boulder, CO: Paradigm.

Koch, A.M. (1997). Max Stirner: The last Hegelian or the first poststructuralist? *Anarchist Studies, 5,* 95–107.

Landstreicher, W. (2005). Against the logic of submission. Retrieved from http://theanarchistlibrary.org/library/wolfi-landstreicher-against-the-logic-of-submission

Langellier, K.M. (1989). Personal narratives: Perspectives on theory and research. *Text and Performance Quarterly, 9,* 243–276.

Levine, C. (1979). 'The Tyranny of Tyranny. Retrieved from http://theanarchistlibrary.org/library/cathy-levine-the-tyranny-of-tyranny

MacKinnon, C.A. (1989). *Toward a feminist theory of the state.* Cambridge, MA: Harvard University Press.

Malo de Molina, M. (2004). Common notions, part 1: Workers' inquiry, co-research, consciousness-raising. Retrieved from http://eipcp.net/transversal/0406/malo/en

Martin, P. (1996). A WWF view of education and the role of NGOs. In J. Huckle & S. Sterling (Eds.), *Education for Sustainability* (pp. 40–54) London, UK: Earthscan.

Mignolo, W. (2009). Dispensable and bare lives: Coloniality and the hidden political/economic agenda of modernity. *Human Architecture: Journal of the Sociology of Self-Knowledge, 7*(2), 69–88.

Motta, S., & Cole, M. (2014). *Constructing 21st century socialism in Latin America: The role of radical education.* Harmondsworth, UK: Palgrave.

Ndlovu-Gatshemi, S.J. (2012). Beyond the equator there are no sins: Coloniality and violence in Africa. *Journal of Developing Societies, 28*(94), 419–440.

Newman, S. (2001). War on the state: Stirner and Deleuze's anarchism. *Anarchist Studies, 9,* 147–163. Retrieved from http://theanarchistlibrary.org/library/saul-newman-war-on-the-state-stirner-and-deleuze-s-anarchism.pdf

Noddings, N. (2010).Moral education in an age of globalization. *Educational Philosophy and Theory, 42*(4), 390–396.

Randolph, B.M., & C. Ross-Valliere, C. (1979). Consciousness raising groups. *American Journal of Nursing, 79*(5), 922–924.

Reger, J. (2004). Organizational "emotion work" through consciousness-raising: An analysis of a feminist organization. *Qualitative Sociology, 27*(2), 205–222.

Reimer, E. (1971). *School is dead: Alternatives in education.* Harmondsworth, UK: Penguin.

Reynolds, T. (2002). Re-thinking a black feminist standpoint. *Ethnic and Racial Studies, 25*(4), 591–606.

Rorty, R. (1991). *Objectivity, relativism and truth.* Cambridge UK: Cambridge University Press.

Santos, B. de Sousa (2007). Beyond abyssal thinking: From global lines to ecologies of knowledges. *Review, 30*(1), pp. 45–89.

Sarachild, K. (1975). Consciousness-raising: A radical weapon. In Redstockings (Ed.), *Feminist Revolution* (pp. 144–150). New York, NY: Random House,.

Schiller, F. (1794/2006). *Letters on the aesthetical education of man* (New York, NY: Gutenberg, Retrieved from http://www.gutenberg.org/files/6798/6798-h/6798-h.htm

Shreve, A. (1989). *Women together, women alone.* New York, NY: Ballantine.

Simola, H. (1998). Constructing a school-free pedagogy: Decontextualization of Finnish state educational discourse. *Journal of Curriculum Studies, 30*(3), 339–356.

Spring, J. (2004). How educational ideologies are shaping global society. Mahwah, NJ: Lawrence Erlbaum.

St. Pierre, E.A. (2004). Deleuzian concepts for education. *Educational Philosophy and Theory, 36*(3), 283–296.

Stepelevich, L.S. (1985), 'Max Stirner as Hegelian', *Journal of the History of Ideas, 46*(4), pp. 597–614.

Stirner, M. (1845). *The ego and his own.* Retrieved from http://theanarchistlibrary.org/library/max-stirner-the-ego-and-his-own.pdf

Stirner, M. (1977). Stirner's critics. *Philosophical Forum, 8*(2–4), pp. 66–80.

Stirner, M. (2009). The false principle of our education, or, humanism and realism. Retrieved from http://theanarchistlibrary.org/library/max-stirner-the-false-principle-of-our-education.pdf

Zembylas, M. (2002), Structures of feeling in curriculum and teaching: Theorizing the emotional rules. *Educational Theory, 52*(2), 187–208.

CHAPTER 4

Creating Transformative Anarchist-Geographic Learning Spaces

Farhang Rouhani

I n recent years, radical geographers have increasingly turned to critical pedagogy to develop feminist, poststructuralist, and postcolonial
approaches to teaching that critique binary models in education, politicize
the learning process, and develop new models that do not simply incorporate
new people and places into existing models of learning. Such a move requires
critical attention to the false separation of teaching and research as distinct
spheres of work, bringing an end to the valorization of research as a form of
activism superior to teaching, and at the same time call for a more extensive
engagement with the classroom as a socially transformative place. While rich
in theoretical development, discussions of pedagogy in geography, with a few
exceptions, tend to be abstract, underdeveloped, and not particularly imaginative when it comes to classroom learning spaces. This is very unfortunate
given that one of the earliest examples of a radical geographic pedagogy was
the highly imaginative, anarchism-inspired Detroit Geographical Expedition
and Institute of the early 1970s. It is also especially urgent when we consider
the ways in which geography as a discipline can provide essential insight
into how the neoliberalization of education works through an institutionalized erasure of place identities, and how this placelessness can be countered
with an emplaced, politically situated pedagogy.

For insight into the practical, creative, liberatory possibilities, geographers can draw significant inspiration from such pedagogic experiments
as well as the long history of creative anarchist work on education. In this
chapter, I argue for a combined critical anarchist-geographic pedagogical
approach that appreciates the challenges of building alternative learning
models within existing neoliberalizing institutions, provides the necessary

tools for finding uniquely situated opportunities for educational change, and emplaces a grounded, creative, student-led critical pedagogy. I will begin by critically examining the relationships between the three relevant areas of knowledge: radical geography, critical pedagogy, and anarchism. I will evaluate three projects that have implicitly attempted to bring the concerns among these three areas into practice and conclude by arguing for the creative, emancipatory potential of a critical, radical pedagogy that explicitly weds geography and anarchism in its vision.

As with many other disciplines, such a transformative pedagogy in geography is essential and urgent at this moment when there are ongoing demands for the commodification, quantification, and technicalization of learning. In the midst of all these pressures for change in classrooms and institutions of learning, the critical geographic drive to understand the world through creative, imaginative exploration may be lost. While geographical imaginations have historically been the basis for some very repressive systems (such as colonialism), they have also served as vehicles for creating anti-hierarchical spaces of liberation. Anarchist pedagogies hold much promise, as examined below, to work against the dominant imperatives in favor of the critical re-enchantment with places in the world that geography should provide.

Radical Geography, Critical Pedagogy, and Anarchism

Critical pedagogy, as a set of approaches geared toward social change through education, revolutionized learning by advocating for the politically transformative power of education and for more horizontal relations in knowledge production (Freire, 1970; Giroux, 1997; hooks, 1994). While varied in the degree of social change they advocate, supporters of critical pedagogy perceive education as a political act that can empower both teachers and students to question given social hierarchies and create the conditions for participatory democracy (McLaren, 1998; Kincheloe, 2008). In this way, critical pedagogical perspectives offer the tools for critiquing, politicizing, and transforming existing educational systems.

In the past two decades, radical geographers have increasingly turned to critical pedagogy, especially by way of feminist, poststructuralist, and postcolonial perspectives on teaching that critique strict binaries in how education should occur, develop new models of learning that focus on transforming the existing process of education rather than simply adding new techniques within old ways of doing things, and move beyond the unquestioned portioning of the world into places and regions. While works in critical pedagogy have significantly influenced these geographers, the radicalization of the discipline that occurred after 1968 and the growing social justice–oriented desire among some scholars to integrate teaching, research, and activism also significantly frame their work.

The Detroit Geographical Expedition and Institute's (DGEI) radical pedagogy served as a particular inspiration for transforming geographic pedagogies (Heyman, 2007; also see Merrifield, 1995). It began in the late 1960s when some geographers felt compelled to respond to the racial, economic, and political injustices facing Detroit's African-American communities. A group made up of residents, activists, students, and academics formed the DGEI, with the goals of directing geographic inquiry and pedagogy toward the issues of survival and self-determination of the marginalized communities of color in Detroit. The collective mapped capital flows, rat bites, children's injuries, and all sorts of everyday phenomena that revealed the uneven patterns of development and access. This project was truly revolutionary in simultaneously operating as an "expedition," an invitation for diverse publics to participate in learning about underrepresented communities in need, and an "institute," an active, collective site for the gathering of knowledge to be used to inform political action and policy.

Heyman (2007) argues that geographers have tended to neglect the extent to which the DGEI was as much about transforming how we teach and learn as about participatory democratic research methods. He writes, "The DGEI was founded not simply to refocus the topics of research towards poverty and ghettoization, but towards breaking the cycle of expert knowledge production as a central goal of radical geography. Such a goal was fundamentally a pedagogical project, one that has been largely ignored as radical geography grew in prominence" (Heyman, 2007, p. 101). As such, it not only revolutionized the subjects and practices of geographic research but also showed how the processes of learning can and should occur in more participatory, horizontal ways.

Geographic perspectives on critical pedagogy have served to critique the separation of academic spaces and have argued for the relevance of the discipline and the study of space, place, and scale to radicalizing our pedagogies. Some scholars have critiqued the extent to which, even in the most critical, radical geographic work, geographers perpetuate a false divide between academia and the rest of society and between research and teaching. This problem appears in even more radical forms of participatory research that perceive knowledge production and research as deeply interconnected, but still prioritize the world "beyond the classroom" in ways that reify the classroom and "the outside" as separate social spaces and limit the perception of the classroom space itself as transformative (Autonomous Geographies Collective, 2010). Such a vision does not take into account the critical ways in which the classroom itself can be a location of participatory political action that can enable students to engage with the social relations of research ethics and to question the boundaries between spaces of learning and spaces of research (Heyman, 2007; Askins, 2008). A connected critique concerns the "ivory tower syndrome," the notion of the university as an exceptional social space, which curtails the development of critical research on the neoliberalization of education systems. In essence, as Castree argues, our attention to the world "out there" has prevented us from truly delving into what happens "in here" (Castree, 1999, 2000). To truly understand the impact of neoliberalization on our education systems, we need to shatter this perceptual divide.

As a result, we need a situated pedagogy that can more effectively both critique the impacts of neoliberalization on our education systems and develop a situated pedagogy that advocates change via the classroom and other spaces of education. Kitchens, for example, reveals the ways in which current trends in education, especially the growing incorporation of universalizing, standardizing information and knowledge delivery systems, have led to the pervasive problem of placelessness, resulting in an erasure of the uniqueness and situatedness of learning practices as they become increasingly replaced with those dictated from above (Kitchens, 2009). We geographers often talk about how place matters; it is crucial that we include learning spaces within that discussion, in critical and transformative ways.

But rather than just responding to larger-scale processes with local scale, emplaced pedagogies, Merrett argues that an emancipatory pedagogy cannot be fixed to one scale (Merrett, 2008). He critiques the extent to which scholars of pedagogy, drawing primarily from Kropotkin and Freire, often view the problems of status quo education systems at the universal scale and truly emancipatory education at the local scale. "This requires critical geographers to understand that progressive ideals are not tied to any particular scale," he writes, "and that, consequently, a critical pedagogy needs to consciously incorporate a dialectical understanding of scale and tolerance of ambiguity" (Merrett, 2009, p. 708). In the context of the neoliberalization of education, it has become crucial for universities to connect with one another in resistant solidarity. While the solution to placelessness may lie at the local scale, truly transforming our education system requires action at multiple scales. Responding to neoliberalization requires mobilization at multiple scales of praxis. Radical geography can, as such, draw from an extensive, critical toolkit that examines our existing education systems through critical, politicized perspectives on space, place, and scale for critiquing and transgressing our existing educational system. While a critical focus on these geographic concepts can aid greatly toward these ends, geographers can also draw inspiration from the long history of anarchist perspectives on education for creative, practical, liberatory inspiration.

Anarchist pedagogies actively seek out possibilities for new, practical, and different ways of learning and relating to others, refusing to settle for our existing institutional arrangements. This refusal in itself is an essential difference that anarchism makes in education: to begin by stating that our education systems need much more than technical fixes and reforms (Suissa, 2010). In his introduction to the edited volume *Anarchist Pedagogies: Collective Actions, Theories, and Critical Reflections on Education*, Haworth argues that there is an urgent and essential need for anarchist-inspired intervention on pedagogy given the rapid universalization of global capitalism at all levels of society (Haworth, 2012, p. 4). There appear to be fewer and fewer alternatives, as capitalism encroaches on more and more spheres of everyday life, and as such, anarchism can serve an immediate, vital source of inspiration for creative, sustainable alternatives. Thus, an anarchist perspective on pedagogy begins with a call for educational transformation and a demand for its urgency.

As Armaline (2009) neatly identifies, there are three central characteristics for an anarchist approach to pedagogy: humility in approaching the education process; a call for creating spaces for education that are organized along more horizontal, less hierarchical lines; and an awareness of all people as capable learners, teachers, and creators in different, multiple ways (p. 139). Humility requires us to be able to talk openly about our capabilities and limitations, actively aware of how we are always simultaneously learners and teachers, not one or the other, and to admit the ways in which we are forced to capitulate to maintain livelihoods in a capitalist world economy, while being critical of it at the same time. Attempting to build a new world in the shell of the old is a necessary but difficult, some may say impossible, process, and we need humbly to be aware of the limitations of what we can accomplish at any given time, without losing sight of the necessary goal of transformation. Humility, as such, requires a deep engagement with self-reflection and self-critique in the process of configuring new and alternative learning practices (Haworth, 2012, p. 9).

Second, in discussions of power within pedagogical processes, I think it is essential to approach education with an anti-hierarchical, rather than a non-hierarchical, perspective so often perpetuated by some anarchists. The problem with the non-hierarchical perspective that some scholars of anarchist pedagogy espouse is that the absence of hierarchy in an unequal society is impossible in our capitalist society. While it is so important to always be working in opposition to hierarchy, a non-hierchical stance almost obscures existing hierarchies from view, hierarchies which can pop up even in the most horizontally organized educational arrangements. An anti-hierarchical stance, by contrast, takes as its mission to break down, challenge, and discuss hierarchy whenever it appears, whether it is about discussions of course content or about the mechanics of classroom activity that may lead to the emergence of certain hierarchies. When I introduce this issue in class, I present it as analogous to the difference between being anti-racist, as a vigilant stance that fights against racism, and being non-racist, "not seeing color" to use the uncritical cliché. As such, when it comes to power dynamics, our focus should include an anti-hierachical stance that is always vigilant about the presence and emergence of unequal power relations.

Third, paralleling the work of scholars of critical pedagogy, we need to expand what we think of as worthy of learning and teaching, to incorporate an ever-enlarging set of educational needs, desires, and talents that people have. An example I often like to use in an introductory human geography class is how the statistics we conventionally use about global human literacy patterns would read differently if they were based on, say, people's knowledge of the plant and animal species in their local ecosystems. To see literacy in a larger sense would include more people in the pursuit of learning and teaching and work against perceptions of who is more or less capable based on their level of knowledge. It also serves to question our existing educational objectives and to argue that there are other ways to prioritize learning based on the things that directly impact people's daily lives. Anarchist pedagogy, as such, promotes creative learning, sociality, community, and autonomous interactions with others and with the environment over established modes of learning (DeLeon, 2006). While anarchist pedagogy comprises a great diversity in historical perspectives, these three characteristics of humility in approach to knowledge, concern for creating spaces free from coercion, and a belief in human capabilities, provide a useful opening for understanding what an anarchist pedagogy can encompass.

The other important part of the triad in this paper is the relationship between geography and anarchism. As Simon Springer (2013) notes, "Anarchism and geography have had a long courtship" (p. 46). From the early works of anarchist geographers such as Peter Kropotkin and Elisée Reclus to the anarchist inspirations of the radical geography movement of the 1970s to the revival of interest in anarchism since the late 1990s, the two have experienced a long, but disjointed relationship. Springer convincingly argues for the need to more fully synthesize the two within a contemporary approach to anarchist geographies. Geography can critically aid in understanding the significant spatial implications of diverse anarchist projects such as Occupy Wall Street, the spectacles of street theater, mutual aid formations such as co-ops, and the multi-scalar organizational capacities of groups such as Indymedia. Similarly, anarchism offers geographers important theoretical perspectives on topics ranging from statehood to social justice to urban gentrification (Springer, 2013, p. 56). Specifically with regard to pedagogy, geographers have much to gain from anarchist pedagogical perspectives (Rouhani, 2013). Anarchism provides radical geographers a more complex approach to understanding power relations, our institutional limitations, and our capabilities to resist institutional limits in creative and liberatory ways. This requires taking the classroom itself seriously as a space of activism and social change, while expanding what spaces count as the geography classroom and what kinds of learning count as geographic knowledge. Anarchists, too, have much to gain from geographic insights into understanding of the places, spaces, and scales of education. At present, though, both sets of perspectives suffer from the same problem of abstractness and a lack of engagement with the specificities of teaching and learning (Rouhani, 2013). While there is a wealth of discussion of pedagogical ideas, there is very little written on insights from pedagogical practices. For shedding light into the potential of a combined anarchist-geographic pedagogy in practical terms, I will now turn to three recent works by geographers that describe different critical pedagogical experiments. While these scholars do not explicitly discuss anarchist pedagogies, their works are certainly within the anarchist spirit of pedagogy and as such can aid in conceptualizing what an anarchist-geographic pedagogy can look like.

Practices and Possibilities

Examining enactments of liberating pedagogies by radical geographers can usefully illuminate the practices and possibilities of anarchist-geographic pedagogies. In this section of the chapter, I will examine the work of three scholars, Anne Godlewska, Laura Pulido, and Rachel Pain, as they discuss such experiments in their classes. I think that their works can provide inspiration and insight into the possibilities of a more conceptually developed framework for how we can create transformative classroom spaces.

In her account of "dislocation pedagogy," Anne Godlewska (2012) discusses learning experiments in a course focused on "research and philosophies of place and space" (p. 384). In these experiments, students at Queens University were dislocated from urban environments with which they were familiar and re-placed in key unfamiliar locations, with local guides who had different kinds of expertise in that location as their guide in the city of Kingston. She frames the experiments with the idea that being dislocated from familiar places and relocated in unfamiliar places has important pedagogical value in prompting students to learn about place in a comparative, reflective way and to provide students with the opportunity to critically engage their learning with places in the city that are not conventionally a part of a university education. Like Kitchens (2009), she identifies the forces of neoliberalization and standardization at work that contribute to a trend toward the devaluing of place-based learning, which makes a pedagogical project such as this also a political project to attempt to recapture a critical, material place-based form of learning. In the end, she states that students' visits to places including a nursing home, prison, and local business had the effect of creating a vital space of mutual teaching and learning: "The knowledge and experience of the place experts excited them, and the place experts in turn were engaged by the students' questions and observations" (Godlewska, 2012, p. 388).

Godlewska's (2012) course learning experiment enacts some of the important dimensions of an emancipatory anarchist-geographic pedagogy, namely through an openness to exploration and the unexpected, a critical revaluing of an emplaced education, and the expansion in the number of people involved in the processes of learning and teaching. She mentions at several points in her review of the experience that the novelty and creativity of the explorative dimensions of dislocation in the class greatly excited both her and her students, in a way that would have been less possible in a conventional graduate school classroom setting. They constantly wanted to learn and explore more and bemoaned the fact that they did not have time to discuss the various aspects of the meanings of place that they experienced. In addition, this dislocated pedagogy helped everyone involved to understand the everyday spaces that surround them, whether they regularly get to interact with them or not, in deeply meaningful ways. It allowed them to connect places that have been made disparate through an educational system that values specialization and quantification, to counteract the tendencies toward placelessness through a learning process that actively engages and makes connections between different parts of a city. Moreover, by incorporating local guides as an essential part of the course, students learned the importance of experiencing their education beyond the confines of the standard learning delivery methods, in a way that incorporates the university into a whole array of possible learning spaces and prevents the "ivory tower syndrome" from emerging. Godlewska mentions that the local guides' experience also was greatly enriched, by being given the opportunity to teach what they know and to learn new things through students' questions. In this way, this experiment in dislocating pedagogy allowed for a much more recursive and reflexive set of learning spaces.

Another productive discussion of such a learning endeavor is the discussion by Rachel Pain and others about their experiences engaging in participatory action research, a collaborative approach to research, education, and action geared toward social transformation, with organizations in the community (Pain, Finn, Bouveng & Ngobe, 2013). Specifically, their account considers the benefits and challenges of a multi-term undergraduate module in participatory geographies, which had students co-produce research with community partners though a series of interactive and dynamic classroom and community activities. The module actively challenges the conventional information delivery modes of undergraduate geographic education by creating multiple decentralized spaces of learning, teaching, and research, with the argument that such community engagement has the potential to greatly enrich both students and non-university community members. It is important to note that the academic article itself is a part of the participatory action process, authored jointly by a faculty member (Pain), a student who undertook the module (Finn), and two members of an asylum seeker and refugee support organization where students participated in research (Bouveng & Ngobe).

The greatest strength of their account, building inspiration toward anarchist-geographic pedagogies, lies in their mission to actively engage with the tensions in achieving the module's aims, rather than simply glossing over them. In a highly self-reflective conclusion, the authors identify five key areas of tension that emerged from their engagement.

The first is the value of engagement itself through building relationships with the people involved. The module required students to engage in the research with their whole intellectual, emotional, and social selves in a meaningful way that is often not possible in our alienating education systems. They recount, for example, a moment in which a student from a privileged background confessed his ignorance about the prejudices and injustices facing refugees and asylum seekers and publicly apologized on behalf of the British people for their mistreatment. Such a personally transforming and life-changing experience can only occur in such a context that allows for deep, meaningful interaction.

A second challenge is the issue of time, with students ultimately realizing the tremendous investment it takes to build meaningful relationships and carry out reciprocally meaningful research. This challenge aided students in honing their research skills, realizing the problems inherent in the conventional learning and research system, and learning how to share resources with community members in a way to make more efficient use of time.

The third tension is between teaching and learning styles, especially between the traditional knowledge transfer and more reflexive, decentered modes. Here Pain discusses both the tremendous value of decentering the classroom as much as possible, as well as the limitations given her role as instructor within the confines of a regulated university system that, for example, does not allow students to be involved in the development of course aims.

The last two tensions discussed concern failure. On the positive side, they argue that discussions of where participatory action research can often fall short in accomplishing its goals is productive in assessing the methods of teaching and research, realizing the complex political and social relations of conducting this work, and informing future research. On the negative side, students and teachers must contend with the fact that our education systems do not value failure in how grades are rewarded. While in this project, students were rewarded for how they discussed their limitations and were not graded down for failing to accomplish their goals fully, they still felt uneasy talking about failure, given our conventional systems of learning assessment. These conclusions provide valuable insight into an emancipatory anarchist-geographic pedagogy by illuminating the strengths and limitations of a sustained, participatory mode of learning and doing.

The last pedagogical project I would like to highlight is A People's Guide to Los Angeles (PGTLA), a collaborative, multi-modal endeavor aiming to document the city's underrepresented, marginalized histories of community, solidarity, and struggle. Strategically, the project "began in casual conversation, developed into a poster, expanded into a website, and has been utilized in walking tours and exhibits" (Pulido, 2008, p. 709). Most recently, participants organized the work into a coffee-table book, published in 2012. While this project did not begin in the geography classroom as the other two did, I find it to be useful in thinking through anarchist-geographic pedagogies for a few important reasons. First, it was a collaborative project that brought together faculty from different disciplines, undergraduate and graduate students at the University of Southern California, and a diverse group of other community members involved in the different conceptual, technical, and practical aspects of the project over the years. Pulido identifies this collaboration as both rewarding and frustrating, in having to give up control over some aspects of the project based on differing expertise and interest. This is a challenge in any kind of collaborative pedagogical project. The collective's use of popular media and content in the project is also very impressive. The posters, website, tours, and book have been able to reach a significant international population, and in a way that presents the marginalized peoples' histories of Los Angeles in a visual, accessible way. Lastly, the PGTLA is an educational tool for empowerment, having impacts in public policy, non-profit work, and public education in Los Angeles, but in other cities as well. In fact, it also contains information about tools, ranging from accessing local archives and repositories to conducting oral histories and landscape analysis, whereby collectives in other places can undertake similar projects.

While not explicitly anarchist in their pedagogical aims and practices, these three projects certainly correspond with some of the major aims and concerns of anarchist pedagogies. In different ways, they all convey the need to be humble in the execution of objectives, to be open to reflection and self-critique, to actively work toward decentering the power relations of learning and teaching as much as possible, and to open higher education up to a larger number of people and forms of knowledge, in a way that makes education a more populist, less elitist endeavor, incorporating the modes and content of education that matter to people's lives. From a geographic standpoint, too, these works provide insight into how to counter the neo-liberal tendencies toward standardization, quantification, and placelessness by providing vibrant, dynamic, emplaced ways to channel our teaching and learning. It is important to note, though, that these are not emplaced pedagogies that isolate education in place, but rather ones that seek to make connections between places and expand our pedagogic horizons. Whether through making connections between traditional and nontraditional learning spaces that matter to understanding the places we live, or encouraging others in other places to use the tools of local social thought and action to form people's geographies around the world, these authors identify some of the salient ways in which our emplaced pedagogical projects are, and need to be, connected across different spaces and places.

This combination of frames goes far in conceptualizing what an anarchist-geographic pedagogy can look like. At the same time, I am left with some concerns and questions about how to develop it further. One question concerns how students of such projects can emplace what they have learned in their future lives toward goals of social justice and transformation. Pain and others, in the article discussed above, suggest that this is one of the potential strengths of a participatory action research module like theirs, but it would be important to carry out more detailed research on how formers students can and do incorporate what they have learned in this kind of a pedagogic setting in their futures. A second important concern is how to deal with resistance on the part of administrators, colleagues, students, and community members if and when it appears. These are the contexts in which admitting our limitations is important, but we also need to think through and develop spaces of mutual emotional support for the significant problems of academic and activist fatigue that often develop out of radical pedagogical projects. Lastly, I find myself deeply inspired by the calls for a socially transformative pedagogy that cuts across spaces and scales, and I think that this is a particularly important area about which to think and act. There are so many inspiring, revolutionary education practices being enacted around the world without the sufficient network through which to share, learn from, and adopt them. While an anarchist-geographic pedagogy can go far in suggesting the importance of spaces and places and the connections between them, within an anarchist framework, it can also aid in suggesting the importance and ways to connect pedagogic projects around the world.

References

Armaline, W. (2009). Thoughts on anarchist pedagogy and epistemology. In R. Amster, A. DeLeon, L. Fernandez, A. Nocella & D. Shannon (Eds.), *Contemporary anarchist studies: An introductory anthology of anarchy in the academy* (pp. 136–146). New York, NY: Routledge.

Askins, K. (2008). In and beyond the classroom: Research ethics and participatory pedagogies. *Area* 40(4), 500–509.

Autonomous Geographies Collective. (2010). Beyond scholar activism: Making strategic interventions inside and outside the neoliberal university. *ACME, 9*(2), 245-275.

Castree, N. (1999). Out there? In here? Domesticating critical geography. *Area, 31*(1), 81-86.

Castree, N. (2000). Professionalism, activism and the university: Whither critical geography? *Environment and Planning, A 32*(6), 955-970.

DeLeon, A. (2006). The time for action is now! Anarchist theory, critical pedagogy, and radical possibilities. *Journal for Critical Education Policy Studies, 4*(2). Retrieved from http://www.jceps.com/archives/521

Freire, P. (1970). *Pedagogy of the oppressed*. New York, NY: Seabury Press.

Giroux, H.A. (1997). Pedagogy and the politics of hope: Theory, culture, and schooling. Boulder CO:Westview.

Godlewska, A. (2012). Dislocating pedagogy. *Professional Geographer, 65*(3), 384-389.

Haworth, R. (2012). Introduction. In R. Haworth (Ed.), *Anarchist pedagogies: Collective actions, theories, and critical reflections on education* (pp. 1-10). Oakland: PM Press.

Heyman, R. (2000). Research, pedagogy, and instrumental geography. *Antipode, 32*(3), 292-307.

Heyman, R. (2007). Who's going to man the factories and be the sexual slaves if we all get PhDs? Democratizing knowledge production, pedagogy, and the Detroit Geographical Expedition and Institute. *Antipode, 39*(1), 99-120.

hooks, b. (1994). *Teaching to transgress: Education as the practice of freedom*. Boston, MA: South End Press.

Kincheloe, J. (2008). *Critical pedagogy primer*. New York, NY: Peter Lang.

Kitchens, J. (2009). Situated pedagogy and the Situationist International: Countering a pedagogy of placelessness. *Educational Studies, 45*, 240-261.

McLaren, P. (1998). *Life in schools: An introduction to critical pedagogy in the foundations of education*. New York, NY: Longman.

Merrett, C. (2008). Pedagogies of scale—universality and particularity in geographic education. *Progress in Human Geography, 32*(5), 704-708

Merrifield, A. (1995). Situated knowledge through exploration: Reflections on Bunge's "geographical expeditions." *Antipode, 27*, 49-70.

Pain, R., Finn, M., Bouveng, R., & Ngobe, G. (2013). Productive tensions—engaging geography students in participatory action research with communities. *Journal of Geography in Higher Education, 37*(1), 28-43.

Pulido, L. (2008). People's Guide to Los Angeles—an experiment in popular geography. *Progress in Human Geography, 32*(5), 708-714.

Rouhani, F. (2013). Practice what you teach: Facilitating anarchism in and out of the classroom. *Antipode, 44*(5), 1726-1741.

Springer, S. (2013). Anarchism and geography: A brief genealogy of anarchist geographies. *Geography Compass, 7*(1), 46-60.

Suissa, J. (2010). *Anarchism and education: A philosophical perspective*. Oakland, CA: PM Press.

CHAPTER 5

The Wretched of the Network Society: Techno-Education and Colonization of the Digital

Petar Jandrić and Ana Kuzmanić

D igital colonialism has many faces. There is traditional colonialism in the digital format, where a stronger country exploits a weaker country using information and communication technologies. Then there is ideological digital colonialism, where one country or even company (such as Google) implements its own interpretation of freedom of information toward another country (such as China). We can talk about cultural digital colonialism, which is based on the transfer of music and films from emitting countries such as the U.S. and the UK to receiving countries such as our native country, Croatia. The internet is based on Latin letters and the English language, so linguistic colonialism underlies the whole of virtuality. The internet is a new cybernetic frontier (Brand, 1974), and we are all colonizing its vast open (cyber)spaces—simultaneously, all aspects of our lives are being colonized by the use and underlying principles of the network. In certain parts of the globe, predominantly in the global North, digital colonization is quite advanced—slowly but surely, these parts are entering the age of digital postcolonialism. Other parts of the globe, predominantly but far from exclusively in the global South, are still awaiting a sweeping wave of digital colonization. Inspired by parallels between geographical migrations of the past and our collective migration into cyberspace, in 2014 we established the research project entitled Digital Postcolonialism aimed at exploring human migration into the digital through the lens of postcolonial theory.

Our research enterprise emerges from convergent traditions of critical theory, radical education, postcolonialism, and anarchism, and shares the spirit of Manuel Castells's (2001) and Jan van Dijk's (1999) network society with other similar attempts such as postcolonial digital humanities (2014).

According to Suman Seth (2009), "the relationship between technoscientific knowledge and *post*-colonial orders has been the subject of increasing—if, until recently, rather sporadic—discussion in science and technology studies (STS) in the last two decades" (p. 376). In the realm of critical pedagogy, such interest offers significant opportunity for transformation, as "the challenge that postcolonialism presents to educators and cultural workers calls for new ideas, pedagogical strategies, and social movements capable of constructing a politics of difference within critical public cultures forged in the struggle to deepen and extend the promise of radical and cultural democracy" (Giroux, 2005, p. 13). However, digital postcolonialism significantly differs from the aforementioned theoretical frameworks in one important respect: instead of applying postcolonial theory to human migration into the digital, it is developed literally on/around the metaphor of human colonization of the digital. Certainly, such a theoretical context makes significant advances in terms of the reach, scope, and validity of digital postcolonialism. However, we do believe—and our recent research has been fairly supportive of this belief—that digital postcolonialism might provide a novel perspective on the relationships among contemporary technologies, human beings, and society.

In the context of "hard sciences," theorists such as Thomas Kuhn (1970) and Sandra Harding (2008 & 2011) have clearly shown that our "laws of nature" are far from mirror images of nature that passively waits to be described and classified. By extension, the conviction that information and communication technologies are far from value-neutral, and reflect a complex web of economic, social, and political relationships, has been shared by various generations of critical theorists (Horkheimer & Adorno, 2002; McLaren & Jandrić, 2015), anarchists (Kropotkin, 1912; Illich, 1971 & 1973) and technologists (Himanen, 2001; Stallman, 2002). Educational systems contribute to this web in various, often conflicting capacities: as producers of knowledge, as transmitters of values, as (re)producers of socioeconomic relationships, as players in the global market, and as sites of formal and informal critical resistance. At all these (and many more) levels, education is dialectically intertwined with the ways we use, perceive, and develop information and communication technologies. Therefore, it seems only natural to explore their mutual relationships through the lens of digital postcolonialism.

According to Itty Abraham (2006), "'postcolonial techno-science' as a way of doing science studies may not be commensurable with 'postcolonial techno-science' as a way of thinking about alternative and local knowledges" (p. 211). In our recent paper, we started developing digital postcolonialism as a way of doing science in and against the prevalent logic of information and communication technologies (Jandrić & Kuzmanić, 2015). In this chapter, we reach beyond the existing state of affairs and explore radical educational alternatives using the metaphor of decolonization. This research is focused on three interlocking questions. First, it briefly explores some initial thoughts and considerations about digital postcolonialism. Second, it identifies the main insights of digital postcolonialism regarding the relationships between education and information and communication technologies. Finally, it uses the identified insights to point towards transformative possibilities of radical learning in the network society.

Digital Postcolonialism

In the most general sense, decolonization is the undoing or reversal of colonial relationships. Traditionally, the focus of decolonization has been on the physical displacement of populations (usually the return of colonists to their motherlands), and aimed against political, economic, and other forms of colonial dependence. However, as the last ship with ex-colonists leaves the horizon, it immediately becomes obvious that the undoing or reversal of colonial relationships cannot be further from the return to previous, often romanticized ways of life. Colonialism brought about new approaches to work, new religions, new ways of thinking, and new expectations. Close interactions between the colonists and the colonized have developed strong mutual relationships and hybrid identities—in words of Frantz Fanon (2001), "decolonization is the encounter between two congenitally antagonistic forces that in fact owe their singularity to the kind of reification secreted and nurtured by the colonial situation" (p. 27). Therefore, decolonization is not a struggle between two distant enemies, but a reinvention of politics, economy, national identity and culture.

Following the same line of argument, decolonization of human learning from information and communication technologies cannot be reduced to rejecting computers and microchip-based gadgets in one or another version of a techno-primitivist utopia, such as that advocated by John Zerzan (2004) and the anarcho-primitivists. Instead, digital decolonization is a process of reinventing new forms of (semi-)digital identities, such as Donna Haraway's cyborgs (1991), and new vernacular digital cultures, such as Stallman's Free Software movement (2002). It provides the colonized with a shared history, critical approaches to understanding their present, and tools for shaping their futures. It transfers technology-related decisions from economic, political, and technological superstructures to the people. Digital decolonization is critical praxis aimed at our emancipation from the forces of global neoliberal capitalism, individually and socially, and geared towards the active democratic reinvention of present and future techno-social realities.

The wretched of the network society are not a new social group—in various forms and under various names, they have existed since the dawn of humanity. They are Marx's and Bakunin's proletariat, and Fanon's wretched of the earth, and Freire's oppressed, and Guy Standing's precariat—all imbued with the age of the network. This chapter combines the theoretical insights of Frantz Fanon and Paulo Freire for two main reasons. First, the fundamental nature of their works is particularly suitable for early research attempts at digital postcolonialism. Second, the strong theoretical links between Fanon and Freire make possible a conversation between traditional postcolonialism and radical pedagogy. For instance, in the introduction to the thirtieth anniversary edition of Freire's (2005) masterpiece, Donaldo Macedo testifies that "reading *Pedagogy of the Oppressed* gave me the critical tools to reflect on, and understand, the process through which we come to know what it means to be at the periphery of the intimate yet fragile relationship between the colonizer and the colonized" (p. 11). However, digital postcolonialism reaches far beyond the important body of work developed by Fanon and Freire, and includes contemporary developments in postcolonial theory coupled with radical insights into the relationships among education, technologies, and society. Therefore, digital postcolonialism is not a new theory or research methodology—instead, it is merely another lens for understanding radical education in the age of digital technologies.

During the twentieth century, critical theorists have developed several approaches to the relationships between human beings and technologies. Among the most popular is technological determinism, which implies that the values of global neoliberal capitalism are somehow "naturally" embedded in technologies. If the question concerning technologies can really be understood through one or another technologically determinist position (as suggested by several generations of Frankfurt School researchers from Horkheimer & Adorno [2002] to Marcuse [1964]), than we can only agree with Martin Heidegger's assertion that "only a God can save us" (1981). However, the third generation of Frankfurt School thinkers rejected technological determinism as inherently dystopian (Feenberg, 2002, p. 183) and sought other solutions.

A popular alternative, shared by critical theorists and anarchists, is based on various design critiques. From Ivan Illich's *Tools for Conviviality* (1973), to Richard Stallman's *Free Software, Free Society* (2002), these critiques assume that the "proper" design of the internal workings of technologies has the power to bring about emancipation and freedom. In spite of their attractiveness, design critiques are clearly utopian—from dynamite to genetic engineering, people have always managed to use technologies against their inventors' visions and ideals (a good case in point is Alfred Nobel and his prize). Obviously, the question of real social change is much more complicated than totalizing discourses based on dystopian technological determinism and/or utopian design critiques (Jandrić, 2014). According to Fanon (2001), decolonization also cannot be further from a totalizing discourse as it consists of "a programme of complete disorder" (p. 27). Developed in complex and often chaotic (post)colonial circumstances, digital decolonization rejects Lyotard's grand narratives (1984) and represents an attempt to develop a nuanced critical approach to contemporary relationships between human beings and information and communication technologies.

Postcolonial science and technology studies place strong emphasis on the role of the researcher. Working in academia, we actively contribute to the digital colonization of our society (as an employee of the Department of Informatics and Computing, for instance, one of the co-authors is directly engaged in various local and global "informatization" projects). Simultaneously, by being subjected to various "objective" measures such as the H-index, our work is systematically colonized by the global neoliberal concept of "progress" through information and communication technologies (Burrows, 2012). Similar dialectics can be found in all postcolonial relationships. Edward Said's "orient" is a co-creation of the East and the West (1993), Frantz Fanon's "primitive" Algerian arrives into being in interaction with the French colonist (2001), and contemporary academic researchers are simultaneously causes and products of digital colonialism. Therefore, our relationship to this research cannot be further from positivist tradition of cold-minded outsiders.

In the framework of digital postcolonialism, academic researchers are in the position similar to Frantz Fanon's "native intellectuals." Born in the East but educated in the West, Algerian native intellectuals during 1950s had a very important role in the struggle against the French colonists: they were needed to provide theoretical guidance for native emancipation, legitimate the claims of a nation through development of a national culture, and develop practical strategies for decolonization (Fanon, 2001, pp. 166–167). As academic researchers we are insiders, immersed both in the digital worlds of the internet and in the positivist tradition of the contemporary academia—yet we are also outsiders, because our studies of digital postcolonialism clearly breach commonly accepted research patterns. In this position, we need to take an active role in the struggle against global neoliberal techno-imperialism to develop the theoretical framework of digital postcolonialism, legitimate its relevance for contemporary relationships between education and technologies, and create strategies for decolonization.

Analyzing the important tasks facing native intellectuals, Fanon identified three main phases of decolonization. For the purpose of this research, we shall call them recognition, historicization, and active resistance (Fanon, 2001, pp. 166–167). (While we believe that these names adequately sum up the main features of Fanon's three phases, this is not how he originally called them—we invented these names for the sake of brevity.) Developed in the context of French colonialism in Algeria, these phases have been identified in numerous studies of decolonization throughout the globe (i.e., Smith, 1999,

p. 70). Inspired by their common appearance in postcolonial studies, Noor Al-Abbood (2012) has recently inquired whether Fanon's phases are mere products of the specific socio-historical context or represent a general "paradigm of native cultural and literary anti-colonialism" (p. 121). Upon extensive comparative analysis of available sources, he concluded that his "narrative does indeed provide indispensable insights in illuminating specific moments or in critically explaining certain themes in the native culture of opposition." However, Al-Abbood also warns that Fanon's conception of colonial power as absolute does not "take into account the various ways in which this power has been exercised and resisted at different times and in different places" (Al-Abbood, 2012, p. 121). While Fanon's three phases indeed appear in all processes of decolonization, the internal power dynamics within individual phases might greatly vary.

Recognition: The Technological Empire of Contemporary Education

In the first phase of decolonization, "the native intellectual gives proof that he has assimilated the culture of the occupying power" (Fanon, 2001, p. 166). Analyzing the depth and extent of colonization, the colonized develop a critical understanding of their circumstances which is a prerequisite for the further development of decolonizing praxis. Thankfully, the relationships between education and information and communication technologies have been thoroughly researched by various critical theorists including, but far from limited to the Frankfurt School and its successors. In the phase of recognition, therefore, we will blend these insights with a generic definition of colonialism. In this process, we will compare the insights of critical pedagogy, postcolonial science and technology studies, and (post)colonial studies. While each of these potent currents of critical theory inevitably brings new and important insights into the debate, it is their shared theoretical base which methodologically enables such collaboration. (A good case in the point is the phase of recognition, which—under various names such as *conscientizacao* (Freire, 1972)—is a constant theme within each of these trajectories.)

Fanon shows that one of the main weapons of colonizers is the fragmentation of discourse into distinct economic, social, or religious issues. Therefore, it is only a complete, well-rounded recognition of various colonization processes that breaks the colonizers' power and opens spaces for decolonization (Fanon, 2001, p. 167). In order to reach this level of recognition, we obviously need to start from a general, overarching definition of colonialism—unsurprisingly, a suitable definition can be found in the field of good old-fashioned conceptual analysis. According to Roland Horvath (1972), colonialism is always a form of domination, and it operates at three main interconnected levels—non-group domination, inter-group domination, and intra-group domination (pp. 46–47). As it happens, simplicity of this definition is both beneficial and restrictive for this analysis. For instance, Aidan Southall (1972) clearly shows that "the categories are not really water-tight, but many times reflect to complex continua" (p. 53). In spite of obvious drawbacks, however, Horvath's definition provides a good fit for Fanon's first phase of decolonization by drawing a full account of the colonial relation-ships between education and technologies.

At an individual (non-group) level, citizens of the network society are fully dominated by information and communication technologies: our time has been appropriated by various gadgets, our eyes have been captured by our screens, our attention span has been colonized by the need for more and more information, and our bodies have been colonized by artificially created expectations. Some researchers, such as Donna Haraway (1991), would assert that each and every member of the human race has literally been re-created and turned into a cyborg—"a cybernetic organism, a hybrid of machine and organism, a creature of social reality as well as a creature of fiction" (p. 291). Others are more cautious, and argue against the essentialism inherent in Haraway's claim (Soper, 1999). One way or another, it is indisputable that information and communication technologies significantly impact the ways we learn, unlearn, and utilize what we learned. Therefore, colonization of education starts from the very mind, soul, and body of the learner.

For one reason or another, not everyone has been drawn into the Faustian bargain of digitalization. Some people live in places that have not (yet) been reached by the long arm of information and communication tech-nologies, others cannot afford technologies, and some consciously reject technologies in spite of their ready availability. In the language of coloni-zation, the digital divide, the difference between the digital haves and the digital have-nots (Van Dijk & Hacker, 2003), has created two distinct classes: the new colonists, or the new citizens of the network society; and the new savages, people originally excluded from the electronic banquet who have slowly but surely joining the table. Just like in the old days, one does not need to personally engage with the colonists in order to become a part of the techno-colonial order. In the world of global neoliberal capitalism, you can ignore technologies, but technologies will never ignore you.

Intergroup domination happens at various dialectically interrelated levels. At the level of global economy, Wittkower (2008) shows that the majority of know-how and profits from information and communication technologies are firmly situated in the global North, while the bulk of the "dirty work" related to industrial production is done in the global South. In order to maintain this domination, the global North uses various neocolonial strategies in order to keep the global South from using information and com-munication technologies for their own emancipation: "Industries based on or around computers, especially the software industry, are in this way akin to empires. They must struggle in order to ensure that colonists who find themselves surrounded by free and available means of production do not use these means for their own subsistence and independence, but rather to support the motherland" (Wittkower, 2008).

This struggle simultaneously happens in various dimensions. At the level of the design and construction of digital machines, educational domination is produced by parallel "dumbing down" of user interfaces and the increasing complexity and obscurity "under the hood." In the words of Ivan Illich, it is in industry's best interest to make information and communication technologies as non-convivial as possible. This creates profound consequences: "To understand the rising cost of education, we must recognize two facts: first, that non-convivial tools create educational side effects which at some point become intolerable and, second, that education which employs non-convivial tools is economically unfeasible" (Illich, 1973). Certainly, the increasing non-conviviality of information and communication technologies is constantly being counter-balanced by their built-in convivial features such as the relative freedom of internet information and open educational projects (Himanen, 2001; Stallman, 2002).

In the dimension of international legislation and intercorporate relationships, the colonization of information happens through various forms of regulation. "The systematic colonization of information is being accomplished through (a) closed-sourcing, (b) governmentally guaranteed encryption, (c) licensing, and (d) the assumption of copyright. Through these means the digital colonist, while she cannot be separated from her land, is kept as much as possible from mining it, from trading or selling it, and from sustainably farming it" (Wittkower, 2008).

This regulation is backed by a strong set of values such as the idea that knowledge can be owned and that the government's right to surveillance is above individual right to privacy. Peddled by international corporations and governments of colonist countries from the global North, this set of values represents the very essence of global neoliberal capitalism. However, colonization is a double-edged sword insofar it transforms both the colonized and the colonist—therefore, it is hardly a surprise that digital colonialism has profound effects all over the globe. If knowledge is property, than education is indeed a commodity. It follows that some people have more rights to access this commodity than others, and educational institutions should predominantly be based on economic principles. At the level of intergroup domination, information and communication technologies have also become proponents of the logic of neoliberal capitalism.

The last form of domination, intra-group domination, refers to power relationships within various institutions. In order to describe the acceptance of information and communication technologies in schools and universities, educational managers (Bates, 2000) and e-learning practitioners (Zemsky & Massy, 2004) have developed various versions of Everett Rogers's (1995) theory of the diffusion of innovations. In brief, these theories classify employees in five categories usually called innovators, early adopters, early majority, late majority, and diehards (or laggards), and conveniently pastes them onto one or another Gauss curve of technology acceptance. At the first glance, this popular statistical distribution merely outlines the current state of affairs. Underneath, however, lies a complex value system which prefers technological innovators to technological skeptics (Fejes & Nicoll, 2008), and educational techno-managers such as Tony Bates (2000) make great efforts to develop complex systems of reward and punishment to encourage the first and punish the latter.

Besides the diffusion of innovations, there are at least a few competing models of technology acceptance such as evolutionism (Jandrić, 2012) and Gartner's (2014) hype cycle. In spite of differences in approach, reach, and scope, models examined in these studies share an important common feature: they praise innovators for their "progressiveness" and blame laggards for their "backwardness," thus evoking the familiar colonial discourse of personal responsibility for structural inequalities. In ancient times, the savage was guilty of being poor, dirty, and ill; according to contemporary common sense, the pre-digital savage is (at least in part) responsible for her own inability to use computers. On that basis, our recent article shows that digital postcolonialism has created its own version of "the myth of the lazy native" (Alatas, 1997), and paraphrases it into "the myth of the lazy pre-digital savage" (Jandrić & Kuzmanić, 2015). This myth is hardly ever questioned in public discourse—the obedient acceptance of the constant flow of new technologies has become the new normality. Within certain parts of academia, however, it is faced with strong resistance, as lecturers and professors throughout the globe are showing that many aspects of their work cannot be technologicized without significant losses (Fejes & Nicoll, 2008).

At all levels, information and communication technologies are linked to the introduction and maintenance of values and ideologies pertaining to global neoliberal capitalism into contemporary education. On that basis, we will tentatively name this structure the technological empire of contemporary education—and look into historical explanations for its development and maintenance.

Historicization: The Advent of Techno-Education
At the grassroots level, systematic digital colonization provokes plenty of grassroots resistance such as piracy, the open source movement, and various policy initiatives and global movements (Stallman, 2002; Himanen, 2001).

Through the important work of digital revolutionaries such as Julian Assange and Edward Snowden, information and communication technologies have become the sites of important social struggle (Assange, Appelbaum, Müller-Maguhn & Zimmermann, 2012). The commodification of schooling is counterbalanced by informal learning through the internet and the rise of informal radical education. Some battles are lost, and others are won—in the complex web of postcolonial relationships, it is hard to determine which one is more important than the other. In order to identify cracks in the technological empire of contemporary education, therefore, digital postcolonialism rejects various dystopian and utopian simplifications, and seeks more nuanced approaches. According to Feenberg (2002),

> the hegemony of capital does not rest on a particular technique of social control but more fundamentally on the technical reconstruction of the entire field of social relations within which it operates. The power of the business-man or bureaucrat is already present in the fragmentation of the various social spheres of production, management and labour, family and home life, economics and politics, and so on. The fragmented individuals and institutions can be organised only by agents who dominate them from above. (p. 183)

Fanon's second stage of decolonization, historicization, challenges the fragmentation and builds a theoretical framework for grassroots, bottom-up critical emancipation. According to Fanon (2001), "decolonization, we know, is an historical process: In other words, it can only be understood, it can only find its significance and become self-coherent insofar as we can discern the history-making movement which gives it form and substance" (p. 27). On that basis, we shall conduct the second stage of digital decolonization by historicizing the relationships between education and information and communication technologies. Such a historicization of discourse, claims Jennifer Lavia (2006), "makes connections between the past, present and the future as a necessary philosophical and methodological endeavour of educational practice" (p. 281). Therefore, it is hardly a surprise that the historicization of the technological empire of contemporary education has already spontaneously begun in worldwide schools, universities, and research institutions around the world. During recent decades, the field of e-learning (also known by similar but non-synonymous names such as technologically enhanced learning, networked learning, learning-at-a-distance, etc.) has slowly but surely transformed from a community of practitioners predominately interested in how to use technologies into a field of researches interested in digital cultures, and the psychological, sociological, and philosophical effects of technologies on individuals and society (Zemsky & Massy, 2004; Jandrić & Boras, 2012). In Fanon's second stage of decolonization, therefore, we will blend theoretical insights identified in the phase of recognition into a brief, well-rounded postcolonial narrative.

Information and communication technologies have a long-standing relationship with education. The first electronic message between two computers was exchanged between UCLA and Stanford. Literally and metaphorically, the internet was conceived in the academic ethos of the mid-twentieth century, which includes openness, the free sharing of information, and horizontalism. Immediately after their release into the public arena, however, information and communication technologies had been taken up by digital pioneers such as Steve Jobs and Bill Gates who openly embarked on the crusade to colonize the world. The process of colonization is equally transformative for the colonized and for the colonist. The colonized industrial society has been utterly transformed by information and communication technologies and has evolved into the network society. The colonists, creators and peddlers of information and communication technologies, have abandoned their initial research ethos and have succumbed to the ubiquitous logic of the market.

In a constant feedback loop, information and communication technologies have repeatedly oscillated between promoting markets and educational systems as vehicles of progress, and, each time, their ideological baggage has been one step closer to the values of global neoliberal capitalism. In this way, they have perpetuated the continuous technological reconstruction of social relations in all areas of human activity. During this process, information and communication technologies have significantly contributed to the commodification, McDonaldization, and precariatization of education. While academics have been busy with developing shiny machines that would change the world, the machines have created an ecosystem based on very different values from their developers'. In this way, the shared history of education and technologies arrives at a common theme of (science) fiction: children that turn against their parents, and machines that turn against their creators.

As can be seen in various works of fiction such as Karel Čapek's R.U.R. (2014) and Mary Shelley's Frankenstein (2008), this complex relationship includes science, facts, beliefs, ideologies, and feelings. In this way, digital postcolonialism has broken the boundaries of analytic research and lost some of its traditional neutrality. According to Warwick Anderson (2002), this is a built-in feature of postcolonial science and technology studies, as they suggest "a means of writing a 'history of the present', of coming to terms with the turbulence and uncertainty of contemporary global flows of knowledge and practice" (p. 644). A shared history of education and information technologies written through the lens of digital postcolonialism is an attempt to come to terms with the complexity of their relationship, in order to get a well-rounded picture, it inevitably sacrifices various features of traditional positivist science.

The identities of technologies have been strongly shaped by education and the identity of education cannot be thought of without reference to technologies. This interconnected view of education and technologies is the prime example of Homi Bhabha's (1994) hybridity. The process of hybridization is central to resistance, as it enables postcolonialism to disrupt the exclusionary binary logic that enables the discourse of postcolonialism (technological optimism versus primitivism, good versus bad technologies, and dystopia versus utopia). According to Rizvi, Linguard, and Lavia (2006), "this is where postcolonial literature and work of creative arts assume an important task of interrupting received ways of thinking about the world, and articulating the hybridity and difference that lies within" (p. 254). On that basis, our postcolonial analysis of education and technologies offers spaces for critical resistance in hybrid forms of knowledge and identity that might disrupt the logic of colonialism by offering subversive meanings and spaces for radical action.

So, where should we seek new knowledge and identities? In digitally colonized societies, pre-digital schools and universities are obsolete. (While we all know plenty of places in the world that are still technically pre-digital, full escape from the long arm of technological globalization seems impossible.) Those who insist on working in a strictly pre-digital manner will eventually occupy a small niche of 'traditional crafts' such as blacksmiths and umbrella makers who exhibit ancient ways of production in historic towns and museums. While that kind of occupation might provide a nice life for a few, its subversive potentials are close to nil. The developed postcolonial narrative clearly shows that the divorce between education and information and communication technologies is impossible. Our knowledge of human biology cannot be separated from our microscopes, our insights into nuclear physics cannot be separated from our Geiger counters, and conclusions presented in this chapter cannot be separated from the internet technologies that enabled its production. Therefore, following the same line of argument that created techno-science (Feenberg, 2002, p. 164; Latour, 1987), educators might adopt a well-rounded concept aimed at designating this dialectic. Perhaps, for the sake of brevity, it might provisionally be called techno-education.

Resistance: Towards a Critical Decolonization of Techno-Education

Following recognition and historicization, we finally leave complex theoretical territory and arrive at Fanon's last stage of decolonization: active resistance. While the majority of postcolonial thinkers share the general ethos of non-compliance and urgency, their analyses and decolonizing strategies range from postmodernist benevolence towards various modernizing practices (During, 2000) to Frantz Fanon's (2001) insistence on the violent nature of resistance. Looking at important work developed by contemporary critical theorists of education (Giroux, 1991; Hill, McLaren, Cole & Rikowski, 1999), there is no doubt that postmodernism has significantly contributed to our understanding of contemporary education. In a strict epistemological sense, digital postcolonialism is also based on postmodern concepts such as the "geography of the digital" (Jandrić & Kuzmanić, 2015). However, recent developments in critical theory put forward a convincing argument about the necessity to divorce educational thinking from dismissive, paralyzing readings of postmodernism and provide more attention to traditional Marxist concepts such as class and race. In the words of Peter McLaren, "We need to use our labor capacity outside and beyond capitalist production relations. This is what critical pedagogy is all about—that is why it is often called revolutionary" (McLaren & Jandrić, 2015, p. 213).

Similar argument can easily be found in the field of postcolonial studies. According to Simon During (2000), many versions of postcolonialism have come to signify something rather remote from self-determination and autonomy. By deploying categories such as hybridity, mimicry, ambivalence or James Clifford's "newly, traditionally"—all of which have interlaced colonized and colonizing cultures—postcolonialism effectively became a reconciliatory rather than a critical, anti-colonialist category. It invoked modernity's triumph over so-called traditional societies, with the twist that this triumph radically unsettled modernity, most of all by dismantling the notion that historical temporality enacts reason's unfolding, a notion that had underpinned colonialist developmental values and practice in the first place (p. 386).

In the context of techno-education, it is easy to draw a parallel between McLaren's critique of educational postmodernism and During's critique of reconciliatory postcolonialism. On the one hand, reconciliatory postcolonialism provides many valuable insights into the dynamics of domination and power—after all, digital postcolonialism looks for spaces of resistance exactly in the postmodern notion of hybridity. At the other hand, hybridity might lead to the passive acceptance of hegemonic technological "modernization." On the road to the decolonization of techno-education, therefore, digital postcolonialism should take special care to avoid the traps of educational postmodernism and reconciliatory postcolonialism. In During's terminology, techno-education should seek opportunities for decolonization in the praxeological framework of critical digital postcolonialism. In that spirit, we shall sum up its insights into the relationships between education and technologies in four main points.

First, information and communication technologies are far from neutral; their design and usage opportunities reflect the worldviews, values, ideologies, dreams, and hopes of their designers. In spite of built-in biases, however, the majority of technologies may still serve as vehicles of diverse values and ideologies; more often than not, these may be in stark contradiction with aims of their designers. The nature of information and communication technologies is neither fully determinist nor fully non-determinist, therefore, the question concerning technologies cannot be resolved by mere replacing one simplification (such as technological determinism) by another (such as design critique). While contemporary information and communication technologies indeed serve predominantly as vehicles of global neoliberal capitalism, it is more accurate to describe them simultaneously as the colonist and the colonized, the oppressor and the oppressed, the battlefield and the warrior.

Second, contemporary education is dialectically intertwined with information and communication technologies—in the network society, one cannot be thought of without the other. Therefore, radical theoretical inquiry and practical resistance should be based on the notion of techno-education, a hybrid concept which reconnects human reasoning about technologies and education, and provides insights into the complex web of their mutual influences and power dynamics.

Third, colonization and decolonization are historical processes, and the path to understanding them lies in the constant (re-)historicization of the technological empire of contemporary education. While the existing colonial domination of information and communication technologies coupled with the ideology of global neoliberal capitalism indeed offers a bleak picture of our reality, it is the wider historical context that offers theoretical spaces for resistance through the notion of hybridity. At the practical level, however, spaces for resistance do not reside in opposing or accepting various simplifications and determinisms, but in local power disturbances and their places within global networks.

Fourth, digital postcolonialism provides a nuanced view to reality which inevitably involves complex ideas—it is based on various postmodern images such as "migration" into the digital, and employs hybrid concepts such as techno-education. However, its theoretical complexity should not paralyze us in the shallow "triumph" of modernity. In spite of the apparent "remoteness" of digital postcolonialism from everyday reality, it is firmly based in the conceptual framework of critical theory and we should always remember the important message from Paulo Freire that man's ontological vocation (as he calls it) is to be a Subject who acts upon and transforms his world, and in so doing moves toward ever new possibilities of a fuller and richer life individually and collectively. This *world* to which he relates is not a static and closed order, a *given* reality which humanity must accept and to which it must adjust; rather, it is a problem to be worked on and solved. It is the material used by mankind to create history, a task which it performs as it overcomes that which is dehumanizing, at any particular time and place, and as it dares to create the qualitatively new (Shaull, 2005, p. 32). In this tradition, the trap of reconciliatory postcolonialism should be avoided, and radical techno-educational learning spaces should be sought in the conceptual framework of critical/radical/Marxist/anarchist digital postcolonialism.

Radical Education in the Age of Digital Postcolonialism

Out of the ruins of digital colonialism, this chapter historicizes the relationships between information and communication technologies and education and offers a postcolonial perspective aimed at decolonization of our techno-educational practices. At the theoretical level, digital postcolonialism poses some grand questions about the nature of techno-scientific knowledge. At the practical level, it rejects common simplifications such as technological determinism and points to small power imbalances as the main sites of resistance against the pairing of techno-education with global neoliberal ideologies. As a research approach, digital postcolonialism exhibits some significant advantages over more traditional forms of radical inquiry into techno-education. According to Warwick Anderson (2002),

> Too often the "postcolonial" seems to imply yet another global theory, or simply a celebration of the end of colonialism. But it may also be viewed as a signpost pointing to contemporary phenomena in need of new modes of analysis and requiring new critiques. Some older styles of analysis in science studies—those that assume relatively closed communities and are predicated on the nation-state—do not seem adapted to explaining the co-production of identities, technologies, and cultural formations characteristic of an emerging global order. A postcolonial perspective suggests fresh ways to study the changing political economies of capitalism and science, the mutual reorganization of the global and the local, the increasing transnational traffic of people, practices, technologies, and contemporary contests over "intellectual property." The term "postcolonial" thus refers both to new configurations of techno-science and to the critical modes of analysis that identify them. (p. 643)

Unsurprisingly, the listed advantages of postcolonial science and technology studies arrive with a high methodological price. Digital postcolonialism is based on the assumption that human beings literally migrate into virtuality. In our recent article, we identified two main methodological problems with this assumption: the transfer of theories and conclusions from geospatial migrations of the past into digital migrations of the present, and the nature of relationships between the digital territories and the digital settlers. On that basis, we concluded that digital postcolonialism should be interpreted merely as another lens for viewing our reality, and it is only with great caution that it might be transformed into a research methodology (Jandrić & Kuzmanić, 2015).

This study is based on phases of decolonization identified by Frantz Fanon more than half a century ago in *On National Culture,* and later on it became the second chapter in his most famous book *The Wretched of the Earth* (2001[1961]). In spite of Al-Abbood's (2012) assurances that Fanon's phases are common for all decolonization processes, theories developed in the context of mid-twentieth century African nation-states cannot be transferred into the contemporary network society without caution. The feasibility of such a transfer strongly depends on one's views on the universality of human nature and cannot be determined analytically. Furthermore, Fanon's work is strictly phenomenological inasmuch it arises from direct observation— therefore, it is methodologically unable to offer predictions. Digital coloni-alism has indeed gone through the stage of recognition and has already dug well into the stages of historicization and active resistance. However, there is no guarantee that it will follow in the footsteps of its pre-digital nation-state models. Humankind will never be able to abandon its earthly territories, but its history is packed with abandoned technologies from gramophones to magnetic tapes. Therefore, it is easy to imagine the advent of a new techno-science that would bring digital postcolonialism to a halt and start a new cycle of techno-colonization (recent advances in biological sciences seem to be a good case in the point).

In spite of strong methodological restrictions, digital postcolonialism does not seem to contradict the existing body of knowledge on education and technologies. Starting from the existing body of radical critiques, it weaves a complex historical narrative, which places our understanding of techno-education into the context of past and future and uses that narra-tive to identify cracks in the technological empire of contemporary edu-cation. Methodologically, digital postcolonialism is very far from a coher-ent research methodology. However, it definitely makes a contribution by providing another lens for analyzing contemporary phenomena—perhaps this lens can be used as inspiration for developing new radical emancipa-tory activities. Our explorations of digital postcolonialism are in their very infancy, and it is very hard to predict the scope and extent of their power to challenge the pairing of education with the logic of global neoliberal capital-ism. Looking at important achievements of postcolonial theory in other areas, however, the time to explore its potential in the context of contemporary techno-education has definitely arrived.

Acknowledgments

We are grateful to Sarah Hayes and Joe Hayes for their important input into our work on digital postcolonialism. We extend our special thanks to Sarah

Amsler, whose insights and recommendations have proved of inestimable value in developing this work further.

References

Abraham, I. (2006). The contradictory spaces of postcolonial techno-science. *Economic and Political Weekly, 41*(3), 210–217.

Al-Abbood, N. (2012). Native culture and literature under colonialism: Fanon's theory of native resistance and development. *English Language and Literature Studies, 2*(3), 121–133.

Alatas, S.H. (1997). *The myth of the lazy native: A study of the image of the Malays, Filipinos and Javanese from the 16th to the 20th century and its function in the ideology of colonial capitalism.* London, UK: Frank Cass.

Anderson, W. (2002). Postcolonial technoscience. *Social Studies of Science, 32*(5–6), 643–658.

Assange, J., Appelbaum, J., Müller-Maguhn, A., & Zimmermann, J. (2012). *Cypherpunks: Freedom and the future of the internet.* New York, NY: OR Books.

Bates, A. (2000). *Managing technological change: Strategies for college and university leaders.* San Francisco, CA: Jossey-Bass.

Bhabha, H. (1994). *Location of cultures.* London, UK: Routledge.

Brand, S. (1974). *II Cybernetic Frontiers.* London, UK: Random House.

Burrows, R. (2012). Living with the h-index? Metric assemblages in the contemporary academy. *The Sociological Review, 60,* 355–372.

Čapek, K. (2014). *R.U.R.* Adelaide, Australia: University of Adelaide.

Castells, M. (2001). *The internet galaxy: reflections on the internet, business, and society.* Oxford, UK: Oxford University Press.

During, S. (2000). Postcolonialism and globalisation: towards a historicization of their inter-relation. *Cultural Studies, 14*(3–4), 385–404.

Fanon, F. (2001). *The wretched of the Earth.* London, UK: Penguin.

Feenberg, A. (2002). *Transforming technology: A critical theory revisited.* New York, NY: Oxford University Press.

Fejes, A., & Nicoll, K. (2008). *Foucault and lifelong learning: Governing the subject.* London, UK: Routledge.

Freire, P. (2005). *Pedagogy of the oppressed.* New York, NY: Continuum.

Gartner (2014). Research methodologies: Hype cycles. Retrieved from http://www.gartner.com/technology/research/methodologies/hype-cycle.jsp

Giroux, H.A. (1991). Border pedagogy and the politics of postmodernism. *Social Text, 28,* 51–67.

Giroux, H.A. (2005). *Border crossings.* New York, NY: Routledge.

Haraway, D. (1991). *Simians, cyborgs, and women: The reinvention of nature.* New York, NY: Routledge.

Harding, S. (2008). *Sciences from below: Feminisms, postcolonialities, and modernities.* Durham, NC: Duke University Press.

Harding, S. (Ed.). (2011). *The Postcolonial Science and technology studies reader.* Durham, NC: Duke University Press.

Heidegger, M. (1981). "Only a god can save us": The *Spiegel* Interview. In T. Sheehan (Ed.), *Heidegger: The man and the thinker* (pp. 45–67). Chicago, IL: Precedent Press.

Hill, D., McLaren, P., Cole, M., & Rikowski, G. (1999). *Postmodernism in educational theory: education and the politics of human resistance.* London, UK: Tufnell Press.

Himanen, P. (2001). *The hacker ethic*. London, UK: Random House.

Horkheimer, M., & Adorno, T.W. (2002). *Dialectic of enlightenment: Philosophical fragments*. Stanford, CA: Stanford University Press.

Horvath, R.J. (1972). A definition of colonialism. *Current Anthropology, 13*(1), 45-57.

Illich, I. (1971). *Deschooling Society*. London, UK: Marion Boyars Publishers Ltd. Retrieved from http://www.preservenet.com/theory/Illich/Deschooling/intro. html

Illich, I. (1973). *Tools for conviviality*. London, UK: Marion Boyars Publishers Ltd. Retrieved from http://www.preservenet.com/theory/Illich/IllichTools.html

Jandrić, P., & Boras, D. (2012). *Critical e-learning: struggle for power and meaning in the network society*. Zagreb, Croatia: Polytechnic of Zagreb & FF Press.

Jandrić, P., & Kuzmanić, A. (2015). Digital postcolonialism. In P. Kommers & P. Isaias (Eds.), *Proceedings of 13th International Conference on e-Society* (pp. 87-94). Madeira: IADIS.

Jandrić, P. (2012). The diffusionist-evolutionist model of e-learning development. *Journal of Baltic Science Education, 11*(1), 67-77.

Jandrić, P. (2014). Deschooling virtuality. *Open Review of Educational Research, 1*(1), 8498.

Kropotkin, P. (1912). *Fields, factories, and workshops: or industry combined with agriculture and brain work with manual work*. London, UK: Thomas Nelson and Sons.

Kuhn, T. (1970). *The structure of scientific revolutions*. Chicago, IL: University of Chicago Press.

Latour, B. (1987). *Science in action: How to follow scientists and engineers through society*. Cambridge, MA: Harvard University Press.

Lavia, J. (2006). The practice of postcoloniality: A pedagogy of hope. *Pedagogy, Culture & Society, 14*(3), 279-293.

Lyotard, J.F. (1984). *The postmodern condition: A report on knowledge*. Minneapolis MN: University of Minnesota Press.

Marcuse, H. (1964). *One-dimensional man*. Boston, MA: Beacon Press.

McLaren, P., & Jandrić, P. (2015). The critical challenge of networked learning: using information technologies in the service of humanity. In P. Jandrić & D. Boras (Eds.), *Critical learning in digital networks* (pp. 199-226). New York, NY: Springer.

Postcolonial Digital Humanities. (2014). Mission Statement. Retrieved from http://dhpoco.org/mission-statement-postcolonial-digital-humanities/

Rogers, E.M. (1995). *Diffusion of innovations*. New York, NY: Free Press.

Said, E.W. (1993). *Culture and imperialism*. New York, NY: Vintage Books.

Seth, S. (2009). Putting knowledge in its place: science, colonialism, and the postcolonial. *Postcolonial Studies, 12*(4), 373-388.

Shaull, R. (2005). Foreword. In P. Freire, *Pedagogy of the oppressed* (pp. 29-34). New York, NY: Continuum.

Shelley, M. (2008). *Frankenstein; or, the modern Prometheus*. Project Gutenberg. http://self.gutenberg.org/articles/eng/Frankenstein;_or,_the_Modern_Prometheus

Smith, L.T. (1999). *Decolonising methodologies*. London, UK: Zed Books.

Soper, K. (1999). Of oncomice and female/men: Donna Haraway on cyborg ontology. *Capitalism Nature Socialism, 10*(3), 73-80.

Southall, A. (1972). Comments on Horvath's definition of colonialism. *Current Anthropology, 13*(1), 53.

Stallman, R.M. (2002). *Free software, free society: Selected essays of Richard M. Stallman*. Boston, MA: Free Software Foundation.

Van Dijk, J. (1999). *The network society*. London, UK: SAGE.

Van Dijk, J., & Hacker, K. (2003). The digital divide as a complex and dynamic phenomenon. *The Information Society, 19*, 315–326.

Wittkower, D.E. (2008). Revolutionary industry and digital colonialism. *Fast Capitalism, 4*(1).

Zemsky, R., & Massy, W. (2004). *Thwarted innovation: What happened to e-learning and why*. Philadelphia, PA: The Learning Alliance, University of Pennsylvania.

Zerzan, J. (2004). Why primitivism? *Anarchy: A Journal of Desire Armed, 21*(2).

The Emergence of Radical Informal Learning Spaces

"Using the Institutional Space without Being *of* the Institution"

CHAPTER 6

What Do We Mean When We Say "Democracy"? Learning towards a Common Future through Popular Higher Education

Sarah Amsler

> "Now we have to start."
> —Ernst Bloch, *The Spirit of Utopia* (2000)

There is a coming community of counter-capitalist educators in England—one that belongs to longer-standing traditions of critical pedagogy and popular education in the global North, but that is striving to respond to particular problems created by British neoliberalism. We long to understand how higher education can contribute to the liberation of human flourishing, co-operative action, and autonomous living. We seek to learn what replaces capitalism as an organizing principle of social life, and to practice overcoming it inside and outside the institutions. We know that we are not yet a "we" but share enough experiences in common to recognize each other prior to feeling the collective identity that we suspect is just over the horizon. We complain of disempowerment and under-liberation; we feel depressed, oppressed, frustrated, and confused by the difficulty of resisting dehumanizing systems of power, which already seem to be in crisis. But we also experience liberation and enlightenment and attempt to understand what makes them possible. We realize that the colonization of educational institutions by capitalist rationalities and the foreclosure of spaces for democratic forms of governance manifest themselves in multiple ways that defy simple counter-strategies. And from somewhere amidst all this activity, a phrase reverberates from the lips of teachers, academics, artists, carers, and other cultural workers: I am suffocating. People are looking for ways to break out.

The rich traditions of critical pedagogy and popular education tell us that there is something about learning which promises a radical shift in consciousness that generates possibilities for undertaking practices of freedom against domination and determination (*conscientização*) (Fanon, 2008; Freire, 2000, 2005). But public spaces for engaging in critical thinking and transformative learning with other people have been cramped in the mainstream institutions where most people are educated. They have contracted even further through the decades-long movements to economize higher learning and academic life (Clegg, 2010; Collini, 2011; Gagnier, 2013). While the school or university classroom will always have the potential to become a place for engagement and surprise, the neoliberal classroom can neither be relied upon as a space for social learning and critique nor as an appropriate institutional structure for the production of humane and useful knowledge. Here critical pedagogy is returned to its roots: the creation of conditions for democratic education, practical-critical learning, and pedagogies of enlightenment and justice is at once made necessary by the contraction of such conditions by capitalist rationality, and is a constitutive part of struggles to reopen the future to educational alternatives. There have not yet been any maps made from the vantage of this conjuncture other than the ones we are drawing as we work through it. We have ceased being students of critical pedagogy and become project-makers in our own right. It dawns on us that this was always the point; that as the German critical theorist Ernst Bloch (2000) once wrote: "I am. We are. That is enough. Now we must begin. Life has been given into our hands."

To say that life is placed into our hands does not mean that it is given willingly or intentionally or with care. It only means that life is our gift to take and it is important to take part in steering its direction. Yet as Bloch (1995) also wrote, "All beginnings are difficult" (p. 129) and in many cases, conditions of possibility are unequally distributed, murky, and only ever partially materialize. Moreover, contemporary neoliberal forms of institutional organizations are maintained partly through the policing of "possibilities." Unfortunately, breaking from these institutional constraints in order to live differently is a difficult endeavor, particularly if we are not used to disobeying authority, challenging normative social expectations, or refusing economic ultimatums. Yet daring to act, even in situations that do not feel emancipatory, can open up revolutionary possibilities. Indeed, if our pedagogies do not challenge "the societal and epistemological paradigm that has shaped the current horizon of possibilities within which we fashion our options, the horizon within which certain options are possible while others are excluded or even unimaginable," then they can only offer what Portuguese sociologist Boaventura de Sousa Santos calls "weak" answers to strong questions (Santos, 2014, p. 20). So, what types of learning can regenerate democratic possibility within neoliberal contexts today?

Something New in Freedom

This chapter responds to this question of regenerating democratic possibilities by considering the accomplishments and issues of a local project in popular higher education, situated in a small English city—the Social Science Centre. The Centre was established as a cooperative in 2011. It was initiated as an academic and activist response to a conjuncture involving the intensified "ruining" of the liberal public university, the opening of possibilities for radical critique of and beyond this system, and an uncertainty which permitted a new wave of social experimentation in democratic politics and education. As I once remarked to a reporter, the Social Science Centre is an attempt to create "something new in freedom" that is at once a counter-capitalist learning space, an imminent critique of neoliberal education, and a contribution to the development of alternative forms of knowledge for democratizing everyday life (Bonnett, 2013, p. 42). The Centre is not a novel endeavor. Higher education cooperatives have existed in the past. Rather, the Centre's unique qualities stem from our ability to have relative autonomy over our practices, because the Centre is without either direct institutional control or explicit institutional privilege.

This has compelled us to articulate new answers to fundamental questions about the purpose of education, defining or redefining democracy, and what it means to be-in-common and to learn. Once we dislodge an idea—the idea of the university, of higher education, the definition of the scholar, the idea of social change—from the material infrastructures that shape and purpose it, then we have to dream and to ultimately choose and act on those ideas. So what is it that we need to learn, and how can we approach these ideas if we do not already know about them? If we could practice any kind of education we want, of what activities would it consist and why? What can these educational spaces do? Who is it for? How was it developed? How is it gendered, classed, raced, colonial, or epistemologically exclusive? Whose expression does it wear, in whose voice does it speak? What is its relationship to traditional, or even neoliberal, education? Are there spaces and cracks to work within and are they enough? How are the roles of student and teacher defined, if at all? What is to be done with intractable reproductions of power? How shall we subsist? Who is affected by our commitments? What are we willing to give, and to lose?

Here I will consider only one of many questions currently on the table during this project. During an evening class called the Social Science Imagination, a friend and fellow scholar posed a question about democracy and the meaning of alternative education. As the official note taker for the class, I elaborated on the small group discussion: we concluded, full of these questions, with something profound: When people use the word "democracy" in this class, what do they (we) mean? A few scholars were quick to say they did not mean representative democracy or one-person-one-vote. Is it then used more "anarchistically"? What could it mean? This question about what democracy means, and whether we use it, and the question of how we ground and justify and have confidence in our thinking and action in the struggle for humane and liberating education, and social life seem critical ones for us to continue answering together (Amsler, 2014).

The question felt significant because it was asked in a space where the word "democracy" had been reverberating, and making an impact, for over three years. The spirit of democracy has historically been central to this project of building a system of free, cooperative, higher education in the city. It is inscribed into the organization's constitution (Social Science Centre, 2011). It also encourages members to privilege non-hierarchical and delibera-tive decision-making systems. It underpins, and is sometimes used to explain and justify a common interest in sharing and cooperating. Additionally, it works to inform the Centre's antipathy towards economic exclusion in the form of commodified learning and relationships of monetary exchange. Thus, the notion of democracy opens onto multiple traditions of critical and femi-nist pedagogies and inflects members' relationships with a political ethic of friendship, fellowship, and solidarity.

At the same time, the deeper philosophical or political meanings of democracy are rarely discussed publically by the Centre's members. As one member of the cooperative said, it is still a "tender" project. While much of the published work regarding the Social Science Centre describes it as a radical political alternative "dedicated to the democratization of higher edu-cation in a time when access to universities is being closed," it also cultivates a less-visible kind of radicality. This is particularly evident in the formation of a collective subject that has to find new ways of "going on together" in the face of uncertainty, difference, and disagreement (Kompridis, 2006, p. 236). Overall, this process requires a commitment not to turn away from specific negotiations and fears. One of these fears is that placing fragile understand-ings of democracy on the table and under the knife will destroy them; the other is that not struggling to articulate these principles will destroy them just the same. Within these spaces, some ideas and practices of democracy make people feel empowered and connected, while others feel shunned like naked nerves or undetonated grenades.

Negotiating between what can be spoken and what remains unsaid, amidst different democratic sensibilities, relationships, practices, forms of organization and ethics, is an important part of practicing democratiza-tion. Rather than focusing attention only on democratic procedures or the micropolitics of democracy, these relationships alert us to the constitutive power of a democratic metapolitics (i.e., what people believe democracy is and is for) and to the interplay between these levels of activity. It is also an important space for revitalizing the radical (i.e., root-ful or essential) because it forces critical theory and critical pedagogy out of their epistemological homes and into the worlds of new friends who may find the academic languages of emancipation unfamiliar, unintelligible, or unimportant. It demonstrates how dominant theories "lose their composure and serenity when they are interpolated by questions, no matter how simple, that they did not ask themselves" (Santos, 2014, p. 107).

Much of what we think we know about how radical democracy works comes from studies of actually existing groups, projects, situations, and radical-democratic experiments (Coles, 2006; Fielding, 2013; Gibson–Graham, 2006). We have good knowledge about how capitalist thinking and power became hegemonic in education, and how counter-capitalist forms have been created and sustained. However, examples that presume there is already a political will and desire to pursue such projects may fail to offer useful maps of possibility in societies characterized by the destruction of democratic sensibilities, social collectivities, and experiences of critical learning. In this context, it is not processes of radicalization but of democratization—micro and meta-political activities of creating, negotiating, and sustaining new democratic and post-capitalist subjectivities and forms of sociality—which illustrate why John Dewey (1939) once argued that all democracy is always-already radical.

It is through these practices that members of the Social Science Centre define what they mean when they say "democracy." Unlike more explicitly radical educational organizations which confidently proclaim a narrow set of political principles, and equally unlike cooperative organizations that claim political neutrality, the Social Science Centre is organized to be both radically open and cooperatively governed. This combination of values pushes democratic cooperation to its limits in three ways. First, it minimizes the formally required preconditions for partaking in cooperative governance and learning. In other words, the possibility of destabilizing encounters with criticism and alterity are structured in rather than out. Second, it insists on the possibility of building cooperative relations among individuals in groups that are not "communities" of location, social interest, or political struggle, and who therefore share little common political ground. Finally, it recognizes that democratizing the conditions for democratic learning is a critical part of democratic politics, but that we do not already know how to achieve this outside familiar institutional forms, and that our democratic common sense is distorted by a multiplicity of privileges, inequalities, and habits.

In this way, the learning ethos of the Social Science Centre resonates with the organizational politics of the World Social Forum, which by promoting the flourishing of an ecology of knowledges, "has refused to reduce its openness for the sake of efficacy or political coherence" (Santos, 2014, p. 42). It is a zone of perpetual proximal development in which a group of people work, as the philosopher Nikolas Kompridis argues, to grasp as learning—which is to say, as an activity of reason—those accomplishments through which we acquire new tongues with which to say what cannot be said and new ears with which to hear that which cannot be heard. Through these accomplishments we overcome epistemological crises, and partial, one-sided, interpretations of ourselves and others and accomplishments through which we are able to "go on" learning from our interaction with one another and our interaction with the "world" (2006, p. 236).

Tributaries, Capillaries, and Blockages of Democratic Diversity

[trib·u·tary]: a vein that empties into a larger vein
[cap·il·lary]: one of the many very small tubes that carry blood within the body [block·age]: something that stops something from moving through something

The development of emergent learning spaces and projects—and within this, the articulation of meanings of democracy-in-practice—is not easy to trace or record with the blunt instruments of logocentric social science. What is coming is often invisible and unsayable, and when it finally appears, it is likely to conceal the full conditions of its own possibility. This makes it hard for informal groups to capture the many different processes through which they construct and make sense of themselves over time. It is even harder for groups like the Social Science Centre, in which many different histories are contemporaneously constructed by people with competing interpretations of collective experience. While people can sense that some interpretations of this experience influence individual and collective action ("tributaries" and "capillaries") and that others are blocked or become blockages themselves, the dynamics of these processes are difficult to comprehend without some sort of analysis. Understanding the diversity of democratic sensibilities, and being able to see the absences and exclusions that make their circulation possible, demands the development of methods for tracing the tributary and capillary influences. Imprinted within these blockages and flows are struggles over meaning, power, and purpose, which need methodologies for designing democratic methods.

From its inception, work in the Social Science Centre has been inflected by epistemological and political flows coming out of the neoliberal (and primarily English) university on the one hand, and radical (mainly British anarchistic and autonomist) social movements on the other. These flows frame how members determine what democracy means together. In many ways, the Centre fulfils the intellectual and social functions of an autonomous social center despite the fact that most of its members do not identify as either autonomists or anarchists or have direct affiliations with the social centers movement. Social centers are spaces created for "giving us space to breathe, take action and experiment with managing our own lives collectively." They "come from a demand for spaces for radical political debate and action, meetings, eating together, grass roots music, mutual support, information and skill sharing, and collective education. They come from a common desire to build networks, solidarities and movements, make connections and develop our politics with our communities and cities" (What's this place? 2008, pp. 2–3).

Through the work of the project, these anarchistic and autonomous flows have enabled the Centre to share affinities with other social centers, (e.g., drawing early inspiration from some of the country's historical social centers such as Sumac and the Cowley Club); "free university" projects, (such as the Really Open University, Free University of Brighton, and Free University Network), Tent City University, (which operated throughout the 2012 London Occupy events); international networks of radical educators and higher education activists, (including the Education Activist Network and European Edu-Factory Collective); the Transition Towns movement in the UK and beyond; and with the international cooperative movement.

However, academia, anarchism, and autonomism are not the only frameworks of meaning, practice, and identity at work in the Social Science Centre. They are the most visible in part because they have been the most proactively inscribed into academic publications, referenced in media interviews, discussed at public conferences, and incorporated into organizational documents and course materials. Yet they interact constantly with others that flow together through the inclusion—and at times, the exclusion—of the experiences, knowledges, desires, and needs of the Centre's members, who themselves flow in and out of the process of its constitution according to the rhythms of their lives and in response to the politics of the project.

Other philosophies of cooperativism are also in play. A participatory photography project run by one of the Centre's members with homeless and formerly homeless men, for example, is described in a local newspaper article as having "started out with a simple plan—people meeting once a week to shoot sites of interest (Our Priorities) and learn more about photography" (Lincolnshire Echo, 2014).

For the project's coordinator, however, this "simple plan" was informed by a theoretical analysis of the role that art and photography can play in the cultivation of humane social relationships and environments, of the power of transgressing class divisions through non-politicized activities, and of the centrality of cooperation in the evolution of functional societies (McAleavey & Amsler, 2012; Ostrom 1990). The application of this analysis to a form of popular higher education that transforms social exclusion into a critical voice and that promotes a particular kind of democratic inclusion called "pro-sociality" is accomplished through the facilitation of dialogues among theories of neurological creativity (Anderson, 2010), John Dewey's (1910) philosophies of problem-posing education, Peter Kropotkin's (1902) anarchist theories of mutual aid, Richard Sennett's (2012) theories of cooperation and civic life, and historical and contemporary projects in cooperation and pedagogy. Just as the horizons of autonomist and anarchistic politics orient the Centre's affiliations with other groups and movements in certain ways, so the horizon of "pro-sociality" orients them in others—particularly towards the formation of patient, long-term, reciprocal, and often quiet relations of mutual aid, and even more particularly, those that have the potential to transgress and dissolve social divisions.

The belief that "co-operation" is a principle of democratic and counter-capitalist governance and education also flows from other members' interests in the international cooperative movement. This is evident in an early decision to constitute the Centre as a formal cooperative organization, and in a current project to establish a cooperative university in the UK (Juby, 2011; Winn 2014a, 2014b). This positioning prompted the development of relationships with experienced cooperators in the UK Cooperative and Radical Routes organizations, although localized understandings are also being developed through the Centre's own courses on cooperative education and organization. Discussions of cooperativism are pluralistic and exploratory. The scope includes women's cooperatives, international principles and practices of cooperation, the history of various cooperative movements, cooperative curriculum and pedagogy, and cooperative schools (Facer, Thorpe & Shaw, 2011). The latter is framed as an explicitly Marxist project that seeks to develop relations of ownership, governance, and pedagogy that enables the organization to be one that "attacks the 'groundwork' of capital, i.e., labor and private property, through worker democracy" (Winn 2014a).

In addition to these intersecting flows, the spirit of cooperation also informs the centre's work via other tributaries of sociology (specifically U.S. and Eurocentric traditions), popular education (via Latin American movements), and critical pedagogy (a hybrid of U.S. and Latin American lineages). From its inception, the project has attracted people who identify themselves as "critical" or "popular" educators, or whose own modes of learning and desires for education draw them to humanist, democratic, problem-posing, and experiential forms of education. The Centre's curriculum is designed collaboratively through activities to facilitate the processes of problem-posing, critical, politically activating, and co-operative learning (Amsler 2012a, 2012b; Hall 2014; Social Science Centre, 2014; Winn, 2012). This hybrid ethos of critical pedagogy and popular education has also grounded feminist workshops in voice, exclusion and privilege, and anarchistic, consensus-oriented approaches to decision-making and organization.

However, this does not necessarily lend (or demand) coherence to the pedagogical work undertaken within the Centre. On the contrary, the diversity of interpretations of co-operative, critical, and popular education is contested terrain. While knowledge, learning, and education are inherently political activities, not everyone interprets emancipatory learning as an explicitly political project. Pedagogical philosophies are inflected by relational positions of class, race, and gender inequality, our dis/abilities and ages and sexualities, our geopolitical locations, and our personal stories. To theorize and translate these discoveries into collective learning practices, we turn to the wisdoms of John Dewey (1910), Paulo Freire (2000), bell hooks (1994, 2003), C. Wright Mills (1959) and other classical teachers of transformative learning (Keeble, Peaceful Warrior & Saunders, 2014)—not to help us teach others, but to help us learn to teach ourselves.

On one hand, the meaning and practice of democracy within the Social Science Centre is diverse and complex. Yet, on the other, even this diversity has been made possible by acts of epistemological exclusion and social marginalization which create parameters of homogeneity—boundaries around what is deemed possible to navigate, and that which is interpreted as unnecessarily, or rather uncontrollably, disruptive. The effort required to negotiate differences among members, when this is undertaken in the spirit of deep democracy, often siphons time and energy away from efforts to address antidemocratic tendencies in the project which may only be visible through attention to absences and omissions and through conversations with those who are not in the room or, more importantly, feel that they do not or cannot belong. From its inception, the Centre has striven to be an "alternative to privilege" in education (Amsler 2011; Neary & Winn, 2011) by offering tuition-free opportunities to learn which are shaped by the learners themselves; thus constituting public higher education as a practice of simultaneous economic and cognitive justice. Yet the discursive democratization of this structural formula for participation (the commitment to opening it up for discussion as a matter of concern) reveals as many power struggles, moral dilemmas, and conceptual perplexities as it resolves. The experience has clarified some specific points:

- The inaccessibility of higher education for poor and working-class adults in this country, as in others, is not rooted simply in the imposition of tuition fees but in the injustices and violence of hegemonic schooling, and the practice of critical pedagogies in higher learning must go hand in hand with the struggle for the abolition of these injustices.

- When educationally privileged and educationally disadvantaged people get together to talk about their experiences of, and desires for, education, mutual and convivial dialogue—happy pedagogies—are not immediately possible or desirable, and a break from "learning" into politics is required.

- The idea of public higher education which so many people across the world are struggling so hard to preserve is deeply contested and perceived by many others as being implicated in the production and reproduction of social and epistemological hierarchies, economic and political inequality, the domination of status, and the legitimization of discrimination.
- If people occupy hegemonic positions of power and privilege, and are not consciously vigilant in seeking out and prioritizing the voices of thinkers and authors from subordinated and marginalized groups— such as women in social theory or the co-operative movement, and co-operative struggles located in the global South; such as black feminist theorists and authors writing about education and politics and relationships from non-heteronormative and queer perspectives—then they are likely to be blind to both the absence and the presence of these critical knowledges.
- When we are vigilant about seeking out these knowledges and facilitating critical self-reflection in relation to them, but not careful to create conditions in which dominant subjectivities and ontological securities can be productively transgressed or minor ones expressed, we are more likely to respond by shutting them down when they create discomfort, confusion, and complexity.
- It is possible to shut democratic possibilities and resistances down through other democratic processes which keep them tightly framed within pre-determined, but not necessarily publicly acknowledged, parameters of what democracy means, what its purposes are, and who is permitted to determine these issues.
- That fighting privilege; working to overcome inequality, injustice, and the foreclosure of possibilities in learning; and creating spaces for transformative thinking and practice cannot be accomplished only by "creating spaces" or by desiring democratic relations.
- At times, we will be unable even to imagine what we need to learn in order to radicalize our common-sense democratic subjectivities, organizations, and forms of sociality, and that this wider learning is an essential part of the transformation of limitations into new possibilities.

Don't Mention the Democracy: Principles, Practices and Letting Be

Given this diversity in intellectual and political sensibilities, it is remarkable that the Social Science Centre hangs together as a democratic educational space. As one of its members remarked,

> Each of us has our own reasons for being a part of the Centre. We all share progressive political values, based on the principles of social

justice and democracy, but the key issue is what we do rather than what we say we believe in. (Neary, 2011)

There are, of course, some discussions about what these "progressive political values" are, about what we mean by "social justice" and "democracy," and what to do with knowledge of both commonality and difference. For whenever the lack of articulation prohibits rather than enables movement and hastens exclusions and withdrawals rather than keeps doors open for strangers and surprises, it becomes a democratic liability. Yet in conditions of neoliberal fragmentation and diversification of struggles against it, we also cannot risk grabbing too tightly onto the "inexhaustible experience of the world and indirect communication" (Santos 2014, p. 13). Democratic diversity is a great pedagogical asset, for it harbors a "repertoire of the modes, models, means, and ends of social transformation" (Santos, 2014, p. 46). In addition, in conditions of rising conservatism and depoliticization in this part of the world, there must be ungoverned spaces in which people who do not desire explicitly political forms of personal or social transformation can also encounter, learn about, struggle with, and perhaps become receptive to critiques of their own ways of seeing the hegemonic present, and become active in bringing forth its many alternatives.

Contemporary critical education must be popular, in that it must find a way of responding to neoliberal common sense without corresponding to it (Marcuse 1998). Therefore, scholars of the Social Science Centre and other autonomous and cooperative organizations may strive to foster a "potential unconditional inclusiveness" such as that of the World Social Forum, which creates a "new political culture that privileges commonalities to the detriment of differences and fosters common action even in the presence of deep ideological differences, once the objectives are limited, well defined, and adopted by consensus" (Santos, 2014, p. 43). However, the privileging of commonalities and common action can only be democratic if it is complemented by the recognition of differences and the will to work through them towards unpredictable ends. What is called for, therefore, is a pedagogy of democratic dissonance which fosters "the conditions of possibility for speaking, listening and voice, not as a means to name and shame others but rather opening the conditions for the possibility of anti-authoritarian practices in all aspects of movement reproduction" and educational politics (Motta & Esteves 2014, p. 11).

Embodying Being-in-Common: It's a Reasonable Education

The activity of being-in-common with others, with an aspiration to becoming cooperative, radically democratic, egalitarian, theoretically informed, and politically engaged is a kind of popular education in its own right. Most of the work that is formally recognized as "learning" in the Social Science Centre takes familiar forms (pedagogy, curriculum, texts for reading, seminars, and workshops). While experimental around the edges, this work is inspired by experiences of mainstream education, critical pedagogy, and critical theory. Yet the act of organizing these activities generates a deeper kind of learning about the cognitive, social, and emotional conditions of radically democratic association itself. This work—which constitutes both a subterranean pedagogy and counter-hegemonic hidden curriculum—sheds light on how important it is to understand the reasons that we develop when working autonomously and counter-hegemonically. The critical philosopher Nikolas Kompridis has suggested that we must insist on the possibility of another kind of reason, another way of living in practice, which is not merely an abstraction or something impossibly utopian but an actual possibility that we can locate in existing, if marginalized, practices of reason (Kompridis, 2006, p. 237).

He argues that "if we are to overcome the negative effects of the dominant forms of reason, we need to weaken our attachment to them to make room for neglected, devalued or suppressed forms of reason" (ibid., p. 237). I suggest that the experiences of the Social Science Centre reveal five forms of reason that form a rudimentary architecture for deep democracy in self-organizing, cooperative projects in the context of neoliberal higher education in England. These are: participating reason, receptive reason, reflective reason, co-operative reason, and anticipatory reason.

Participating reason enables what Paulo Freire called "committed involvement" in the world, what Maxine Greene called "wide-awakeness," Marx called "human emancipation," and what John Dewey called "present-ness." In other words, this type of reason enables us to be present as a subject of history with a commitment to its cooperative formation, to mediate the world with reflective, creative, and critical activity, and to be thrown-into-what-is-becoming rather than being a spectator, a subordinate, or a consumer of ideas, policies, products, and so on (Dewey, 2005; Freire, 2000, p. 68; Greene, 1995, 2005; Tucker, 1978, p. 46). In a section of a book called *The Principle of Hope* dedicated to "militant optimism," the German philosopher Ernst Bloch wrote:

> precisely the defeated man [or woman] must try the outside world again. That which is coming up is not yet decided, that which is swamp can be dried out through work. Through a combination of courage and knowledge, the future does not come over [us] as fate, but [we] overcome the future and enter it with what is [ours]. (Bloch, 1995, p. 198)

Participating reason is not only what enables us to form independent purposes and reasons and to engage in practices of freedom, but it is what enti-

tles indignation when possibilities for this mode of living are foreclosed in
our concrete circumstances, whatever they may be.

This committed "investment in the present" (Santos, 2014) demands
that we cultivate a kind of receptive reason which allows us to comprehend
both the visible and the not-yet-articulated possibilities of our internal and
external environments. Reflective reason then makes it possible to make
critical judgments about how to work with these environments. Encounters
with new ideas, people, and possibilities can disclose previously unthinkable alternatives; this in turn can open opportunities for making decisions
about whether to maintain a status quo or take the risk of questioning it. As
a result, however, the reality is new and uncertain—the kind of newness
which is an object of desire in revolutionary politics—has a dual character
which makes us feel alive but also "arouses our suspicion . . . anxieties and
fears" (Kompridis, 2011, p. 257). "Thinking from a new stance is essential
to the democratic form of life," yet people are not necessarily receptive to
thinking in radically new and destabilizing ways (Kompridis, 2011, p. 257).
Being thrown into situations or states that are unfamiliar and uncontrol-
lable, working with knowledges, tools, and other people that we have not
mastered, learned to predict, or even fully understand, is hard. Kompridis
suggests that "the work of reworking ourselves can feel overwhelming,
threatening and unnecessarily demanding. No one should have a right to
demand such a change in us" (Kompridis, 2011, p. 262). However, "since no
one lives in a world that is unencumbered by expectations that arise from
sharing a life with diverse human and nonhuman others, such demands for
change will be unavoidable" (Kompridis, 2011, p. 262). Neoliberal forms of
social organization, with their privileging of competitive individualism and
hedonistic power, have a tendency to obscure the political, intellectual, and
ethical demands of being-in-common with and for others. Those who work
predominately in such organizations have become deskilled in dealing with
moral, intellectual, social, and communicative differences and uncertainties, and opportunities to practice this work are denied in the interests of
economic rationality and in order to reduce the chances of individual and
institutional power being "encumbered" by the social, epistemological, or
ethical demands of an (anti-capitalist and democratic) other.

In a radically democratic context, however, the question is not whether
we will encounter possibilities to learn through such alterity, but how to
respond when we do—and further, how to desire and invite such encounters.
It is easy to practice a kind of "disengaged curiosity" about the world, allowing ourselves to have "an intense engagement with something or someone
that leaves lots of room for disengagement." There are plenty of situations
in which we mindfully, but privately, "take notice of the assumptions, tensions, anxieties and random musings that come to the fore as we sit, quietly

noticing for the first time what goes on in the background . . . allowing something to emerge . . . that may have been previously inaudible, invisible or unthought." These exercises carry no "normative baggage" and are unaccountable to anyone else. However, they do not call upon us to practice any kind of radical receptivity or co-operation with others, and thus cannot catalyse socially transformative sense-making in practice (Kompridis, 2011, p. 263). An alternative is to become more answerable to "the call of an other," which means that we are "facilitating its voicing, letting it become a voice that we did not allow ourselves to hear before" and consider doing things that did not occur before (Kompridis, 2011, p. 262). It allows us, requires us, to potentially abandon whatever carefully constructed self-understandings that we have successfully relied on for being-in-common.

Cooperative reason is therefore vital as it orients our thinking about how to do this work with, for, in relation to, and in the company of others. Here I am referring to radically democratic cooperation rather than cooperation in its other forms. I do not mean the vague liberal notion that cooperation makes people happier than competition or conflict, or that democratic governance works best if people all "get along," or that we feel happier if we participate in self-governance, or that happiness is a valid indicator of democratic vitality. I do not mean the kinds of cooperation—mostly reproductive co-operation—that are required for capitalist competition to function (Federici, 2010, 2013). I do not mean the coercive cooperation that persuades those with minority needs, interests, and views to conform to the will of dominant majorities by silencing themselves or one another in order to ensure the smooth cooperation of the whole. All of these are shallow appropriations or distortions of cooperative reason which legitimize the hegemony of anti-democratic civility over loving and agonistic public dialogue, deliberation, and where necessary, struggle.

I am referring to the more critical forms of cooperative reason that have been marginalized, devalued, and in many cases explicitly suppressed in neoliberal institutions and societies, and whose recovery is an essential resource for the strengthening of radical democratic politics. There is, for example, a wisdom that comes from understanding that we are always-already cooperating in the world with others. We cannot survive without care, communication, and love; we perish faster if our social relations are organized to promote neglect, misrecognition, and harm. Giving birth, learning to eat, communicating with others, playing, getting around—none of this can be accomplished without cooperation. In 1902, the Russian anarchist Peter Kropotkin even argued that "in the practice of mutual aid, which we can retrace to the earliest beginnings of evolution, we . . . find the positive and undoubted origin of our ethical conceptions; and we can affirm that in the ethical progress of man, mutual support, not mutual struggle, has had the leading part." The future can only be undetermined so long as everyone is free and able to alter it. As Simone de Beauvoir (1991) pointed out, "My freedom, in order to fulfil itself, requires that it emerge into an open future: it is other men who open the future to me; it is they who, setting up the world of tomorrow, define my future." And further, "What happens to me by means of others depends upon me as regards its meaning; one does not submit to a war or an occupation as he does to an earthquake: he must take sides for or against, and the foreign wills therefore become allied or hostile. It is this interdependence which explains why oppression is possible and why it is hateful" (p. 82).

We must believe in the desirability and possibility of cooperation to pursue radical democracy. Yet it is a "weak muscle" in neoliberal societies ("John," personal communication, 2012). In neoliberal systems, ideologies of individualism and the "entrepreneurial" learner-self diminish, devalue, and render invisible the dense web of cooperative labor that makes all of our lives possible. Channeling faith in human capacities for cooperation into cooperative practice therefore requires other knowledges, skills, values, and sociocultural infrastructures than the ones we can acquire through hegemonic education, and it falls to us to relearn these elsewhere.

Anticipatory reason keeps us oriented towards enlarging our possibilities rather than mourning closures or reproducing the parameters of the present. It is a consciousness that encourages us to attend to what is dawning, unintelligible but palpable, and what is "striving to become articulate" (Dewey, 2005, p. 69). It is a mode of reasoning that fosters generous, curious, and critical attitudes towards the "undecided material" of the present as it is in process. It is not limited to the explicit imagination of alternative futures, but it is a more general "utopian function" that makes daydreams, desires, fantasies, utopias, and ultimately radically democratic practices possible. Like cooperative reason, anticipatory reason is an integral part of human experience (although not necessarily an inherent tendency of human nature), and "represents the actual space of receptivity of the New and production of the New" (Bloch, 1995, p. 116). However, it often takes repressive forms that devalue processes of intending, desire, fantasy, longing, and utopia, and, on the contrary, privilege either the fetishization of past accomplishments or seek to predict and control what happens in the future. Radical democratic futurity, however, is not fatalistic or voluntaristic, not cynical or optimistic, and neither calculated nor careless; it is the revolutionary reason of people who are "aware of their incompletion" and strive, through critical learning to "more wisely build the future" (Freire, 2000, p. 84). Strengthening anticipatory consciousness enables us to produce the kind of knowledge we need to practice a politics of possibility: "not only knowledge . . . in the sense of an excavation of what was, but knowledge in

the sense of a planning of what is becoming; knowledge . . . which itself deci-
sively contributes to this becoming, becoming which changes for the good"
(Bloch, 1995, p. 132; see also pp. 198–200). This knowledge is neither the same
as hope nor reducible to it; however, the hope that we can create something
new in freedom from within conditions of capitalist enclosure is not possible
where the education of critical anticipatory reason is devalued, denied, or
taken for granted as a natural capability.

Conclusion

In a paper on what he calls the "educational commons and the new radical
democratic imaginary," Alexander Means argues that progressive educators
across the world are under pressure to "reconstruct common educational
institutions against their imaginative and political enclosure," and that this
commons "should ideally be oriented to the diverse needs and aspirations of
plural communities" (2014, pp. 122, 123). He also suggests that the creation of
common institutions can only be accomplished "through a process of organized common action based on the principles of democratic-egalitarianism"
which "requires an insurrectional theory of democracy" as well as a "revolution in values, culture and pedagogy," and some "difficult work of organizing
and agitating for alternative visions of living and learning within and beyond
the historically inflected locations that we inhabit" (2014, p. 134). Finally, he
argues that we cannot escape the present conditions of our existence in
doing so, and that we therefore must direct our energies towards thinking
through how new forms of democratic-egalitarian educational organization
and subjectivity might emerge through the patient work of collaboration,
movement building, experimentation, and the strategic cultivation of the
values and constituent desires for lives and livelihoods in common (Means,
2014, p. 135).

As the work of the Social Science Centre illustrates, these processes
are taking place not only in high-profile anti-capitalist movements, but in
ordinary places where "the pedagogical does not refer [only] to a method
of learning but rather a political project of struggle in which practices of
learning are embedded' (Motta & Esteves, 2014, p. 11). It also demonstrates
the need—even, or especially, amidst the enthusiasm often generated by
social experiments—to remain vigilant about how democratic metapolitics
inadvertently contribute to either the reproduction or the overcoming of inequalities, exclusions, and injustices in education (Luchies, 2014). Becoming
conscious of these fault lines in our own relationships and transforming
them into political learning opportunities is essential for ensuring that radically democratic pedagogy is also a critical pedagogy of dissensus, resistance,
and dignity among groups who are at once united, diverse, divided, and
aspiring to be in common—who are travelling only with what Santos calls

"crude maps" and learning to embrace the uncertain liberations that they afford (2014, p. 2). As a Social Science Centre scholar noted in her write-up of another evening class:

> Scholars commented on how much they appreciated the rotating role of note-taker: it consolidates our learning, which tends to be quite "messy", and shifts the power in the group. In particular, scholars appreciated last week's notes—the author had captured uncertainty, honesty and the liberating messiness of our learning. One radical thing about this space is that there is the right to experiment, and have revelations about anything, not just about what is being taught. Scholars agreed that being conscious of SSI learning and cooperative processes was valuable, and worth checking in on. Cooperation is a process, and is not necessarily conclusive. (Stratford, 2014)

Learning what we mean when we say "democracy"—even if this remains an unanswerable question that is only partly about democracy itself—is an important part of sustaining the "growing global movement against the commodification of knowledge and hope to create a space for people to think about and experiment with alternative models of higher education" (Saunders & Ghanimi, 2013). To understand the potential of this emergent tendency, it is instructive to examine the micropolitical and metapolitical processes of democratization in localized projects of informal education where people are creating common spaces to think about, and experiment with, cooperative learning and living spaces for learning how to break with relations of domination, to breathe, and to begin being-in-common together.

References

Amsler, S. (2011, June 23). Inequality, power and privilege in the struggle for the humanities. *The Guardian.*, Retrieved from http://www.theguardian.com/higher-education-network/2011/jun/23/new-college-of-humanities-and-social-inequality

Amsler, S. (2012a). Notes from the curriculum working group meeting of 22 June 2012. Social Science Centre. Retrieved from http://socialsciencecentre.org.uk/blog/2012/06/27/notes-from-the-curriculum-working-group-meeting-of-22-june-2012/

Amsler, S. (2012b). Studying with the Social Science Centre curriculum workshop. 30 June, Social Science Centre. Retrieved from http://socialsciencecentre.org.uk/wp-content/uploads/2012/06/Studying-with-the-Social-Science-Centre-curriculum-workshop-30-June-2012-2.pdf

Amsler, S. (2014). Notes on the SSC course, February 6, Week 4—Alternative Education. Retrieved from http://socialsciencecentre.org.uk/blog/2014/02/09/notes-on-the-ssc-course-february-6th-2014-week-4-alternative-education/

Anderson, M.L. (2010). Neural reuse: A fundamental organizational principle of the brain. *Behavioral and Brain Sciences, 33*, 245–313.

Beauvoir, S. de (1976). *The ethics of ambiguity*. New York, NY: Citadel Press.

Bloch, E. (1923/2000). *The spirit of utopia.* Stanford, CA: Stanford University Press.

Bloch, E. (1995). *The principle of hope.* Cambridge, MA: MIT Press.

Bonnett, A. (2013, May 23-29). It's really exciting to create something new in freedom. *Times Higher Education.*

Clegg, S. (2010). The possibilities of sustaining critical intellectual work under regimes of evidence, audit, and ethical governance., *Journal of Curriculum Theorizing, 26*(3), 21-35.

Coles, R. (2006). The wild patience of radical democracy In L. Toender & L. Thomassen (Eds.), *Radical democracy: Politics between abundance and lack.* Manchester: Manchester University Press.

Collini, S. (2011, August 25). From Robbins to McKinsey. *London Review of Books, 33*(16), 9-14.

Dewey, J. (1910). *How we think.* Retrieved from http://rci.rutgers.edu/~tripmcc/phil/dewey-hwt-pt1-selections.pdf

Dewey, J. (1939). Creative democracy—The task before us. In J. Boydston (Ed.), *The Later Works, 1925-1953* (Vol. 14, pp. 224-230). Carbondale: Southern Illinois University Press.

Dewey, J. (2005). *Art as experience* New York, NY: Penguin.

Facer, K., Thorpe, J., & Shaw, L. (2011, September). Co-operative education and schools: An old idea for new times? Paper presented at the British Educational Research Association conference, London, UK.

Fanon, F. (2008). *Black skin, white masks.* New York, NY: Grove Press.

Federici, S. (2010). Feminism and the politics of the commons in an era of primitive accumulation. In C. Hughes, S. Peace & K. van Meter (Eds.), *Uses of a whirlwind: Movement, movements, and contemporary radical currents in the United States* (pp. 283-294). Oakland, CA: AK Press.

Federici, S. (2013). A feminist critique of Marx. Retrieved from http://endofcapitalism.com/2013/05/29/a-feminist-critique-of-marx-by-silvia-federici.

Fielding, M. (2013). Beyond the betrayal of democracy in schools: Lessons from the past, hope for the future. *Research in Teacher Education, 3*(2), 47-50.

Freire, P. (2000). *The pedagogy of the oppressed.* London, UK: Continuum.

Freire, P. (2005). *Education for critical consciousness.* London, UK: Continuum.

Gagnier, R. (2013). Operationalizing hope: The neoliberalization of British universities in historico-philosophical perspective. *Occasion: Interdisciplinary Studies in the Humanities.* Retrieved from http://arcade.stanford.edu/sites/default/files/article_pdfs/OCCASION_v6_Gagnier_100113.pdf

Gibson-Graham, J.K. (2006). *A postcapitalist politics.* Minneapolis, MN: University of Minnesota Press.

Greene, M. (1995). *Releasing the imagination: Essays on education, the arts, and social change.* San Franscisco, CA: Jossey-Bass.

Greene, M. (2005). Teaching in a moment of crisis: the spaces of imagination, *The New Educator, 1*, 77-80.

Hall, R. (2014, January 26). On alienation and the curriculum [Web log post]. Retrieved from http://www.richard-hall.org/2014/01/26/on-alienation-and-the-curriculum

hooks, b. (1994). *Teaching to transgress: Education as the practice of freedom.* New York, NY: Routledge.

hooks, b. (2003) *Teaching community: A pedagogy of hope.* New York, NY: Routledge.

Juby, P. (2011, September). A co-operative university? Paper presented at the UK SCS conference Cardiff, UK.

Keeble, R., Peaceful Warrior, Saunders, G. (2014). Social Science Centre Podcast #2: Education [Audio podcast]. Retrieved from http://www.sirenonline.co.uk/archives/4959.

Kompridis, N. (2006). *Critique and disclosure: Critical theory between past and future.* Cambridge, MA: MIT Press.

Kropotkin, P. (1902). *Mutual aid: A factor of evolution.* Retrieved from http://www.marxists.org/reference/archive/kropotkin-peter/1902/mutual-aid/

Lincolnshire Echo. (2014, June 4). Homeless and ex-homeless people capture Lincolnshire through the lens for new photography exhibition. Retrieved from http://www.lincolnshireecho.co.uk/Homeless-ex-homeless-people-capture-Lincolnshire/story-21187549-detail/story.html

Luchies, T. (2014). Anti-oppression as pedagogy: Prefiguration as praxis. *Interface: A Journal for and about Social Movements, 6*(1), 99–129.

Marcuse, H. (1998). The new German mentality. In D. Kellner (Ed.), *Technology, war and fascism* (pp. 139–190). New York, NY: Routledge.

McAleavey, D., & Amsler, S. (2012, October). A practice that aspires: Pedagogies of creativity, democracy and inclusion in popular higher education. Paper presented at Creativity and Democracy (the 3rd IJADE and NSEAD research conference), Liverpool John Moores University, Liverpool, UK.

Means, A. (2014). Educational commons and the new radical democratic imaginary. *Critical studies in education. 55*(2). 122–137.

Mills, C.W. (1959). *The sociological imagination.* New York, NY: The Free Press.

Motta, S., & Esteves, A.M. (2014). Reinventing emancipation in the 21st century: the pedagogical practices of social movements. *Interface: A journal for and about social movements, 6*(1), 1–24.

Neary, M. (2011, October 7). The Social Science Centre: A radical new model for higher education. Retrieved from http://www.opendemocracy.net/ourkingdom/mike-neary/social-science-centre-radical-new-model-for-higher-education

Neary, M., & Winn, J. (2011, June 23) An alternative to privilege. Retrieved from http://www.timeshighereducation.co.uk/416602.article

Ostrom, E. (1990). *Governing the commons: The evolution of institutions for collective action.* Cambridge, UK: University of Cambridge Press.

Peaceful Warrior. (2013). R+evolution in Lincoln [Web log post]. Retrieved from http://acloudcuckooland.blogspot.co.uk/2013/05/revolution-lincoln.html

Santos, B. de Sousa (2014). *Epistemologies of the South: Justice against epistemicide.* Boulder, CO: Paradigm.

Saunders, G., & Ghanimi, A. (2013, September 23). From Edinburgh to Brighton: Britain's free, alternative higher education network offers lifelong learning without lifelong debt. Retrieved from http://www.ragged-online.com/2013/09/edinburgh-brighton-britains-free-alternative-higher-education-network-offers-life-long-learning-life-long-debt-gary-saunders-ali-ghanimi/

Sennett, R. (2012). *Together: The ritual pleasures and politics of co-operation.* New York, NY: Penguin.

Shore, C. (2010). Beyond the multiversity: Neoliberalism and the rise of the schizo-phrenic university. *Social Anthropology/Anthropologie Sociale, 18*(1), 15–29.

Social Science Centre. (2011). Constitution of the Social Science Centre. Retrieved from http://socialsciencecentre.org.uk/wp-content/uploads/2011/05/constitution-final.pdf

Social Science Centre. (2014). Notes on "co-operation and education" class: Week 2, curriculum design and pedagogy. Retrieved from http://socialsciencecentre.org.uk/blog/2014/01/27/notes-on-co-operation-and-education-class-week-two-curriculum-design-and-pedagogy/

Stratford, L. (2014, February). Notes on the SSC course, February 13th, Week Five: Co-operative values and principles [Web log post]. Retrieved from http://socialsciencecentre.org.uk/blog/2014/02/15/notes-on-the-ssc-course-february-13th-week-five-co-operative-values-and-principles/

Tucker, R.C. (1978). *The Marx–Engels reader*. New York, NY: Norton and Co.

What's this place? Stories from radical social centres in the UK and Ireland. (2008). Retrieved from http://socialcentrestories.files.wordpress.com/2008/06/whats-this-place_lo-res.pdf

Winn, J. (2012). Creative projects [Web log post]. Retrieved from http://socialsciencecentre.org.uk/blog/2012/07/13/creative-projects/

Winn, J. (2014a, June). *The co-operative university: labour, property and pedagogy.* Paper presented at the Governing Academic Life conference, London School of Economics.

Winn, J. (2014b). Is the worker co-operative form suitable for a university? Part 2 [Web log post]. Retrieved from http://josswinn.org/2014/03/is-the-worker-co-operative-form-suitable-for-a-university-part-2/

Your Lincoln. (2012). Live like common people. *Your Lincoln* magazine, Spring 2012, p. 16. Retrieved from https://www.lincoln.gov.uk/your-council/news-and-media/your-lincoln/

The Space Project: Creating Cracks within, against, and beyond Academic-Capitalism

Andre Pusey

"To survive and flourish we have to build creative alternatives."
—Really Open University, 2010a

Higher education is increasingly subject to extensive processes of neoliberalization, marketization, and privatization (Giroux, 2014; McGettigan, 2013). The effects of this have included rising tuition fees and student debt, the introduction of a variety of metrics mechanisms, and the increased precarity of academic working conditions (Caffentzis, 2010; De Angelis & Harvie, 2009). This situation has been characterized by some as "academic capitalism" (Slaughter & Rhoades, 2009), while others have proposed that the university is in "ruins" (Reading, 2007) and the contemporary university has increasingly been compared with a "factory" (Aronowitz, 2001; Edu-Factory, 2009; Raunig, 2013).

In response to this increased enclosure (Harvie, 2000) and commodification of education and the perceived "assault on the universities" (Bailey & Freedman, 2011), there has been widespread resistance, in the form of workplace organizing, student protest and occupations, and extensive social unrest (Hancox, 2011; Solomon & Palmieri, 2011; Zibechi, 2012). Concurrent with this activity *within* and *against* academic capitalism, there have also been attempts to go *beyond* it, and we have witnessed the emergence of a plethora of radical informal learning spaces. Some of these have been operating within what Moten and Harney (2013) term the "undercommons" of the university, and others have operated outside institutional space altogether, thus creating a "critical pedagogy in, against and beyond the university" (Cowden & Singh, 2013).

In this chapter, I discuss the development of an "autonomous education" project and informal learning space called "the Space Project," which was established by a group called the Really Open University (ROU) in Leeds (UK), of which I was a founder-member and formed the basis of an extensive militant research project (Pusey, forthcoming). I argue that the Space Project represented an example of a crack in academic capitalism (Holloway, 2010), a space for the self-managed, collective, and collaborative development of learning autonomous from the university.

This project was informally embedded within a wider history of autonomous education projects, such as anarchist "Free Skools" (Shantz, 2012) and "autonomous universities" (Kanngieser, 2008), yet it was also distinct from these formations, being placed within the interstices of the contemporary crises of capital and higher education. The Space Project also drew on the tradition of autonomous social centers and squatted spaces (Chatterton, 2010; Hodkinson & Chatterton, 2006; Pusey, 2010), but as I discuss below, it wished to avoid some of their perceived pitfalls. I explore the context of the development of this project, within the higher education crisis, and the politics informing its development, before finally moving on to some of the obstacles and barriers that autonomous education projects such as the Space Project face in their attempts to create cracks within, against, and beyond academic capitalism.

Cracking Capitalism through Doing

In *Crack Capitalism* (2010), John Holloway suggests that through everyday acts of transgression, negation, and creation we create "cracks" in capitalism. He suggests these cracks could create a strategy for us to break with capitalism, and to stop our autonomous and self-directed "doing" being transformed into the alienation of "abstract labor" which is the source of capitalist (re)production. For Holloway, "a crack . . . is a moment in which relations of domination were broken and other relations created (2010, p. 31). These "other relations" are those in excess of capital, which overflow the codified and exploitative relations of domination that we inhabit in our lives under the domination of value—the substance of capital, the substance of our domination (Postone, 1995).

Central to *Crack Capitalism* is the desire to understand capitalism not simply as domination, but from the perspective of its weaknesses and contradictions, and, even more importantly, to understand ourselves as those contradictions (2010, p. 9). This then is an empowering view of our abilities to resist capital and create other worlds. For Holloway, the "argument is clear: the only way to think about revolution is in terms of the creation, expansion and multiplication of cracks in capitalist domination" (2010, p. 51). We create cracks in capitalism every day, through everyday acts that refuse the rule of money, that are not about work, and that refuse the tyranny of measure. Holloway includes examples ranging from reading a book on a park bench instead of going to work to starting a course in a university about social activism.

Central to Holloway's method of cracking capitalism is the idea of "doing" as opposed to abstract labor. Abstract labor is one part of the dual nature of labor under capitalism, with concrete labor producing use value and abstract labor producing exchange value. Holloway counterposes abstract labor with "doing." Doing, Holloway tells us, is activity that is not determined by others or activity that is potentially self-determined (2010, p. 84), and "the story of the cracks is the story of a doing that does not fit into a world dominated by labour." Despite the bleak picture of the domination of capitalist value over our lives, Holloway suggests that "our doing is not totally subsumed into abstract labour" (Holloway, 2010, p. 97). This "doing" then forms an excess. It exceeds the parameters of the social relations dominated by value, and "the crack is the revolt of doing against labour" (Holloway, 2010, p. 85):

> The pivot, the central fulcrum, in all of this is our doing: human crea-
> tion. One form of doing, labour, creates capital, the basis of the society
> that is destroying us. Another form of doing, what we call simply
> "doing," pushes against the creation of capital and towards the creation
> of a different society. In both cases, our doing is at the centre. By focus-
> ing on doing, we put our own power at the centre of our understanding
> of society: our power-to-do (and therefore, our power not to do, and
> our power to do differently). By focusing on doing, we also state clearly
> that the argument of this book is not for "more democracy" but for a
> radical reorganisation of our daily activity, without which the call for
> "more democracy" means nothing at all. (Holloway, 2010, pp. 85–86)

By correlating his concept of "cracks" with "doing," Holloway successfully grounds the "other relations" which are constitutive of these cracks with the refusal of abstract labor and value, and therefore, the negation of the sub-stance of capital. By attaching his conceptualization of "cracks" in capitalism with "doing," and therefore, social production, Holloway ensures the spaces of negation and creation that form these cracks are well situated to refuse the means of our subjugation. These cracks, then, are not just forms of protest, but forms of creation and excess, social activity not orientated towards the reproduction of capital, but also refusing its capture through measure.

In the next part of this chapter I outline the work of the Space Project as an example of a radical informal learning space that was developed out of the struggles of students in 2010 and 2011 around university space. In the fol-lowing section I argue that the Space Project provides an example of a crack in academic capitalism and of the doing, which Holloway suggests can help us refuse our subjugation.

The ROU and the Space Project

> It is the goal of ROU to carve out a slice of space and time in which to experiment and find something new. Everything is up for reinvention. We are rejecting prescriptive dogma so that we can promote innovation and creativity, and build the future into the present. Only by constructing alternatives can we make them feel normal. (Really Open University, 2010b)

The Space Project was conceived as a six-month experiment in creating an informal autonomous learning space and was initiated by a group called the Really Open University (ROU). The ROU had been formed in January 2010 as a means not only to protest against budget cuts and the increase in tuition fees, but also to push against the further instrumentalization and neoliberalization of higher education more generally (Pusey & Sealey-Huggins, 2013; Sealey-Huggins & Pusey, 2013). The ROU's motto "strike, occupy, transform!" embodied the groups desire to merge a praxis based on political antagonism and resistance with a transformative and affirmative politics of desire. The ROU was a forerunner to the UK student protests that erupted in the autumn/winter of 2010, and the group participated in this emergent movement (Amsler, 2011; Brown, 2013; Burton, 2013; Hancox et al., 2011; Hopkins & Todd, 2013; Ibrahim, 2011; Rheingans & Holland, 2013; Robinson, 2013; Salter & Kay, 2011; Solomon & Palmieri, 2011). But in addition to turning up at local and national protests about issues facing higher education, many of the activities organized by the ROU attempted to blur the lines between events-as-protests and protests-as-events (Lamond & Spracken, 2014). An incomplete list of the group's activities includes constructing a papier maché costume depicting the "general intellect" and storming a live television debate about the tripling of student fees; the production of an irregular free newsletter called the *Sausage Factory*, taking its name from Marx's *Capital*; a three-day conference of varied talks, workshops and other activities around the theme of "reimagining the university" timed to coincide with a large demonstration against the increase in tuition fees and reduction in further education maintenance grants proposed by the Browne Review which saw the occupation of a lecture theater on the University of Leeds campus; and finally the establishment of the Space Project, which forms the focus for this chapter.

ROU operated on the "edge" of the university (Noterman & Pusey, 2012), attempting to act within what Deleuze and Guattari understood as the "cramped" spaces or "bottlenecks" which provide fruitful opportunities for transgressive creation and the generation of rebellious subjectivities (Pusey, 2016). The Space Project served as a continuation of this endeavor. It was a self-managed and horizontal space which provided an example of a "crack" in academic capitalism, and where the collective doing that emerged from the project was in excess of capital's measure. The Space Project was not only an example of an autonomous education project, but it also attempted to go beyond some of the limitations of activist "free skools" (e.g., bike repairs and campaigns) which ROUers associated with the sharing of practical skills and an activist subculture it did not wish to reproduce. Although it grew out of the tradition of self-managed social centers, it also attempted to go beyond their limitations as perceived by members of the ROU. Again, these spaces were associated with the reproduction of certain forms of activist practices the group wished to move away from.

Early discussions around the relative merits, pitfalls, and aims of establishing such a space were not always met with an easy group consensus. There were fears among most ROUers about merely repeating the social center model, rather than superseding it. Nobody wanted to create a space that merely reproduced an insular activist subculture. There were also important concerns about the amount of time and energy needed to sustain such a project, especially by those about to embark upon the final year of their research/studies. This extract from ROU minutes reflects these concerns:

> Problems we want to avoid a sub-cultural space where we are inundated with lifestyle politics and the dream that one space isn't capable of facilitating all our needs. We also don't want to be bogged down with upkeep (which we think we can avoid if we are not having a café or gig space). We also want to move beyond advertising this to our immediate 'activist' community and figure out how we can open this to different audience/participants. (ROU Minutes, 2/9/12)

A participatory element of the Space Project had initially planned to be brought about through an open meeting held in the newly acquired space, organized for the day in which the keys were handed over to the group. This public meeting was attended by around forty people. The meeting was kept short, with an introduction about the ROU, the origins of the Space Project and some of our ideas for it.

Before this event, there had been a discussion in a ROU meeting about how to present the project:

> Tone will be set during the first public meeting. We don't want just another community space. Go beyond same spaces that already exist— community spaces and activist spaces. Need to achieve a balance. Work on outreach.
>
> Back to conversation about what the space is for. . . . Being an *educational* space rather than a space (in broad terms). (ROU Minutes, 9/9/12)

These comments indicate some of the tensions in the group about the desire to resist becoming an "activist ghetto," but also the anxieties about becoming "just another community space." There were tense discussions in meetings before this about fears that the project could become, in some way, "less political" than many of the group wanted. Sometimes this focused on design and the way we were attempting to publicize the project. At other times, it was about how we would explain enough to attract people, but not define it so that it predetermined who might be interested in getting involved, or what sorts of focus or events might happen.

These tensions arose out of the ROU's origins in struggles within and beyond the university, and out of individuals' involvement in activism across the city, including squatted spaces and social centers. They reflected the desire to maintain the political antagonism at the heart of the ROU project, but to avoid the sometimes formulaic and over-coded forms of political identities offered by activism and political militancy more generally (especially what Foucault labeled the "sad militant"). Equally, however, there was a refusal to become part of the community sector. One of the ways some within the group described their wishes for the space was in terms of "cross contamination." This meant that the space was not simply a resource in which different groups could have their meetings or events, it was also an invitation to create new relations and interests between groups and individuals. This was not intended to be on the basis of political networking or with the requisite appeal to organize something together, but it was assumed to be a messy pedagogical process with no explicit aim in sight, only the organization of becoming.

The Space Project effectively ended up developing into two distinct periods, and having established the context from which the ROU and the Space Project emerged, I will now outline these stages and what constituted them.

First Stage of the Space Project: October–December 2011

The first stage of the Space Project began when the space opened in October and lasted until closing for the winter holidays. This initial period consisted of a wide range of events, mostly put on by individuals within the collective, based on their interests. These ranged from a film festival about Italian workerism, included as part of a fringe for the Leeds International Film Festival, to visiting speakers talking about a diverse range of radical topics, including the revolution in Egypt, the 1984-1985 UK miners' strike, and the eviction of Travellers from Dale Farm in Essex. It gave birth to a local radical history group and, briefly, a radical pedagogy study group. The space was also used by activist groups, such as No Borders and Occupy Leeds.

There was a lot of discussion within the group about how to launch the space, and people were keen to organize a radical history bike tour. This event launched a radical history series at the space. Another early initiative was a regular film night called Militant Cinema. Initially a small group of us had envisaged this as a one-off series of films to act as a fringe to the Leeds International Film Festival (LIFF). Having worked with the LIFF in former years as part of previous collectives, several of us had good contacts with the organizers, and they agreed that the Space Project could be a venue where we could show films. This meant the film showings (and the Space Project) would be listed in the LIFF program, which we hoped might reach a broader audience, and therefore, promote the Space Project. Another project that many wished to initiate was a regular critical pedagogy group although, in practice, this was short lived.

In November, the Space Project was host to a public lecture by John Holloway. Holloway had delivered two public Leverhulme lectures at the University of Leeds, and the third and final part of the lecture series was held at the Space Project because a national strike by the University College Union meant that higher education workers were out on strike that day. Around 150 people attended. Holloway's talk and this event were by far the best attended at the Space Project and included some heated exchanges that had been notably lacking from the question and answer sessions after the previous two talks held at the University of Leeds.

One of the things I noted at this event was the apparent disjuncture between those who were used to traversing activism/radical politics and academia, and those who were experienced with activism, but not necessarily with these radical left political traditions. Some were critical of the traditional speaker format, which was felt not to be in keeping with horizontal approaches to political discussion that was expected of us as a project. This is interesting to note given the project's stated desire to go beyond neatly defined political traditions and identities. Generally the ROU and the Space Project engaged in a range of formats for events and meetings and drew on political traditions which, although loosely aligned to forms of "autonomous" politics, definitely were not located explicitly in anarchist or horizontalist repertoires.

The first stage of the Space Project came to a close at the end of the year as the holidays approached. This period had been characterized by an intensive period of organizing the self-management of the space. With the second stage of the Space Project came the implementation of many of the more ambitious ideas the group had envisaged before moving into the space. These included reading groups and courses that continued over several weeks, rather than simply one-off talks and workshops. In many ways, this built upon some of the ROU's earlier initiatives, such as public meetings focused on discussing specific topics.

Second Stage of the Space Project: January–March 2012

One of the ideas that had been mooted in Space Project meetings since the initial planning stages was to host a course on radical economics and understanding the 2008 crisis. This not only came to fruition in the second phase of the project, but it was well attended and widely deemed a successful project. The curriculum reproduced below gives a good indication of the depth and breadth that the course encompassed:

Crashing through Capital: An Introduction to Economics

As we face austerity and what seems like an ever changing global economic situation, understanding the reasons behind it all can seem daunting.

Really Open University will be hosting a 2 month crash economics course at the Space Project. We present a beginners guide to economics through lectures, discussions, film showings and workshops unravelling the financial jargon, examining the history and analysing the causes of the crisis whilst also collectively creating our own resistance to this new stage of capitalism.

Each session works on its own so you are free to come to as few or as many as you like. For further readings and discussions around a specific area of economics, check out the New Weapons reading group on 'Crisis'.

6th Feb— 'Economists and commoners: an introduction to the capitalist "science"' David Harvie

A brief historical introduction to the ways in which economists have remade the world, and remade us in their image—and are continuing to do so. And why we should care.

David Harvie is a senior lecturer in finance and political economy at the University of Leicester, political activist and member of the Free Association collective.

13th Feb— 'Inside Job' Film Showing

Film highlighting the systemic corruption within the financial system and how it led to the debt crisis. This will be followed by a discussion on the central role played by debt in Neoliberalism. The session should explain the ideology of debt and how it is inherent to the capitalist system, a great introduction to the following workshop . . .

20th Feb—Corporatewatch Debt Resistance Workshop

As we all face more and more debt, this is a practical workshop on how we can resist it in our everyday lives. Corporatewatch is a research group providing information on corporations and supporting campaigns against them.

27th Feb— 'What we got for £850 billion: finance and its functions'
David Harvie.

The second lecture from David Harvie, focusing on financial institutions and the technicalities (in everyday language) of the financial markets. How do they work? What does the jargon mean? Why did the British state commit £850 billion to bailing out the banks and why is finance so essential to neoliberal capitalism.

With the creation of courses such as this, the Space Project and the ROU were developing ongoing forms of autonomous education that went beyond our previous, less sustained, efforts. As noted, this was part of the intention for the project when we were conceptualizing it, but it had taken several months to establish the space and encourage newcomers to become involved. In this second part of the Space Project, much of this hard work came to fruition.

In addition to the Crashing Through Capital course, a new reading group called New Weapons was established, which hosted a Really Open Course in Crisis. Again, we can see the plans for the project discussed over the previous summer coming to fruition with several courses which went beyond the one-day events which had previously been more typical of what we had organized at the Space Project.

This is how it was promoted to potential participants on the Space Project website:

> From bankrupt PIGS, revolting Greeks and an £1 trillion hole in Italy abroad, to riots, banker bailouts and strikes at home, wherever you look these days there's banter about "crisis." But what crisis? Where, and for whom? Facilitated by Leeds Radical Library, this first discussion series, The Really Open Course on Crisis, aims to provide a lively forum for debate about some of the key issues of our time: what is capitalism and does it seem to break again and again? Taking short, weekly texts as a starting point, we want to explore the history of capitalist crisis to find out what "our crisis" has in common with previous crises, and what might be unique about it. While economists and bankers whom we've never met or elected seem able to make more and more decisions about the way we run our lives, The Really Open Course on Crisis will aim to unravel from the very beginning the modern day myths about "finance," "capital" and "democracy." (Space Project, 2011)

The outline reproduced below, taken from the Space Project website, gives an indication of the scope and structure of the course:

Week 1. January 19th History of Crisis—Mapping the Crisis to the present day

What caused the current crisis of capitalism we're living through? Where did it come from? What makes it a 'financial' crisis? Here we seek to define our terms and understand the roots of the burgeoning debt, gaping inequality and mass unemployment that characterises the UK today.

Week 2. Crisis Theory—Capitalism as Crisis

Why does capitalism seem so accident prone? Here we'll look at the way capitalism functions as a method for generating wealth and try to diagnose what about capitalism, if anything, sends whole economies spiralling into recession.

Week 3. Crisis and the Everyday—Precarity, austerity and debt

Building up debt? Unstable employment? We will be looking at how capital reconfigures our daily routines and what this means for our everyday interactions, work patterns and material conditions.

Week 4. Feminist Perspective on Crisis—Capital and the crisis of reproduction

By taking a feminist perspective, we will analyse what we mean by reproductive and affective labour? What role does unwaged labour have in the reproduction of capital? What is meant by the crisis of reproduction and what does this mean for anticapitalist resistance?

Week 5. Resistance, movements and struggle

How do we resist? How do we gain class power? What strategies and methods of struggle are appropriate in our current political context?

The Space Project had been an interesting experiment drawing on the social centers and free school and free universities traditions as well as the surge of struggle around higher education. Running concurrently were similar projects emerging from this context with links to these traditions, such as the Social Science Centre in Lincoln and the Tent City University which emerged from the Occupy St Paul's protest (Halvorsen, 2015; Neary & Amsler, 2012; Pickerill & Krinsky). These illustrate the desire for elements of student and higher education movements to exceed being protest-based movements and develop into broader experiments with autonomous education that embody the radical and antagonistic nature of critical pedagogy.

The Space Project Creating a Crack in Academic Capitalism

Through the Space Project, the ROU created a space that enabled all participants to engage in practices of resistive-learning and knowledge production that was in-against-beyond the university. This space enabled a collaborative form of "doing" that was operating in a "cramped space" (Deleuze and Guattari, 1986). This space was a crack in (academic) capitalism (Holloway, 2010; Slaughter & Rhoades, 2009).

It can therefore be argued that the "doing" of those in the ROU was produced as a reaction against the alienating classroom life experience. This reaction encompassed both resistance and creation. Rejecting the false dichotomy of defend or destroy offered by some in the Californian student occupation movement of 2009, which exerted an early influence on many in the group, the ROU sought instead to start from within and against, whilst creating liminal spaces, cracks that could help form a tentative "beyond."

This is a process of "exodus," of creating what Deleuze & Guattari (2004) call "lines of flight," not in order to flee, but in order to produce. To produce an actually existing "really open university" through the prefigurative praxis of our various projects—the everyday doing of our lives. This doing attempted to resist its subjugation as abstract labor and become concrete. It also attempted to exceed abstract labor and become doing.

How do we change the world? How do we stop making capitalism? John Holloway suggests that "there is no right answer, just millions of experiments" (Holloway, 2010, p. 256). The Space Project was one of these experiments. Not only was the Space Project a site of self-education through design, as a dedicated space for the proliferation of self-managed education, knowledge production, and exchange, it was also a collective process of self-education in self-management. The difficult and often mundane process of everyday autonomous self-management was also a project of collective self-education about the tensions and hard work involved in (re)producing the commons (Pusey & Chatterton, 2016). Despite being all too aware of the hard work involved in managing a project such as the Space Project, and having wanted to avoid some of the pitfalls of group members involvement with autonomous social centers, the project had taken its toll on the group, and over the six months the Space Project had been running, a number of people had taken a step back from involvement. All the participants in the group had other commitments, including childcare and jobs, and several were in the final stages of writing their PhD theses. The Space Project was a self-managed and horizontal space which provided an example of a "crack" in academic capitalism, and where the collective doing that emerged from the project was in excess of capital's measure. However, although the Space Project was funded and was therefore free of many of the usual financial concerns that plague autonomous projects, the real cost was in our time. The fissures began to come to the surface (the cracks began to show) when there was less of it, when the rule of money and value came back into our lives. We had jobs to do, courses to finish. PhD time was running out. PhD funding was running out. There was abstract labor to perform.

The experiments of the ROU broke with the rule of academic capitalism. In its place, the Space Project provided a collectively organized and horizontal experiment in knowledge production and exchange. Ultimately, however, capital reimposed its measure and the majority of ROU participants were coerced back to conventional study and work. The challenge is how to collectively rid ourselves of the tyranny of capitalist value and its disciplinary regime of measure, so that we can create new values based on new, liberatory social relations.

References:

Aronowitz, S. (2001). *The knowledge factory: Dismantling the corporate university and creating true higher learning*. Boston, MA: Beacon Press.

Bailey, M., & Freedman, D. (2011). *The assault on universities: A manifesto for resistance*. London, UK: Pluto Press.

Browne, J. (2010). Securing a sustainable future for higher education: an independent review of higher education funding and student finance. Retrieved from: http://www.bis.gov.uk/assets/biscore/corporate/docs/s/101208securingsustainablehighereducationbrownereport.pdf

Caffentzis, G. (2010) The future of "the commons": Neo-liberalism's "Plan B" or the original disaccumulation of capital? *New Formations, 69*, 23–41.

Chatterton P, (2010) Autonomy: The struggle for survival, self-management and the common. *Antipode, 42*(4), 897–908.

Cowden, S., & Singh, G. (2013). *Acts of knowing: Critical pedagogy in, against and beyond the university*. New York, NY: Bloomsbury Academic.

De Angelis, M., & Harvie, D. (2009). "Cognitive capitalism" and the rat-race: How capital measures immaterial labour in British universities. *Historical Materialism, 17*(3), pp. 3–30.

Edu-Factory. (2009). *Toward a global autonomous university: Cognitive labor, the production of knowledge, and exodus from the education factory*. Brooklyn, NY: Autonomedia.

Giroux, H.A. (2014). *Neoliberalism's war on higher education*. Chicago, IL: Haymarket Books.

Halvorsen, S. (2015) Taking space: Moments of rupture and everyday life in Occupy London. *Antipode, 47*(2), 401–417.

Hancox, D. (Ed.). (2011). *Fight back! A reader on the winter of protest*. London, UK: openDemocracy.net. Open Democracy UK. Retrieved from https://www.opendemocracy.net/ourkingdom/ourkingdom/fight-back-reader-on-winter-of-protest

Harvie, D. (2000). Alienation, class and enclosure in UK universities. *Capital and Class, 71*, 103–132.

Harvie, D. (2004). Commons and communities in the university: Some notes and some examples. *The Commoner, 8*, 1–10. Retrieved from http://hdl.handle.net/2381/3288

Hodkinson, S., & Chatterton, P. (2006) Autonomy in the city? Reflections on the social centres movement in the UK. *City, 10*(3), 305–315.

Holloway, J. (2010). *Crack capitalism*. London, UK: Pluto Press.

Moten, F., & Harney, S. (2013). *The undercommons: Fugitive planning & black study*. London, UK: Minor Compositions.

Neary, M. (2014) *The university and the city: Social Science Centre, Lincoln—forming the urban revolution.* In: The physical university: contours of space and place in higher education. New York, NY: Routledge, pp. 203–216

Neary, M., & Amsler, S. (2012). Occupy: a new pedagogy of space and time?. *Journal for Critical Education Policy Studies*, 10(2), 106–138.

Pickerill, J., & Krinsky, J. (2012). Why does Occupy matter?. *Social Movement Studies*, 11(3–4), 279–287.

Postone, M. (1995). *Time, labor, and social domination: A reinterpretation of Marx's critical theory.* Cambridge University Press.

Pusey, A. (2010, summer). Social centres and the new cooperativism of the common. *Affinities: A Journal of Radical Theory, Culture, and Action*, 4(1), 176–198.

Pusey, A. (2016). Strike, occupy, transform! Students, subjectivity and struggle. *Journal of Marketing for Higher Education*, 26(2), 214–232.

Pusey, A. (forthcoming). A cartography of the possible: reflections on militant ethnography in and against the edu-factory. *AREA.*

Pusey, A., & Sealey-Huggins, L. (2013). Transforming the university: Beyond students and cuts. *ACME: An international journal for critical geographies*, 12(3), 443–458.

Pusey, A., & Chatterton, P. (2016) Commons. In Jayne, M., & Ward, K. (Eds.). (2016). *Urban theory: New critical perspectives.* New York, NY: Routledge.

Raunig, G. (2013). *Factories of knowledge, industries of creativity.* Cambridge, MA: MIT Press.

Readings, B. (1997). *The university in ruins.* Cambridge, MA: Harvard University Press.

Really Open University. (2010a) Support the UCU Strikes. Retrieved from: https://reallyopenuniversity.wordpress.com/2010/02/24/support-the-ucu-trike/

Really Open University. (2010b) Do it yourself. Retrieved from: https://reallyopenuniversity.files.wordpress.com/2010/03/sausage4.pdf

Sealey-Huggins, L., & Pusey, A. (2013). Neoliberalism and depoliticisation in the academy: Understanding the "new student rebellions." *Graduate Journal of Social Science*, 10(3), 80–99.

Slaughter, S., & Rhoades, G. (2009). *Academic capitalism and the new economy: Markets, state, and higher education.* Baltimore, MD: The Johns Hopkins University Press.

Solomon, C., & Palmieri, T. (2011). *Springtime: The new student rebellions.* London, UK: Verso.

Space Project. (2011). *The Space Project presented by the Really Open University.* Retrieved from http://spaceproject.org.uk/

Zibechi, R. (2012). *Territories in resistance: A cartography of Latin American social movements.* Oakland, CA: AK Press.

CHAPTER 8

Anarchists against (and within) the Edu-Factory: The Critical Criminology Working Group

Jeff Shantz

This chapter examines anarchist pedagogical approaches in practice, through organizing, engagement, and struggle against neoliberalism and corporatization within new universities in British Colombia. More specifically, it offers a critical analysis of organizing efforts to develop an anarchist working group that is fighting marketization; "job ready" curricula, programs, and degrees; and administrative inaccessibility in a new university (converted from a community college) structured within a two-tier postsecondary model (research versus "special purpose" universities geared towards the labor market) by a neoliberal government.

The Critical Criminology Working Group (CCWG) at Kwantlen Polytechnic University (KPU) in Surrey, British Columbia (Metro Vancouver, unceded Coast Salish territory) is a collective of faculty, students, and community members who organize public events, engage in community organizing, and maintain public media venues. They are now in their fourth year of organizing successful events under difficult circumstances. The Critical Criminology Working Group organizes and hosts a variety of substantial public discussions, including panel discussions, book launches, film screenings, spoken word, and mixed-media presentations. It has also organized community actions, including a blockade against a highway through a residential area. The objective has been the engagement of academic work and analysis with issues of broader community concern and the development of participatory, critical pedagogical praxis. It is applied theory in the service of a public criminology bringing together community members, students, and faculty for conversation and action.

Events are an active expression of applied critical knowledge. These events present a participatory, open, engaged version of a polytechnic mandate to bring academic work to bear on understanding public issues and contribute to a community-based approach to address social questions. This is counter to the notion of polytechnic education as job training asserted by administration and the government.

All events have involved participation from community members, students, and faculty, bridging the gap between campus and community. The working group has built alliances with community organizers, as well as created spaces and practices on campus to pose critical pedagogical practices and perspectives. The working group has opposed, within the context of a criminology department, the construction of students as future criminal justice systems workers (and along the way produced some anarchist scholarship and a thesis within and against that structural framework).

Anarchism and Criminology

Criminology is often viewed, with some justification, as a conservative, even reactionary discipline. This is due to the association among some faculty with criminal justice system institutions as well as the role, historically and currently, of criminology and, especially, criminal justice programs in recruiting and training future police officers, prison guards, lawyers, and security personnel. It also relates to the tendency of too many criminology scholars to take the statist criminal justice system for granted as a legitimate and proper (even beneficial) institutional framework for defining, addressing, and solving social problems.

At the same time, there have been important critical, indeed radical, traditions within criminology. These traditions have often drawn explicitly from anarchism. Indeed anarchism provided some of the earliest criminological theories and offered some of the first opposition to conservative and statist criminology (as represented in the works of Lombroso, for example).

Yet these histories are often forgotten or overlooked within criminology itself, never mind outside the discipline. Thus some are surprised to hear of an anarchist grouping of criminology faculty and students active around a range of social issues in a suburban area out of the activist spotlight.

For the Working Group members, if criminology is to be at all meaningful in addressing social harms, the theoretical and scholarly research tools of criminology can best be used to identify, understand, explain, and respond to the real sources of most social harms: the economic and political power holders and institutions of economic and political power, states and capital.

The Critical Criminology Working Group has attempted to bring anarchist principles, politics, and pedagogies to bear on social struggles in an area otherwise lacking in activist resources. Along the way, it has provided

growing infrastructures for community organizing while also shifting perceptions of the discipline and challenging the conventional labor market
focus of the postsecondary institution in which it is situated.

Students have additionally undertaken innovative research to uncover
and resituate anarchist approaches within ongoing practices of criminology,
from the early days of the discipline through to the present. They have also
carried out original research on corporate and state crime and injustices
within dominant criminal justice systems and institutions (and relationships
of these with the KPU administration).

The Critical Criminology Working Group

As noted above, the Critical Criminology Working Group is a collective of
Kwantlen faculty, students, and community members who organize public
speaking events and a public criminology website. They are now in their
fourth year of organizing successful events. The CCWG organizes and hosts
a variety of substantial public discussions, including panel discussions,
book launches, film screenings, spoken-word, and mixed-media presentations. These typically take place over two to three hours. The objective is the
engagement of academic work and analysis with issues of broader community concern. It is applied theory in the service of a public criminology, and
critical activist pedagogy, bringing together community members, students,
and faculty for conversation.

All CCWG events have been, and will continue to be, open to faculty,
students, and the general public. There has been regular attendance from
community members from Langley, Richmond, Surrey, and Vancouver. In
addition, there have been visitors from Central and South America, several
states in the U.S., and Quebec. Attendees have a range of ages and backgrounds. Working Group events have been attended by between thirty to one
hundred people with the average attendance around sixty.

CCWG events are an active expression of applied critical knowledge,
in keeping with a polytechnic mandate to bring academic work to bear on
understanding public issues and contributing to community-based approach
to addressing social questions. All events have involved participation from
community members, students, and faculty, bridging the gap between
campus and community.

KPU students are overwhelmingly from blue-collar backgrounds and
live in a lower income suburb of Metro Vancouver. A large proportion of
these students are from migrant backgrounds, and most are the first generation in the family to attend post-secondary education. They have a gut level
sense of being exploited and oppressed but often lack means to articulate
their frustration or anger. Students benefit greatly by having opportunities
for rich and lively discussions of issues of public relevance as developed

through the Working Group. They are introduced to speakers and ideas to which they might not otherwise have access. This expands their own personal awareness and understanding while also introducing them to practical solutions by which people and communities are attempting to address these issues. Students have gained access to materials (research reports, pamphlets, books) that have been useful for class projects and term papers. Students have made it clear that participation in Working Group events has opened them up to perspectives and social situations of which they would otherwise not have been aware. Events have made a real contribution to the development of an intellectual culture at Kwantlen in which learning takes place outside the classroom as well as inside.

Faculty members have gained by building research and pedagogical relationships with community members and international scholars. Connections have been made between Kwantlen faculty and community groups in Surrey. This has in turn contributed to opportunities for community-based learning for students. It has also helped with the groundwork for other projects such as the proposed Centre for Social Justice which faculty members in criminology and sociology have been busy working towards. Ongoing projects, such as the Climate Teach-ins about local road and pipeline developments, which involve community members of diverse backgrounds, have been initiated through Working Group events.

Events have had participation from recognized academics as well as public intellectuals allowing for the cross-pollination of ideas. This is a characterization of polytechnic education. Participants consistently report that the events have raised their awareness of Kwantlen and left them with a highly favorable view of the university. Indeed, past out-of-town presenters (including Yves Engler and Test) have contacted the Working Group to host other events in Surrey. They now include Kwantlen as a potential site for a visit during national tours, a development that has only resulted from the efforts of the Working Group. These public figures with high profiles of their own bring many people to Kwantlen who otherwise have not had occasion to attend the campus.

Kwantlen has benefited from increased positive exposure and notice within a range of local and international media. Kwantlen has also benefited from increased connections and strengthened relations with the communities in which we work and serve. There has also been the benefit of providing students with enriched learning experiences beyond the classroom. In keeping with Kwantlen's polytechnic mandate, Working Group events involve a productive intersection of theory and practice.

The Working Group maintains a website and mailing list with news postings and notices of their events. It also produces an original journal of radical theory and practice that brings together academics, community, and prison activists. The journal, *Radical Criminology*, is now into its sixth issue since launching in 2012. The CCWG also has an active Twitter account with more than 1,700 followers. They have also established a YouTube channel and publish videos from some of their events (http://www.youtube.com/user/RadicalCriminology). They have published the video from the September 17, 2013, event on Palestinian Political Prisoners as well as the October 8, 2013, presentation by Layla AbdelRahim on "Crime and Reward from an Anarcho-Primitivist Perspective." The November 26, 2013, event on "Human Rights and Community Advocacy in the Age of Extreme Energy" was recorded by a community videographer and is also presented on YouTube (http://www.youtube.com/watch?v=88zE_cElbxw). Working Group events have generated media attention. The "Scrap the So-Called 'Terror List!'" event was featured in the *Georgia Straight* (with notice on the cover).

The Working Group has also given rise to related longer-term projects including the Kwantlen Center for Anarchist Studies (KCAS). A new, still evolving, project, KCAS will provide digital online copies of rare movement documents as well as provide library space for hard copy originals. The KCAS will eventually provide research support for activists and scholars interested in anarchist movements. Some of the documents made available at KCAS represent the sole remaining copies of the publication. This includes numerous photocopied zines and pamphlets that were produced in relatively small numbers.

The CCWG also hosted the North American Anarchist Studies Network Fifth Annual Conference. Over the past two decades, there's been a growing interest, both inside and outside the academy, in research done on anarchism (or by anarchists), and we have seen a resurgence in related multidisciplinary reading, study, and theory. As the conference call suggested:

> It is hoped that this conference will build upon the work of the four successful previous NAASN conferences; first, as a wonderful opportunity for head-to-head gathering, with lively discussion and comradely debate, and then at conclusion, will leave an open archive of all published papers & presentations intended to stand as a positive contribution to the further flourishing of anarchist ideas and action.

As part of the conference, the CCWG organized the first ever anarchist book fair in Surrey. This was a major move for organizing in the area. Indeed, upon hearing that an anarchist book fair was being organized in Surrey, many local activists expressed disbelief. "Seriously, an anarchist book fair *in Surrey*?" was a common response. The general disdain with which Surrey has been held among activists is discussed in greater detail below. Yet the book fair and conference were major successes, bringing more than five hundred people to Surrey for several lively days of engaged discussion, debate, music, art, and revelry. Several participants proclaimed it the best anarchist book fair they had attended, more engaging than several longer-standing, larger fairs.

KPU, as a former community college, is also a commuter school without student residences and lacks even a student center as a space where students might congregate and interact. Part of the culture at the school has been that students go to class and then go home without lingering. The Working Group has worked, with success, to change this culture. People now organize their schedules around Working Group events. While the first few meetings were sparsely attended (a dispiriting experience that has caused other groups to give up hosting events), the Working Group has committed to put on events on a regular basis and to follow through with compelling presentations and discussions regardless of attendance. Over time, the Working Group has become known for hosting lively, engaging, interesting, and meaningful events.

Structures of Collaboration

As is true for most anarchist collectives, the Working Group operates according to a horizontal organizational approach. There are no designated positions such as director or convener. All members discuss plans for events, take an open approach to events (avoiding sectarianism), and share labor in organizing. As an anarchist organization, the Working Group favors participatory, egalitarian, flat (or multidirectional) organizing practices.

The Working Group is organized on an affinity group basis. Rather than a formal, unified, membership, it brings together a core of people with shared interests and perspectives—social affinity—and some level of trust. The Working Group consists of a core of organizers who plan and organize events, do outreach, and organize solidarity actions with community groups around specific campaigns. The core is made up of faculty, students, and community members who have a shared (informal) basis of agreement around specific issues and perspectives (anti-statism and anti-capitalism). Membership, while informal, is not open to all initially, but new members can become part of the organizing core after some time involved with Working Group events and when there is affinity among themselves and group members (on a political rather than personal basis). These are relationships based on mutual respect and trust. Beyond the organizational core, there are participants of all types who support the group and help with events, but who do not want to be involved in organizing. Events are open to all.

The affinity-group approach for the organizational core, with an open approach in solidarity alliances, has been taken in order to provide some insulation against uncritical tendencies among criminology faculty—to keep a radical and activist orientation and commitment in a discipline that has marginalized both. Indeed, some liberal faculty, who are not particularly committed to activism, community organizing, or critical perspectives have sought to join the group and to water down its principles. They are, of course, welcomed at meetings, where they are invited to engage with the debates and discussions. At the same time, the dual approach allows for members to maintain critical support in alliances with non-anarchist groups. Thus a comradely and collegial anarchist perspective can be offered in alliances without hiding or watering down the anarchist orientation in strategy and tactic.

This dual approach allows for development of what some anarchist-communists refer to as theoretical and tactical unity. Rather than cobbling together a mishmash of contradictory or opposing perspectives, in a false or limited consensus, and diluting the commitment to libertarian pedagogy and action, the Working Group approach favors strong internal debate to develop more critical analysis and action. This does not mean that sameness or complete agreement is sought but rather that some agreement is had around key issues *after* and *through* discussion and analysis. The context is always active involvement in real world struggles.In practice, the group has been very open to supporting groups that have different opinions and perspectives, and in public events, the group seeks lively engagement over pressing issues as a means to develop more critical or radical (getting to the root of social challenges) approaches. Experiential learning is also valued, and tasks are rotated and shared where possible. Skill sharing is a means to facilitate a spread of capabilities and skills, rather than keeping a strict separation of skills among members.

Surrey What?! Anarchy in the Suburban Hinterland

Anarchism in North America has largely been viewed as an urban, indeed downtown, phenomenon. Very little attention has been given to and very little written about suburban anarchist projects (apart from a few zines and blogs produced by suburban anarchists themselves). There have been very few discussions of the particular issues facing suburban anarchists.

In addition to the political economic context of the polytechnic university under neoliberal marketization, attention must be given to the suburban context in which the CCWG organizes. There are the specific challenges posed by the sociopolitical context of organizing in a blue-collar multi-ethnic suburb, far away (culturally and politically as well as spatially) from the activist hubs of downtown Vancouver. The CCWG has worked to overcome these obstacles and provide a useful pedagogical and resistance infrastructure.

Surrey is a much-reviled working-class suburb of Metro Vancouver, a shadow city, though far from economically peripheral. It is an epicenter of capitalist megaprojects and strip malls, a sprawling convergence of seven superhighways, and a massive port expansion. With multiple rail lines and pipelines already, it's not enough for developers' greed; the vultures are now running in overdrive mode: politicians in pocket, and ready to roll out twice as many lines. They're pressing hard in order to facilitate the extraction and shipping of megatons more of dirty coal—dug up in Montana and Wisconsin, shipped via rail lines through Washington, out to port here in Surrey, and then sold and burned across the Pacific to return as acid rain. The battle over LNG expansion and fracking is also heating up. Add that to the battle over heavy fossil fuel transport and leaks. Major pipeline expansion projects are actively being fought all the way from Surrey to the Alberta tar sands; the Fraser River and the Salish Sea are tangibly threatened by their refineries and supertanker traffic.

Surrey is a city of migrant settlers. Besides English, Punjabi and Mandarin are the most commonly spoken languages. It is a rapidly growing suburb which became a city itself with sprawling satellite suburbs. Surrey is often outside of the activist cultures of downtown Vancouver, but it has its own overlooked, unrecognized, histories of working-class radicalism. Surrey started urbanity as a gas station, really, on what was a gold miners' trail. It had been, for many thousands of years, the site of indigenous peoples' settlements. The year-round warmth of the green, wet valleys provided excellent shelter and became regular "wintering" villages. The middens adjacent to these settlements can still be found in the rainforest valleys along the southern shore of the Fraser River. These settlements were displaced by British colonial expansion during the nineteenth century. Although that process continues to unfold through gentrification and industrial expansion, Surrey remains one of the oldest known settlements in the world.

The Kwantlen peoples ranged all across these territories, and they still play a vital role in the interconnection and welcome at any All Nation Gathering. Recently, there have been some preliminary steps towards a Truth and Reconciliation Project aimed at uncovering and beginning to address the horrors of colonial rule in the form of residential schools (which were genocidal institutions that stole language and children for too many decades throughout these lands). This area, on the Pacific Ocean, is also Semiahmoo territory (particularly in the south, directly adjacent to the U.S. border). It is—partially ceded, partially hotly contested—Musqueam territory (particularly in North Surrey, which is also now a site of a gentrification push by new condo developments). It is Tsawassen land (to the west, all along the delta where the Fraser River flows into the Salish Sea). It is Katzie territory in the east and up into the mountains. Surrey is unceded territory, contested in multiple layering complex ways.

Surrey is looked down upon by more privileged activists living in activist enclaves in neighborhoods rich in progressive sub/cultural capital (collective cafes, anarchist bookstores, artist studios and galleries, organic food shops, alternative theaters, etc.) and used to more activist-influenced (and familiar) environs. Reliable meeting spaces, let alone cultural venues for shared experiences and discussions, are absent or unavailable in Surrey. The CCWG is attempting to use educational venues and practices to organize infrastructures of resistance in a context in which these necessary resources for struggle are largely absent or inaccessible.

The Working Group has also supported lower-income groups without resources by funding external events, providing organizing space and promotional materials, and by getting funding to individuals and groups through university honoraria. This allowed a significant redistribution of resources for groups and individuals engaged in social struggles. In an area in which durable, reliable, shared spaces for organizing and awareness raising, shared experiences, and mutual aid are too often lacking, the Working Group has provided an often crucial infrastructure of resistance.

The CCWG has played vital roles in specific campaigns in Surrey. For example, the CCWG was a main organizing center for a blockade and occupation camp against development of the South Fraser Perimeter Road, a key artery in the government's planned network of free trade/export processing zones in British Columbia. The free trade zones will be spaces in which environmental and labor protections in the province are suspended for multinational corporations that establish themselves in the province. The road itself had a significant impact on local ecosystems and poor neighborhoods, which faced evictions. The CCWG provided meeting space, organizational work, website support, and material support for the campaign. Even more, CCWG members were active participants in the blockade and provided logistical support (building supplies, food, labor) for the camp, which lasted for several weeks on a road development site. Working Group members also engaged in door-to-door information canvasses in neighborhoods along the road route to provide information about the harms associated with the road. Notably, many people who would go on to take part in Occupy Vancouver and campaigns against pipelines in British Columbia got their feet wet with the anti-road camp; thus this shows the important developmental part played by such direct action campaigns.

The Working Group was also instrumental in launching a broad campaign against the federal government's terror list. The terror list is a political tool used by the government to criminalize people, particularly migrants, involved in peoples' liberation or community defense groups by labeling such groups as terrorist (even when they have no history of terrorist activity). The campaign researched and publicized the political nature of the list (targeting progressive groups rather than actually terroristic reactionary ones) and built solidarity campaigns for people targeted by the government. This has been significant given the migrant, working-class background of many Surrey residents and the fact that groups connected to the migrant communities in Surrey have been listed.

The CCWG has been successful in breaking down some of the barriers to connecting and organizing that have separated not only activists within Surrey, but also activists in Surrey from those in Vancouver. Activists in the downtown have reported to CCWG members that the first or only time they travelled to Surrey (only thirty minutes by SkyTrain rapid transit) was for Working Group events.

Surrey, like most of British Columbia, is unceded indigenous territory. Lands were never negotiated through treaties, and native communities did not give up title to their lands. This fact has been of significance for the group, and it has taken anti-colonialism as a key organizing principle. Many Working Group events are opened with a greeting and welcome from a member or members of the Kwantlen First Nation. Events are opened with an acknowledgment of the land and the first people on whose territories events are held. Numerous events have directly addressed colonialism and resistance to colonialism. Many events have built solidarity with indigenous communities in various parts of Turtle Island (North America) who are struggling against resource extraction, neo-colonialism, violence against indigenous people, and legal system injustices.

People have come to see the Working Group as a valuable and necessary resource for organizing in the Fraser Valley and suburban Vancouver. Notably, in the absence of the Working Group, there would have been no Surrey organizing at all for the anti-terror list campaign, and no anarchist or radical organizing for the Climate Camp against the SFPR.

"Special Purpose Teaching Universities" and the Neoliberal Edu-Factory

The CCWG also operates within a specific post-secondary educational context. It is one that highlights changes occurring within the post-secondary sectors in the Canadian state context. The neoliberal austerity framework and the push to convert universities from institutions of critical engagement to places of industry service (either for jobs training or research geared to commercialization) has shaped Kwantlen's development from a community college in the 1980s to a university college (a near-university institution with a vocational emphasis but a new capacity to grant degrees in limited areas) in the 1990s, to a polytechnic university in 2008. KPU was designated a new "special purpose teaching university" in 2008 along with four other former colleges in British Columbia. As a polytechnic university, among the special purpose new universities, KPU is envisioned by the British Columbia government as an extension of the industrial regime in the province, a labor-market training site.

The Liberal government's intention in converting former colleges and university colleges into the new universities is expressed directly within the legislation that governs the "special purpose" institutions. The new University Act, created at the time the new universities were launched in 2008, states that these are "special purpose teaching universities" and their purpose is to meet the labor market demands and the needs of industry within the specific regions in which the new universities are located. They are distinctly hybrid institutions, retaining trades and technology programs and facilities along with continuing education, university preparation, and university degree programs.

At the same time, the "special purpose teaching universities" are granted fewer rights and opportunities than the established "traditional" universities, which include the University of British Columbia (UBC), Simon Fraser University (SFU), the University of Victoria, and the University of Northern British Columbia (UNBC). Their "special purpose" is clearly labor-market-driven job preparatory institutions. This purpose is reflected in the fact that they are denied government funding for research and scholarship. Research is said to be allowable in the special purpose teaching university's mandate only "so far as and to the extent that its resources from time to time permit" and then as "*applied* research and scholarly activities" (read *job-related*). This applied research and scholarly activity is further limited "to support the programs of the special purpose, teaching university" rather than for the sake of knowledge production, intellectual inquiry, critical thinking, or curiosity. Furthermore, while the research universities are global in scope, the special purpose universities are mandated to serve the (labor market) needs and are their specific local school districts, thus reinforcing their role as job training institutes. The Act further states that the new special purpose teaching universities are not permitted to grant PhDs even where institutional capacity and local need might favor it.

Funds can be raised or saved by the institution for the purposes of research and scholarship, but this is not granted directly by the government for these purposes. This is itself a distortion of what a university is and what purpose it has. It is fundamentally a two-tiered structure of haves and have-nots. This has been challenged in various ways by faculty at each of the institutions.

In addition, the two-tiered university structure in British Columbia is also reflected in the fact that faculty salaries are legislatively capped at the special purpose teaching universities. Faculty there are also denied tenure, although through collective agreements they achieve similar protections.

The neoliberal market focus of the special purpose teaching universities as expressed in the Act is given further form and content in KPU's Aims and Principles and Mission and Mandate Statement. The Mission and Mandate

Statement proclaims: "We value scholarship as a socially relevant obligation and opportunity. We support multiple approaches to research and innovation to address community, industry, and market needs." The Vision Statement explains its vision of the polytechnic university: "A Polytechnic: We emphasize applied education within the context of broad-based undergraduate learning to prepare our students for successful and rewarding careers." And further: "Kwantlen provides learning opportunities that support professional and personal enrichment by responding to the needs of the workforce and the interests of our broader community."

Neoliberalism and Criminology

In the present period of political economic austerity, post-secondary institutions like Kwantlen are pressured by governments and businesses alike to provide dual functions. On the one hand, they serve a function of training the working class to accept increasingly labor-market-oriented, job-related tasks (rather than critical thinking) within a market that is dominated by lower skill, perfunctory, service sector roles. At the same time, the schools also function to provide a detour from the tightened job market for a proportion of the working class, keeping unemployed youth off the streets in a holding pattern that they pay for. For some students, the schools hold the promise of the relative privilege of low-level managerial positions in private industry or state agencies, depending on the discipline. Anarchists have long argued that formal schooling involves inculcation into the dominant norms, values, and beliefs of state capitalist society. Students are taught to internalize acceptable behaviors within this context (rather than to develop values and behaviors that oppose it or provide an alternative). Mainstream criminology has been viewed as a discipline particularly suited to this sort of moulding of dominant, particularly statist, values and priorities.

One might note, in this regard, the veritable explosion of criminology programs designed to prepare working-class students to be police, prison guards, border security, or private security guards. The neoliberal context has propelled the rise and expansion of criminology and criminal justice programs to service the expanding repressive state institutions. Thus these students are prepared to police their fellow working-class neighbors. This is particularly poignant in a blue-collar suburb with a large South Asian immigrant population like Surrey, where KPU is located. Surrey has been subject to numerous moral panics over crime, especially around racialized gang discourses centered on Indo-Canadian male youth.

Notably, this has accompanied a shift away from critical theory and social movements courses in sociology, the department in which many criminology programs are housed and from which others have emerged. While sociology is typically politically of the left and activist influenced, criminology is often more right-wing or conservative. While criminology expands, sociology recedes in some institutions.

The Working Group fights back against all of this. It uses the tools of criminology to analyze and challenge state institutions and practices in the neoliberal period. This includes research into university relationships with industry and the character of corporate agreements with the institution. Thus students and faculty have undertaken research looking at questionable agreements between KPU and Sodexo for food services on campus and exclusivity agreements such as the one that allows for a monopoly of Coca-Cola products on campus. Research uncovered a correspondence between the timing of the Coke exclusivity agreement and the absence of water fountains in a new campus building and the lack of repair on existing fountains in other buildings.

The Working Group also supported a student led campaign against Sodexo. When a student associated with the CCWG tried to distribute leaflets outlining Sodexo's history of labor abuse, racism, prison contracts, and unhealthy food, he was assailed by campus security taking directions from the Sodexo management to stop him from speaking with other students and distributing the information sheets. That campus security should be taking direction from an outside corporate manager was clearly a troubling situation. In response, the CCWG printed thousands of leaflets and began a mass leafleting campaign with information tables on campus. The CCWG also challenged administration to uphold academic freedom for students and call off security, thus allowing anyone to freely disseminate information on campus. Another group of students from the CCWG started a grassroots, cooperative free food distribution on campus, providing healthy vegetarian food for free each day. The group, Friends for Food, was eventually shut down when Sodexo called the health inspector to fine the students and insist on a permit. These struggles are ongoing. Notably none would have been undertaken or pursued without the active presence of the Working Group on campus.

Conclusion: Breaking Free

In addition to providing a needed resource for community organizing, the Working Group has provided a crucial opportunity for undergraduate students to develop a range of skills, both related to their academic interests (research, writing, communicating publicly, etc.) and to their social justice concerns as community members and activists. It has also served as a space to support students who are questioning their future careers as state agents in training. Several students have changed their perspectives on the police and guards as well as institutions such as courts and prisons through Working Group events, discussions, and actions. Several have changed career paths as a result of involvement with the Working Group and its organizing efforts.

Many students from blue-collar backgrounds, who had been told repeatedly that they could not succeed at graduate school or would be wasting their time and should focus on a job, have developed and successfully pursued their interests in grad school and/or gone on to study to become teachers. This is something of a direct material outcome of Working Group organizing. It has some ideological as well as real world consequence in diverting a potential recruit away from a repressive state agency (police, border services, security, prison guard, etc.) and actually results in their active organizing (with fellow students and beyond) to undermine those agencies.

Even more, students and others involved in the Working Group are explicitly engaging with anarchist theory and practice. Anarchism is not an afterthought. It is openly, actively, and centrally present within Working Group activities and discussions. Participants engage with anarchist ideas and analysis and develop anarchistic forms of organizing and interrelating in activist projects.

Students involved with the Working Group have been inspired to do innovative research uncovering hidden histories of anarchist contributions to criminology as a discipline. This work has been presented at numerous conferences and has been taken up by scholars elsewhere who have been provoked or encouraged by the Working Group students' works. Thus the Working Group shows one way in which organizing within a specific academic discipline at a post-secondary institution, even a polytechnic labor-market oriented one, can have a subversive impact with real-world effects counter to those promoted by the institution and government.

CHAPTER 9

Teaching Anarchism by Practicing Anarchy: Reflections on Facilitating the Student-Creation of a College Course

Dana Williams

Introduction

What would happen if a college instructor asked students to design their own syllabus, figure out what they wanted to learn, and run a class on their own? In other words, how would a classroom work if established on anarchist principles? I conducted my own socio-pedagogical experiment within a class on the subject of anarchism to answer these very questions.[1] I wanted to know if the daily practice of anarchy within a course could actually help students to learn more about anarchism (and even become anarchist).

Much teaching scholarship has focused on student learning through service learning projects outside the classroom that make course subject matter "come alive," but very little research has been done on how students learn when the course *structure* is designed to help them learn about a particular subject. This paper presents preliminary findings and reflections on one attempt to do this at a large research-level university in the U.S. Midwest. I conclude that while most students expressed a favorable opinion of the class structure, they also had many concerns and frustrations with its many challenges (e.g., lack of direction and the challenge of making collective decisions).

In 2010, I taught a student-requested course, called the Sociology of Anarchism. Some students I knew from a local bike ride called Critical Mass, with whom I had occasionally discussed anarchism, approached me about teaching a class on the subject. Since no similar class existed at the university, I agreed. The interim chair of the Department of Sociology generously offered to host the class as a special topics course. The students' request indicates that anarchism has been a relatively "hot" subject during the last decade, due to the anarchist movement's growing prominence throughout the world and increased visibility in the mass media.

I identify as an anarchist and as a public sociologist, and I sought to share the many ideas and practices of anarchism with my students. To do this, I wanted students to experience anarchism firsthand in a challenging learning environment. There have undoubtedly been university-level classes that have included or even focused explicitly on anarchism, but to my knowledge none have attempted to *practice* anarchism in the classroom. To rectify this gaping chasm between knowledge and experience, this paper discusses the possibilities for alternative, anarchist learning techniques in college classrooms. What are the opportunities for creating an empowered, self-managed learning environment for students? Specifically, I analyze the varied results and outcomes of this experiential learning course on anarchism. First, I situate the anarchist tradition in respect to sociology (my professional discipline), society, higher education, and learning.

Anarchist Theories and Anarchist Education

Anarchism and sociology share common origins in the modernism of the Enlightenment (Purkis, 2004). Although the two share some common roots, anarchism and sociology have had starkly different domains of influence and objectives. Whereas post-Durkheim sociology mainly sought to *understand* and *manage* society, anarchism sought to *transform* society through the maximization of human freedom (both individual and collective). Like sociology, anarchism has been founded upon both classical liberal and radical aspirations. But modern sociology has been driven by the scientific method and academic interests, while anarchism—in its classical and modern versions—has been led by certain key values, which guide movement participants (Williams & Shantz, 2011).

The values of anarchism stand in opposition to the major institutions that dominated social life during the mid-nineteenth century including hierarchically organized religions, the centralized nation-state, and industrial capitalism (see Dolgoff, 1996; Goldman, 1969; Malatesta, 1995). The traditional aspirations of classical anarchists from this time period have been broadened, and contemporary anarchists seek alternatives to structures and manifestations of patriarchy, white supremacy, heterosexism, bureaucratization, ecological destruction, and other relations that they argue inhibit human freedom (Ward, 1996; Ehrlich, 1996; Milstein, 2010).

In the place of domination, authority, and centralization, anarchists sought (and continue to seek) to transform the social order to create horizontal, decentralized, cooperative, and egalitarian relationships. These values are represented in several key ideas. Anarchism is premised upon a strong form of anti-authoritarianism: no one should be able to tell others what to do or be able to coerce others (e.g., employers, government officials, religious leaders, teachers and principals, military officers, and police). In place of authority figures, anarchists value self-management. People are capable of determining, and should determine, for themselves what they do and when. Individuals should be able to reserve the ultimate authority to decide something for themselves, and not have to rely on bosses or experts. Since individual freedom requires others' help, anarchists also value egalitarian cooperation. People are born equals and should be able to help each other for the common good (i.e., "mutual aid"). Such cooperation requires direct democracy, where people can participate together in such a way that individual and collective needs and responsibilities are satisfied. It is more efficient, empowering, and practical to do something yourself (and collectively with others) than ask or wait for someone else in a higher rank to do it for you. Thus, anarchism prioritizes the worth of direct action, as opposed to indirect, representative action taken on behalf of others.

Most major institutions, including education, have found themselves in anarchism's analytical crosshairs. Anarchists believe that the formal institutions of education tend to be premised upon domination and do not serve the interests of students or learners but rather those of elites. For example, Paul Goodman (1960) argued that the American education system trains students for ends determined by the dominant social system, not the students' own interests. Anarchist educators William Godwin, Francisco Ferrer, and Ivan Illich argued that compulsory, mass education has generally served the purposes of societal elites. Thus, the intention and structural result of such education is to instill obedience to capitalists within the labor market and patriotism toward nation-states (Spring, 1998). While most criticism has targeted primary and secondary education, anarchists have also focused upon universities: Martin (1998) has described the ways in which higher education acts as a complex system of interlocking forms of domination, each resulting in constrained, stunted, and non-free participants.

Anarchist responses to the authoritarian character of standard education do not preclude their agreement with valuing learning, socialization, and knowledge acquisition. Instead, education ought to be motivated and driven by different logics, while being conducted in far different, more liberatory ways. Deschooling has been one prominent position for anarchists: thus Illich (1970) argued for avoiding formal education altogether, perhaps instead pursuing homeschooling or learning in freer environments. Anarchists have experimented with many different types of environments. For example, teach-ins and "skill share" sessions allow people to directly interact with other interested learners and share ideas, without a hierarchical authority figure, while focused on a topic of practical concern. Radical study groups are another space for learning to take place (Rouhani, 2012). Others have organized more permanent projects called "free skools" where learning takes place in a non-hierarchical environment away from official education sites, among learners who want to be there (not have to be there) and want knowledge rather than a degree or a job (Antliff, 2006). Classical-era anarchists actually developed sizable school systems of this character. The "Modern Schools," which provided secular education for working-class children in a liberal and class-conscious environment, are an example from the U.S. (Avrich, 2006).

Anarchist influence can also be found in U.S. universities. During the late 1960s and 1970s, anarchists projected radical New Left ideas into the student movement, influencing both the occupations of university buildings and the foundation of alternative education institutions, such as the anarchist Tolstoy College within the State University of New York at Buffalo. Of particular relevance in this history is the tradition of anarcho-syndicalism which argues that workers ought to try to gain control over their own labor and workplaces (Rocker, 2004). These syndicalist ideas were promoted by non-anarchist New Leftist Carl Davidson (1990) in his essay "Student Syndicalism." According to student syndicalism, learners should control university decision-making, abolish the grading system, and thoroughly incorporate the ideology of participatory democracy. Anarcho-syndicalist ideas applied to an educational setting suggest that students ought to be in control: learning is their responsibility, their project, and done for their own reasons. In other words, learning needs to be controlled, executed, and inspired by students themselves.[2]

Anarchist activists have developed practical techniques for working collaboratively. By prioritizing direct democracy, anarchists value the need for large numbers of people to be empowered to collectively clarify ideas, stake out positions, and work with each other. When many people are involved in direct democracy, anarchists prefer "popular assemblies" that are run by popular will, not by the direction or manipulation of leaders. Preferably, people can find ways of coming to a consensus in decision-making. To practice consensus decision-making, activists have created processes and techniques that help make the decision-making time and space as egalitarian, group-centered, empowering, and effective as possible. A key contribution here is the structural process of consensus-building, spatial tactics (like sitting in circles), small "break-out" groups, a reconciliation method for dealing with minority dissent, and the creation of formal (yet non-authoritarian and rotating) roles including facilitators, timekeepers, and scribes (see Butler & Rothstein, 1991; Cornell, 2011; Gelderloos, 2006). The types of organization desired by anarchists are those that deliberately create such egalitarian, non-coercive, and participatory structures and processes. The anarchistic traditions of student syndicalism and direct democracy were intentionally employed in the aforementioned course that I describe next.

Planning For and Preparing Anarchy

With the ideas and values of anarchism in mind, I realized almost immediately that it would be disingenuous to teach about anarchism in a hierarchically organized classroom. Typically, my teaching is pretty standard-fare for American college classes—complete with PowerPoint lectures, quizzes on assigned readings, and periodic exams composed of multi-choice and essay questions. I understand all the critiques of such a pedagogical approach—and how I am often guilty of perpetuating what Freire (1970) famously called the "banking method"—but I still retain the pedagogical practices that I was educated with during my college experience. I was and remain very uncomfortable with this paradox, thus I wanted to expand my repertoire and test new class formats.

I decided to turn the Sociology of Anarchism class into a mini-laboratory, a social experiment on how to learn without authority figures (i.e., students acting as anarchists to learn about anarchism). I first had to establish some ground rules that would facilitate the experiment. Although I was still responsible for giving a grade to the students at the end of the semester, and the Sociology department required that 25 percent of the grade be based on out-of-class writing, I decided that students should be responsible for deciding how the rest of that grade was to be assigned. For the purposes of the class, I considered anarchism to exist at the intersection between individual freedom and collective responsibility, and that the class structure should reflect that insight. Thus, I followed Students for a Democratic Society's advocacy of student syndicalism (Davidson, 1990); since students were the ones who (hypothetically) wanted to learn about anarchism, they should be in control of that learning. And, since they were going to be sharing the experience with each other, the class needed to be democratically managed. After initially creating some basic course infrastructure and ground rules (see below), I attempted to "turn over the reins" to the students. It wasn't perfect, and all our hierarchical socialization got in the way of the project more than once (Williams 2011), but the class was an amazing experience.

I hoped learning about anarchism by *doing* anarchism was a novel approach. One of the major conditions that determine whether we "learn" something the first time we encounter it is the extent to which we interact with it, appreciate it, reflect on it, and have to take responsibility for learning it. Thus, experiential learning—learning that occurs via our experiences, physical actions, and our own choices—is bound to be more thorough, long-lasting, and hopefully powerful learning. I took for granted that learning through intimate, practical, and firsthand experience was a form of learning more effective than traditional approaches. While my approach was akin to experiential learning, it did not necessitate leaving the classroom environment, thus differentiating it from service learning, field trips, or other simulations.

The class roster filled up immediately, including many students who were not sociology majors.[3] The course overflowed with students, as I continued to sign override requests for students who wanted access to the packed class; I did this on the principle that I should not turn away interested persons simply because of an arbitrary class "cap." Then, most surprisingly of all, three others showed up regularly to the class who weren't even signed up and some who were not even students. Curiously, most of these students attended more consistently than some who were officially enrolled. Apparently, there was a healthy interest in anarchism among students. But, apart from a very small handful of knowledgeable students, very few were aware of what anarchism actually was.

Working on the principle elegantly articulated by Dorothy Day and Peter Maurin of the *Catholic Worker*, that "we must make the kind of society in which it is easier for people to be good" (cited in Day, 1954, p. 217), I decided the most important design imperative for this class was to consider what structure and social norms would allow students to *be* the best possible learners. The structure of a class determines how things work on a daily basis and influences what the general outcomes may be. The social norms of class are what create inertia and establish typical social relations. Thus, by creating a classroom infrastructure that encouraged non-coerciveness, popular democracy, and free will, I hoped students would become empowered learners. With these cultural values in place, students could then focus on the task of addressing the substantive design questions of class objectives and requirements—and thus the true experiment began.

From the beginning of the course, I developed various strategies to accomplish these goals. My first effort was non-interactive: I created a twenty-page, single-spaced syllabus that was packed with ideas for what the course *could* include. I had a lengthy multi-page description of the course's design and just as many suggestions of what I considered useful strategies to have a successful course. There were two sizable blank spaces—course objectives and course requirements—for students to fill in once they had collectively made their decisions regarding these crucial components. Most of the remaining section headings in the syllabus were qualified by the word "possible" (possible readings, films, topics, assignments/projects, etc.) The daily class schedule was completely blank after the first week. On the first day of class, I handed out this lengthy "syllabus" and asked students to study it and use whatever they found useful.

My one imposition of instructor authority was to begin each class period with a short "this day in anarchist history" presentation. For example, on January 12, I presented information about the reading of the "Anarchist

Declaration" during the 1883 Lyon Trial (which included Peter Kropotkin) and the 1996 police raid of the Jacksonville Anarchist Black Cross. My objective was to generate interest in various issues, events, and persons related to anarchism, as well as to inform the students. I asked the students early on if they wanted me to continue this practice and they did.

During the first week of the semester I give a presentation about myself and my history as an anarchist. Then, I gave another presentation critiquing educational systems and different specific pedagogical strategies, which I ended with a description of various alternate strategies used by anarchists in the past. In subsequent weeks, with student permission, I gave other presentations about what anarchism *was not*, presented different models for understanding anarchism, and even a PowerPoint presentation complete with dozens of photographs depicting anarchist protest banners. Later, after class discussion and voting, students requested additional lectures from me, which I happily presented, although I remain unsure of their benefit. Some students were able to listen to a lecture on a subject they were interested in and were able to "soak it up," but what about the uninterested students? Even for interested students, being lectured to can cause them to turn off their critical faculties (being passive is, in many respects, antithetical to anarchist principles of self-determination). And who is to say that I have a definitive interpretation of anarchism that is better than what students might read about, that they may organically develop on their own by acting as anarchists, and so forth?

Perhaps the two most crucial decisions I made to accomplish the goal of "self-empowered students learning about anarchism" was to (1) "require" all students to continue their discussions and decision-making after class time, and (2) utilize the same kinds of decision-making practices that the anarchist movement does. First, I set up a website for the class that used a groupware software system designed by the radical technology collective Riseup.net, called CrabGrass.[4] Via CrabGrass, students were able to (productively, I hope) interact online and further their decision-making processes. CrabGrass allows for discussions, wikis (universally editable documents), and a wide variety of decision-making tools, including surveys, approval votes ("is this good, OK, or bad?"), and ranked votes (where many options can be prioritized at once). Many students were enthusiastic about this software—which is a more interactive and collaborative form of social networking than something like Facebook or course management software like Blackboard—and took it upon themselves to work intensively with the discussions and activities occurring online. For some, online discussions of this nature may be less intimidating than those in a face-to-face setting.

Second, during the first week I discussed the various justifications and strategies for anarchist decision-making in organizations, particularly direct democracy and consensus decision-making. I introduced activist practices, such as the rotating meeting roles (e.g., facilitator, scribes, and timekeepers), sitting in a circle, and even the idea of nonverbally showing agreement by "twinkling" one's fingers. Students widely adopted these strategies in class meetings and justified these adoptions on the basis of utility to addressing the challenges of making decisions among forty-five individuals. I expect it would have been difficult, if not impossible, for students to meet my challenge of making collective decisions without having such strategies and tricks in their repertoires. The students eventually settled upon a super-majority model (two-thirds consent required), where the minority's senti-ments would have to be addressed somehow while the majority would still be able to move ahead with their decision.

Students were given all the necessary rope to pull themselves *almost* all the way clear of the quicksand of academia. Of course, the more rope, the greater the possibility of "hanging themselves" with it, too. I frequently found myself having existential experiences: it was challenging to trust students to do "the right thing" for their learning, even in ways that fly in the face of well-established pedagogical research. More than once, I sat on my hands and bit my tongue when students wandered down paths that I *knew* would be fruitless and frustrating. I regularly felt the impulse of a hierarchically trained instructor to interrupt and forcibly redirect students in a "better" direction. To the extent that I remained silent,[5] I hoped students would be able to discover on their own practical ways of collective problem solving. When I did intervene, it was only to do one or both of the follow-ing tasks: to summarize the overall discussion and thereby illuminate the general sentiment and to make pointed (and often multiple) suggestions that were meant to show possible ways forward. In doing so, I tried to never make my "informed" opinions known and to instead emphasize that the decisions they faced were theirs.

Students designed their own syllabus.[6] They spent the first six weeks of the semester determining the learning objectives, what they would require of themselves and each other, and how I should give out grades. They did all of this democratically, while achieving a near-consensus (with a class of over forty students)! In doing so, they acted completely different from any other collection of students I have ever taught. Students acted as if they were in charge of the class and they took seriously my promise to not act as their boss. Consequently, most students were excited, active, engaged, reflexive, and creative.

Critics might argue that a month and a half is an incredibly long time to dedicate to accomplishing this "preliminary" task, and even that it was a reckless waste of valuable class time.[7] I disagree. My objective was different from the average college instructor: to empower students to have the kind of class *they* wanted. While, surely some students would have preferred to avoid this front-end work, they were in control of it all.[8] Other critics will note that I asked students to do (in an intensive and democratic environment) what a trained instructor does in an essentially authoritarian environment (i.e., decide their own course parameters). Although students may have an intuitive appreciation of course structure from their own classroom experiences, they are unlikely to have any prior experience designing courses. Students' lack of experience and pedagogical theory deficit likely made the whole exercise a bit unfair. Of course, many situations in life are "unfair," yet people find impressive collective solutions to problems and thus learn in the process. I wanted my students' learning experiences to be liberatory: knowing they could actually do this work (create and govern a course as well as learn), and, most impressively, they could do it in a collaborative environment. I next analyze the outcomes of this pedagogical experiment and present evidence that supports my conclusions.

Anarchy in Action

My pseudo-experiment in classroom anarchy was fascinating, exhilarating, frustrating, and more than a little scary. My own reactions often mirrored some of the varied impressions, feelings, and conclusions of my students. There are several important observations that I made from the experience, and I think that these observations illustrate some of the strengths of my approach, as well as some of the predictable weaknesses.

Before describing the course's outcomes, I need to explain the sources upon which I base my observations, arguments, and conclusions. As a participant observer (of a kind) in the course, I watched closely how students responded to stimuli, including each other, and took note of daily activities and notable responses in a detailed diary. I also administered surveys to students at the beginning and end of the course, which addressed a variety of attitudes, opinions, and experiences—the two data points allowed me to track changes in students over the course of the semester. Finally, my own critical and reflexive analyses about this experience, over the course of the last few years, have also been included in the descriptions that follow.

The conscious attempt to decenter my authority was a curious experience. I asked for students to call me by my first name and all did (at least those who addressed me by name). Although this is only a symbolic example of decentering my instructor authority, I think it is important: symbols do have meaning and the prestige attached to a formal label like "doctor" would have modified the classroom environment considerably due to the implications of that word "Dr.," regardless of how much I would insist that it was just a formality. Thus, emphasizing my first name only, (at least) symbolically placed me on a more level playing field with my students. I encouraged students to only use me as a resource and not the final arbiter when they were having class discussions,[9] so I was pleased when students would reference me as "Dana" when I was sitting in a circle with students. They usually did not attach any greater significance to my role, except to acknowledge the fact that I was generally more knowledgeable about anarchism and was the person who would ultimately assign grades (based on their instructions, of course).

From the beginning of classwide decision-making, I encouraged students to form their desks into a circle—a very large, almost unwieldy circle. After a few times doing it, it became the norm and no one even had to encourage others to do it—students simply created a circle on their own. However, few people contributed during these early discussions, so one day I suggested breaking the class into smaller groups. While ostensibly done at random, I encouraged them to count off by traversing the room in such a way as to collect students who do not usually sit next to each other (thus: in groups an equal number of students who chose to sit close to the front who are generally more enthusiastic students and those who isolated themselves in the rear, i.e., often less interested). As soon as students formed these smaller groups, they became useful. Students expressed feeling more empowered in the small groups and they subsequently chose to break the larger class "assembly" into the smaller groups to work out certain problems more intensively, and then reaggregating those groups back into the assembly again.[10] The small groups generated an impressive diversity of ideas that was often helpful for the large assembly, although some ideas would occasionally conflict with other groups' ideas.

My assigned classroom could have held another dozen students. Since students with lower levels of engagement tended to sit toward the back of the room and more engaged students toward the front, there were many empty chairs spread through the room. The students in the rear used their distance from the front of the room (from me, but also from the more talkative students) as a means to "free-ride" during class discussions. In doing so, they were left out and probably deliberately left themselves out more often.[11] This is what Shor (1996) referred to as the Siberia Effect—the isolating geography of classrooms that generates hostile relations simply by their spatial configurations. The assembly's circle helped a bit, as students were all facing each other, but most of the Siberian students were sitting next to each other (silently) and were thus easily ignored. Had the room been more compact and if students had been more interspersed, the free-riding dynamics of the Siberian Effect could have been somewhat mitigated.

I considered calling on students sometimes, to integrate them into class discussions, but I held back, deciding that to do so would have been coercive. If they did not want to participate, why should I force them? In retrospect, I believe I made a mistake. I (or others) could have easily posed questions towards students who had not spoken much, asking if they wished to contribute anything.[12] This is an old facilitator trick (to "spread out" the discussion and allow those remaining quiet to talk), but I tried to act too "principled" in my role of a non-authoritarian instructor. I am afraid my inaction backfired and I compromised my principles of making an empowering classroom for all students. Instead of standing back and relinquishing all obligations, I could have actively used my authority to help create more egalitarianism.[13]

I realized early on, and I understand even more clearly in retrospect, that it is important to give people access to a lot of useful "tools." It is expecting too much of people for them to accidentally develop strategies that took activists generations to perfect. However, it was not enough to simply introduce a "tool" once and expect that it is obvious to use. I sometimes forgot that my own experiences in the anarchist movement took place over many years and that I developed a certain anarchist instinct about things that could not be simply "taught" on a one-time basis. I should have also done a more in-depth tutorial about meeting facilitation, including the values behind it, various strategies to help the group come to consensus, and so on. Yet I expected people to learn facilitation skills easily. I instructed people on how to facilitate and I even modeled it twice, but people usually need many opportunities to experience facilitation—people often need to experience meeting facilitation that works well and experience getting stuck and frustrated. Not enough people in the class were able to become facilitators for the large assembly and thus were not able to have those experiences.

Many people joined the course with the desire to learn about anarchism and were ready to engage with the assumptions that undergird anarchist thought. Such students had satisfactory levels of curiosity, but most still had preconceptions that got in the way of them getting as much out of the experience as I had hoped. In educational theory language, students had previously designed "schema" that already had information hanging on their "anarchism" hooks, likely involving popular misconceptions related to "chaos," "disorder," "craziness," and maybe even "violence". Some of these misconceptions were particularly interesting. For example, I had several criminology and criminal justice students in the class, who I feared would have a hostile orientation towards the course content from the beginning, since surveys suggest that police have abnormally high levels of right-wing authoritarianism (Haley & Sidanius, 2005; Gatto, Dambrun, Kerbrat & de Oliveira, 2010). Surprisingly, many of these students found the subject matter and the course challenges to be stimulating, and even recoiled at instances of extreme police brutality in a film on European squatters that was shown in the class (essentially, the *opposite* of the reaction I had expected). Another student had Libertarian values (which in the U.S. means something very different than much of the rest of the world), while another was very interested in the so-called Zeitgeist movement. I wonder what conclusions such students acquired about anarchism. I expect that some probably decided that "anarchism" was all about "do your own thing," "anything goes," or even DIY (do-it-yourself) politics.

As mentioned above, I administered surveys to students in my class and I discovered that many had very unique and curious definitions of anarchism by the end of the course. Due to my objective of creating an almost completely non-authoritarian setting, I *never* told students exactly what anarchism was or even gave them a basic definition. In retrospect, I wonder if I eventually should have, after they had spent part of the course mulling over the things they were learning and experiencing. I could have helped put the course into broader context and helped tie together many of the disparate threads that I helped to orchestrate, but that they may have never understood, perceived, or took to their logical conclusion. By dancing around definitions throughout the semester, I succeeded in decentering my voice and in allowing students to come to their own conclusions. But, ultimately, there *are* certain core values and tenets to most strains of anarchist thought, and I'm not convinced that students were able to figure this out or learn what those key ideas were.

Constraints of "Anarchy" in a Classroom

Few college classes have likely been entitled the Sociology of Anarchism. In fact, I have never heard of such a class at an established university. Consequently, the experiences in this class can only be characterized idiosyncratically. But, even idiosyncratic observations are revealing and can point the way towards more liberatory methods in other, more widely offered courses.

A universal constraint present in any course that tries putting student syndicalism into practice, regardless of the course's official subject matter, is the hierarchical nature of the university. All college classes offered at tuition-based universities are, on one level, at least, concerned with financial matters. In order for most instructors to spend their time teaching classes, they expect some kind of remuneration (unless they have other employment or economic support). This need tethers most instructors to traditional pedagogical paradigms. They (reasonably) expect that if they are too "unconventional" they will lose their employment. This is particularly true for contingent/adjunct/part-time faculty members, as I was for this course. Such instructors teach only by the good graces of people in power.

When I first received permission to teach the course, I expected to receive some kind of blowback from other university employees, especially administrators. The course was listed with the word "anarchism" in the course catalog, where thousands of students could (and likely did) see it. Surprisingly, most of my colleagues or people with whom I discussed the course had a liberal attitude about it and expressed a certain intellectual curiosity about how I planned to design it. I only received one critical warning, delivered to me in a joking manner. I laughed at the joke (which cautioned me to be careful with teaching student "anarchy" and having them get "out of control,") but I also realized that this joke was, in fact, an *actual* warning, too, and this colleague was probing me to see what my plans were and whether or not they should be concerned.

Since I ultimately had to assign some sort of grades to the students (only the officially enrolled students who would be receiving college credit), hierarchy had already intruded into an otherwise egalitarian classroom. Even if I decentered my role, I still had to be responsible for assigning grades and would be in trouble with students and administrators if I did not. I was also putting myself in a position to create inequality within the classroom if I gave different grades to students. Even though I entrusted this question to my students, their solution was surprising. Before the class began, I strongly expected the students to decide that they would ask me to give them all A grades, something I was willing and prepared to do, if that was what they decided. But, I never mentioned that possibility and—even though I'm certain many thought of it—no one ever seriously raised it during class discussions. Instead, they decided to design a conventional course based around a minimal level of meritocracy and student performance. Students assigned requirements to themselves, including a final project that each individual would choose. I asked students to direct me (in writing) on how to grade each of these projects. While many students did not really know how to do this (and gave me vague direction like "If I do a good job, I should get a good grade,") many established rigorous standards for themselves. But this was still rather arbitrary: one enthusiastic student wrote at the end of their final project report that they felt their work in the class deserved a C only, while another student wrote an almost embarrassingly brief and poor paper and simply stated they should be awarded an A. As the executor of my student's will, I did exactly what was requested in both instances, but I personally felt the grades should have been reversed. Upon reflection, I am not sure what end this unfairness served: the free-riding A student likely learned they could exploit an open situation to their advantages without consequences, while the harder-working C-student perhaps learned the same lesson after realizing the negative consequences for their honesty.[14]

The trouble students had establishing standards for themselves illustrates a broader constraint the entire class faced throughout designing the course: most students have nearly no experience or knowledge about how to do these kinds of tasks. Even though students have *taken* college courses, they have not designed them and do not always possess an understanding of pedagogical reasons for doing certain activities. Thus, my mandate to design the course was more than a bit unfair to the students, since I was asking them to do something independently that they had never done before. Combined with the lack of experience with other sorts of skills, like consensus decision-making, this challenge put students outside their comfort zones—for some this might have inadvertently generated a self-fulfilling prophecy about how they are not good at collectivity. American culture tends to value individualism, although it is usually conceptualized as consumerist independence.[15] When it is time to do other tasks, such as work, pray, or make decisions, many Americans turn to authority figures. Thus, except for already radicalized or anti-authoritarian students, the culture they had been socialized into repeatedly created barriers and inhibited quicker progression.

A lot of time was spent trying to solve problems and address issues, all within confines to which many people normally wouldn't want to be subjected (such as designing a syllabus or figuring out how to grade). The tedium of working under these circumstances exasperated many students, as did the radicalness of their endeavor (designing the entire framework of their course). In this respect, the course differed from Ingalsbee's (1992) "design-a-utopia" course, in which students focused their semester-long efforts on theorizing and planning a more perfect society. In my class, students designed the very "society" they were presently part of, but within strict limits (the room, the grades, a writing requirement, etc.). In this respect, I regret not more thoroughly presenting my lengthy syllabus, which was filled with ideas, on the first day of class. I hesitated because I did not want to unduly influence students with my ideas or preferences, but I now believe that in a situation that has a vacuum of ideas, any ideas (even from authority figures) are good for reacting to. I fear the open-endedness I created paralyzed some of the students.

Another constraint centers on the issue of free will. Before the semester began, I sent all enrolled students an e-mail, describing in detail my plans for the course. I expected some to drop the class (a few did); because of this, I assumed the remainder were, in essence, submitting themselves to these terms and the challenge of designing the course.[16] But, this assumption deserves to be more closely examined. Did the students all *really* want to be there? Judging by the responses of some (especially those in Siberia), they did not. I assume that some were taking the class because they need more elective hours for their degrees and my class fit into their schedule. Thus, were they taking this class because they wanted to or because they "had" to? I would like to assume that all the students took the class in preference to other electives offered at the same time, but I cannot know this for certain. Even more fundamentally, we could debate whether all students in college even *want* to be enrolled. Many students during my years of teaching have told me that they dislike being students in college, but they feel like they must and that college is today required to get even entry-level jobs.[17] Thus, in an unequal, capitalist economy where there is severe labor market competition and where education attainment is a principal way of differentiating between workers, how much free will do college students really have?[18]

Students experienced a sentiment different from having no personal control, as many began to interpret "anarchism" as a form of extreme individualism, which could not and should not compel people to contribute to the overall class. Many students resisted assigning themselves things to read for the class (even though I proposed many pages worth of interesting and pivotal readings in the syllabus) and I suspect that had a two-thirds majority ever been obtained many would still have not read the assignments. I was dismayed to witness this, since so many important things about anarchism can be learned from the countless readings (scholarly or activist) written on the subject. By absolving themselves of collective responsibility to raise the level of class discourse, students were also cheating themselves of resources that would have aided their individual learning (had they wanted to). This illustrates a paradoxical situation between individualism and collectivism, and how limiting or exaggerating one can adversely affect the other.

One final constraint of the class has led me to a troubling political conclusion. I gave students as much power and control as I felt I could, yet not all took or even accepted this power. It was difficult to have a robust direct democracy and, thus, an empowered class of students, if not all were active participants. Unlike the majority of anarchist collectives and affinity groups where there is at least minimal participation or contribution from all members, my class had numerous *entirely passive* members who never spoke in class. This raises the troubling issue of whether or not to *force* people to be collectivist, radical, or participatory if they choose not to be. Presumably, people in a future liberatory society could choose not to participate regularly in matters that affect their daily lives; but, there would also seem to be a breaking-point at which too many non-participants would threaten the liberatory character of that society. I have wondered many times about whether things that I said or did somehow dissuaded greater participation from some of my students, or whether there was an honest lack of desire to participate?[19] If the latter was the case, what are the sources of this deficit (e.g., half the students were first-generation college students with lower-levels of cultural capital), and what could be done to raise the desire for additional responsibility and collective power? However, this criticism may also be unfair since, in a more realistic situation, students would self-select their presence in such a classroom and would have intrinsic motivations for being there and for participating in a framework outside of a meritocratic institution such as a university.

Further Reflections and Future Aspirations

My little pseudo-experiment was not perfect, and there are lots of things I would do differently next time. But it changed my perspective on what is possible (and, judging from exit surveys the students filled out, it changed them, too): students *can* be trusted with control over their educations. At the end of the semester, students reported believing that student involvement in course design was both practical *and* empowering (both 94 percent affirmative).[20] My experiences also validated many of the anarchist assumptions about human nature and potential that I hold dear. But such experiments can also be scary, since teachers are placed outside of their safe space. I found myself in a learning environment that all my professionalization told me shouldn't be allowed to exist. I haven't designed a class like that since, although I've thought seriously about how to democratize many aspects of certain classes. It turns out that I am, like most of my colleagues (and higher education itself), presently too invested in hierarchical social order. But, as an anarchist-sociologist, I'm trying my best to mature my pedagogical approach and teach more anarchistically more regularly.

If most sociologists are using their "sociological imagination" (Mills, 1959) to help them teach (and I think the good ones do this), then anarchism definitely has a lot to offer in the classroom. Transparency in the classroom is essential for students to be informed and brought in to the mechanics of a course structure. It is important to give students opportunities to practice new, liberatory skills, especially those they can use later, outside the academy. Students used all sorts of anarchistic organizing models to accomplish formidable, complex tasks: from small/affinity groups and large assemblies to formal consensus decision-making techniques as well as the CrabGrass software to help prioritize projects, rank preferences, debate options, and so on. Exposing students to alternative forms of social order and new ideas is crucial.[21] As a feminist colleague of mine tells her classes, her job is not to make students feel comfortable in their old beliefs, but rather to provoke critical thought, reflection, and action. A sizable minority of my students were often visibly uncomfortable with the control they were given (45 percent reported experiencing frustration during the semester, according to the survey)—a few times throughout the semester there were subtle requests to end all the democracy and revert back to a typical, predictable course with me making all the decisions. But, in the midst of those discomforting moments, students expressed learning a lot about education, the subject of anarchism, and even themselves and their own collective potential.

Creating a memorable class is important. Just as anarchist artists have introduced giant puppets, stencil graffiti, or guerrilla theater into stagnant protest, anarchist teachers need to create novel environments that will create lasting impressions. Doing something anarchistic (or democratic, or justice-oriented) is going to leave a stronger mark upon students and influence them to think differently in the future than just learning *about subjects* like anarchism (or democracy or justice). To follow this logic, civics or political science classes would be better organized as active democracies, just like most sociology classes would be best structured as practical exercises in creating social justice.

One last, crucially important point for teachers seems to be finding ways to decenter their own roles and voices, especially as "bosses" and "experts." This doesn't mean pushing volumes of empirical research aside (although being critical of academically produced knowledge ought to be permissible) or allowing an "anything goes" environment. The best way for a teacher to self-decenter would be to create a more horizontal, democratic course framework. It seems sensible to allow students (within the reasonable confines of the course subject, I suppose) to select topics that they find more interesting, pick or create projects or assignments that interest them most, and when there are discussions in the classroom, especially among students, a teacher ought to play more of a "facilitator" role than that of a "final arbitrator" (Atwater, 1991). The amazing thing is that any of these things can be done without even mentioning the word "anarchism," although talking about anarchism wouldn't necessarily hurt either. In other words, acting anarchistically is often as important to anarchists as self-identifying as such.

Despite its flaws, the course described here was still a wonderful and important social experiment, one that I would relish the opportunity to replicate. After the semester, I held a potluck at my house. (What could be more anarchist, I asked my students, than a potluck meal?) Students and I then started an anarchist reading group, reading and discussing Cindy Milstein's *Anarchism and Its Aspirations*, and I still hear from my former students to this day. As my first experiment with such a course design I am pleased with many of the positive outcomes and have thought much about how to improve upon the experience.[22] Anarchism is a creative, flexible intellectual framework that can illuminate various pathways to collective liberation, inside and outside the college classroom.

Acknowledgments
Kathryn Feltey, Mark George, Kathleen Lowney, Kathy Slusser, and Suzanne Slusser all graciously provided helpful comments.

References
Antliff, A. (2006). Breaking free: Anarchist pedagogy. In M. Coté, R. Day & G. de Peuter (Eds.), *Utopian pedagogy: Radical experiments against neoliberal globalization* (pp. 248–264). Toronto, ON: University of Toronto Press, 2006.

Atwater, L. (1991): Trading places: Teaching with students in the center and profes-
    sors on the periphery of the principles course. *Teaching Sociology*, 19(4), 483–488.
Avrich, P. (2006). *The modern school movement: Anarchism and education in the United
    States*. Oakland, CA: AK Press.
Bakunin, M. (1970). *God and the state*. New York, NY: Dover.
Bovill, C., Bulley, C.J., & Morss, K. (2011). Engaging and empowering first-year stu-
    dents through curriculum design: Perspectives from the literature. *Teaching in
    Higher Education*, 16(2), 197–209.
Butler, C., Lawrence, T & Rothstein, A. (1991). *On conflict and consensus: A handbook on
    formal consensus decision making*. Portland, ME: Food Not Bombs.
Cornell, A. (2011). *Oppose and propose! Lessons from Movement for a New Society*. Oakland,
    CA: AK Press.
Davidson, C. (1990). *The new radicals in the multiversity and other SDS writings on student
    syndicalism*. Chicago, IL: Charles H. Kerr.
Day, H.C. (1954). *Not without tears*. New York, NY: Sheed and Ward.
Dolgoff, S. (1996). *Bakunin on Anarchism*. Montreal, QC: Black Rose Books,.
Ehrlich, H.J. (1996). *Reinventing anarchy, again*. Edinburgh, Scotland: AK Press.
Freire, P. (1970). *Pedagogy of the oppressed*. New York, NY: Seabury Press.
Gatto, J., Dambrun, M., Kerbrat, C., & de Oliveira, P. (2010). Prejudice in the police: On
    the processes underlying the effects of selection and group socialization. *European
    Journal of Social Psychology*, 40(2), 252–269.
Gelderloos, P. (2006) *Consensus: A new handbook for grassroots political, social, and envi-
    ronmental groups*. Tucson, AZ: See Sharp Press.
Goldman, E. (1969). *Anarchism and other essays*. New York, NY: Dover.
Goodman, P. (1960). *Growing up absurd: Problems of youth in the organized system*. New
    York, NY: Random House.
Greenfield, K. (2011). *The myth of choice: Personal responsibility in a world of limits*.
    Hartford, CT: Yale University Press, 2011.
Haley, H., & Sidanius, J. (2005). Person organization congruence and the maintenance
    of group-based social hierarchy: A social dominance perspective. *Group Processes
    & Intergroup Relations*, 8(2), 187–203.
Hudd, S.S. (2003). Syllabus under construction: Involving students in the creation of
    class assignments. *Teaching Sociology*, 31(2), 195–202.
Illich, I. (1970). *Deschooling society*. New York, NY: Perennial Library.
Ingalsbee, T. (1992) Conceive-a-community: A group exercise for teaching the theory
    and practice of communitarianism. *Teaching Sociology*, 20, 298–301.
Janer, F. *Dawn of the dead: A student narrative on collective classrooms*. In J.A. Meléndez
    Badillo & N.J. Jun (Eds.), *Without borders or limits: An interdisciplinary approach to
    anarchist studies* (pp. 241–258). Cambridge, UK: Cambridge Scholars Publishing,
    2013.
Knapp, T., Fisher, B., & Levesque-Bristol, C. (2010). Service learning's impact on
    college students' commitment to future civic engagement, self-efficacy, and social
    empowerment. *Journal of Community Practice*, 18(2), 233–251.
Malatesta, E. (1995). *Anarchy*. London, UK: Freedom Press.
Martin, B. (1998). Tied knowledge: Power in higher education. Self-published,.
    <http://www.uow.edu.au/~bmartin/pubs/98tk/>
Mills, C.W. (1959). *The sociological imagination*. London, UK: Oxford University Press.
Milstein, C. (2010). *Anarchism and its aspirations*. Oakland, CA: AK Press.

Purkis, J. (2004).Towards an anarchist sociology. In J. Purkis & J. Bowen (Eds.), *Changing anarchism: Anarchist theory and practice in a global age* (pp. 39–54). Manchester, UK: Manchester University Press, 2004.

Rancourt, D. (2007). Academic squatting: A democratic method of curriculum development. *Our Schools, Our Selves, 16*(3), 105–109.

Reddiford, G. (1993). Autonomy and interests: The social life of a curriculum. *Oxford Review of Education 19*(3), 265–275.

Rocker, R. (2004). *Anarcho-syndicalism: Theory and practice*. Edinburgh, Scotland: AK Press.

Rouhani, F. (2012) Practice what you teach: Facilitating anarchism in and out of the classroom. *Antipode, 44*(5), 1726–1741.

Saines, S.B. (2002) The radical syllabus: A participatory approach to bibliographic instruction. *Journal of Library Administration, 36*(½), 167–175.

Shor, I. (1996). *When students have power: Negotiating authority in a critical pedagogy*. Chicago, IL: University of Chicago Press.

Spring, J. (1998). *A primer of libertarian education*. Montreal, QC: Black Rose Books.

Ward, C. (1996). Anarchy in action. London, UK: Freedom Press.

Williams, D.M. (2011).Why revolution ain't easy: Violating norms, re-socializing society. *Contemporary Justice Review, 14*(2), 167–187.

Williams, D.M., & Shantz, J. (2011). Defining an anarchist-sociology: A long anticipated marriage. *Theory in Action, 4*(4), 9–30.

Notes

1   This is not an experiment in the classic sense, since there is no explicit control group. Instead, I compare outcomes from this class to the typical outcomes of college classes, generally.

2   Student syndicalism and student-controlled learning environments are not simply hypothetical—for example, Janer (2013) describes his positive experience with this kind of situation.

3   Students were also disproportionately male (67 percent), white (over 90 percent), and half were first-generation college-students (i.e., lacked college-graduate parents).

4   The software is currently being used by countless radical social movement organizations throughout the world to facilitate decision-making.

5   I usually *did* remain silent during class discussions, but I was only physically absent from class one day, when students executed plans (successfully, I was told) they made the class period prior.

6   A few scholars have written about their experiences allowing students to compose parts of course syllabi (Hudd, 2003; Saines, 2002) or even curriculum design (Bovill, Bulley & Morss, 2011). However, none were as far-reaching and democratic as my students' experience, nor did these other classes synergize the act of composition with the course subject matter.

7   Some of my more conventional academic colleagues expressed alarm about how "long" this took and for how long students were "without" a syllabus.

8   Other skeptics might suspect students were trying to stall the inevitable work that awaited them once course design matters were decided. While possible, my anecdotal observations in class suggest this is unlikely: after even three weeks of discussions there was noticeable apprehension and impatience on the part of

many students. Even those who advocated for prudence and patience seemed sincerely motivated to find the best and most democratic solutions.

9   Mikhail Bakunin (1970) argued that one could consider the intellectual "authority" of a bootmaker when it came to the task of creating footwear, but that final decisions about one's own footwear rested with the wearer of the boots.

10 This process, of course, reflects classic anarchist principles of federation, wherein multiple working-groups or collectivities hash-out specific details that are then channeled back to the overall whole. Incidentally, these efforts seemed to have had an impact: 85 percent of students reported experiencing feelings of liberation during the semester and 88 percent experiencing excitement, according to the survey.

11 While this was clear from body language and posture, it was also shown by my observations of low levels of participation from students in the rear. This should not be interpreted to mean disinterest, however, as only one student indicated experiencing boredom on the survey, while the rest experienced interest.

12 I was pleased that less-participatory students from class tended to contribute more online.

13 This has a more Marxist-Leninist feel to it, however, but it may have been immediately practical if only done once or twice.

14 But I strongly suspect the "C-student" still learned more in class and had a more empowering experience, and thus the impact of the average grade may be less important than other lessons learned.

15 Reddiford (1993) claims that an [individualist] anarchist priority in the classroom or curriculum ought to be autonomy; while not unimportant, this prioritizes individual action over collective creativity and collaboration.

16 Rancourt (2007) describes how his students came "on board" to his project of "academic squatting" a physics course (and then treating it as an activism course). Squat "occupants" had to consent with his project and with mine.

17 Anecdotally, an amazing 93 percent of survey respondents indicated that they felt knowing more about anarchism would be useful in their life after college.

18 See Greenfield (2011) for a critical discussion of "choice."

19 I have suspicions that the former was true, as most of the non-participatory students also regularly attended class; it is *not* that they do not care about the class. Instead, I think their interest was only in receiving a grade and not learning. But, I have no empirical evidence to prove this.

20 Empowerment is important, since it is linked to commitment for future participation (Knapp et al., 2010).

21 According to survey responses, 95 percent of students agreed that participating in designing the course gave them familiarity with methods that "could be used to create a more democratic society."

22 One final observation of note: 95 percent of my students stated they had a more favorable view of anarchism after the course than before and 69 percent even said they had learned things during the semester that made them interested in *identifying* as anarchists.

Of the Streets and the Coming Educational Communities

Toward an Anti- and Alter-University: Thriving in the Mess of Studying, Organizing, and Relating with ExCo of the Twin Cities

Erin Dyke and Eli Meyerhoff

Introduction

When the administration of Macalester College, a liberal arts institution in St. Paul, Minnesota, pushed to end "need blind" admissions in 2005, dozens of students responded with protests, calling this policy "affirmative action for rich people." The administration initially framed their policy of "need aware" admissions as a "financial necessity," but continued protests forced them to shift their rhetoric to a "balance of priorities" between "access and quality," while framing "quality" in terms of a higher ranking in *US News and World Report*. The protesters questioned the legitimacy of such rankings and argued that, instead of a tradeoff, "access equals quality."[1] Despite broad support across campus, the protesters failed to stop the policy change. Yet, rather than seeing this as the end of their struggle, they took their failure as a spur for reflecting on the struggle in a semester-long process. Through their collective study, they found that the inequity they were fighting at Macalester was not unique but part of broader trends across higher education in the U.S.: increasing racial and economic inequalities in access to, and success within, colleges and universities, while those institutions compete for rankings that have little relation to their impacts on local communities (Berg, 2010).

During this time of reflection, the participants came to desire a radical alternative to Macalester: an institution that could serve as both a critical contrast and a base for studying and organizing that would continue their resistance movement. They found a model for such an alternative in the Experimental College (ExCo) at Oberlin College in Ohio, and were inspired to start their own ExCo of the Twin Cities as a social justice–oriented infra-structure for supporting free classes that anyone can take or teach. One year later, a second collective branch of their project emerged at the massive public university in the Twin Cities, the University of Minnesota (U of M), out of three overlapping struggles: an attempt to save a program for racial and economic equity called General College, a graduate student unionization campaign, and a clerical workers' union strike. Despite resounding failures in each effort, the organizers sought to continue their relationships and their movements. In a "People's Conference" for reflecting on the failure of the strike in fall 2007, the protest organizers heard a presentation from an ExCo organizer, inspiring them to create a local chapter of it. Within two years, a third chapter emerged from ExCo course participants in the South Minneapolis Latin@ community, which offered free classes in Spanish.

After eight years of existence, hosting over five hundred courses with thousands of participants, ExCo of the Twin Cities has blazed a unique path for radical study projects. What distinguishes ExCo from most of the fifty or so contemporary free universities and free schools in North America is that it emerged out of struggles within and against normal education institutions. From continuing to engage with those struggles while creating an alternative, ExCo's organizers have developed a particular kind of political project that, if strengthened and spread, could become a powerful infrastructure for radical movement-embedded study. Yet they have faced many challenges. Writing from the perspectives of ExCo organizers (Erin, currently, and Eli, formerly), we offer selected narratives and critical analyses of the challenges ExCo has faced, leading towards our conclusion with a proposal of strategic guidance for organizers of ExCo and other projects of study within radical movements.[2] Taking inspiration from its formative struggles, a driving motivation for many ExCo organizers over the years has been the opportunity to create an alternative university that would, among other things, avoid reproducing the modes of teaching and learning and the overall composition of higher education institutions in the Twin Cities. Instead of the predominantly white, middle- and upper-class knowledges and bodies that were valued at local universities and colleges, we would create ExCo as a working-class institution that centered ways of knowing and learning that resonated with peoples' everyday lives and histories, especially people who existed only on the margins, if at all, within higher education. Despite these desires and our experiments to envision and create a critical university utopia, we often failed in our attempts, with organizers and class facilitators being mostly white and college-educated.

We focus our study on ExCo's first six years (2005–2011) in order to highlight what we interpret as a major shift in its organizing practices. ExCo began through practices of collective, messy studying in-and-through organizing and building "a/effective relationships" of creative resistance to higher education.[3] However, this messy studying of questions and controversies—

around access to or exclusion from higher education and around whom ExCo should serve—often became a source of discomfort. Our analysis highlights the various ways in which organizers tended to short-circuit, or take short-cuts around, these messy, collective inquiries.

Our reflections and analyses of ExCo's early years in this chapter are acts of care and love for the many people, over the years, with whom we have built relationships, agonized over values and vision questions, biked and bussed all over the Twin Cities to put up fliers, studied in ExCo classes, and cooked countless community meals. Our intellectual work is deeply situated within our experiences as longtime organizers, class facilitators, and class participants. In our lives as academics, it is often easy to avoid acknowledging the ways in which the questions we engage are constructed in and through our bodies, places, affective desires, and webs of relationships. The university often claims itself as the "zero-point," or some heavenly location from which we, "academics," have the potential to discover and produce knowledge about the "communities" below, while we are rarely required to reveal our location, our intentions, or our desires (Mignolo, 2011).

Writing this chapter became, for us, an opportunity to question the kinds of simplified and celebratory histories we (ExCo organizers) often tell ourselves about how ExCo came to be. Instead of recirculating triumphal or teleological narratives that would smooth over the tensions that shaped ExCo in practice, we dug into ExCo's archive, excavating seemingly lost conversations and disagreements, in order to paint a more insightful picture. We conducted formal interviews with fifteen past and present organizers as well as numerous informal interviews with current organizers and collected and analyzed nearly nine years of meeting notes, proposals, and other documents. Also, Erin is participating in ongoing visioning discussions that the ExCo collective is undertaking this summer (2014)—visioning discussions that were, in part, ignited by our excavations. The following more detailed retellings and analytical interludes attempt to reveal the labor and relationships of organizers as they unfolded over time. While stories or analyses of radical, autonomous projects tend to skip over or de-emphasize these everyday, affective modes of relating and organizing, they are critically important for understanding how such projects can be sustained and can move closer toward fulfilling their visions. Given our political commitments to the project, we are writing this analysis of challenges that ExCo organizers have faced in order to offer guidance for grappling with these challenges in practice.[4] We construct particular stories about ExCo that we hope will help it come closer to realizing its potential as an infrastructure for fostering radical, movement-embedded study.

In telling stories of ExCo's origins, we find a kind of *indeterminacy* about when and where the project begins. In the first part of the paper, a retelling of ExCo's beginnings, we highlight how ExCo's growth and change cannot be easily ascribed to linear narratives of intentionality and action or clean arcs of progress/growth and failure/decline, but were embedded within the place- and body-political relationships and study of those who were attracted into its project. In the second part, we narrate how, in ExCo's expansion, organizers grappled with tensions from trying to hold together both elements of ExCo's mission: its engagement with university struggles and its creation of a radical alternative. Attempts to deal with these controversies through structural transformation, unfortunately, ended up reproducing some of the technocratic, patriarchal features of the education system within ExCo's own approach.

ExCo's Emergence: Intertwining Organizing, Study, and Affective Relationships

Throughout the struggles around Macalester's "need-blind" admission policy, what at first seemed like a failure became an object of study, inspiring the creation of a radically new project. Miriam, one of ExCo's early organizers, saw a silver lining in this failure to prevent Macalester's "need aware" admission policy: "It cultivated a lot of conversation around access to education." Through these discussions, the participants cultivated desires for creating something new that could realize their ideals. Miriam shared her motivations for this constructive turn:

> there was a handful of us who were interested in continuing the work of thinking about access to education at Macalester and it wasn't me, but someone else had heard of the Experimental College as something that had been done before. I was interested in the fact that it was constructive as opposed to reactive. Some of the ideas that we started to talk about were that it shared Mac's resources with the rest of the community. It was a chance for us to get to know the community better. (M. Larson, personal communication, June 23, 2014)

Although most of the initial organizers were involved in the struggle against the end of need-blind aid, some, such as Callie, were not. She got involved with ExCo when she was a sophomore at Macalester because she was living with her friend, Miriam, who connected her with the project. Before it became ExCo, Callie participated in visioning discussions that led to its birth. She saw it as "a way for people involved in the end of the need-blind aid struggle to put their energy into something else. Over the years, it's become a bigger thing" (C. Recknagel, personal communication, June 5, 2014). On a personal level, she saw ExCo "as a way of exploring education more deeply." On a more collective level, through many visioning sessions, they defined its goals of "challenging the lack of access" and of "trying to get people to think critically about higher education." She saw ExCo making this critical contrast through creating spaces for "participatory education," in which "everyone would have a voice."

The story of the beginning of the second ExCo chapter at the U of M is not a linear narrative of protesters learning about ExCo from a kind of Macalester ExCo missionary. Rather, some of the U of M organizers and Macalester organizers had already built relationships with each other through involvement in other activities, such as the struggle to save the General College at the U of M, which was a program with supplemental instruction and advising to facilitate the transition to college for many working-class people of color who initially did not meet the university's academic requirements. One of the eventual U of M organizers, Arnoldas, had participated in the General College fight, and he also learned about ExCo through reading a zine, *Dames With Frames*, which members of an ExCo class, "Bike Feminism," had created (Arnoldas, personal communication, June 9, 2014). He then took an ExCo class, Anarchist Anthropology, and through that reading group, he became friends with some of the ExCo-Macalester organizers.

A few years ago, Arnoldas moved back to his home country of Lithuania, where he has been involved in organizing the Lithuania Free University. When he tells people about why ExCo was successful, he "often emphasizes the importance of people developing certain relationships over time," such as doing things together after the class, where "it's not always the result or end product that is so visible," but "relationships happen . . . that create a web or network of people doing things together." Arnoldas's own involvement in ExCo started through a complex web of connections: meeting ExCo organizer, David Boehnke, through the Anarchist Anthropology class, then bringing David to the post-strike People's Conference to talk about ExCo, which inspired the creation of a new ExCo chapter at the U of M. Arnoldas's relationship with David, and his desire for the study of anarchism, converged with another political trajectory in his life: he engaged in solidarity with the clerical workers' strike, most dramatically by participation in a four-day hunger strike that involved an encampment in the middle of campus where hunger strikers spoke with passersby to raise awareness of the main strike. Over six years after the failure of this strike to achieve the workers' demands, Arnoldas reflected that one of their main motivations for creating a new chapter of ExCo was "continuing to have a certain space where either confrontation or critique or a different kind of engagement with the U could happen." Reflecting on their "feeling of failure," they wanted to address the seemingly intractable problem that "not only the U administration is the oppressor but also a certain disengagement of all the other actors that were constituting the U"—e.g., when on hunger strike, they heard "occasional comments from passersby such as 'these workers are a labor aristocracy.

We are in an even more precarious position."' They felt it was important to create "a critical space" for engaging strategic questions inspired by these experiences. Similarly, Lucia describes the need for this critical space out of her experiences organizing in support of the clerical workers' strike: "And thinking about who the university is for is what made me think about starting ExCo because I wondered if the University isn't for the people who work here, is it even for anybody who doesn't work here? So, who is the University for?" (L. Pawlowski, personal communication, June 1, 2014) In their quest to build an alternative and anti-university, for Arnoldas, Lucia, and many others in ExCo, anxieties then surfaced about who ExCo should be for.

During ExCo's first two years, centered around student groups at Macalester and the U of M, its organizers created an alternative organization for radical study and insurgent relationships, built out of reflection on the failures of university-focused struggles. Organizers not only created spaces for such study in classes, but they also made space-time in their own meetings for study of the messy tensions that striated their mission—especially between ideals of changing the existing higher education institutions and creating alternatives to them. These tensions were present in its beginning, but organizers discussed them in increasingly serious ways in relation to ExCo's organizational structure, building to a crescendo in 2009. Their collective study was both motivated by and gave rise to concerns over *how* they would avoid becoming just another exclusionary university. These discussions dove into complex controversies over how to understand "community" and "education," which interwove with tensions over values and principles (e.g., Should ExCo be "politically neutral"?) and organizational questions (e.g., How should ExCo define its structure in relation to the university and various communities?).

From ExCo's beginning at Macalester, its organizers had expressed desires to diversify the demographics of who was organizing, who was facilitating, and who was participating in classes. Organizers saw a contradiction between their ideal of opening access to higher education and the reality of mostly white, mostly class- and education-privileged participants in the project. With the expansion to a second organizing chapter based at the U of M, this contradiction sharpened, as the doubling of the organizers merely replicated another university-centered collective and failed to significantly diversify ExCo's demographics. Organizers' anxieties about this tension were heightened in 2008. David talked about the need of "a plan for how to make a more diverse group of participants and organizers" (D. Boehnke, personal communication, February 8, 2008). At a visioning session, organizers articulated multiple tensions within our definition of how what education should be: "Free. . . . A process of community resource mapping, and as such, build upon and strengthen existing communities and movements. . . . A good in itself. . . . A way of bringing people together for social equality and justice" (notes from visioning session, June 22, 2008). Amy, an organizer and grad student at the U of M, described a tension: "how much do we want ExCo to be attached to the university and how much do we want it to be attached to communities outside the university?" Arnoldas also spoke about this tension and argued for an approach of "one foot in, one foot out," recognizing the need "to keep ties to the historical origins of our chapters (Macalester with exclusion and U of M with labor)," and "to do the community work, but also to simultaneously challenge the structure of the university." Eli noted, "We need to problematize the distinctions and boundaries between university and community."

The organizers' discussion of these important tensions was prompted by questions about how to define ExCo's shared values and vision. Yet they articulated so many controversies across their different desired ways of defining these values and visions that they were unable to agree upon a proposed organizational structure. In response to a proposal of autonomous chapters and class-creating collectives around different issues, Miriam raised the questions of "how we communicate our relationship to social movements," and of how social movement–oriented classes could "break down fragmentation" between movements. She argued that "the more important issue is setting the tone for teachers about what we're looking for . . . not so much about disapproving classes, but about being proactive about what we're approving." In this discussion, a central question was how chapters should define their autonomy from each other and their relations with each other while having a citywide core that shares common resources and values. Some attempted to shortcut around this discussion: for example, Dan from Macalester argued for extreme autonomy of the chapters—that "each chapter is free to decide" on how it defines its political approach. By contrast, others argued for continuing to engage these tensions in further collective study, such as in Arnoldas's plea that "whether we work more apart or closer, we need a time where we can autonomously communicate with each other." He acknowledged that this "communication contributes to this feeling of ambiguity that is frustrating," yet he insisted that we should continue to reflect and "try to work out a way to have both communality and autonomy." The group as a whole sided with this plea for continued study.

With their organization structure remaining informal and improvisational throughout the summer of 2008, some organizers embarked on experiments envisioning ExCo's relations to communities and universities. They built relationships with communities that were marginalized from higher education. They talked with workers at already established nonprofit institutions, including Project for Pride in Living, the U of M's Community Service-Learning Center, and the Waite House Community Center. The latter focused on serving a primarily Latin@ community in South Minneapolis. Relationships with people in this community, mediated through the Waite House and its staff, eventually blossomed into a major innovation in ExCo's organization: a new chapter called Academia Comunitaria.

After a class on media representations and independent media was scheduled in Spanish at the Waite House, participants in the class approached the director and asked for more.[5] Enthusiastic about this development, the director approached ExCo organizers to fill in their Saturday programming with ExCo classes. Several productive tensions soon emerged. First, while ExCo offered an outlet for the community center to create the types of politicized programming that it otherwise would not have been able to create, the legal restrictions on the space in relation to childcare and food, both of which they wanted to offer, made the organizing unexpectedly expensive and bureaucratic. Moreover, by starting immediately, they did not develop the base of awareness, relationships, and community involvement—particularly as organizers—from the breadth of the population they were trying to serve. Productively, this meant that the organizers refused to stand in for the community and its desires, but it also resulted in two sets of classes that, while impressive, were not thriving as much as the director hoped. What resulted was the closing of open Saturdays for education, as well as the withdrawal of the time of the two paid staff organizers at the center. This could have been a disaster for the project. What saved it was twofold. First, the community center had compiled the phone numbers of past participants, which ExCo was given when the collaboration ended. Second, a set of innovations emerged from the process: volunteer infrastructure for providing free childcare (which became the Twin Cities Childcare Collective), doing public presentations at food shelf distribution days, and having a seasonal reflection dinner where past participants, facilitators, and their friends and family, as well as organizers, were invited to come together to talk about what they had to share, what they wanted to learn, what they envisioned for ExCo, and what it would take to make it all happen. The Academia Comunitaria emerged out of these discussions, becoming ExCo's third organizing chapter. By the spring of 2011, a quarter of ExCo's courses were in Spanish.

The expansion of ExCo to three chapters greatly increased its organizers' capacity to host classes—building up to over seventy courses in spring 2011. Yet their shift in operations also forced the organizers to confront anew the messy controversies about their shared vision, values, and organizational structure. They began to revisit these discussions in May 2009, as Academia Comunitaria was getting started (notes from Visioning Session, May 14, 2009). They discussed whether ExCo's organization should be seen as a network of autonomous collaborating chapters, a collective of collectives, or a single organization. Despite having intense, elaborate discussions about these tensions, they were unable to reach consensus. They sent the question to a committee for generating a proposal, but the committee seemed to have lost its charge, and thus the questions about ExCo's organizational form were left open. At another visioning session a year later, some organizers felt that their capacities were overloaded with the work their expansive mission forced them to take on.

Analysis Interlude 1

Drawing together threads from the narrative above, we believe that the most important aspect of ExCo organizers' approach was their messy, mixing up of organizing with studying and relationship-building. In response to the complex mess of the world in which they found themselves situated, ExCo organizers created space-times—in classes, meetings, and other events—for grappling with their controversial questions around how to understand and engage with the world.[6] In their ongoing discussions about ExCo's values, visions, and organizational structure, despite "failing" to come to a settled, unified agreement, ExCo organizers still developed makeshift understandings that guided their fluid, informal approach.

Reflecting on these messy practices of studying-organizing-relating, we can better understand what was good about them through drawing lenses from theoretical literatures. The constituent moment for ExCo organizers involved, simultaneously, a "yes" and a "no." They said "yes" to the pleasurable experiences of studying and relationship-building that higher education institutions (sometimes) offered, and they said "no" to the limits on that studying, in terms of its limited access, quality, and associated modes of making the world. After dealing with the tensions between this "yes" and "no" through their attempts to reform the institutions, and reflecting on the failures of these attempts, they regrouped to form new practices for grappling with their tensions. These practices of study coalesced into the relatively more settled, formal institution of ExCo—yet, through continually studying these tensions, they forestalled any finalizing or fixing of ExCo's institutional form.[7] Organizers had unwittingly innovated a way to avoid reproducing one of the main functions of education institutions: the pressuring of students to subscribe to the fixed identities and life-trajectories of liberalism (e.g., a student becoming a graduate, pursuing a career, making a heteronormative family, becoming a voting, law-abiding citizen in a liberal democracy, etc.).[8] Rather than inscribing students with desires for "unified, coherent, bounded selves," ExCo's messy studying-organizing-relating corresponds with practices of affirming and grappling with "ambivalent, incoherent, porous selves."[9]

An expression of these "ambivalent selves" is seen in the tensions within ExCo organizers' understandings of their motivations for ExCo—e.g., between loving experiences of studying and hating the alienation in normal education. At ExCo's best, the organizers made it into a project for creating space-times in which they could play/work with these tensions, in meetings and classes (Dyke & Meyerhoff, 2013; Katz, 2011). Organizationally, their desire to grapple with such ambivalences was seen in their discussions of overlaps between the "roles" of organizers, facilitators, and participants. Also, this was seen in their discussions of relations between universities and communities, and of their ambivalent and transgressive memberships within/across/against/beyond the normalized borders of these groups.

The intertwining of these affective relationships in and through studying in ExCo classes and organizing was the basis for the organizers, particularly the new ones from Latin@ South Minneapolis, to decide to form Academia Comunitaria as a means for continuing their messy organizing-studying-relating. Thereby, the organizers did not resolve their ambivalent selves into some new coherent unity but rather opened up new channels for communicating about these tensions with each other. The relationships and discussions across the chapters were across the usual segregations between people who experienced their "ambivalent educational selves" in significantly different ways: the Academia Comunitaria organizers/facilitators/participants, many with undocumented status that excluded them from higher education, and organizers from university-based chapters with privileges in terms of race, citizenship, class, and education. The "no" of Academia organizers enacted implicitly through their embodied experiences of crossing colonial borders and evading police, and their many "yeses"—desiring study to maintain their communities and learn skills and knowledges—offered new tensions for ExCo organizers. The burning question for ExCo organizers, then, was how to reenvision their institution in ways that could expand their messy study-organizing-relating around these new tensions—while, simultaneously, maintaining their capacities for engaging with such messiness against the continual pull to give in to their anxieties from inhabiting ambivalent selves in contrast with modernist, liberal fantasies of unified selves.

The Shift to "Community-Led" Chapters: Slippages, Short-Circuits, and Aversions to "Mess"

After the expansion of ExCo to three chapters, organizers were able to host, publicize, and support many more classes. Yet with this quantitative expansion came critical questions around whether and how ExCo could maintain integrity to its principles. The increase of classes lived up to one half of ExCo's constitutive mission: its ambition to create an alternative institution for study. Yet they had no clear connection with the other half of ExCo's mission: to become a means for resisting the dominant education institutions. In 2010, organizers theorized this split as a tension in their imagined possibilities for ExCo's future. Based on our reading of meeting notes, we saw these tensions in the form of three narratives simultaneously in play. One narrative was that, in the U of M chapter, organizers attempted to reconnect their ExCo organizing with struggles at the U of M.[10] The other centered on efforts to create "community-led chapters," taking a model from Academia Comunitaria and trying to replicate it with other "communities." The third involved discussions of the structural transformation of ExCo's organization.

In spring 2010, the organizers in the U of M chapter anticipated that their group was entering a period of crisis. They noted that "there are only a few organizers who are students at the U; we need at least 5 to re-register as a student group" (U of M chapter meeting notes, May 26, 2010). In addition to this pragmatic concern, they were most focused on reconnecting the chapter with its "rooted history in the struggles at the U," aiming "to get more participation, build coalitions, and take part in struggles from within the University." As an idea for how "to get people involved and participating," David suggested that "we have a concrete goal, like working for course credit." The pursuit of this concrete goal, as well as several others, became the U of M organizers' focus throughout that summer and fall. At another meeting, they fleshed out the goal of getting course credit into a multi-pronged strategy: students would get credit at the U for taking classes through ExCo and the content of these classes would engage the participants in organizing at the U, such as classes on "speed-up, access, and organization at the U in the last 50 years," on "radical history at the U," and on "visions for a new university" (U of M chapter meeting notes, June 30, 2010).[11] Getting credit would be a way to give people "more time to do the organizing they want to do and also as a way of having more organizers," while being "self-reflective . . . about involving different people from across the U." The organizers recognized that "the really hard part is the credit part," particularly through building relationships with faculty at the U who could give students credit, such as through an independent study course or service learning. To address this challenge, they devoted several meetings to planning a reflection dinner with professors and others who might be interested in receiving credit and organizing projects.[12] The principle behind this project was the idea of "inflating the credit," which we borrowed from a social center in Rome called ESC.[13] They framed this project in relation to a wider aim of "Building a movement for free education and a democratic university at the U of M."[14] In planning for the reflection dinner, one of the guidelines was to "talk up the point that we're experimenting; we're running it ourselves, so it's going to be a little messy."[15]

The reflection dinner resulted in a rich discussion with several current undergraduate and graduate students at the U. Despite having months of preparatory planning and outreach, however, no faculty came to the meeting, thereby reinforcing the organizers' sense of frustration at the challenge of inspiring faculty involvement. Over the years, a few students figured out ways to gain credits for involvement in ExCo as either facilitators or organizers, but ExCo has yet to implement a program with the expansive scope and ambition to "inflate the credit." Yet the discussions at the reflection dinner did lead to another project: a "Disorientation Gathering" at the U of M, which took place on October 7, 2010, the National Day of Action in Defense of Education, and during Ethnic Studies Week. Picking up on the "disorientation" concept from Disorientation Guides that radical student groups had made at other universities to counter the usual orientation that new students receive, the Gathering sought to "disorient" people through "unsettling dominant understandings of the U and its history" as well as to "reorient" through "helping situate current organizing in relation to a broader history of struggles at the U."[16] Ideally, the Gathering was also supposed to channel "some of these new relationships and collective energies into creating new classes through ExCo." The Gathering event went well—with around forty attendees who participated in a popular education–style activity, discussed their ideas for issues around struggles at the U that they would like to study, and heard speakers on contemporary and historical struggles.[17] Despite the Gathering not clearly resulting in any new ExCo classes, it did contribute to building relationships and collective passions that coalesced into the most powerful project around education organizing at the U that year: the "Whose University?" movement, which was a massive collaboration of over a dozen student groups focused on struggles at the U around access, maintaining cultural space for students of color, and saving the Ethnic Studies departments in the face of budget cuts.[18]

Although much discussion at U of M chapter meetings focused on reconnecting ExCo with struggles at the U, organizers devoted equally as much, if not more, energy to creating new community-led chapters on the model of the Academia Comunitaria. We tried to see overlaps between these two narratives—e.g., to "think about the U of M chapter as a communities-based chapter itself with goals to be involved in struggles with wider U community and surrounding communities like Cedar-Riverside."[19] Yet in practice, they had little overlap.

At the peak of ExCo's organizing strength in fall 2010, the U of M chapter decided to split its energies into two directions: one relating to struggles at the U of M and the other toward creating a new ExCo chapter grounded in "the South Minneapolis radical/anarchist community."[20] Looking back at this decision, its timing seems quite strange, immediately after the Disorientation Gathering, an event to which we had devoted three months of planning. Perhaps we felt disappointed, as that event had not lived up to our expectations of serving as an incubator for ExCo classes around U of M struggles—piling another failure on top of the attempts to collaborate with faculty on inflating the credit. The rationale that the organizers gave for creating this second chapter was that we had "two bases of relationships," one at the U of M and the other in the DIY/anarchist community, and some in the group, those who were not students, were not well-connected or invested with the U base and struggles. At least some organizers said that we should prioritize building the U of M chapter and its organizing base, because of its constituent mission in those struggles, and to make the anarchist chapter a second priority. However, the course of the next few months would see the organizers veering away from their focus on the U of M and moving towards a focus on the new anarchist chapter, which became known as the South Side Free Skool (SSFS).[21] Part of their reasoning for this move was framing the SSFS through the "community-led chapters" model, seeing it as having a more clearly defined "community" in comparison with the U of M.

Another reason to expand to community-based chapters beyond the U was that organizers wanted to break out of ExCo's centering of higher education institutions, which reinforced their self-validating position at the top of the education pyramid. The creation of the SSFS chapter as well as two other attempts to create community-based chapters in particular neighborhoods—Cedar-Riverside and Hamline-Midway—allowed for the possibility of broadening ExCo's mission to include engagement in struggles around education more broadly, in the realm of P–12 education, an area that is often treated in more feminized ways. Many Macalester ExCo organizers were gearing up for graduation and felt that since their institutional membership was nearing its end, they wanted to create a community-based chapter that they and others could be involved in long-term. Jason explained that he was also tiring of the "not-so-sexy" work of logistics and e-mailing facilitators and wanted to engage in "relationship-based activism that's about changing hearts and structures."[22] He said he felt the most energized in ExCo when he was doing neighborhood-based organizing. They attempted to reach out to community residents and leaders in Hamline-Midway, a diverse, working-class neighborhood nearby Macalester to find potential class spaces and facilitators. Similarly, some U of M organizers built what initially seemed like a solid base of organizers within Cedar-Riverside, a border neighborhood bordering the U of M whose residents were mainly East African refugees. Yet in both neighborhoods, decreasing organizer capacity, and the complex politics and desires of neighborhood residents that did not quite fit the model that Academia had created, led to their eventual collapse.

The third simultaneous narrative in play was a kind of meta-narrative in relation to the other two. The organizers attempted to figure out how to maintain and strengthen their capacities to organize together in light of challenges brought on from the multiple, new directions in which they were taking ExCo, while continuing to provide their regular level of support for courses each semester. Their approach took two main forms. One approach was simply to expand and intensify the messy process of relating/studying/ organizing in the space-times of reflection and visioning meetings. The other approach, proposed in and through such meetings, attempted a structural transformation of ExCo's organizational form.

At a citywide organizer retreat in November 2010, the organizers articulated their diverse experiences with these challenges. Jason, a Macalester organizer, noted that "citywides are not convenient for both chapters [Macalester and Academia]," and that student organizers have difficulties making time for citywide meetings, especially when they are located far from their homes (Rodney, J., personal communication, June 12, 2014). Andrew M. emphasized the challenges of becoming involved and fitting in as a new organizer: "despite hearing that there is so much to potentially be done, but we don't have the organizer energy or capacity, I'm unclear about who is doing what and what's not getting done." Ayanna echoed this concern: "People might not get equal access to organizing." Christian, an Academia organizer, emphasized the strain on their capacities in the Academia chapter: "It's only three or four people doing everything, and mostly just two people doing it by phone and email. There's a lot of ignorance about Latin@ culture. It's hard to invite people into ExCo—people are looking for resources, trying to work and deal with needs, not enjoying life." Rita raised her concerns "around balancing energy levels—I want to give more and to also take care of myself, and not ask too much of others." Erin and others echoed this burnout concern and also pointed to the need for better communication among organizers.

In response, they also suggested various approaches to these problems. Reflecting back on them now, we see two general tendencies, as either more formal or informal. The more formal approach was to argue for structural transformation with new organizational roles: inter-chapter liaisons, go-to persons, treasurers, and secretaries. In the most extreme version, some organizers built on the concern with fundraising problems to push toward creating a nonprofit, a 501c3 organization. The other, more informal tendency was to create more opportunities for communication. This was seen, for example, in Kelly L.'s call for more "cross-chapter participation, and citywide communication" and in Erin's noting that "citywide meetings are a good space, but there is not enough time. Could they be more often and more regular?"[23] These formal and informal tendencies overlapped and some organizers pushed for both: e.g., Kelly called for "inter-chapter liaisons" and Erin said that, "We could use more clearly defined roles." Yet certain organizers, particularly a few male organizers (including one of us, Eli), pushed more heavily than others for the more formalizing, structural transformation approach, which ended up winning out.

The tension between these two approaches was expressed repeatedly at meetings. In a discussion at a U of M chapter meeting, everybody expressed that they felt low energy.[24] This was problematic because we had just implemented a new organizing structure that required each of us to put in more energy to take on new roles. Despite talking so much about the organizing structure, organizers' bodies and affective relationships were not energized sustainably enough to give life to that structure. Going into 2011, the organizers ran out of steam and could not continue to hold together all three of the narratives at once. Since the plan for structural transformation was biased toward the parts of its mission that were replicable (the "community-led chapters" model), when the plan became relatively solidified, that part of the mission won out: de-emphasizing struggles at the U of M and focusing on creating new chapters while continuing the usual "business" of ExCo's operations. Faith in the new structure and a replicable model allowed organizers to take shortcuts around dealing with ExCo's controversies. Yet its tensions continue to bubble to the surface.

Analysis Interlude 2

Reflecting now on the problems that we saw arise during and after ExCo's transition from the height of its capacity in 2010 to its structural reorganization in 2011, we make a similar diagnosis to the one we made about ExCo's earlier period. Again, the things we can look back and affirm about ExCo emerged in and through the organizers' messy process of organizing with studying and relationship-building, while its failures occurred from attempts to take shortcuts around, or short-circuitings of, this messy process. These shortcuts and short-circuitings were multiple and complexly interconnected, but we can group them into two main types.

First, the eventual gendered dominance of the formal organization tendency was legitimated and effected through a structural proposal that was written from the perspective of top-down, technocratic expertise. Although ExCo organizers were facing problems in realizing ExCo's mission as a whole, in both the oppositional and propositional parts, rather than focusing on the failures in all of these parts, the various forms of the proposal highlighted the successes of one form of the propositional part, the "community-led chapters" model, and sought to "transform all of ExCo on this model."[25] The proposal took on a kind of "zero-point epistemology," i.e., seeing the world from a "God's eye" perspective above rather than from perspectives grounded in people's particular embodied, place-located experiences (Mignolo, 2011). Such an approach also relies on a view of the world as split into a binary of the realm of representations, correct knowledge of which is produced by experts, and realm of the represented (Mitchell, 1999). This desire for the certain settled knowledge of expertise was seen in the proposal and in discussions promoting it. Concerns about the current organization were expressed as "a tendency to get stuck in uncertainties" and "confusing communication dynamics." In contrast, the proposed new organizational form (of community-based chapters and citywide organizing teams with go-to people) was to have "chapter functioning that is much more simple," and deploying abstract phrases to signify this desire for certainty in organizing relationships, such as "a critical mass," "a solid place," and "structure."[26] In previous visioning sessions, organizers grappled collectively with and built affective relationships through their *disagreements and debates* on ontological-political controversies between organizers at the citywide level (especially the questions of what *are* ExCo's political values and how should those *be* implemented through organizing). These discussions drew on their body-and-place particular epistemologies and emotionally grounded motivations for commitment to the ExCo project. With the top-down structural proposal, what were seen as political-ontological conflicts and arguments between organizers (as emotional, historical beings) over ExCo's composition—i.e., the ontological questions of what values *are or should be* in its constitution— became reframed as problems of distorted communication (on a collective level) and uncertainty (on an individual level) over a pre-settled, correct knowledge of an already agreed upon set of values and visions.

Second, directly related with the expertise-driven, top-down proposal approach was a move to implement *roles* in the organization, including the citywide secretaries, treasurer, and the go-to persons. Organizers were expected to develop expert knowledge of how to perform their role. The euphemism "go-to persons" *intentionally* masked the technocratic aspects of the role; they also considered calling them "managers" or "coordinators." They reproduced a key element of the higher education institutions against which ExCo's mission had been in antagonistic relation (i.e., expert administrators who rule over hierarchies of persons and knowledge). Taking on subscriptions to such fixed identities served to deaden ExCo's messy, playful experimentation. More settled roles in the organizational structure hardened the distinction of organizers from facilitators and participants. Also, the "community-led chapters" model engendered more settled identities of particular "communities," and a tendency for university community chapters to take on a "privileged allies" identity in relation to "oppressed" communities.

Looking back through the meeting notes, we see that, generally, female organizers tended to push for holding the reflection and retreat meetings, where playful, messy studying-organizing-relating had room to take place, while male organizers pushed more for the structural transformation meetings that were centered on business and perceived as solutions to problems of inefficiency. This gendered division of labor reproduced patriarchal norms that associate femininity with emotional, reproductive labor and masculinity with supposedly emotion-free rationality and getting business done. A related trend of how such patriarchal norms infiltrated ExCo organizing practices is seen in how women organizers (especially Kelly Lundeen) tended to contribute the bulk of the reproductive labor of translating and interpreting English and Spanish at the citywide meetings. Likewise, the Childcare Collective was women-led and mostly women offered their caring labor through it.

These contributions of non-cis-gendered-male organizers—renewing relationships in retreats, translating, and childcare—were all essential ways of fostering and maintaining affective relationships across normalized segregations of race, class, citizenship, age, language, etc. These more micropolitical practices could be seen as creating potential points of synergy with a more macro-political institutional shift that ExCo was attempting in its shift to "community-led chapters." That is, against the pyramidal education system's norm of feminized P–12 education and masculinized higher education, ExCo's shift toward a "community-led" model was at least partly motivated by a desire to de-center the universities. Unfortunately for the prospects of the projects undertaken with that shift, the organizers did not clearly articulate this motivation, and other motivations dominated that were more about pragmatically *avoiding* rather than engaging the challenges of ExCo's complex political controversies, both within and beyond its organizing group.

Conclusion

To enable this subtle move from political-ontological debates to epistemological, expert-led problem-solving, the organizers subscribed to certain abstractions as guiding ideals in their model: "community-owned education" and a "diverse, community-based institution" with "community-led chapters." These abstractions were seen as representing an already agreed upon core set of values, in contrast with how these values were continuously up for debate, disagreement, and study in ExCo's early years. Subscribing to abstractions of "education" and "community" offered shortcuts around the difficult controversies over ExCo's political values and visions. Organizers' romanticizing of "community" was seen in their assumption of a coherent "South Minneapolis DIY/radical/anarchist community" around which to organize the new South Side Free Skool chapter (though some critical questions were raised about its internal differences).[27] Likewise, in talking about Academia Comunitaria, they often reified the idea of a "South Minneapolis Latin@ community."[28] Their romanticizing of both education and community was seen also in their name change to Experimental Community Education of the Twin Cities, in response to the threat of being fined by the Minnesota state government for having "college" in their name. Alternative possibilities were suggested that would have avoided formalizing the community education model: including "Experimental College of the Twin Cities," "ExCo of the Twin Cities," and "using an indigenous word for school."[29] Also, the Spanish translation that we decided on ("Educación Comunitaria Experimental de las Ciudades Gemales") contains an interesting reinterpretation of "community" as "communitarian," which shows a tension in our understanding.[30]

Instead of settling on abstractions of "university," "community," and "education," radical study projects simultaneously within, against, and beyond education institutions should make more and better opportunities for the messy processes of studying, organizing, and a/effective relationship-building. The move toward a more "efficient" organizational structure with expert management roles enabled us to avoid the discomforting challenges of relating with people at the U of M and in surrounding neighborhoods who embodied different worker positions and demographics. This also reinforced our romanticization of "education"—we avoided dealing with the ways in which participating in ExCo was seen by some communities as a luxury activity; communities (folks in Academia, and in the fleeting Cedar-Riverside and Hamline-Midway chapters) that were more focused on surviving, finding resources, trying to work, and dealing with needs, as Christian, an Academia organizer, pointed out in one of our visioning sessions.

Presently in ExCo, this research, and the conversations and histories it has uncovered, has contributed to a collective move to return to these messy, unsettled questions around ExCo's values and practices and its relationship to struggles within and against education institutions. With increasing organizer turnover and frustration with feeling bogged down in the semesterly "business" of putting on classes, many current organizers felt that they could not continue to do work for ExCo without knowing or discussing why or for whom they were laboring. This summer (2014), organizers decided to step back from "business" and hold a series of intensive visioning potlucks. Through sharing meals and meeting in different organizers' homes, ExCo organizers are prioritizing affective relationship-building and studying. Yet some have raised concerns that once the summer ends, we will still have to get back to "work." Given that organizing ExCo is our "third shift," how do we make space-times for the messy work/play of studying-organizing-relating versus seeing these as separate activities where study and relationship-building is often feminized and given short shrift to the more masculinist "action" of organizing? This question is not necessarily solvable but an ongoing problematic that, kept at the fore, can enable radical study and education projects to carve out space-times to continuously revisit and reimagine our transformative political aspirations and build more effective movements.

References

Berg, G. (2010). *Low-income students and the perpetuation of inequality: Higher education in America*. Burlington, VT: Ashgate Press.

Dyke, E., & Meyerhoff, E. (2013). An experiment in "radical" pedagogy and study: On the subtle infiltrations of "normal" education. *Journal of Curriculum Theorizing*, 29(2). Retrieved from http://journal.jctonline.org/index.php/jct/article/view/491

Joseph, M. (2002). *Against the romance of community*. Minneapolis, MN: University of Minnesota Press.

Katz, C. (2011). Accumulation, excess, childhood: Toward a countertopography of risk and waste. *Documents D'anàlisi Geogràfica*, 57(1), 47–60.

Latour, B. (2005). *Reassembling the social*. Oxford: Oxford University Press.

Lavin, C. (2013). *Eating anxiety: The perils of food politics*. Minneapolis, MN: University of Minnesota Press.

Law, J. (2004). *After method: Mess in social science research*. New York, NY: Routledge.

Lensmire, T.J. (2010). Ambivalent white racial identities: Fear and an elusive innocence. *Race, ethnicity, and education*, 13(2), 159–172.

Mignolo, W. (2011). *The darker side of western modernity: Global futures, decolonial options*. Durham, NC: Duke University Press.

Mitchell, T. (1999). Society, economy, and the state effect. In George Steinmetz (Ed.), *State/culture: State-formation after the cultural turn*. Ithaca, NY: Cornell University Press, pp. 76–97.

Moten, F., & Harney, S. (2013). *The undercommons: Fugitive planning and black study*. New York, NY: Minor Compositions.

Moten, F., Harney S., & Bousquet B. (2009). On study: A *Polygraph* roundtable discussion with Marc Bousquet, Stefano Harney, and Fred Moten. *Polygraph*, 21, 159–175.

Papadopoulos, D., Stephenson, N., & Tsianos, V. (2008). *Escape routes: Control and subversion in the 21st century*. Ann Arbor, MI: Pluto Press.

Rasmussen, C. (2011). *The autonomous animal: Self-governance and the modern subject*. Minneapolis, MN: University of Minnesota Press.

Shukaitis, S. (2009). *Imaginal machines: Autonomy & self-organization in the revolutions of everyday life*. New York, NY: Autonomedia.

Notes

1   From conversations with an organizer of the protests, David Boehnke. For more on the Campaign to Defend Need Blind Admissions at Macalester, see http://tinyurl.com/DNBAM.

2   We are writing this version of the paper for a broader audience but we are also writing another version of it as a report for ExCo organizers specifically. Rather than present a false appearance of comprehensiveness with our narratives, we acknowledge our selectivity in choosing these particular narratives for the political purposes of composing guidance that could be useful for such projects.

3   On "a/effective relationships," or the importance of attending to affective, everyday relationships for effective organizing, see Shukaitis, 2009.

4   A note on pronoun usage: We take up ExCo as the object of our study, yet our selves and our past experiences are deeply entangled in its history and present (Eli began working with ExCo in 2007 and Erin in 2009). Throughout the text, we attempt to mark when "we" refers to Eli and Erin, the authors, or when "we/us" refers to our identification with and participation in ExCo as organizers. However,

we used the third-person in almost all of the narratives. Although we want to avoid the distance and feigned objectivity that this perspective implies, we used it in order to provide greater clarity for our readers.

5 This account of the beginnings of Academia Comunitaria is based mostly on former ExCo organizer David Boehnke's writing about the project in 2010.

6 For our call for engagement with this "complex mess," we are influenced by Actor-Network-Theory, such as in John Law's *After Method*, which promotes diving into messiness in social science research, and Bruno Latour's *Reassembling the Social*, which offers guidance against taking short-cuts around the challenges of describing the messy controversies encountered in attempts to compose the world (Law 2004; Latour 2005).

7 For an ideal of continual circuits of study, teaching, and knowledge, forestalling "preparation for governance," we draw on Moten and Harney (2009; 2013).

8 On subverting normative life trajectories, see Papadopolous et al., 2009. On how modernist liberalism's institutions, including education, construct such autonomous, responsible, sovereign selves, see Rasmussen, 2011.

9 We draw the concept of "ambivalent selves" from Tim Lensmire's theory of the "ambivalent racial self" in Lensmire (2010). On the liberal anxieties produced from subscribing to fantasies of the bounded, unified self, see Lavin, 2013.

10 We focus on the U of M chapter here because we have much better capacities for interpreting the notes from their meetings, as we were both present at most of these meetings and were ourselves often the note-takers. For the sake of space in this paper, we are foregoing a close reading of the Macalester chapter and Academia chapter's meeting discussions during this year. Yet we are taking into account the perspectives of organizers from those two chapters through interviews with some of them.

11 The list of potential class projects expanded later to include: "Joining existing organizing . . . Supporting existing organizing . . . Opening up research and organizing on key issues . . . Student workers and the university, Undergraduate solidarity with graduate student organizing, Organizing for a National Day of Action in Defense of Education on October 7, Military research and the university, Corporatization of the university: Rise of an Administrative Class, Relationships between Cedar Riverside and U of M, Making U of M resources accessible, Un/equal access at the U of M, Immigration issues at the U, Educational segregation in the Twin Cities, High Schools and U of M Student Demographics, U of M Donors, History of X struggles at the U, History of departments created through struggles, General College Lessons and Application, Gender, Labor, and Affect at the U, Corporate vs Open Source: the University's Software, University research: patents and corporate control, Responding to staff firings, developing a flying picket squad, Student unionizing, Cross-sector organizing: understanding different positionalities, Student apathy, why?, Branding: the University of spectacle, Corporate accountability struggles at the U: Coke, Arrowmark, TCF Bank, The U and the Prison-Industrial Complex, The Schools-to-Prisons Pipeline, The casualization of academia: potentials for contingent faculty organizing, Mental health at the U of M, Connecting Immigrant Rights Struggles and Education Struggles . . . among many others!" (E-mail blurb about the project, 7/16/10).

12 U of M chapter meeting notes, 7/14/10, 7/21/10.

13 We explained the source of the idea in an e-mail overview of the project: "This would be similar to what can already happen in the university with 'service learn-

ing,' independent studies, and internships, but ExCo would facilitate the building of more direct relationships between the students, movements, and communities for organizing and valuing their collaborative projects on their own terms, rather than mediated through the disciplinary metrics that the university mandates. We have adopted this strategy of 'inflating the credit' from conversations with Claudia Bernardi and Paolo Do, based on their work within the Eccedi Sottrai Crea (ESC) Atelier, a social center and militant research collective in Rome, Italy, which creates a radical interface between their university—La Sapienza—and the wider metropolis: http://www.escatelier.net. Through occupying an administrative building, they forced the administration to grant University credit for the projects of self-education and self-organizing that they facilitate through connecting sympathetic professors with movements, such as around precarious labor and migrant struggles. They are following the Italian autonomist Marxist tradition of struggling to 'inflate the wage' to value all laboring activity, including that in the home, not only that within the traditional workplace." (E-mail, Eli to the U of M chapter, 7/16/10).

14 E-mail regarding "Re-imagining ExCo at the U" reflection dinner, 8/25/10.

15 U of M chapter meeting notes, 7/21/10.

16 U of M chapter meeting notes, 8/30/10. For examples of Disorientation Guides that were particularly inspirational for ExCo organizers, see those of the Counter-Cartographies Collective: http://www.countercartographies.org/category/disorientation-guides/.

17 These included struggles to save the General College, the AFSCME strikes, the IWW Jimmy John's Workers Union, the founding of the Black Student Union through occupying a campus administrative building, and contemporary struggles around space for students of color on campus.

18 The "Whose U?" crew rekindled the campus conversation around institutional racism through creating a documentary and putting on a major event that included over six hundred undergraduate and high school students who were bussed in for the event.

19 U of M chapter meeting notes, 5/26/10.

20 U of M chapter meeting notes, 10/18/10.

21 The counter-spelling of "skool" signifying their affiliation with the wider network of anarchistic "free skools." For a list of North American free skools, see: http://freeskoolsproject.wikispaces.com/.

22 Notes from organizer retreat, 11/14/10.

23 Notes from organizer retreat, 11/14/10.

24 Notes from U of M chapter meeting, 12/14/10.

25 Proposal for "Transforming ExCo's Structure," 3/18/10.

26 Structure proposal, 3/18/10, and meeting notes from U of M chapter, 12/14/10.

27 Notes from U of M chapter meeting, 10/18/10.

28 For a thorough critique of such romanticizing of "community" in a different context, see Joseph 2002.

29 From e-mails in preparation for upcoming citywide meeting, 12/2/10.

30 Notes from citywide meeting, 12/5/10.

CHAPTER 11

What Is Horizontal Pedagogy? A Discussion on Dandelions

Authors: David I. Backer, Matthew Bissen, Jacques Laroche, Aleksandra Perisic, and Jason Wozniak

Participants: Christopher Casuccio ("Winter"), Zane D.R. Mackin, Joe North, and Chelsea Szendi Schieder

Introction

Horizontal pedagogy is an approach to learning with roots in the work of many activists, scholars, and educators through their various encounters within teaching and learning (Freire, 1972/2000, Guattari 2005).[1] This chapter presents horizontal pedagogy as a prefigurative educational experiment that emerged from the Occupy University in New York City's General Assembly. This experiment drew together several traditions of facilitation practice in order to work against neoliberal-capitalist relations of production, but also to learn what other kinds of relations of knowledge production might be possible. The following chapter offers one description of the pedagogy's history and practice during 2011-2012. The chapter first outlines the emergence of the horizontal pedagogy (HP) group in the Occupy Wall Street movement (OWS), followed by an annotated dialogue from a horizontal pedagogy session which occurred in 2014. Through this history and dialogue, the chapter addresses the question:

What Is Horizontal Pedagogy?

This particular approach to horizontal pedagogy emerged from the initial call to action of OWS. It then moved swiftly to meet the concerns of OWS's Empowerment and Education Working Group, out of which formed a group that would explore pedagogical issues during more than two years of workshops. To understand the formation of this group, a minimal amount of OWS context is necessary. An event description published in *Adbusters* in July 2011 read "#OCCUPYWALLSTREET: On September 17th, flood into lower

Manhattan, set up tents, kitchens, and peaceful barricades and occupy Wall
Street." This initial call continued with the following description:

> A worldwide shift in revolutionary tactics is underway right now that
> bodes well for the future. . . . The beauty of this new formula, and
> what makes this novel tactic exciting, is its pragmatic simplicity: we
> talk to each other in various physical gatherings and virtual people's
> assemblies . . . we zero in on what our one demand will be, a demand
> that awakens the imagination and, if achieved, would propel us toward
> the radical democracy of the future . . . and then we go out and seize a
> square of singular symbolic significance and put our asses on the line
> to make it happen.
>
> The time has come to deploy this emerging stratagem against
> the greatest corrupter of our democracy: Wall Street, the financial
> Gomorrah of America.[2]

On September 17, the occupiers established a community through a complex
organization of working groups, which used direct-democratic facilitation
procedures centered on the daily meeting of a general assembly. The nascent
community considered proposals brought to its general assembly, moving
forward with actions after its members expressed consent. Hundreds of
working groups emerged from the activists' interests in this way, including
a group called Empowerment and Education (E&E). E&E became the main
working group for those interested in educational issues. A number of sub-
committees formed within E&E, including Open Forum, Occupy the DOE,
and the Occupy Student Debt Campaign. Another subcommittee, formed
early in the occupation, was known as the Nomadic University.

Nomadic University (which changed its name to Occupy University in
January 2012) drew artists, intellectuals, professors, students, and workers
to its meetings. Members of this subcommittee formed task forces devoted
to particular organizational goals for creating a university. There was a task
force devoted to curriculum (what subjects, themes, or ideas would the university address?), a task force devoted to outreach, and another task force to
analyze particular concepts and definitions necessary for the creation of an
educational institution consistent with the Occupy movement. In addition
to the larger working group meetings and the smaller Nomadic University
subcommittee meetings, these task forces met weekly. The Concepts and
Definitions Task Force (C&D) of the Nomadic University subcommittee of the
Empowerment and Education working group held meetings to discuss the
meaning and significance of words like "nomadism," "university," "hospitality," and "emancipation."

In an effort to stay true to the movement's habit of occupying public
space at symbolic centers of Wall Street and financial power, C&D met in

privately owned public spaces around midtown Manhattan. The task force eventually made Trump Tower on 57th Street and 7th Avenue its home. The group read texts and composed its own writings to create satisfactory understandings of the above terms, which it then presented to the larger Nomadic University. After a month of thinking through these concepts and definitions, C&D became interested in ways of practicing the ideas it had discussed. As one reflective arm of a project devoted to creating an educational institution, the group wanted to experiment with ways of learning, studying, and teaching consistent with its social and political values and those of the Occupy movement. The group agreed that different members of C&D would facilitate a series of interactions, using whatever techniques each member saw fit. Members drew from student-centered facilitation practices such as Harkness pedagogy, from the community of inquiry model of philosophy for children (in particular a model practiced by Walter O. Kohan in Brazil[3]), techniques used in Lacanian psychoanalysis, as well as the direct-democratic consensus-oriented procedures widely practiced in Zuccotti Park. On the first night of the experiment, the group examined a passage from Sen. Carl Levin's report (2011) on the 2008 financial crisis.[4] At the end of the experiment, another member volunteered to facilitate the following week. The group did not describe this pedagogical activity as "horizontal" until later.

Pedagogy was first described as "horizontal" in the body of an e-mail summarizing Nomadic University's first series of foundational proposals. Describing a pedagogical proposal, the author of the e-mail (North, J., personal commication, November 20, 2011) wrote: "Nomadic University classes would follow many different pedagogies—we wouldn't try to impose one 'correct' pedagogy on every class. But in line with OWS's general commitment to horizontal and consensual processes, we would encourage/stipulate that NU classes try to adopt a more horizontal and non-hierarchical pedagogy than conventional education offers."

C&D used its Levin experiment as a model for this proposal. The group attempted to practice education that was "in line with OWS's general commitment to horizontal and consensual processes" which it took to be "more . . . non-hierarchical than conventional education." After this proposal passed, members of the newly formed horizontal pedagogy workshop facilitated interactions over the course of a month. Each encounter resulted in a new question, topic, or text that the group would study the following week with a different facilitator. These horizontal pedagogy workshops had two functions. First, Horizontal Pedagogy was an ongoing course offered by Nomadic University. Second, members of this workshop facilitated other courses that Nomadic University offered such as: Studying May Day, Poetry and Political Feeling, Radical Economics, Critical Walking, and Occupied Algebra.[5] While members of the horizontal pedagogy workshop wrote down certain procedures and habitually used them during Occupy University's courses, "horizontal pedagogy" came to refer not only to the procedures themselves, but also to the way in which the group had come to them, since the basic impetus of the pedagogy, as practiced, is to learn, teach, and study in line with a general commitment to non-hierarchical conventions and procedures, such as those used by the occupiers in Zuccotti Park. Though the pedagogy itself is contested and provisional (as the following dialogue demonstrates), before describing its procedures, we may say some general things about its history.

First, members of the HP workshop mostly identified as belonging to the Occupy movement. This sense of belonging created a shared sense of purpose: protesting, demonstrating against, and manifesting discontent with the "financial Gomorrah of America." Second, the group believed that creating an educational institution, with its own pedagogy and curriculum, was a critical and necessary project for OWS. These two conditions would eventually inspire "horizontal pedagogy," a way of learning, teaching, and studying that is committed to non-conventional, non-hierarchical educational approaches.

Procedures

These are the routines and procedures HP facilitators would follow during workshops.[6]

- **Introduction**: The facilitator or participants begin by describing the group, the purpose of the meeting, and what has happened at previous meetings. We answer the questions: *who we are, what we are doing, why we are doing it, what we have done thus far*.
- **Check-in**: Each participant says their name and how they feel at the moment.
- **Physical Education**: The facilitator asks participants to propose some form of movement. Most occasions of formal learning require the body be a certain way: sitting, hunched, tensed, generally still. This procedure is meant to draw participants more into their bodies than they might otherwise be.
- **Examination**: The group looks at a text. "Text," however, is a very flexible term referring to anything interpretable: the room, a poem, a piece of clothing, a memory, etc.
- **Collective Questioning**: After examining the text, the group asks questions about it (and only questions, no comments). The facilitator writes these questions down and reviews them aloud after the group cannot think of any other questions.
- **Discussion**: Discussion requires that participants address the questions with one another, ideally with an equality and variety in the sequence of turn-taking so no one lectures or leads a recitation.[7]

- **Final Remarks**: Final remarks are closing thoughts. Though the group might not have reached a definite conclusion, participants report whether any ideas congealed for them, or what understandings/questions they might take away from the interaction.
- **Debrief**: Participants do their best to discuss the discussion itself. They reflect on the dynamic of the interaction, who spoke, how it felt, and what it was like. Also, the group may find certain habits of speech that worked well or did not. Finally, during debrief, the group plans for the next interaction.
- **Check-out**: Each member of the group reports how they feel at the end of the interaction.

What follows is an annotated transcript of an HP session from 2014, held both as a celebration of the group's friendship and camaraderie as well as to ask the group the question, *What is horizontal pedagogy?* As the discussion unfolds, themes of consent, ritual, process, ideology, collectives, community, capitalism, listening, and questioning emerge. However, the group arrives at the following critical position:

> It seems important that as we represent it, we don't fix it. That it is this constant movement, and it's a constant fight to preserve the right to have this kind of movement. And the best we can do is offer others a glimpse or a taste, so that they can bring that to whatever they're doing.

Check-in

The "check-in" for horizontal pedagogy sessions situates participants in the space, acknowledging participants' emotions and states of beings at the start of the interaction. This moment prior to examining the text recognizes that everyone approaches the process from different perspectives and states of mind. This may seem like a minor point of beginning, but it works to establish that everyone's state of mind is of value and worthy of expression within the group. This moment also moves the center of expression and knowledge from the facilitator and the text to the gathered participants as a whole. This experience is expressed by Chris during this session's check-in:

> Winter/Chris: I'm sometimes Winter, sometimes Chris. This can be very confusing, to know which one I am. In contrast to Jason, I love this part of the practice; I think it's crucial for people to acknowledge where they're at when they come into a space.[8] There are very few spaces in our lives that create that, and in my last few months of doing experimental forms of education with teenagers I've found that that piece was actually very powerful for them. It gave me some new ideas

and concepts about this form of education that we do, so hopefully I'll try to weave them into the conversation. In terms of how I'm actually doing, I'm kind of a wreck [chuckles]. Um, I'm extremely disoriented. I'm feeling like I'm having layers of existential crises all at the same time, at the level of life, career, love, like, sanity . . . all at the same time. It's actually hard to stay focused and present with you guys, but all the things you've said resonate with me, and so parts of me feel all the things that you've been saying.

The perspectives of nostalgia, excitement, joy, and sadness emerged during this check-in due to the fact that many of the participants were leaving New York City soon. The emotions that resonated through what was termed a developing HP "diaspora" can be heard in the following exchange between Jacques and Chelsea:

> Jacques: Okay, which way? Okay I'll go. This is Jacques. I'm really excited that everyone is here, the assortment of people that are here, it sucks that we're all leaving, but I'm also not really sad about it. It's just the new chapter, the way I'm looking at it. It's as if there's pollen being blown across the wind . . .
> Chelsea: Like the dandelion?
> Jacques: Yeah, like we're all going to different places and we're going to see things in different areas and I'm feeling a bit sad about my perceived drop in momentum for certain things, but, that's about it. Feeling good in general.

Inclusion and the position of the other has been a continual topic during these horizontal pedagogy sessions and its relevance is present here in Joe's check-in.

> Joe: But it's also odd to have these two different things happening at the same time, which is that everyone is moving away and so it feels like it's a little bit of a moving-away feeling, which isn't the same thing as an HP-feeling at all, but it seems really relevant, and that's very much what I'm thinking about. And it's also odd to not be moving away, given that I don't feel like . . . I still feel very foreign in New York, like I've just moved here even though I've been living here for eight years, and I'll be here for at least one more, and other people are moving away and it feels odd, like I should be the one moving away, but I'm not.

Physical Education

For this session, physical education entailed sharing a meal prior to and during the discussion.

Examination

Examination is time spent looking at something together, closely, as a group. Looking was focused upon a "text"—conceived broadly to include the written word, spaces, images, movements, experiments, etc. The text for this session would be the reactions of each member to the question: "What is horizontal pedagogy?" Each participant was asked to respond to that question briefly, after which, the group would collectively question the responses as a whole. We include each response in full.

Matthew: I guess I will start. The strength I got over the last two years, the empowerment I felt to come together to struggle through concepts, as a young teacher, as a student, as a person. I think that the HP approach was one of the few times I could struggle in the open and struggle with support. And whether that's the people or the structure, I don't know, the approach to HP or you all, I don't know, but I ended up coming back. I'm curious how movement in and out of space, in and out of classes—classroom classes, not class class—how HP can support the ability to transfer in and out productively in a supportive way, and I'll stop there since this isn't a novel, but a distilled statement.

Jason: Yeah, the question of horizontality is important. It's been critiqued in some interesting ways, defended in some interesting ways. And I kind of mentioned this in my presentation that David said he had recorded,[9] but I like the metaphor of the horizon. One walks towards the horizon but as you walk towards it, it keeps getting farther away. Nevertheless, what matters is that you walk towards it even though you never really reach it. And I think this is an important aspect of the idea of HP: I've never thought that it is horizontal, but that's okay. Because I think the attempt to try and reach horizontality is what changes the practice in some pretty radical ways. The only other thing I'll say is that I really think it's very important that there are attempts to get together and collectively question, then collectively think about these questions, with no particular ends in sight. The openness to create collective concepts that come out of these questions is an absolutely vital part of HP. One of the space-times that HP opens up is the space-time of collective questioning, collective thinking, and possible collective conceptualizing.

Aleks: I can go. There are a few things that I really appreciate about this process. One of them is that I, like Winter, actually like the check-in, which moves the process beyond the purely intellectual discussion. It leaves room to look at oneself and others, and that's why I also liked the physical education part of it, there is an attention to different aspects of ourselves. I also like that it pushes the idea of what a text is, what a text can be, and what can be used as a text. I, however, have a few questions. I've tried to use different parts of the process in the classroom, and one of the things I saw was that the check-in was important, because students have a lot of trouble saying how they're feeling. Even though you specifically say that's the question—and I think we all do this—they revert to recounting what they've done the previous day. So I think that's important work. But I did have questions about horizontality and direction. Collective questioning is important as it opens up various avenues, but then I'm not sure that's enough. Maybe it is, but sometimes it does feel like it's a constant opening with a lack of direction. I've been struggling with that a little bit.

Jason: Just a footnote, because this is the second time someone has mentioned that they like something I don't like—can we address this at some point? [Laughter]

David: We can get to that in the questions . . . [Chuckling]

Chelsea: When Aleks brought up the classroom, I was thinking about an anecdote, or what I was going to say. I've been thinking a lot about the classroom since I just got finished writing syllabi that I'll use with students in Japan next year and I'm not sure how—it'll be English language courses, but I'm not sure how good their English language will be. And I want to have challenging discussions, I mean they'll be challenging since they'll be speaking in a language that's not their native language already, but I want to be able to have debates and discussions about things that might be difficult for them to talk about, and I want to create a safe space for this where I'm not directing the conversation, where I'm decentered, and so, for me, a question has always been facility, with language, not just a mastery of the subject but: how can I decenter myself when students will always be questioning themselves in terms of expression? That's something I've been thinking about and that's my big question for HP: when students have trouble talking about how they feel, that's one thing, but when there's this other gap in expression. . . . I mean I think even native English speakers feel this, the gap between their ability to express something in language that they're thinking and feeling, so, how do we think about that gap in the classroom specifically?

Winter/Chris: I never liked the phrase "horizontal pedagogy." I'm not sure I've said that before. When we started using it, I went along with it because it seemed to fit some of the things we were trying to do. But when I hear the phrase "informal learning" I kind of like it, or maybe "informal unlearning" seems more like what we were doing. And I think we run into trouble when we try to formalize it, and when we try to institutionalize it, I think that's when we run into trouble, when things get ugly, or tricky. But, um, you know I never really thought of myself as much of an education person when we started doing this, still didn't seem like pedagogy to me—it just felt like people coming together about how they were feeling and then questioning the hell out of everything, and making that the basis for a certain unraveling and untangling of all the ways that we've been unable to see each other and hear each other and be with each other in a real way, so for me, it was always just about coming to a place where I knew I'd be in a group, in a collective, where I'd be seen and heard in a way that never felt possible before. And that felt like a certain kind of unlearning. And there was a phrase that Joe once said to me after we were finished, like there was all this talk about empowerment in Occupy—we came out of the Education and Empowerment Working Group—but it feels much more like disempowerment to me, in a really productive way, in the way that like maybe, you know, maybe sometimes you just need to shut up and listen, and I think half of what I got out of this process is just having to listen to people and see and hear people in ways that we're not taught to, and that we had to teach ourselves. Towards the end, it really became clear to me that the learning we were doing was learning how to be in a community, how to hear and see each other and feel each other, and not necessarily have to know where that was going to go. And I think that was scary. I think that was scary when people came in, I think it was very unclear what we were doing, we had trouble articulating it—I think we still do—but that's what I think is the beauty of it. And I still think there's a ton of potential to be unraveled in it, and a bunch of different directions to go with it.

David: It's important for me to think about the history of HP. And I don't want to say that it's a new thing, but certainly something emerged, out of a task force of the Nomadic University subcommittee of the Empowerment and Education Working Group of the Occupy Wall Street movement in New York City. And it was originally the concepts and definitions task force, I think. That feels important to me because something that people say, when I tell them I was involved in Occupy, they say, "Oh you know, I'm not really down with the whole disorganization thing." But we were so organized! [Laughter] So, I like to repeat that as frequently as possible. And I think HP is a way of teaching, learning, and studying wherein the people who are teaching, learning, and studying have a share in the administration and deliberation of whatever it is they're going to learn.[10] It turned out that when we got together to learn, the procedures looked like what we're doing now, but I think HP could look differently depending on whomever got together. What I mean is that the process of HP isn't necessarily the Intro, Check-in, etc., but rather what happens when people get together and they are committed to collectively consent to the way in which they will learn. And in that way, I think it was prefigurative for learning to be in a community, as was said: it was a political thing for us to do that together in New York City at Trump Tower.

Jacques: I feel a little strange weighing in on this because I feel like you all have been doing so much more work on HP formally, and at the same time, I kind of like when Jason and others talk about it. Right now, your definition, it feels natural—you know on the one hand I feel unnatural, like, "What do I have to say about this?" but on the other it's like, this is what we've been doing since Occupy and, like we've said, people from way before us have been doing this. What I like about this is the ability to create a space where people of all levels are being really heard and everybody has a say in the conversation without pushing anyone else out, and that's really important. But figuring out the best means of speaking to each other and learning from one another and disseminating information to others depends on the configuration of the group. So then, yeah, echoing what's been said before, it just depends on who is there, and asking the right questions in that context seems to be the most important thing for me. Instead of yammering on, there's a tendency for people to get together and throw out their experiences into a vacuum and then think that that's magically going to disseminate knowledge to other people. Instilling a sense of self-awakening is probably more effective and the "asking questions" seems to get to that—the right questions at the right time. Those are my thoughts.

Zane: In my experience, HP was always inherently radical and political because it's horizontal. The subject of study in HP, at least as we practiced it, was really itself. I think it was, as Jason or David said already, it was learning how to be together. I found that to be a really valuable exercise: how to be with other people and listen radically, and how to be honest with yourself with other people. I overheard, when I just came in, people talking about whether HP can help destroy capitalism.[11] I don't think that HP is inherently directed towards destroying capitalism. It can't be because destroying capitalism, or the desire to destroy capitalism, is really an ideology. And HP is inherently anti-ideological. It's very real. It may turn out to do so, which would be cool, but I don't see it directed towards that particular idea. You guys talked a little bit about inheritance, and I think there's two sides to that coin. I think that in Occupy we tended to neglect our inheritances, and it has something to do with, you know, this idea of "everybody's voice has value." So we make David Graeber sit in silence down on Beaver Street just because, you know . . . which to me seemed a little strange.[12] But at the same time, I think there was a pedagogical value to reinventing the wheel. We built a lot of stuff from the ground up that other people probably had models for, but we just kind of did it. And that was a really wonderful way to own things. Of course, when you build something like HP, and new people come in that somehow don't like the structure or whatever, and want to change it, we can't go back to reinventing the wheel all the time. So we developed something of a culture. Sorry, I've already talked a lot. I'll leave it there.

Joe: I'm the last one but I don't really know what to say. I really found the whole process very moving, but to say something more conceptual and not just nostalgic, I felt that . . . I like what David was saying about it being a way of different people getting together and all consenting to the means by which they were going to learn. But it seems to me also that there are all sorts of groups that get together and, because consent is a really problematic thing, and that individuals feel that they're consenting to things that they don't in fact consent to, and volition is a really complicated thing. . . . I wonder, it seemed to me that there would be a lot of cases where people get together and all feel that they're consenting to something that's oppressing them pretty badly. And I wouldn't want to think of that as being horizontal, if by horizontal, we mean, a lot of the time, that it has something to do with the leveling off of power relations. And there's an aspiration at least, as Jason was saying, there's a direction towards equality as a value. So, if we all consented to being unequal, that wouldn't seem very horizontal to me. But then it seemed to me also, since we had that emphasis on equality that I really value, there's also an emphasis on freedom and the sort of openness towards, you know, questions that haven't arisen yet, or answers that haven't arisen yet, and I really value that too. But one of the things I think we got to sometimes, though not always, was not just not oppressing each other, which can sometimes feel like community-building, but often it can feel like community-dissolving, it can be a kind of libertarian thing that I'm always paranoid about, where we're all just individuals consenting and never entering into any relationship that we don't consent to, which actually doesn't seem right because people are always in relationships that they don't get to consent to, like being in the world . . . [Laughter] Anyway, so it seems as if one of the things that was really good about HP, and that the phrase "horizontal" doesn't really catch, but something that the word "pedagogy" catches, is that there is some commitment to trying to help each other in an active way, and that getting together might be a good thing. Not just getting together in a way that doesn't oppress each other, but actually getting together in such a way as to help one another learn something about the world. Somehow that's how the Occupy sense of mutual aid, or whatever you want to call it, or the older revolutionary thing of the brotherhood of man—getting into very gendered terms—but that there's a sense, not only of liberty and equality, but the sense of actually trying to help each other, which seemed very important.

Collective Questioning

The typical educational encounter gives priority to resolution: as soon as the unfamiliar is presented there is a rush to escape it by resolving it, and this often prematurely closes questions off from deep exploration. It could be said, however, that HP prioritizes questions, and the process of questioning over answers and answering. Questions (if they are genuine and not merely rhetorical) put into doubt the familiar, they create fissures in the familiar, thus opening up an unfamiliar space of thinking and feeling to be explored. Importantly, however, it is not merely the asking of questions that HP prioritizes. HP, by carving out space-time in the educational encounter, a space-time that cannot be measured chronologically, nor geographically, but is situational and has a logic of its own, encourages learners and teachers to develop relationships with questions/questioning. Of this relationship, little can be stated in the space allotted here. Perhaps, Rilke said it best. To paraphrase: one must learn to live questions.[13] *But, we can also suggest that questioning in a collective manner is a type of collective poetics: it provokes the process of collective creative thinking about new ways of being, and in a political sense, such questioning often provokes people to begin thinking together about new ways of creating culture. What follows is a diagram depicting the questions the group asked during this session.*

Discussion

Below we include a large excerpt of the discussion, which addressed the questions depicted above. The transition between questioning and discussion is typically fluid and opaque, so we include the transcript here at the moment when comments first emerged:

Matthew: The concept of idea-thing-entity-individual, keeps coming back, but I'm wondering: isn't this a process? Is all this a process? We didn't produce a thing. This is a community coming together, and that's where the issues of inclusion and exclusion are because we think, or people think, it's a thing. But it's a process. It's learning, it's being together. Shifting that thought, we might be able to maintain open some of these other issues. And so, Jason, I'm reading Mr. Horton and Mr. Freire's book . . .

David: *We Make the Road by Walking*? I love that book.[14]

Matthew: It's basically a book of them talking to each other. So I thought this was a way to, that writing isn't about . . . writing is talking. It's not fixing an idea to a page, but a record of conversations.

Jason: This might be one of the ways in which it's [HP] anti-capitalistic, in that—what Zane said and what you just said—it's a way to prevent reifica-

Consent
To what extent do the steps
(Intro, Check-in, etc.) represent the
value that we all consented to?
Does that go out the window if we accept the
definition of perpetual consent, or is there
something more universal about what we do?
About consent: what does it mean to think about
freedom as a collective rather than an individual?
Do we fetishize the individual rather than
compromising when thinking about collective consent?
We made a thing at a certain moment, but we didn't
perpetually consent to it over and over again, and
that's a problem with democratic theory in
general, did we fall prey to that?
Is perpetual consent a fantasy?

Space
With conscious decisions
to work in certain spaces, how
is HP concerned with the individual
—but not just the community, what
does it mean for the individual to go
through this process?
About communication: what is a text
and what are the key components
of the space necessary to
develop HP?

Purpose
Education in
institutions has a telos,
but does HP work with a
telos?
Does it have many
teloses?

Capital
What does HP really
have to do with
capitalism?
Is community building a
counterweight to
capitalism?

Collective
People organize collective learnings
in a politically-charged environment, but
could you do it in a non-politically-charged
environment—could you do HP outside of a
movement like OWS?
Does collective learning depend on a large-scale political
movement?
What is the relation between HP and collective writing?
Is there an HP for writing, as in the first DROM—was that
horizontal (or just collective) writing?
Where's the balance between including everyone's individual
desire and compromise?
Is an equal and various sequence in the turns taken during
interaction a minimum of sufficient experience for
horizontality in pedagogy?
How does the attempt to come up with collective
learning like HP serve to bring down capitalism,
what role does it play?
Is collectivity something other than the
fetishization of including every
individual?

Inheritance
There were all kinds of
pedagogies and thinking about
education from before, but why
wouldn't we acknowledge those?
Why wouldn't we recognize our
inheritances?
If we're reluctant to acknowledge
our inheritances, does this have
something to do with
individualism in terms of
temporality?

Community
We were originally accountable to
others, that's why we named it, but we
also wanted to share it with others, so how
does a collective thing get represented and does
that representation change the thing itself?
Question about the process of naming: How does naming
HP form HP, and how has that happened over time?
Given that our experience with one another was to keep
meeting with one another, when does a group become
exclusive, inhospitable, and develop barriers to entry?
Certain people didn't come back to HP when we were
doing it, and why was that?
How important is it that HP be repeated with the
same people?
How do we use HP to build community?
Are those even related?
Helping—what does it mean exactly when
Joe says "in HP you help people"?

Structure
How do we apply what we are
doing here?
How do you move beyond the informal
context to formal spaces with HP?
Adapting HP to existing structures: What
about higher education specifically? Can it be
adapted to university without losing its radical
anticapitalist edge, if that is what it has?
In the context of university students who
have to take a class, but what if someone
gets turned off to HP, what does that
mean about the process?
Will HP meet resistance in the
classroom?

tion. And, in another sense, when Zane was talking, I wonder if this is an eternal process of deconstructing, we're always just deconstructing . . .

Chelsea: I wonder if this list [of questions] just represents our own obsessions. I don't know if it's because we are who we are that the C-word (capitalism) comes up, I don't know if, this idea of the individual and the collective, there's no way to guarantee that collectives are radical also, right? Collective behavior can be inherently antithetical to certain forms of liberalism or neoliberalism, but that doesn't mean they'll be radical. They can be really reactionary. So hearing the words that are brought up here: individual, consent, community, capitalism, collective, representation . . . there's a question: is the quality or content of HP caused by this particular group that's getting together and talking, or is it something about what we're doing that these words come up?

David: I think it's a really fascinating tension, Chelsea. In some way, we all think or thought HP has something to do with the fight against capitalism that we're all engaged with, but it seems like at the same time, that it doesn't necessarily have to be. If people were living in some other kind of arrangement, whatever it was, and they were getting together to think about what they didn't know and new ways of being together, it could be the complete reverse. So, then there's this question of "anti-ideology." Are we just confronting our ideologies, and it just so happens contingently that we're confronting capitalism, but if we were living in communism or feudalism, or whatever, and we got together and did this, would we be confronting those things? There's something appealing about both of these options, but it would have to be one or the other, wouldn't it?

Jacques: It seems to go right back to what Jason was saying, whether there's a *telos*, right? So there's definitely also the question about the repeating group or the exclusion or inclusion . . . yeah, this might be because of who we are, but it's hard to tell. I don't know.

Joe: I'd like to think there's something anti-capitalist about it, but now I'm going back to this "it" language and that might not work because it's a process not a thing. But it seems like this is a good moment for it to be a thing rather than a process, which is that: at least everyone who regularly turned up to HP meetings had anti-capitalist aspirations, and seemed to be part of the OWS movement, because they were in some way frustrated or resistant to or looking to challenge something like capitalism, or like "Wall Street," or like "money in politics," or these various things that we can express in this way, and it does seem as if in that context, at least the insistence on a certain kind of collectivity, that's not a rightist or conservative or fascist collectivity, but a more kind of different collective, a less hierarchical one, as if it had a political emphasis that was anti-capitalist, but that doesn't really . . .

Jason: Yeah, I just want to say though that capitalists love this stuff. It's so easy for capital to appropriate a lot of what we are talking about and practicing. Now I will say that the response to this appropriation, what maybe keeps HP from being appropriated by capitalism, and this to me is vital, is the non-productive element of constant questioning. This goes back to the point of what you were saying Zane, and to what you just said, Jacques, regarding *telos*. The capitalist might view HP as a great way to get questions on the table, questions which ultimately might lead to the creation of some creative thinking about new products or new ideas or whatever can be sold and bought, whereas what we were thinking and practicing placed the emphasis always on the questions, questioning. Constant questioning and questioning again, a questioning without end that might not ever lead to a "final" product. And I think that this might actually be a move against capitalism.

Winter/Chris: But I think again, that question I raised before about form and content seems really important to me here. Because the form of HP, clearly, capital would love. Absolutely, why not? But there's the form of it, the content, which is the principles, the questioning, listening, recognizing the body, for instance, there's a whole lot of it that productivity and capital would have a hard time appropriating. There's also the context of it, which is that it was a direct action. We were in a public space talking about capitalism. So I think that there's a danger that we've slipped into as we formalize it, just looking at the form of it, people coming together to form a community, and consenting . . . but we have to go with form, content, and context and take that all as one. Seems like we're skirting around that, but it seems like a good moment to re-tangle those pieces together. So, in a sense, HP is a thing, it is a process, it is an experience, it's all of those things, and if we just take one angle, and only one angle, we lose the radical elements of it.

David: So that was one of Matt's earlier questions: what are the things that we need to make it? It sounded like you were almost gesturing towards the . . . what would be needed.

Winter/Chris: That's what you were asking too, right, what's the minimum?

David: Yeah, what's sufficient for an HP experience? It seemed like you were saying form, content, space, direct action. Maybe the same people over and over again like Chelsea was saying?

Chelsea: Well, okay, just the space thing. I don't know why it hasn't been brought up, it seems so obvious from what you said, Winter. The public spaces, claiming the public spaces, and spaces that were porous where people could just come in. Now we're in a private space, invitation only, nobody could just wander in and say something.[15] Also, just the visibility of it, we've all had the same experiences, during a certain point of Occupy you felt reinforced by seeing things all over the city, even if you weren't involved in planning them, so there's a sense of things like this having gone into people's private spaces, and then in a university, which of course is a space that has its own baggage, so I think that point about the public space was quite important.

Winter/Chris: It was free, it was open . . .

Jacques: There's something that I'm really trying to figure out, and it goes directly to the point we're talking about here, and that's the question about the equal and various sequence in turns: Is that a minimum or sufficient condition? I'd remember times where you'd see clearly someone just walk in that doesn't know the general assembly process, but they really want to say something. And they start to speak, and someone, very kindly, will say "Hey, this isn't the time or place for that," or "we'll put you on stack" or "you can come back next Thursday at 7:45 am," or some shit like that. The point is, and that's happened to me too, the point is there's a certain intuition in HP that I don't know how it can be formalized, where you have to "read" people and understand like, this person gets a little leeway in this way, because of whatever their experience is—which is difficult, because how do you formalize that? Or this person gets, like, one of you said something about David Graeber not speaking? I don't know anything about that, but it just sounds so perfect. It just sounds like people hyper-focusing on privilege, and then excluding him unnecessarily and saying, "You've gotten too much speaking time. You have all this experience, but shut the fuck up!" You know, those intuitive unsaid things need to be somehow acknowledged, if not slightly formalized, at least, given credence in these sorts of engagements.

Chelsea: Does the HP process help those things come out? Because if we say that we feel like we're in danger of ignoring our inheritances, but is there something about this process that makes it possible for those things to come up? Things maybe otherwise would not have come up at all, so we can leave and be like "Hmm, maybe I need to think about my inheritances, or moments when I need to listen, or moments when I exclude someone because I think they have power in another context" or something like that.

Joe: I feel like, I really—those two comments seem really rich and interesting for me. It seems like what we're talking about, in a way, is a kind of habit, or skills or capabilities, or habits of being sensitive, sensitivities, sensibilities, whatever you want to call them, that exist or don't exist in the social body. If you want to talk about HP that way, that does seem to me what we were trying to do, one of the good things we were trying to do, which was—and this comes back to your point about reiteration—you can't change a habit by doing something once, by getting new people, you have to go and practice it again and again and again. When DR was talking about learning to listen more, I realized I felt strongly that way myself: that I was learning to listen more than I had before, and learning to cultivate those kinds of habits that seem really worthwhile. I guess what I'm trying to say is that as a mode of radical action—or if you want to call it resistance to capitalism, coming up with anti-capitalist alternatives, whatever, however one conceptualizes it—cultivating a sense of how that's done in a group, that is, for being sensitive to what everyone in the group needs and what the group needs, seems like a really valuable thing, and in any case a necessary thing no matter what else is also required, which hasn't got quite captured with the sequence of turns thing, because it's not about something that can be quite formalized, nor an effable thing, it's just a set of habits and practices that actually have to exist in a certain mode.

Matthew: That's my distinguishing between thing and process. When we had general assemblies, for instance, the process became a religion. Which then makes the process a thing. It's no longer a social formation. That's when I feel like we lose social formation. We lose the habit-forming ability in our process when all of a sudden we fix it and say, and I think we did have this in HP at some point, we fixed our process, and it became "the HP way," or whatever. That is a tricky threshold for me. That's where I struggle with it. And whenever I'm critically questioning, I'm always looking for those shifts—when we try to make something a thing and not a process, and I think that's a very important place where we stop the ability to question. One of the values of this group is that we've not yet reached the point where we've stopped questioning ourselves. Sorry, not ourselves—this social formation. We've not stopped questioning this social formation.

Jason: I want to say though that I'm not sure we settled on a process, but we did decide there were certain elements that had to be included if it was going to resemble anything we were calling at the time "HP." I think there's a difference, because to say that there are certain elements doesn't guarantee that there will be a certain outcome or certain processes to be followed. We said that there are questions, we said there is discussion. But it seems to me that you could take those elements and mix them up in a multitude of ways that almost seem without end. To me that doesn't seem like a process. Yes it's clear that we determined elements that had to be included in order for something to happen, but I'm not sure that's the same thing as determining how things should happen.

DR: Jason, do you remember talking about rituals of hospitality?

Jason: Yeah, that goes back to the question that Chelsea just brought up. I don't know why we just don't come out and say, for example, that we're heavily influenced by Derrida and Rancière. Hospitality and the equality of intelligence. I don't know why we haven't said that yet.[16]

DR: Yes there's hospitality, but there's also ritual. Ritual is a codified form of behaving: check-in is a ritual process. You know, to say this is a fixed thing, we're going to question it, that's sort of undermining the whole mood that we set through ritual action. My influences of course are ecclesiastical rather than theoretical,[17] but they work, you know? We need to go through, we need to pass through a threshold from the regular, everyday world, the sort of demotic, into a space that we could call a sacred space, in which hospitality is ritualized and radicalized. For me then, the check-in is one of the most important parts of HP.

Aleks: So then I want to go back to the question of how do you, and can you, bring that into an institution? Or, can it only exist outside the institution? You were talking about ritual and Winter was insisting on form and contact and space. Being in the classroom, I've always felt like I can only bring in one or two, but never all of those at the same time. What do you do at that point? Is that a lost cause?

David: I've had good experiences over the last couple years doing some of the things we do in institutional settings. Now there's a class that I teach where I let the check-in go for half an hour. And students come in and they talk about what's going on, but in terms of the purpose of the course, which has a lot to do with what it means to be a student, that ritual is a little more relevant. But it creates, and this is the second part of what I was going to say—theoretically it feels to me like what happens is, if you do HP in the institution, what won't happen is a situation where the structures of dominance just dissolve and there's emancipation or whatever. [Laughter] Rather, the moment of liberation is ephemeral, or evanescent, such that there is a kind of opening where the group has an ability to see the institution anew in some way. It's almost more powerful when you bring it into an institution, I think. Because when you get into this sacred space, that quality allows you to see what's around you, and in other people in a different way, and that's what it means to change institutions, right? An institution to me is just a bunch of language and architecture,

Aleks: And money, of course.

David: Yes, and money, but you can change the language and the buildings. Certainly, different kinds of things happen in the same buildings, even when the same money is available, and it's because people start talking and thinking differently. It seems to me you can do that with HP. It's really hard. Students don't really like it, at first. I remember, when we went to Karen's classroom at SUNY-Purchase, and all her students had a big problem with HP. But I think it can.[18]

Matthew: I came at this not necessarily, I mean we talk about the critique of capitalism, I think this would get into the universality of the classroom— that's when the real sharp critique of capitalism comes, because as much as I want to horizontalize my classrooms, I still have to grade students, and that's the space where the commodity enters, that they need to get a grade which gets them into their job. And that's where my struggle is. And they know that the grades are there too. So it feels like lip service in a lot of ways. They say, "Well, bullshit. You know that and we know that, so don't say otherwise." So that's where my view is: where capitalism comes in really harshly is the grades. Because that three credits is a commodity that is traded, and profited from in various ways. The way I bring HP in, particularly in spatial theory classes, is we constantly question the space over and over and over again.[19] We'll diagram the power balance, and how that room is designed around power over and over again. We won't come together as a group necessarily, but every time we come into a classroom we will question that classroom: how it's influencing our space. That's how I've been able to bring it into the classroom—really question the space we're sitting in. And getting them to see space. But that's relevant to how I'm teaching spatial theory classes, which goes back to David's point, where sometimes it fits more into the context of the class and sometimes it doesn't.

Chelsea: How's that just different from what we call "critical thinking skills"? Or something like that? Because teaching students how to ask questions, I mean, I guess that's another way of thinking about that question: Silicon Valley loves doing something physical while they're trying to brainstorm— all ideas are saved, until you're on track to make the amazing product. But it's a culture of late capitalism. But also in the classroom, what would distinguish a process we would call HP or informal pedagogy, from teaching "critical thinking skills"?

Winter/Chris: That's why the takeaway is the action piece for me. The idea of practicing the thing that I was involved with in a classroom doesn't work, because what I was doing there was certainly not a process that can be brought into a classroom. It is a problem of naming: you name something and you want to reproduce it, but you can't, so is it then that HP is something we suggest that other people should do? If so, do we then expect that they do all the things we were requiring once we've named it? It's this big quagmire. And even challenging teleology, bringing in the body, all that stuff is particularly incompatible with capitalism, one by one. Really, when we bring it all together . . . we learned to listen to each other and be with each other. Once you start taking them apart it becomes problematic. And so, I'm having a hard time thinking about how this goes beyond even our experience: which goes back to the question of whether we can do it with other people, at other times, in other spaces, and if so, should it just get a different name? I don't know. Tricky questions.

Jason: There's an anecdote that I want to offer with regard to this question about the institution that for me provides hope, and also addresses the issue of inheritances. And that is: I was involved in work that is very similar to this in a different context in Brazil, everyone knows about this because I've talked about it before. And we were basically doing very very similar things, though maybe not explicitly addressing capitalism, with young students in marginalized communities outside of Rio. Long story short, we were doing this for about four years and the municipal government decided they were going to cancel what it is that we are doing. But the students themselves had gotten a taste of doing whatever it is we're doing, and they said, "No, we're not going to let that happen." So what they did was they organized themselves outside the classrooms and got their teacher to do what they were doing inside of school, outside of school. And they would meet. But they went beyond meeting and they said, "No, we're going to complain about this." So they told their parents that their classes were cancelled. And then their parents went to the school board and the school board said, "Huh, maybe we should put that back in there." So they put it back in there and then other students started to say, "Why can't we do what they're doing?" [Laughter] Other students started to say, "We want to do what they're doing!" We called this philosophy, but maybe it wasn't philosophy. So, then the school board said, "Yeah, okay, you guys can do this too." And then one school heard about it from this school, and asked, "Well, why can't we do what they're doing?" And so in this area, Duque de Caxias, which has a few hundred thousand people in it, the school board and the city decided, okay, yeah, we're going to allow what's going on at this one school to happen at a multiplicity of schools. And we'll even have public events where anyone can come and do this. To me, this provides a gesture of hope, in the sense that: you get a taste of doing something like this, and once you do, you don't want to go back to doing things the other way. This is obviously very idealistic, but whatever, we need idealism. It's kind of all we can hope for: at some point if you get a taste of whatever it is that we're doing, you fight to preserve that space.

Matthew: I don't see that as idealistic. Because we have a particular space at a particular time in a particular culture that keeps us trying to do things differently, because we really like what we've been doing for the last three years. You just explained a particular place and time and culture that has done the same. That's not idealism: that's practice. And we're a part of that. I teach differently now than I did two years ago because of this group. Not because of, well, for other reasons too, but that's practice. It's not idealism. I'm pushing back a little bit. You just explained two real examples of this working.

Jacques: Winning isn't idealism.

David: We've set up conferences differently so that people at conferences can interact this way. Then other people at the conference, they say "this is great" and they take that back to wherever they're going. It's an interesting way to see the thing propagate. If it is a thing, the way that you were talking about Jason, the "whatever it is that we're doing." It's like it's there but, "I know not what."

Winter/Chris: That seems important though, going back to your question about fixing. It seems important that as we represent it, that we don't fix it. That it is this constant movement, and it's a constant fight to preserve the right to have this kind of movement. And the best we can do is offer others a glimpse or a taste, so that they can bring that to whatever they're doing.

Jason: The word "taste" is fundamental. I think this is a feeling. I think this is very important. It's a feeling of doing something differently. We're not just talking about ideas and concepts here. It's a lived experience that's felt; it cuts deep inside you, and it feels good, and you think, "Yeah, I want to keep doing that," and I think that's essential, to talk about the feeling behind it. Because I think in the end, that's what's going to motivate you to defend it, like I was saying. The idea won't motivate you. It's emotion.

David: What is that feeling, though? And it starts to sound a little religious. Like, some people might find this culty . . .

Jacques: Culty?

David: I don't know . . .

Joe: I really like the emphasis on pleasure. [Laughter] No, because there's something, if you like: the revolutionary value of pleasure is highly underrated. [Multiple voices say "yes!"] And people commit to things when they learn a new mode of pleasurable experience, and then they're denied it. That's really, that's one of the ways in which people become radicalized. I mean they become radicalized through disappointment, but so often disappointment is not just "I was going to get this money and then didn't" but rather "I have these capabilities that aren't being exercised, that I could once exercise, and it was good." So I feel like the emphasis on that is good.

Jason: Joe, that's a great line: "The revolutionary value of pleasure is highly underrated."

Debrief

Debrief establishes, at the first possible moment, a feedback loop of our session and a focus back toward process. The session does not end without a reflection upon how the discussion occurred, issues of process which emerged, and other concerns which may inform our horizontal pedagogy. This is not a reflection on the content of the questioning and the discussion, but a debrief on how we are practicing our particular horizontal pedagogy. Out of this debrief emerged the importance of pace and pause. The reflection ebbed and flowed, but throughout the debrief statements, the importance of pace and pauses can be seen in the following excerpts.

David: So let's go to debrief. How did that go? It felt so quiet and civil and reserved to me. I've been noticing the differences between conversation and discussion a lot more since I've been thinking about it, and during conversation, particularly when I lived in South America, everyone is interrupting each other and breaking up, there's a very dramatic shifting. And when it's like that, there are moments when one person talks really loudly and everyone listens, and then it breaks apart again into two-by-twos and three-by-threes. But when we do HP, and I remember this too, it's very quiet, with an intense focus on who is going to speak next . . .

Chelsea: I like that . . . trying to get away from the words like and don't like . . . but for example if you do meditation or something like that, you just sit in silence for a certain period of time and you don't do anything, but it really does color your day afterward. Yes, in conversation we're not thinking about how we're talking with each other, and in this space I'm really thinking about it, and in particular at the beginning, with the recorder on, which we can talk about with the writing, I was very conscious of that. So maybe you can think of it in that way: it's this extra, hyper-conscious space, but it probably seeps out in colors, perceptions of conversations beyond this space.

Aleks: I agree, one of my favorite things about OccU meetings was that everyone would take twenty or thirty seconds before beginning to speak and I really love that. First of all, there's a moment for everyone to process. A lot of times conversations feel like a race to talk, and weirdly, I can notice that in certain spaces I start feeling anxious, pressured to talk. So I really appreciate the slowness and time in between people talking.

Jacques: Yeah, I'm going to double down on that. I feel like we don't have many spaces to discuss or dissect what a conversation is or should be, or for what reason, what do you want to get out of it, and that kind of stuff. I feel like I've always wanted to have conversations like this, because they just seem to be the best in terms of getting everyone who is participating to get something out of it. For those reasons. I mean there are so many times where you're with people and the loud person dominates, and people get left out of the conversation, or it's the race, and even if you do race and get your point in, is anyone even digesting it? There's all that kind of stuff. I feel like one thing I can throw in there that's a little more helpful is: the problem with this kind of mode of conversation is, with HP, in a sense, getting people to do it. Because people's first nature is not to sit and listen to other people. When I was in Detroit there were some meetings that I went to and remarkably, if all you do is write things on a board and then ask people, "What are the polite modes of conversation?" and people give responses and you write it down [chuckling], everybody follows it. It's really weird. You get those kinds of conversations just by doing that.

Winter/Chris: There's also an assertion of a certain type of culture. I have very strong memories when we were doing HP in Trump Towers where new people would come in, and they'd be really assertive, be loud, or speak too much, and there was a certain kind of normalizing that went on. I could see all of us who were veterans rolling our eyes, and they could see us rolling our eyes, you know, and facilitators would gently shut them up. There's a normalizing process when you come into this space, which isn't to say it's bad, but it's intense for sure, as much as I love it, I wonder, well, if it's a space that I want, is it therefore, a space that others want?

Joe: I've really enjoyed this process at various points, and the waiting between people talking, that's the vast bulk of my feeling about it, but sometimes it can be a bit somber . . . [others say: Hmmm] . . . And I'm wondering if we could find the way to have the same "listen-y" kind of rhythm, that nevertheless was able to be punctuated by another livelier rhythm; a way of enlivening it somehow?

Aleks: I'm still going back to Joe's question about how you can be slow and jovial at the same time! [Laughter] And I feel like I've been struggling with this a lot, with every kind of meeting, or being at a party or a get together with activists and radicals: like there's always a certain kind of weight, and intensity, and I think for a lot of people that intensity is not always easy to handle. And I don't know, I don't think intensity is necessarily bad, but I do appreciate jovialness. I'm not always sure how to bring it into a certain space, but . . .

Joe: Oh really? I would be interested to see how long it took us to establish this slow rhythm. Because I'd be interested to see how the people involved had to learn it, and over what time period. My sense is that we learned it as a group slowly, under various circumstances, some of which were probably good and others of which were bad. Some of them were just being quite afraid of jumping in over anyone else, because in Occupy this was so frowned upon, the whole movement was really into everyone having their chance to speak and not talking over other people. There's a little bit of a tension about it, which is in some ways quite productive because we say: let's pay much more attention to this than we normally do, because normally we'd fuck it up all the time. I'm just really interested, and I wonder if other people. . . . We often think about the people who have been doing this for six months and then people who come in and experience this normalizing, but if we are talking about the benefit of learning different habits of being and modes of interaction, then that seems like a good thing: that a new person is not down to speed yet. That seems like a sign that the group is learning something, and though it might be bad because it might mean we become inhospitable, nevertheless there should be a gap between the group that has practiced something and a new person that hasn't practiced that thing—that's a sign that your educational process is proceeding.

Check-out
We end this chapter with the final procedure: check-out. Each participant says how they feel after the interaction has taken place.

David: I feel really good and this is a great feeling. This is just really nice.

Joe: I feel great, that was really great. I'm really pleased that it happened. And I'm almost pleased that David expressed it as a diaspora. I was like, yeah, that's a really nice way to think about it, it's not like everything has ended, and it's not like a wake or a nostalgia-fest. Let's just meet one more time before spreading outwards.

Chelsea: I seem to remember in the winter, or something, there was, going back in my memory, there was an OccU iconography and it was a dandelion, with the little sprouts going. When Jacques said it was like pollen disseminating. . . . Maybe we can think about that, not in a cultish way where we're all going to be dandelions, but maybe we'll be like the kind of dandelions that disperse and become other kinds of weeds. [Laughter] I feel pretty good about that.

Aleks: You know for a really long time I thought that a dandelion was a live thing that was actually a happy lion [Laughter], never really understood why this image of a dandelion is such a prevalent image in the U.S., and like . . . [Laughter again]

Matthew: I think we found the title to our article: "The Dandelion."

Jacques: I'll check out. I'm just, there was a moment toward the end where I was thinking about other groups that I was involved with during Occupy, and there's this prevailing thought that, "Man, I just wish we could've communicated better with one another." And then I thought, "Wow, that's what HP is." Somebody said earlier "cultivating a set of habits that account for the needs of the group via its participants." I'm paraphrasing, but that's really important. I felt like the groups that I was a part of that did really good work, the moments when the good work was getting done, that was its apex. . . . And then the moments where things didn't get done, where that was at the low point. I'm just really glad that I was a part of this in a tangential form through groups that practiced HP.

DR: I'd like to check out. I think that obviously HP works because it can get a bunch of people who used to talk, back together after two years. I was really looking forward to seeing everyone's faces. And the conversation picked up just as easily as it ever did on any Thursday. So, on that front, I think it was a clamorous success. And I would hope that further experiments would be similarly successful. Also, in some reflection, as we're all talking, I realized how much HP has changed my own ways of discussing ideas. And in really interesting, deep-seated ways. For example, I went to a conference, an academic conference, while we were still doing HP, and I decided not to read a paper. Everyone's seen conferences where we read from papers and we're wanting to shoot ourselves from boredom. I realized that the boredom or stultification, the term we used to use, is counter-revolutionary, to quote some other guy. I remember I refused to read a paper. I talked. I had an idea of what I was saying, but I talked. So there are all kinds of ways, really interesting, and far-reaching effects that HP had on my own pedagogical methods that sometimes were not really directly related to what we were actually doing there, but it was really about militating against boredom, which is important. So it was deeply effective, and maybe sometimes in subterranean ways that we don't even realize. The end.

Matthew: This is very comfortable, which I have to admit that, in the eight years I've been here, I haven't been comfortable a lot. To be honest. And you guys, I'm very comfortable with . . .

[Significant pause]

Aleks: I would like to propose that we do this again in Miami. [Laughter] In the wintertime. Jacques and I promise to bring a hammock. And tropical fruit! [Laughter]

Joe: I second that!

Matthew: A yearly conference? I love it!

Winter: I was going to check out non-verbally with one of these. [Tips his hat]

DR: Does that mean we're done? All right.

Jason: Opa!

[Clapping]

Aleks: Can I just say one thing that's tangential, David, to what you were saying . . .

Notes

1   The term "horizontal" in reference to pedagogy has at least two precedents in the history of philosophy and education. The first is in Paulo Freire's (1972/2000) *Pedagogy of the oppressed*, who utters it in a very different sense than we intend. Freire uses the word "horizontal" to refer to a kind of violence which occurs among the oppressed: when the oppressed oppress one another. However, Freirian dialogical pedagogy, in its attempt to revolutionize oppressive relations, does seek to "equalize" the roles of teacher and student in a way that may bring the concept of horizontality to mind. For example, Freire calls for "teachers-students" to learn

with "students-teachers" in dialogue, rather than teachers talking to students in a banking model of education. We also understand horizontality in education as a pedagogical approach which counters oppressive relations, though we do not mean the term exactly the way Freire did. The other usage is in Felix Guattari's (2004) *Three ecologies*, which includes a concept of "tranversality" very close in kind to "horizontality." The way in which we mean the term may be found in two recent articles on educational practices of the Occupy Wall Street movement: Beery, T., Fischer, N., Greenberg, A., & Polendo, A. (2013). "Occupy museums as public pedagogy and justice work." *Journal of Curriculum Theorizing*, 29(2); and DiSalvo, J. (2013). "Political education—Occupy Wall Street's first year." *Radical Teacher*, (96), 6-15. For further research on horizontalism generally see the work of Marina Sitrin, particularly: *Horizontalism: Voices of popular power in Argentina*. AK Press, 2006; *Everyday revolutions: Horizontalism and autonomy in Argentina*. Zed Books, 2012; "Horizontalism and the Occupy movements." *Dissent* 59.2 (2012): 74-75.

2   #OccupyWallStreet: A shift in revolutionary tactics. *Adbusters*. Retrieved at http://www.commondreams.org/views/2011/07/16/occupywallstreet-shift-revolutionary-tactics.

3   See Wozniak, J.T., & Kohan, W.O. (2012). Philosophy as spiritual exercise in an adult literacy course and the endless evaluation of philosophical experience. In *Educating for Complex Thinking through Philosophical Inquiry*. Napoli: Liguori, 271.

4   Levin, C. et al. "Wall Street and the financial crisis: Anatomy of a financial collapse." Report issued by the Permanent Subcommittee on Investigations, United States Senate. Retrieved from http://www.hsgac.senate.gov//imo/media/doc/Financial_Crisis/FinancialCrisisReport.pdf?attempt=2

5   For an archive of courses offered by the Occupy University, see http://university.nycga.net.

6   The following is taken from a document written in 2012 for use during workshops.

7   See Dillon, J. (1994). *Using discussion in classrooms*. Philadelphia, PA: Open University Press.

8   Earlier in the process, Wozniak expressed some misgivings about the check-in procedure, as well as the physical education procedure. In both cases, he takes issue with compelling, or putting pressure on, members of a group to say how they're feeling or to do things with their bodies, which recalls the forced participation of schooling.

9   Wozniak spoke briefly at a StrikeDebt meeting about HP, which Backer recorded. StrikeDebt is an offshoot organization of OWS groups devoted to the politicization of debt.

10 This phrase "share in the administration and deliberation" is a paraphrase of one of Aristotle's articulations of democracy in *Politics*, 1261b.

11 Mackin came late to the discussion and is responding, in this comment, to a moment of the dialogue that happened as he entered. Though he came during the discussion, we asked him to describe HP as we had done earlier, and we have inserted his remarks in the examination section to keep the flow of the written document.

12 Anthropologist David Graeber was involved in many aspects of OWS, including Occupy University events and discussions.

13 Rilke, R.M. (1993). *Letters to a young poet*. (S. Mitchell, Trans.). Boston, MA: Shambhala.

14 Horton, M., & Freire, P. (1990). *We make the road by walking: Conversations on education and social change*. Philadelphia, PA: Temple University Press. The format of this chapter is loosely based on the format of that text.

15 The discussion took place at one of the participants' apartments in New York City.

16 See Derrida, J., & Dufourmantelle, A. (2000). *Of hospitality*. Stanford, CA: Stanford University Press; Rancière, J. (1991). *The ignorant schoolmaster: Five lessons in intellectual emancipation*. (K. Ross, Trans.). Stanford, CA: Stanford University Press.

17 Zane/Sage is a scholar of medieval Italian literature.

18 "Karen" is Dr. Karen Baird, a professor of political science at SUNY–Purchase. Dr. Baird was a co-founder of Occupy University and a participant in many HP sessions. On the occasion referred to here, Dr. Baird dedicated a day at the beginning of a course on race and politics to pedagogy and communication. Backer and Emily Coralyne, a graduate of Purchase who had studied with Dr. Baird, facilitated an HP session with students at Purchase's campus. This session was part of a "fall campaign" in 2012 where members of the HP workshop facilitated discussions at universities in the New York area, including Bard College and Teachers College.

19 Bissen is an architect and the courses referred to were taught at the Parsons School for Design.

CHAPTER 12

Street Theory: Grassroots Activist Interventions in Regimes of Knowledge

Sandra Jeppesen and Joanna Adamiak

Introduction

We begin this chapter about different spaces of learning with a story that situates us, and our discussion, in one of these spaces of learning. We participated in one of the annual North American Anarchist Studies Network (NAASN) conferences. When we arrived, about two hours after the day had started, we learned from organizers that the opening panel had been extended by two hours. This delayed all subsequent events, including our panel, which would be on anarchist interventions into academic conferences.

We responded to this in two ways. First, it was refreshing that organizers and participants took the intervention seriously, and space was made for some key discussions to take place. However, the flexibility also presented an experience of dissonance. Although we are critical of academia, and therefore, open to fluidity in learning, our institutionalized training around punctuality nonetheless led us to feel stressed by the delay. As the opening panel wrapped up, we felt pressure to get through our workshop quickly, sensing that people had other commitments to get to, whereas the organizers and some participants in our panel explained that we should take all the time we needed. This contradiction presented a profound challenge for us.

We had planned a participatory workshop to unsettle the idea that only workshop facilitators are experts, thus giving space to the expertise of participants. The first step of the workshop was a go-around where we invited participants to introduce themselves and to share a story of their learning experience through storytelling or explication. However, the fact that there were over forty participants meant that the go-around took almost all of our originally allotted time. It seems that in facilitating the workshop, while we were anxious about the delay, we accepted the new structure of fluidity.

The go-around was generative and did the very work we had hoped for—participants had all struggled in different ways to be learners against the structural, affective, and epistemological constraints in the regular school system. From primary to secondary, post-secondary, and beyond, participants came up with very creative strategies for mixed learning models, resistant learning, and psychic survival. The wealth of experiential knowledge, resilience, and resistance shared by the participants in that go-around was overwhelming and quite moving. It was a highly effective and affective moment of learning for us as well as for many participants. After the go-around, we took a break to figure out next steps, since we had not yet completed the content of our workshop.

We regrouped and strategized with our other collective members. We were intensely aware that some people were leaving due to time constraints or disappointment that we had not yet covered most of the points in our notes. During the go-around, we spoke to the fact that we resisted the need to reinsert ourselves as experts, to sum things up, or to interpret the go-around through academic frames. Despite the intention to unsettle this performance of academic expertise, we felt conflicting pressures because of the feeling that as anarchist, feminist, female presenters, there was already a structural assumption that we were not experts, and because of this, we would need to assert our knowledge all the more explicitly to be deemed legitimate by participants. We decided to facilitate a check-in with people about how the go-around had felt for them.

When we called participants back, only a handful returned, perhaps five to seven people. While we were initially discouraged, assuming others had not returned because of our shortcomings, the conversation that took place was again, quite generative. People trickled back slowly, so the group grew to a comfortable size. The conversation centered on strategies used to learn differently, to teach differently, and to encourage our students and teachers to challenge institutional learning models. This discussion also interrogated what our workshop had sought to question: how do we co-create strategies for intervening into learning/teaching spaces? It seems that through the careful work of our participants, and also the work of stepping back on our part and not reinserting ourselves as experts, we had effectively, collectively engaged in the resistant co-production of pedagogical knowledge.

We attended NAASN because it seemed like a space where we could safely engage in co-production of knowledge that is critical of disembodied and individualized academic performance. As our past experiences suggested, more work needed to be done to break the posturing of masculinized spaces for dissemination of research. Whereas much research has been done on co-production of knowledge with research participants through participatory action research, little has been explored on participatory dissemination. However, we had assumed that radical learning spaces such as NAASN could more easily challenge structural forms of learning and power. We were surprised by our own deep-seated, internalized, institutional way of approaching learning, especially with respect to how long it takes to learn, and how engrained it is for some of us to follow a schedule. We therefore found that spaces of radical learning require a challenge on many levels, not just geographically in terms of opening a space and sitting in a circle, but also epistemologically and psychologically.

This chapter examines four types of radical learning spaces with respect to how they might unsettle institutionalized learning. We present experiences as narratives interlaced with critical analysis, and in some places, translate the narrative into theoretical frames. We are intentionally inverting and subverting the classic academic model, using a grassroots anarchist-feminist methodology (Guberman & Greenfield, 1991; McLaren, 1998; Leighton, 1979; Greenway, 2010; Dark Star Collective, 2012; Jeppesen, Kruzynski, Lakoff & Sarrasin, 2014). We first consider radical pedagogies engaged in university settings. However, we argue that while university spaces may be subverted in some ways, there are limits to the types of interventions that can be made because the neoliberal university system is rooted in intensifying state control and capitalist practices. Furthermore, it exists as an ideological space in which systematic interlocking oppressions take place along lines of race, class, gender, sex, colonialism, disability, and other axes (Lorde, 1984; Crenshaw, 1989; hooks, 1989; Collins, 1990; Yeatman, 1995). We then consider: counter-hegemonic formalized learning spaces, informal learning spaces, and events that are not designated as learning spaces at all. We find that radical learning spaces outside the academic system address epistemologies, psychologies, and geographies of space that more profoundly challenge the process and politics of learning.

Interventions into University Spaces
In a Queer Theory course taught at York University in 2007, Sandra organized learning around bringing in guest speakers from the queer activist community in Toronto. This included Maggie's Toronto Sex Workers Action Project, which facilitated a workshop on peer sex-worker harm reduction, trans folks from the 519 Church St. Community Centre who facilitated a "Trans 101" workshop, and writers such as Kristyn Dunnion and Tara-Michelle Ziniuk who read from their work and did a question and answer period with students (Maggie's Toronto, 2011; The 519 Talks: Workshop Series, 2011; Dunnion, 2004; Ziniuk, 2009).

From the beginning, students were encouraged to try out their "half thoughts" or partially formed ideas in the hope that someone else might have the other half, acknowledging that knowledge production is a shared process. Early in the course, we did a session on "the unspeakable" where students wrote down something they personally were not able to talk about. These were collected and read out anonymously. Many students shared superficial taboos such as "don't talk about sex," but a few shared personal details from their lives that they really struggled to put into words. These struggles resonated with the group, and students were motivated to do a second round, digging a bit deeper and opening up with each other. In this discussion, we came together as a close-knit group who could share intimacies. This expanded our repertoire from theory to identity and the affective, reaching beyond texts into people's lives.

Increasingly, students incorporated examples from their own lives, engaging difficult questions, even inventing terms to describe something they had no language for. One such term was *homogeneration*—the generation that has grown up with normative homosexuality and gay marriage. The male inventor of this term said he and his partner could go to Ikea and nobody misread them as roommates or brothers; everyone knew they were partners. At another moment, people asked if there was something such as *homonormativity* or normative standards of what it means to be LGBTQ. Students also started talking to specific friends after class on a weekly basis, and brought in their friends' questions. They weren't the only ones! Sandra was also processing her class with a few close friends each week, generating new ideas and strategies. Bringing in these questions extended the classroom to include many absent others and silenced voices, breaking down geographies of space and social class that police university classroom boundaries.

A few weeks into the course, after agonizing over conversations with a friend who said she would have been devastated if a queer theory professor she related to had then come out as straight, Sandra decided to tell to her class. Framing it as her "unspeakable," Sandra revealed that she had a primary partner who was male and shared her fear that people might think this undermined her legitimacy to teach this course. Sandra spoke briefly about queering heterosexuality, destabilizing gender, and polyamory. Students seemed surprised, especially about the fear of being judged inauthentic. However, it seemed to work two ways. On one hand, it deconstructed the university power hierarchy by decentering Sandra's authority, and by giving academic legitimacy to the students' experiential knowledge. On the other, it demonstrated how claiming ownership over knowledge and deciding when and how to share it does provide the possibility of taking power, although in this case, it was not power-over but power-with-others, inviting their empowerment (Starhawk, 2011). Following this model, students could decide for themselves what to disclose and when.

The final assignment was a group queer theory performance project. These final performances took place outside the classroom, in a lounge, after one of the public poetry readings offered as part of the course. There was food, and we sat on couches and armchairs, which established a much more convivial and intimate atmosphere. People created theoretically informed and profoundly moving sketches that challenged and destabilized sex and gender norms in creative ways. For example, a mock talk show had heterosexual couples fighting for rights in a fictionalized "homonormative" society. By bringing in outside knowledges and challenging who owns knowledge, the class was ultimately able to exit the classroom space and thereby produce profoundly transformative learning.

The second course was Discourses of Dissent taught at Concordia University. The readings for this course built on the Direct Action class Sandra had co-facilitated at AnarchistU in Toronto with Ashar Latif. The books were all written by revolutionaries describing their own process of coming to consciousness, challenging state hegemony, and offering rationalizations for militancy (Fanon, 1965; Bauman, 1981; Shakur, 1987; Hansen, 2001; Churchill, 2007; Gelderloos, 2007). Students were required to engage in a project with a community group and produce a critical discourse analysis of the group's materials. Many of the students got involved in groups they respected, only to find as the semester progressed that the group had inappropriate expectations of their involvement (e.g., fundraising); problematic dynamics (e.g., a male-dominated LGBT advocacy group); stringent design aesthetics (e.g., a poster students designed was rejected as "too mainstream"); contradictory messaging (e.g., a website that invited people to come and chill out versus a space full of signs stating strict rules); or colonial attitudes (e.g., an NGO that sent students from Canada to Africa but was not willing to consider inviting students from Africa to teach in Canada). Space was made to talk about challenges in working within activist groups, especially if you have radical critiques that might lead to conflict, to being singled out, or to not being taken seriously.

This course transgressed the university learning space by valuing radical epistemologies represented in the six texts studied, by bringing in authors to speak with the class, and by challenging middle-class assumptions about pacifism, violence, and structural oppression. Students brought these ideas into their own activist practices, which created profound personal struggles and growth. Like Queer Theory, the class provided a generative affective space. It integrated transgressive content into course assignments, included activist practices, and constructed alternative epistemological spaces that spilled beyond the classroom.

While the first course attempted to bring the community into the classroom, the second attempted to bring the students or the classroom into the community. What becomes apparent through both courses is that this divide between university and community is quite fixed and only partially permeable. This is for three reasons. First, its structure is legitimated by the state (in Canada, the Ministry of Training, Colleges and Universities) which authorizes and funds university programs, oversees their administration, and approves the granting of degrees, which may be understood as an ideological form of knowledge production. Second, universities are legitimated by capitalism through the payment of tuition, to become a student/knowledge producer, and through the receipt of salary, to become a professor/knowledge disseminator. The occupation of these hierarchical positions is controlled not just by the number of degrees obtained, but also by the fees paid or received. Higher fees signify a "better" university; higher salaries signify a "better" professor. Third, universities are structurally implicated in neoliberalism in terms of these organizational (state and capital) forms, and as such, they further enact other ideological and material forms of interlocking oppressions beyond the economic, including reproducing hierarchies of race, class, gender, sex, sexuality, disability, and colonialism (Razack, 1998; Jiwani, 2007; Jeppesen and Nazar, 2012; Smith, 2013; Thobani, 2008). Thus while radical ideas and transgressive practices may be enacted within university spaces, structural inequities are very difficult, if not impossible, to challenge. We, therefore, conclude that radical learning must move outside the university to address these issues.

Challenging Epistemologies of Learning: Formalized Counter-Hegemonic Learning Spaces

Disheartened by the university setting, anarchists and other radicals have established counter-hegemonic learning spaces free from the hierarchies, boundaries, structures, and pressures of educational institutions that tend to serve as ideological state apparatuses (Gramsci, 1971). These counter-hegemonic institutions are often labeled "free schools" after the Ferrer model and may include primary, secondary, or post-secondary classes (Miller, 2002).

Anarchist architect and Toronto free school participant Adrian Blackwell (2000) has constructed a "Model for Public Space." Comprised of a spiraled bench that grows in height as it winds around itself, this seating model sets up hierarchies and then destabilizes them. If you sit at the top of the model, occupying a geographically higher space of power, you will in effect be on the periphery of the conversation, whereas if you sit in the centre, occupying a geographically central location of power, other people will be sitting above and behind you, and you may have difficulty seeing everyone or being heard. There is no single position that geospatially maps onto the position of greatest power, as there would be for example, in a classroom, where the front is the power position. Blackwell's Model encourages people to sit in the middle rows, positioning themselves spatially in relations of equality with others. This is an excellent visual model for thinking through processes of learning in counter-hegemonic spaces, which attempt to eliminate the power position at the front of the classroom, rendering it uninhabitable by those who would exercise control.

In Toronto, Canada, the Anarchist Free University (AnarchistU or AFU) was active during 2003–2012; Sandra was involved as part of the organizing collective or general assembly, as a class participant, and as co-facilitator, during 2004–2007. AnarchistU challenged the limitations of mainstream universities: neither legitimated by the state nor charging capitalist fees, they were committed to counter-hegemonic content and anti-oppression processes in learning. All of the AFU minutes are available online.[1] The notes from the founding meeting open:

> We had a go-around and everyone said what they would like the Free University to be and what they're interested in. Most people want a challenge similar to university. Most people want some kind of structured way of learning but many people spoke against the traditional model of classes with a "professor." . . . Several people spoke strongly about anti-oppression politics and would like an emphasis on issues of decolonization, immigration, race, sex, gender, sexuality. There was some difference in emphasis. Some people want courses that are action-oriented, in effect learning by activism. Other people seem to want something like a course of readings and group discussion. We went inside because it was getting cold and spent the last half-hour on some issues of organization. (AnarchistU, 2003)

Following this mandate set at their first meeting, AnarchistU was committed to free learning more fully connected to real life experience, as indicated by collective member Rob Teixeira (n.d.): "Our experiment in radical education demanded that we make learning relevant to the concerns and needs of those who sought knowledge and engagement with ideas that were not divorced from their everyday lives and acting in the world" (p. 8).

AFU organized as a loosely constituted "general assembly" consisting of whoever attended meetings, and this group would collectively decide on courses by evaluating proposals received:

> Decisions at the Free University are taken at monthly general meetings. There is no executive committee. If we set up any working groups for particular tasks they are responsible to the general assembly. Participation at meetings is open, though later we might decide on

a level of participation in the Free University needed to take part in decision-making. The general assembly decides on all course proposals. The facilitator or group make a proposal in writing and present this to the assembly. After questions and discussion they leave while a decision is being taken. (AnarchistU, 2003)

This model was later modified when people perceived that the structurelessness was causing invisible hierarchies. The fear was that "individuals with greater experience in the collective would have greater power over decisions, and that skills and experience tends to get concentrated in certain individuals due to their repetition of activities" (AnarchistU, 2004). This demonstrates the self-reflection and care taken to challenge unspoken power dynamics.

The experience of AFU was compared favorably to university classes by many participants. One student-participant had intentionally hitchhiked and freight-hopped up from the U.S. to attend AnarchistU for the summer semester, much as one might move cities to attend university. Another participant writes of their experience:

Five of us met weekly over tea in the comforts of a participant's living room. One member of the class was to present to the rest each week. I'd say each class was about as well or better prepared than the handful of paid courses I took over the past year. Though it may not have been as information heavy as some of those other courses, my classmates were engaged and sincerely interested in having a meaningful discourse. The atmosphere was intimate, relaxed and conducive to people opening up and sharing ideas. (Shawn-Caza, 2011)

At the same time, being desirous of creating a university-like experience, university hierarchies may have inadvertently been replicated. There were facilitators proposing classes, who were presumed to have some kind of expertise in contradistinction to those who participated in classes. There were spaces designated for each class, predominantly people's living rooms, or a community space such as Uprising Books. Having read texts selected by the facilitator, people would gather in a given space, at a specified hour, on a continual weekly basis, in a meeting constituted somewhat like a university class, for ten weeks in a row. These blocks of ten weeks were referred to by organizers as semesters. In these ways, AnarchistU classes were structured like those of a university.

On the one hand, facilitators were presumed not to have any special knowledge, presuming that class participants would co-produce knowledge, and on the other, facilitators were needed to propose classes in the first place and to generate discussion. For example, in the Direct Action class that Ashar Latif and Sandra facilitated, there was one week when neither could make it, and the group agreed to self-facilitate, however, there was a lack of focus and little discussion, which was surprising as we usually had lively conversations. Despite establishing a non-hierarchical space, there are "invisible hierarchies" based on presumptions and behaviors inherited from mainstream society.

Although AnarchistU challenged many aspects of state, capital, and interlocking oppressions, our practices raise questions around *epistemologies of space*. How is knowledge produced within certain spaces, how are those spaces constituted as spaces for learning, and by whom? In the case of AnarchistU, classes were constituted as learning spaces through the review of proposals approved by the collective. Does this introduce an alternative hierarchy defined by new criteria such as being legitimated as an activist with the appropriate level of experience, rather than the possession of university degrees? Moreover, can everyone's knowledge be equal when there is a designated facilitator who is authorized to speak on the topic because they have developed the proposal, done the readings before the others in the class, and framed the discussion? Having a collectively legitimated expertise does not mean one person knows better or more, but everyone's knowledge is not equally recognized either. In classroom spaces, power is gained through the expression of knowledge, and the production of power in turn legitimates the knowledge produced.

The attempt to replicate a university structure outside capital and the state can thus be seen as both a strength and weakness of AnarchistU. People could recognize the classes as spaces of radical learning, and this was its greatest strength. Student-participants were an interesting mixture of ages, classes, genders, sexualities, and social locations. Many positioned themselves outside the university system, without high school, college, or university degrees, while some were undergrad or grad students and one of the co-founders, Alan O'Connor, was a professor. On the other hand, while hierarchies of state and capital were eradicated, hierarchies associated with epistemologies of space were only somewhat mitigated.

Radical learning thus runs up against its own limits as it has created geographies of knowledge production or epistemologies that delimit learning spaces. Perhaps by isolating learning in a designated epistemological space, some of the affective aspects of free learning are limited. The affective and spatial issues raised here, we argue, have more freedom to be addressed in less formal learning spaces.

Challenging Psychologies of Learning: Informal Activist Learning Spaces

By removing learning from formalized education spaces, activists often create spaces where learning is intentionally anti-academic and thus more emotionally available. Informal activist learning spaces can be defined as intentionally constructed spaces of knowledge sharing, where activists co-create mostly experiential knowledge. These spaces do not have clearly demarcated borders with other types of learning spaces. Rather, they share some features of formalized learning spaces on one side and non-learning-designated spaces on the other. We argue that this kind of learning space contributes to radicalizing learning by challenging the psychological or affective space of institutional learning.

Activist conferences, teach-ins, anarchist book fair workshops, and organizing weekends are some of the spaces that comprise this category. One example is the explicitly activist conference, Mobilizing and Organizing from Below Conference (MOBCONF) held in Baltimore, Maryland, in June 2012. Unlike NAASN, which was started by academics who self-identify as anarchist, MOBCONF was organized by and for organizers and activists. Similar in format to academic conferences including NAASN, there were simultaneous presentations in different rooms, with panels of two to four people presenting information to a room of people who could choose which presentations to attend or walk in and out as they pleased. The differences from formal academic conference spaces were significant, however.

First, the location of the conference was chosen intentionally to be non-academic, held in a community organizing space, with an open door policy and a pay-what-you-can structure if and when fees were applied.[2] Second, the structure of the sessions was somewhat different. Each room had chairs laid out in a circle. Workshops began with an introduction of each person in the room, thus providing an opportunity for presenters and participants to speak about their organizing work and allowing for the potential for collaborations on the activist projects being discussed. This initial round of introductions had two main effects. First, it broke down the wall between presenters and audience, allowing for an interactive discussion of organizing work. Once each participant had shared how they were connected to the topic, the perception that only the presenters had knowledge to share was quickly broken down. The second, related effect was that the direction of the conversation to follow could be amended based on the interests, knowledge, expertise, and proposals of those in the room.

Despite these structural differences, there was still sometimes an assumption of expertise imposed on presenters by some participants, or a deferral to them. Moreover, some participants voiced disappointment or concern that they did not want to speak about their expertise because they came to learn something from the presenters. We also experienced this in our NAASN workshop. Furthermore, gender dynamics and ageism still played a role in determining who was considered to be an authority. However, these concerns were often explicitly challenged by some participants and presenters, and did not constitute the dominant dynamic.

Academic expertise also played a role in constructing the legitimacy to speak. MOBCONF had many participants and presenters who were undergrad or grad students and academics, who did not necessarily present themselves as such, and who did not use their status as academics to claim expertise. If anything, they tried to downplay this. In Joanna's own experience, this was done partly because of the vehement critique of academics in activist spaces, and partly because of a desire to separate from academic conventions, privileges, and oppressions, preferring to engage solely as an organizer and leaving her academic hat at home. However, Joanna found her internal critiques of some of the panels derived from her academic training, for example, being critical of presentations that did not reference their sources, or that used few if any sources. We might consider how some learning spaces expect us to separate aspects of ourselves which are deemed illegitimate in the space, leaving us only able to mobilize incomplete knowledge. Moreover, if many people are carving off aspects of their experience or expertise, how does this impact the overall generativity of knowledge co-production? Are we weakening our movements by producing limited types of knowledge in particular spaces? For example, only producing academic knowledge in university spaces, and activist knowledge in activist spaces? How can these forms of knowledge interact to strengthen each other without hierarchizing them?

In this informal space, the geographical space was slightly different than an academic space, but the psychology and epistemology of the space was quite different. Joanna was part of a presentation in this conference, with two friends who both have graduate degrees. We presented a performance piece about our experiences participating in anti-G20 protest organizing in Toronto in 2010. The presentation began with reading out a pamphlet about different emotions and behaviors associated with having experienced and recovering from trauma (York University Counselling Services, n.d.). We then wove together in a journal-like style three personal narratives of our experiences during the G20, revealing how the three experiences of trauma were interrelated. Personal conclusions about trauma in large protest events were shared, we concluded with how we learned to support one another through it, despite the fact that none of us had any training in trauma psychology or counseling. The participants seemed to accept that we were experts of our own experience, and the rest of the workshop focused on collaborative strategizing, dealing with future protest trauma through an established shared experience of trauma at large political events. The deferral to us as experts was based on two different things: either we had more hindsight because our trauma had occurred a few years earlier, or because some had not experienced this kind of trauma but were looking for guidance in planning trauma support for upcoming events. This deferral seemed to happen despite the fact that the conversation did not presume we were experts. We did not give advice to participants; we collaborated in thinking through how to address issues raised, and we received input on how to support our communities in their grief and trauma. As experts only of our own experience, we came together with participants to learn from the experiences of other people and to make better sense of our own through collective sharing.

Other informal learning spaces in which we participated, perhaps closer to non-learning-designated spaces, include mass mobilizations against the G20 in Toronto in 2010 and the G8 in Heiligendamm and Rostock, Germany in 2007. At the latter, there were two types of learning spaces. First, there were ad hoc training sessions offered at the entrance to one of two large base camps for protesters. As the need for medics arose, or as people strategized particular actions—e.g., occupying an airstrip, or shutting down the only road to the meeting site—training sessions were spontaneously organized to give activists the opportunity to share skills needed to pull off the action. These were the more formal of the two types of learning spaces, though organized in an ad hoc manner. Second, there was the opportunity to learn by taking action. For example, there were many opportunities to participate in consensus decision-making, art creation, cooking, maintaining security (from police), playing drums in a drum circle, or sharing social movement histories with people you happened to sit beside at dinner or who set up their tent beside you. Furthermore, there were radical vendors set up, and conversations could be engaged in or overheard about books or other merchandise that constituted a sharing of knowledge about movement histories or activist practices in other countries. The participation of many different people in an extremely large spokescouncil showed how consensus decision-making could be translated across many different ethnic and language groups. In the Heiligendamm context, Joanna was a participant who arrived at the camp a few days before the demonstrations began.

Joanna's experience with the G20 in Toronto was much more in-depth as a mobilizer and co-creator of a layer of protest infrastructure, work that started months before the June 2010 protests. In January 2010, we began the work of reaching out to people in Toronto, Southwestern Ontario, and Quebec to consolidate organizing efforts, including establishing infrastructure for the thousands of protesters coming to town, by forming the Toronto Community Mobilization Network (TCMN).

The work of the TCMN had multiple levels of knowledge production and co-production, bridging the less formal learning space in Rostock with the more formal learning space of MOBCONF. For example, participation in meetings meant gaining facilitation, organizing, logistical, counseling, policy-making, and computer skills, as well as experience in consensus decision-making and knowledge about the histories of movement practices. While many institutional learning conventions were not followed, there were still hierarchies of legitimation and expertise within these spaces. Just as at MOBCONF and in Rostock, the psychological space of informal learning tried to challenge institutionalized learning modes, but ran up against the internalized structures of the spaces being challenged. Most importantly, the challenge came when bringing up knowledge that included emotional and interpersonal learning where experiences being shared were contextualized in social relationships. Within the spaces described in this section, the geography of MOBCONF was not significantly different from formal academic spaces, while the geographies of Rostock and G20 learning spaces were quite different. Consultations and workshops were organized for people to share knowledge about protest tactics and theories, medic training and trauma support, political ideologies and power, the role and impact of the G20, economic histories, and government policies. In addition, skillshares were organized to engage in art-making, outreach, creating media and media events, interacting with mainstream media, and cooking. The teaching and learning structure was that those who had activist-oriented expertise shared it with those who did not.

Both Rostock and the TCMN did, however, make a decisive intervention into the *psychologies of space*. By prioritizing learning from experience and flipping the understanding of expertise on its head, the emotional aspect of learning was linked with knowledge-sharing, discouraging theorizing disconnected from practice, social relationships, and lived experience. The psychology of space in such a learning environment challenges institutional spaces of learning in that knowledge being co-created could not be easily separated from emotional and personal experience. A disconnected, rationalized presentation of facts was not given primacy in these spaces, even though there continued to be a struggle for academic authority, with proper citations, or some participants questioning the expertise of some presenters. Not only was there an active disavowal of this kind of institutionalized disembodied engagement, but also the content of the knowledge itself changed the psychology of the space because it was derived from the lived experiences of the people presenting and participating. However, there are still some ways that this new valuing of expertise creates hierarchies, although different hierarchies than academic spaces uphold.[3] This is part of the critique we had offered in the NAASN presentation. Learning spaces where psychologies of space are challenged are also sites of learning songs, chants, interacting with police, and navigating protest sites, which brings us to the fourth space of learning—learning that literally happens in the streets.

Challenging Geographies of Learning: Non-Learning-Designated Spaces

Learning that takes place "in the streets" also takes different forms and follows a similar pattern to that mentioned in the previous section. This style of learning profoundly challenges the geography of learning spaces. While some learning is almost inadvertent, there are also moments of planned learning in the streets. One good example was the Toxic Tour March that took place on the Environmental Justice Day of Action in the week leading up to the Toronto G20 Summit (Casey, 2010). Participants in the march stopped at sites of banks and corporations guilty of environmentally destructive practices and ongoing neo-colonization. Learning was multifaceted. First, using a megaphone, people were given information about the relationship between capitalism and environmental destruction; the relationship between resource extraction and ongoing colonization and genocide of indigenous people, cultures, and land; and practical information about resistance movements and how to get involved.

Second, learning happened in the act of engaging in the march itself. For example, the experience of participating in a march offers lessons about the police. In this particular demonstration, the police were particularly antagonistic toward participants, trying to enforce strict (though arbitrary and changeable) geographical delineations between the "protest zone" and the "police area." This experience included learning how police abuse their power and how to engage with this arbitrary rule-setting, as well as learning personally how to negotiate physical, psychological, and even epistemological space in relation to these representatives of the repressive state apparatus (Gramsci, 1971). Having a theoretical, ideological critique of police, perhaps surprisingly, does not preclude learning a great deal about oneself, including internalized self-policing through contact or conflict with an officer at a demonstration. This offers a window into how we carry ourselves in the face of militarized power, including how we navigate fear, repression, and arbitrary abuses of power.

A second example of "protest pedagogies" derives from a video of participants in the black bloc march on Yonge Street during the Get Off the Fence demonstration on June 26, 2010 (TorontoG20Exposed, 2010). The video features a rapid-fire conversation between two black bloc protesters,[4] who were marching up Yonge Street engaging in "property modification," about whether or not the adult entertainment Zanzibar Club should be targeted. One person was about to modify the light bulb sign when the other asked why they were targeting it. The person answered that the club was a symbol of the exploitation of women. The intervening person argued that sex workers were comrades and attacking their place of work could be perceived as being against sex work. The footage ends with both participants walking away from the club without targeting it. The discussion about sex worker rights as labor rights may have continued later, but the real learning took place in the moment of action, revealing how unstructured learning can profoundly challenge the hegemonic geography of learning spaces that designates schools to be where we learn, and non-school spaces to be, by default, non-learning spaces.

Other examples of "street learning" are consultas and general assemblies that lead up to mass mobilization protests, where collective decision-making takes place among large numbers of people. These will be familiar to anyone who has been in protests against the G8, G20, Free Trade Area of the Americas (FTAA) or other free trade agreement, the World Bank (WB), International Monetary Fund (IMF) or World Trade Organization (WTO), or who has participated in Occupy or the Quebec Student Strike in 2012. Again, drawing on experience, this time from Sandra's perspective, we will take two examples: the Washington DC IMF protest in April 2000, and the anti-FTAA protests in Quebec City in 2001.

The IMF protests were organized using spokescouncils, which are designed like bike wheels, with each group participating in the decision-making being one of the spokes, and the axle being the facilitator(s). According to Jason Del Gandio:

> Spokescouncils enable many different people to participate in their own collective decision making. Usually there is a large circle with a facilitator. Individual activists and members from different affinity groups are given the opportunity to voice concerns and contribute to the conversation. While these conversations can range from friendly discussion to full blown arguments, participants usually strive for some form of consensus, however tenuous and temporary that might be. Spokescouncils often focus on strategic issues, like what type of action to take and when and how to execute that action. (p. 193)

While individual activists may participate in a spokescouncil, they are actually designed for groups to come together and make decisions. Each group designates a spokesperson, and the group sits together around the outside of the circle, with the spokesperson joining the circle. Although only one person from the affinity group is empowered to speak, groups are given breakout time to discuss a contentious topic after which the spokes will bring the groups' position forward.

Amory Starr argues that, "In preparation for a protest, the spokescouncil will agree to 'action guidelines'" (p. 219), giving the following example:

> Action guidelines for the 2000 Washington DC protests (a16) were:
> "1. We will use no violence, physical or verbal, towards any person.

2. We will carry no weapons. 3. We will not bring or use any alcohol or illegal drugs. 4. We will not destroy property (excepting barricades erected to prevent us from exercising our rights)." (p. 219)

These guidelines were hotly disputed by many activist groups who felt the imposition of nonviolence was taking place in an authoritarian manner whereby the facilitators were not allowing people who were not nonviolent to speak or be heard by the spokescouncil. In addition to developing action guidelines, the spokescouncil allowed affinity groups to self-organize protest activities. Washington DC was divided into pie slices, with affinity groups organizing to blockade particular segments of the pie through several consecutive days of spokescouncils, as people converged from points afar.

These spokescouncils thus allowed for two types of learning, similar to the G20 marches described above. The first was that specific topics regarding protest tactics were discussed, and people co-produced knowledge about the efficacy and desirability of various tactics. These were complemented by trainings at the convergence, including legal rights, medics, and nonviolent direct-action tactics, as well as workshops covering global critiques of neo-liberal capitalism.

The second type of learning took place through participation in the spokescouncils themselves. People learned about directly democratic, consensus-seeking decision-making through participating in it. Many of us had not participated in a spokescouncil before, but when we arrived in Washington, a friend in our affinity group who had been there for a week outlined the process. Our learning was then extended to a deeper level when we participated in the spokescouncil, particularly as we joined those offering strong critiques of the nonviolence and anti-property-destruction guidelines. Participating in the organization and planning of protest tactics is empowering and provides for greater safety in the streets. We each reflected on our own comfort level around tactics, and shared these feelings with our affinity group through several affinity group meetings, including one fairly intense one in the street in the midst of action, where some of our group had been arrested, and others were rain-soaked, cold, tired, hungry, and injured. We needed to collect ourselves and move forward as comfort levels were shifting. We learned quickly that consensus is not always possible or even desirable, as we agreed to split into three different groups: one that would leave for the day, another that would go directly back into the action, and a third group that wanted to take an hour to eat and dry off a bit before going back to the protest. This decision-making process taught us how to listen to each other, express our own needs, and make decisions that respected everyone's immediate affective space. It was quite thrilling to participate in such a process of direct democracy fuelled by open debate, deep mutual care, and a genuine desire to find solutions that would meet everyone's differing needs. We also learned issue-based information through trainings. For example, in the legal training, we learned about jail solidarity, and how different people have different risk levels. Specifically, we learned that police may single out a person who speaks with an accent for repression or violence; therefore, in solidarity with them, we should all refuse to speak to the police. For this reason we wrote, "I am exercising my right to remain silent" on our arms. These discussions would feed into the subsequent protest mobilization for Quebec City.

Over the course of the next year, many of us who had participated in the IMF protests began preparing for the anti-FTAA protest in Quebec City. Two groups, CLAC (the anti-capitalist convergence from Montreal) and CASA (from Quebec City), organized a series of consultas that invited groups interested in participating in the protests to consult on how the protest should be organized. In particular, the question of violence versus nonviolence was raised, and ultimately the principle of accepting a "diversity of tactics" was adopted (Starr, 2011, p. 219). During the consultas, we again learned direct democratic process by participating in it, but this time over a longer-term series of consultas. Those of us from Toronto built relationships with people from Montreal and Quebec City. We learned a great deal about capitalism, discussing strategies such as whether to march under an explicitly anti-capitalist banner, and how to implement a diversity of tactics once it had been adopted. Because discussions of protest tactics have the sole purpose of organizing a protest, the stakes are high, and these spaces can be quite emotional. People may be excited or cautious, angry or conciliatory, care-taking or stormy. There is a space for affect and emotion in the process of learning as the distance required in the classroom is removed, and as people consider the risk of arrest, police violence, demands of other protesters and groups, and the like. We must learn quite quickly where we stand in these debates and in the streets; to fail to do so could have dire consequences. Thus in non-learning-designated learning spaces, the psychology and affect of learning becomes explicit, as counter-hegemonic geographies of learning demand that we engage as embodied individuals and groups, balancing intellect with emotional and physical needs.

Conclusion

The experiences we had as academic-activists at NAASN have informed how we think about spaces of learning inside and outside the academy. We want to draw out two specific conclusions. First, more work needs to be done to value the learning of everyday life as much as other ways of learning. Feminist and anarchist researchers have pushed scholarly work to question the power relationship that develops from "expert knowledge," suggesting that no one "expert" exists, and that "expertise" can come from life as much as, or more than, from books. This requires research to take a different form, with methodologies that fall within a framework of social justice and decolonization. This requires methodologies, to borrow the words of Colectivo Situaciones (2007), "whose journey is to carry out theoretical and practical work oriented towards coproducing the knowledges and modes of an alternative sociability, beginning with the *potencia* (power) of those subaltern knowledges" (187). Rooted in the tradition of anarchists and feminists who have worked to acknowledge everyday life as the most important site of politics, we must also reconsider where places of learning exist (Portwood-Stacer, 2013). The anarcha-feminist tradition, grounded in practices of knowledge co-production and sharing that occur in grassroots activist spaces, teaches us to include affective aspects to our learning, to learn in spaces that are not outside of day-to-day life, to see that everyone is an expert of their own experience, and to acknowledge that there is no one right way of knowing or sharing knowledge.

Our intervention here is to specifically point out how learning outside the university is more conducive to counter-hegemonic thought and experience because it is more rooted and embodied. As we saw in the two university course examples, academic spaces may allow for learning related to everyday life, but these spaces are limited by the controlled geographies of knowledge production. Furthermore, university spaces isolate the learner in a particular designated epistemological and psychological space, often removed from affective aspects of learning. The example of offering a workshop at NAASN, somewhere in the fluid boundary between formalized counter-hegemonic learning spaces and non-learning spaces, gives us tools to understand how impossible it is to disconnect our epistemological and psychological selves from spaces of learning. In the "streets" examples, we were reminded of other ways to learn in real life. The consultas and protest spaces were not about listening to the teacher; rather, the reality is that people may be arrested, jailed, subjected to police violence, or otherwise traumatized during a protest, and these possibilities must be discussed openly. Learning in non-university spaces has material consequences, teaching us how to minimize negative impacts on our communities and to maximize our abilities to dismantle neoliberal capitalism, colonialism, patriarchy and racism.

Second, we argue that challenging the kinds of knowledges that are deemed legitimate—which often mimic academic privilege and coincide with Western, gender, race, and class privilege—requires a process of unlearning the internalization of institutional learning, from clock-watching, to hierarchies of expertise. Despite our desire to undo the systems of legitimization that the academy creates, we sometimes bring these same systems to other learning spaces.

Our narratives about non-academic learning spaces show, however, that there continue to be hierarchies of expertise outside the university. One aspect of this that we find in non-learning spaces has been a tendency to fetishize the current actions of "right now" while not necessarily seeing the value of expertise from historical actions, events, and experiences. The consequences are twofold. First, sometimes older activists may be granted more authority to speak than younger ones; other times, older activists may be discredited, regarded as being passé or out of the loop, with more authority granted to younger activists, sometimes based on subcultural credibility including basic things such as fashion or slang. The hierarchy of the university has been reversed but not superseded by a level playing field. This persistent power dynamic can be actively challenged through having go-arounds at the beginning (and sometimes the end) of workshops, skillshares, and other informal learning spaces. This practice foregrounds the wide range of specific expertise and knowledge in the room, legitimating everyone as knowledge holders and producers.

When we take learning to "the streets," boundaries around who can be an expert are further disrupted, revealing how oppressions are interlocking, where different people experience oppressions and access spaces differently because of white supremacy, heteronormativity, capitalism, colonialism, ableism, and patriarchy. It is here that we see the limits of our own experiential knowledge and must also place our knowledge in relation to the knowledge of others. Self-criticism, self-awareness, and self-reflection, coupled with group learning can provide a space of knowledge sharing that connects our struggles to collaborate, theorize, create, protest, think, and organize in solidarity with each other. The three frames of learning spaces (psychological, epistemological, and geographic) that we have discussed here are toolkits for reconstructing learning space, integrating learning into our organizing spaces, and further working to undo the racism, colonization, homophobia, classism, and sexism that many of us have internalized through institutional learning.

Acknowledgments
This research was supported by the Social Sciences and Humanities Research Council of Canada.

References

AnarchistU. (2003). Anarchist Free University Meeting 1 June 2003. Retrieved from https://web.archive.org/web/20040222220402/http://anarchistu.org/bin/view/Anarchistu/MinutesFrom2003June1

AnarchistU. (2004). Meeting Minutes—Sunday 10 October 2004. Retrieved from https://web.archive.org/web/20051220143902/http://www.anarchistu.org/twiki/view/Anarchistu/MinutesFrom2004Oct10

Baumann, M. (1981). *How it all began*. New York, NY: Pulp.

Blackwell, Adrian. (2000). *Model for public space*. Mercer Union exhibitions. Retrieved from http://www.mercerunion.org/exhibitions/front-gallery-adrian-blackwell-back-gallery-alex-morrison-platform-janis-demkiw/

Casey, L. (2010, June 24). A homemade BP oil-spill float, clowns and activists smeared in fake oil wove through downtown Toronto Wednesday in a "toxic tour." *The Toronto Star*. Retrieved from http://www.thestar.com/news/gta/g20/2010/06/24/toxic_tour_protests_environmental_genocide.html

Churchill, W. (2007). *Pacifism as pathology: Reflections on the role of armed struggle in North America*. Oakland, CA: AK Press.

Colectivo Situaciones (2007). On the researcher-militant. In M. Coté, R. Day & G. de Peuter (Eds.), *Utopian pedagogy: Radical experiments against neoliberal globalization*. Toronto, ON: University of Toronto Press.

Collins, P.H. (1990). *Black feminist thought: Knowledge, consciousness, and the politics of empowerment*. New York, NY: Routledge.

Crenshaw, K. (1989). Demarginalizing the intersection of race and sex: A black feminist critique of antidiscrimination doctrine, feminist theory and antiracist politics. *University of Chicago Legal Forum, 140*, 139-167.

Dark Star Collective. (2012). *Quiet rumours: An anarcha-feminist reader*. Oakland, CA: AK Press/Dark Star.

Del Gandio, J. (2013). *Rhetoric for radicals: A handbook for 21st century activists*. Gabriola Island, BC: New Society Publishers.

Dunnion, K. (2004). *Mosh pit*. Markham, ON: Red Deer Press.

Fanon, F. (1965). *The wretched of the earth*. New York, NY: Grove Press.

519 Church Street Community Centre, The. (2014). Retrieved from http://www.the519.org/newsfeed/the519talksnews

Gelderloos, P. (2007). *How nonviolence protects the state*. Boston, MA: South End Press.

Gramsci, A. (1971). *Selections from the prison notebooks of Antonio Gramsci*. G. Nowell-Smith & Q. Hoare (Eds.). New York, NY: International Publishers.

Greenway, J. (2010). The gender politics of anarchist history: Re/membering women, re/minding men. Paper presented at the PSA Conference, Edinburgh, Scotland, April 2010.

Guberman, S.R., & Greenfield, P.M. (1991). Learning and transfer in everyday cognition. *Cognitive Development, 6*(3), 233-260.

Hansen, A. (2001). *Direct action: Memoirs of an urban guerrilla*. Toronto, ON: Between the Lines.

hooks, b. (1989). *Talking back: Thinking feminist, thinking black*. Boston, MA: South End Press.

Indypendent Reader (2012). Mobilizing and organizing from below. Baltimore, MD. Retrieved from https://indyreader.org/mobconf

Jeppesen, S., Kruzynski, A., Lakoff, A., & Sarrasin, R. (2014). Grassroots autonomous media practices: A diversity of tactics. *Journal of Media Practice, 15*(1). 21-38.

Jeppesen, S., & Nazar, H. (2012). Beyond academic freedom: Canadian neoliberal universities in the global context. *TOPIA: Canadian Journal of Cultural Studies, 1*(28), 87-113.

Jiwani, Y. (2007). *Discourses of denial: Mediations of race, gender, and violence*. Vancouver, BC: UBC Press.

Leighton, M. (1979). Anarcho-feminism. In H.J. Ehrlich, C. Ehrlich & D. DeLeon (Eds.), *Reinventing anarchy: What are anarchists thinking these days?*. New York, NY: Routledge.

Lorde, A. (1984). The master's tools will never dismantle the master's house. In *Sister outsider: Essays and speeches*. Berkeley, CA: Crossing Press.

Maggie's Toronto. (2011). Toronto Sex Workers Action Project. Retrieved from http://maggiestoronto.ca/

McLaren, P. (1998). *Life in schools. An introduction to critical pedagogy in the foundations of education*. New York, NY: Addison Wesley Longman, Inc.

Miller, R. (2002). *Free schools, free people: Education and democracy after the 1960s*. New York, NY: SUNY Press.

North American Anarchist Studies Network (NAASN). (2014). Retrieved from http://www.naasn.org/

Portwood-Stacer, L. (2013). *Lifestyle politics and radical activism*. New York, NY: A&C Black.

Razack, S. (1998). *Looking white people in the eye: Gender, race, and culture in courtrooms and classrooms*. Toronto, ON: University of Toronto Press.

Shakur, A. (1987). *Assata: An autobiography*. Boston, MA: Zed Books.

Shawn-Caza. (2011). Anarchist Free University [Web log post]. Retrieved from http://www.t.isgood.ca/learning/anarchist-free-university/

Smith, L.T. (2013). *Decolonizing methodologies* (2nd ed.). Boston, MA: Zed Books.

Starhawk. (2011). *Empowerment manual: A guide for collaborative groups*. Gabriola Island, BC: New Society Publishers.

Starr, A. (2005). *Global revolt: A Guide to the movements against globalization*. Boston, MA: Zed Books.

Teixeira, R. (n.d.). *Creative passion as resistance: A history of the Anarchist Free University in Toronto*. Unpublished manuscript.

Thobani, S. (2008, Spring). No academic exercise: The assault on anti-racist feminism in the age of terror. *R.A.C.E.link*, 3–7.

TorontoG20Exposed. (2010). *Chapter 3—Black Bloc Riot*. Retrieved from http://www.youtube.com/watch?v=8A1wTE3OzTE&feature=youtube_gdata_player

Yeatman, A. (1995). Interlocking oppressions. In B. Caine & R. Pringle (Eds.), *Transitions: New Australian feminisms*. Sydney, Australia: Allen & Unwin.

York University Counselling Services (n.d.). Common Stress Reactions to Trauma [Web log post]. Retrieved from http://pcs.info.yorku.ca/common-stress-reactions-to-trauma/

Ziniuk, T-M. (2009). *Somewhere to run from*. Toronto, ON: Tightrope Books.

Notes

1 The anarchistu.org website is no longer functional but can be found using the Internet Archive's Wayback Machine retrieved from http://archive.org/web/.

2 NAASN has also done this in the past, for example, when organized in Hartford, CT, the conference took place in a local activist-oriented community church and the fee was sliding scale.

3 Joanna's experience as a member of the Toronto Anarchist Bookfair Collective gives a perspective on how informal learning spaces may legitimate presenters. The people we deemed experts were folks involved in activism on issues for which we were seeking presentations, or who had done independent research and writing about these topics. Furthermore, we looked for folks who had offered training or skillshares in the past that could expand the skill base for doing anti-oppression work. While the format of the Bookfair workshops is similar to a

conference like MOBCONF, the process of recruiting presenters shows that a particular kind of expertise was sought.

4   The protest tactic known as black bloc entails dressing in black clothing to be indistinguishable from other participants to protect against police targeting and arrest during militant demonstrations.

CHAPTER 13

Theory Meet Practice: Evolving Ideas and Actions in Anarchist Free Schools

Jeff Shantz

This chapter examines evolving theoretical perspectives and activities in anarchist free schools situating pedagogical commitments within changing activist engagements. Beginning with a critical discussion of anarchist pedagogical approaches the paper outlines how anarchists have adapted their efforts through real world organizing over the last two decades. The chapter offers comparative analysis of organizing within two free schools and how the interaction of theory and practice as well as state response have transformed these spaces as sites of learning and action. Tensions between class struggle and insurrectionary approaches are examined as are issues of identity and social background. Offering a social history of anarchist struggles against neoliberalism and austerity within the Canadian state context the chapter discusses the importance that issues of decolonization and intersectionality have gained within anarchist pedagogical approaches (and the decolonizing of anarchist pedagogies) more recently compared with free school work in the late 1990s. Connections between anarchist pedagogies and community organizing, especially solidarity with indigenous communities and anti-poverty movements are addressed.

Anarchism, Education, and Free Schools

Anarchism has grown dramatically as a part of movements against authoritarianism and inequality, states, and capital over the last two decades. Indeed anarchism has become one of the most important radical movements (in perspective and practice) of the twenty-first century as people seek alternatives to state capitalist austerity in a context in which previously influential alternatives, notably Marxism and social democracy have waned or been exposed as false models.

The development of anarchism has led many to question dominant idea systems and mechanisms by which ideas, perspectives on the world, are constructed and disseminated. This has impelled critical thinking about education and has fuelled, and been fuelled by, a desire to develop alternative educational practices. At the same time alternative educational venues, initiated and sustained by anarchists, have provided important resources in the growth and transformation of anarchist movements more broadly. Among the most significant forms of anarchist real world projects have been free schools, collective efforts to engage critical perspectives on the world and to support community organizing materially.

Anarchist playwright Pat Halley (2013) once wrote in the pages of the anarchist journal *Fifth Estate*, "The purpose of education is to kick the animal out of you" (p. 25). By this Halley made the argument that, for anarchists, formal education in state capitalist societies plays a function of domestication. It works to constrain people's desires, autonomy, and sense of self-determination while inculcating students with systemic values, respect for instituted authorities, and routinization into daily practices of compliance. This is a process that has been illustrated in detail by social theorists such as Michel Foucault (1975) who notes the similarity in structures and practices between schools, prisons, and factories. Each serves to (re)produce ritualized practices of work discipline.

Even more, for Halley and other anarchists, formal education presumes that the current order is a natural and essential one. The current system is portrayed further as "the best of all possible worlds," to use the popular phrase. For the *Fifth Estate*:

> In one such as ours, where everything that it means to be human has been grotesquely twisted to the needs of the ruling order, formal education teaches unquestioning respect for authority, acceptance of hierarchies, carrying out tasks that benefit others but harm yourself and the planet, adherence to work in which you have no interest, measurement in abstractions, militarism and nationalism, an inherent value in the production and consumption of commodities, religious mysticism, and perhaps the most insidious, that the current system is the only possible manner in which the world can be constructed. (*Fifth Estate*, 2013, p. 25)

Modern schooling, as a formal social institution, was created, and has developed, in the context of industrial state capitalism (Matthews, 1980). For anarchists, formal schooling has been made to fit the needs and values prioritized with, and reflective of, capitalist social relations (Bowles & Gintis, 1977). This includes preparation for work, the acceptance of work for wages, worker discipline, management conditioning, and flexibilization. It emphasizes discreet projects over holistic development. Such schooling acts to construct the majority as an exploitable workforce within a specific national state context. It is geared toward the needs of the current economy. It is not so concerned with the development of free and autonomous people in free and autonomous communities (Anonymous, 2013).

For education critic Daniel Quinn (2008), much of schooling serves to keep youth out of the job market, thus manipulating unemployment rates. It also serves to keep them off the streets and busy rather than collectively responding to conditions of need and/or anger. Youth are not taught independent survival skills, which they might desire (knowledge of local environments, food sources, production skills). Rather they are left only with the option to work for wages as mediated means to meet some survival needs (and many others geared only toward the survival of the market, such as many consumer goods).

For anarchists, traditional, compulsory schooling by the state renders children and youth a population to be evaluated, surveilled, controlled, and disciplined (Anonymous 2013, p. 26). Authorities that stand over them are to be respected. A writer in the student movement pamphlet *En suspense*, a publication of the Quebec student uprisings of 2012, suggests:

> According to several parents practicing home schooling or "unschooling" the educational material of one week of primary or secondary school can be reduced to about 8 to 10 hours a week. The rest of the time, we are taught to be submissive and to fear the authority of the teacher, of the director, of the social worker, of youth protection services, of the police detention centers and of juvenile court. (quoted in Anonymous, 2013, p. 25)

In addition to the repressive role, traditional schooling serves a moral regulatory function; what Foucault (1975) terms a productive power, producing identity. Such schooling involves the inculcation of the dominant norms, values, and beliefs of the society in which the child lives—a state capitalist society, in the case of the U.S. It molds acceptable behaviors within this context (rather than values and behaviors that are expressed against or as an alternative to it). Anarchists argue that, as a process of power, people need to be disconnected from their experiences and desires to be made ready for undesirable, often unhealthy, work conditions and procedures to which they will be subjected for most of their lives. For the anarchist social movement critic of education under state capitalism:

> A hierarchical society needs school to teach children to be submissive and to renounce their desires, so that children adopt behaviors

that support the established order. School socialization is primary and principle socialization, since it begins at a young age and becomes the main influence on the child, supplanting the family. Institutionalized socialization is above all a result of the constraints imposed by its agents. Interactions between an individual and their social environment are possible, but they remain under the surveillance and control of the state and corporations since interactions that are not surveilled risk producing a radical social transformation of society. (Anonymous, 2013, p. 26)

It is precisely such a radical social transformation that anarchists seek. In doing so, they have developed a range of organizational practices to make their desires a reality. Among the projects that anarchists have undertaken are cooperatives, working groups, alternative unions, and collective houses. Perhaps the most recurrent, and among the most valued, of anarchist projects have been free schools (typically located in free spaces or anarchist community centers).

Those seeking realistic positive alternatives to state capitalist social relations desire educational experiences that inform their pursuit of alternatives while bringing those alternatives to life in the here and now of everyday experience (rather that "after the revolution"). As one participant in Toronto's Occupy Free School project suggests: "We desperately need education that is free for the development of the individual personality. This means education that is culturally relevant, and teaches peace and self-determination" (quoted in Kinch, 2013, p. 42). Free schools have been a primary means by which anarchists have sought to make these deeply felt needs real. And they work, if imperfectly.

In addition to sites of knowledge and skill sharing, free schools also provide important opportunities for anarchists and other concerned community members to meet and discuss matters of interest in their lives. It provides a participatory democratic sphere in which people can identify various needs and concerns and speak openly with others about how to resolve problems effectively in concert with their neighbors and other residents of the local area. This is a potent resource in a context in which open, participatory democratic opportunities and venues for collaborative problem solving are generally absent for regular folks.

The personally transformative power of anarchist free schools is expressed by many participants. Indeed, I can attest to this from my own experiences over decades (including at several of the venues discussed herein). As rapper and Anarchist Free University alum Illogik (of group Test Their Logik) recounts:

The AFU was amazing vibrant when I first got involved; multiple classes each semester, lot of attendance. The AFU led me to Uprising [bookstore] and then to a now-defunct collective house which all spawned many different activities. It got me plugged into the community and once in, the vehicle that got me there was less important. (quoted in Kinch, 2013, p. 41)

Illogik also highlights the role that free schools can play as connectors for broader anarchist and community organizing and shared projects beyond their role as educational spaces. The Anarchist Free Space and FreeSkool, and its successor the Anarchist Free University in Toronto, would provide important inspiration for different projects initiated in other cities.

Free school participants speak of the sense of conviviality and community that such projects can foster. Free school commentator Niki Thorne, a free school alum who went on to write a master's thesis on free schools, suggests:

FreeSkool, for me, has always been this warm welcoming inspiring space, a community of caring and creative people, and an example of the concrete beautiful projects and initiatives that we can build out of our ideas and ideals. FreeSkool represents creativity and community, and is part of building the kind of world we want to live in. (quoted in Kinch, 2013, p. 42)

This speaks to the prefigurative power of these projects. It reflects a key aspect of anarchist projects: the desire to see that means and ends coincide in practice.

Building Blocks: Locating Free Schools

Kensington Market is a historically working-class neighborhood near downtown Toronto. It had been home to Jewish radicals in the 1930s and 1940s and has maintained its sense of a radical, or at least alternative, haven up to the present. Long a home to anarchists, the Market was the neighborhood in which Emma Goldman spent the last years of her life while in exile from the United States until her death in 1940.

Throughout the 1980s the Market had been home to anarcho-punks who lived and played in the area's several punk venues (from bars to basement parties). The Market punks were important participants in legendary battles against neo-Nazis during that time and through their various efforts drew new generations in the anarcho-punk scene. A number of bands involved in the Kensington scene over the years would go on to achieve widespread acclaim, even internationally. Among these were bunchofuckingoofs and Fucked Up.

Kensington, with its availability of space in historic buildings and its openness to bohemian cultures has provided an important base for anarchist development. When the Who's Emma? Infoshop and DIY punk record shop opened, the anarchists had a significant infrastructural space for organizing, awareness raising, and skill development—usually through workshops and meetings. It also had a reliable space for putting on punk shows and mini festivals.

In 1998, the Active Resistance '98 anarchist gathering and conference was organized largely out of Who's Emma? and by people involved with the space. The size and success of the conference served to bring many more people into the movement in Toronto and beyond. This included people already in Toronto as well as anarchist-inspired activists who moved to Toronto following Active Resistance in order to be involved in the lively movement there. Many, frustrated with the subcultural aspect of Active Resistance, determined to join community based groups involved in anti-poverty work, housing struggles, and anti-racist campaigns.

Within a few years of Active Resistance the Anarchist Free Space and Free Skool, Uprising Books, and the Anarchist Free University had followed in Who's Emma's footsteps, organizing additional spaces in the Market. The Anarchist Free Skool would serve as a crucial entry point for many new anarchists. Dozens of people became radicalized through involvement in the space with many becoming experienced organizers who would make substantial contributions to political movements in the city over a period of more than a decade (right up to the present). The Free Skool effectively combined relevant real world organizing with theoretical and strategic analysis. It provided a lively pedagogical praxis that inspired and challenged many in local social struggles.

The Anarchist Free University emerged from the ashes of the Free Skool following the loss of its physical venue. It would serve as a more tradition-ally educational project focusing almost exclusively on classes on a range of topics, although, of course, participants were also involved in other projects, campaigns, and movements. The AFU shared a house with a radical bike collective (Bike Pirates) sharing labor and resources as well as rent burdens. The AFU would go on to represent one of the longest running projects in Toronto over the last decade. It would contribute to later projects such as Occupy Toronto and the Occupy Free School.

Eventually both the Anarchist Free Skool and the Anarchist Free University would become homeless as rising rents in the city made it hard even for relatively stable collectives to maintain venues such as infoshops or punk clubs. The loss of the spaces had real impacts. As Kinch suggests: "Anarchism went a bit further underground. Without a geographical space or a strong activist movement, the AFU stagnated along with the dispersed anarchist scene in general" (Fifth Estate, 2013, p. 41). At the same time participants in the AFS and AFU would go on to make essential contributions to Occupy Toronto and the Occupy Free School as well as free schools and infoshops in other cities.

Both projects served as hubs of skill sharing about free schools and people travelled from all over North America to visit and learn how to set up and maintain free schools in their own locales. Projects such as the Free School in Hamilton, Ontario, an industrial city located about an hour southwest of Toronto were directly influenced by the AFS and AFU and invited participants from those projects to join them for initial meetings around setting up their new space. Other projects influenced by the AFS and AFU include the Windsor Workers Action Centre in Windsor, Ontario, and farther afield the Twelfth and Clark anarchist salon in Vancouver, which was started by a former AFS participant.

Out of the Ruins: From G20 Protests to Occupy Free School

The formal dissolution of the AFS and AFU did not mean the end of free school activities in Toronto. Indeed, one aspect of free schools projects is that they instill pedagogical and activist approaches that transcend the spaces of the free schools, percolating through other projects and organizing efforts. Those who experience free school practices come, in various ways, to embody them, expressing them as they engage in their local communities. Such is exemplified in the Toronto context through the emergence of anarchist pedagogical projects, including free schools, in the mass mobilization against the meetings of the G8/G20 global powers in Toronto in 2010 and in Occupy Toronto a year later.

Free school projects developed as important parts of the broad mobilization against the G8/G20 meetings of global capital and national states. The Free School provided crucial venues for raising awareness publicly of concerns with G8/G20 politics and policies and provided a horizontal, participatory, and democratic counterpoint to the elite, exclusive, and anti-democratic closed meetings of the G8/G20. At the same time the Free School helped organizers sharpen their own analyses of capitalism, neoliberalism, and austerity, while providing useful organizing practice beyond the smaller anarchist subcultural context in which free schools often operate.

Popular projects emerged that expanded the scope of free school practice and the range of public interaction. A crew of people came together from one AFU media course to produce a high-quality documentary movie, *Tales from the G20*, about the mobilization. This provided a useful resource for organizers in Toronto. It also provides a resource for organizers of future mobilizations and for others seeking information about the G20 and its priorities and policies.

The G8/G20 free school projects took on a life of their own and a Toronto Free School operated for approximately a year after the G8/G20 meetings. Eventually it folded, in part, because organizers had to spend so much time, energy, and resources working on legal defense and popular political-legal education for those arrested and charged during the G8/G20 repression and mass arrests. Yet the desire for a free school did not dissipate and the experiences of the vitality of the free schools remained strong within participants, providing strong impetus to start again. When the Occupy wave of protest camps emerged in the fall of 2011, Occupy Toronto benefited from the efforts of various free school participants in the city. As in other cases, the general increase in involvement of younger or newer or less-experienced political activists in a short period of time, showed a need for educational work to help develop political analysis and share practical skills as well as to learn from the histories of successful and failed struggles in the city and elsewhere. In addition, there was a real need for education about issues of oppression, police practices, economic alternatives, and basic survival skills along consensual, communal, and cooperative lines.

A handful of experienced free school organizers—including some from the AFS, AFU, and the post-G20 Free School—worked to establish the basic infrastructure for the Occupy Free School. Once established, the Occupy Free School was easily maintained by any and all who chose to participate. Anyone could schedule classes simply by listing desired subjects on a whiteboard at the Free School tent and being available at the suggested meeting time.

As might be expected in a case of open struggle, as opposed to day-to-day living under unequal conditions, classes were typically tied into organizing projects underway at the Occupy camp. This included a class on anarchist theory attended by many involved in community safety at the camp (Kinch, 2013). This involvement in the anarchist theory course reflected a real need and desire on the part of participants to develop a theoretical understanding of practical approaches to keeping people safe in a context of the active pursuit of freedom, participation, cooperation, and non-hierarchical decision-making. Notably, as in the Anarchist Free Skool, the most popular courses were on anarchist communism and class struggle. Other courses, showing the mix of theory and practice, focused on gardening and recycled paper arts.

Significantly, the Occupy Free School survived the Occupy camp itself, developing its own life after the camp's collapse. While the loose assembly of Occupy, lacking political coherence and theoretical or practical affinity, fell apart rather spectacularly, the closer, engaged "structure" of the Occupy Free School allowed it to thrive, adapting to radically changed circumstances and providing a common ground for participants to move forward productively in the face of adversity. While the evicted camp dispersed and loose attachments came undone, the Occupy Free School persisted, maintained by people who had learned their theory and practice, strategy and tactics, experientially and collectively. The Occupy Free School still meets in a downtown Toronto park each Sunday. It produces a temporarily open and free space, what anarchist theorist Hakim Bey might term a mobile temporary autonomous zone (TAZ) in the heart of the city.

Sites of Change: Shifting Priorities, Shifting Practices in Free Schools

Free Skools are, almost by definition, heterodox and decentered spaces. Collectives are diverse, changing, and evolving. The viewpoints and priorities of collective members are by no means homogeneous. The Anarchist Free Skool pulsed between two poles that were in creative tension throughout most of the space's existence. On the one hand was an artistic, subcultural, expressive grouping that favored alternative or underground cultural events, dadaesque parties and happenings, and classes geared toward cultural dissent (culture jamming, billboard liberation, etc.) and alternative lifestyles. On the other was a class struggle grouping that favored community-based local organizing and saw the Free Skool as a resource for organizing. The class struggle grouping participated in anti-poverty movements in the city and was active in anti-gentrification struggles in the specific neighborhood in which the Free Skool was located. The art group argued against fighting the businesses that pushed gentrification in the neighborhood, strangely viewing that struggle as one that did not offer a new cultural vision (despite the cultural underpinnings of much of the gentrification promoters and their expressions against the "poverty cultures" of homeless people. The class struggle group favored classes on theory and practice and historical examples (from urban struggles of the 1970s and 1980s to the anarchist collectives in the Spanish Civil War of the 1930s and in Russia in the revolutionary period).

These two groups managed to coexist and coevolve over a period of five years without interfering too much in each other's work. Eventually more class struggle activists became involved in the space and more activists voluntarily drifted to other, typically gallery, spaces. It should be noted that the growth of alternative globalization movements and struggles after Seattle in 1999, and the influx of young activists inspired by or curious about anarchism, played a part in the growth of the class struggle tendency within the Free Skool. Many of the young activists were looking for real-world, practical means to address issues of economic and social injustice and inequality. While artistic and cultural expressions were personally gratifying they did not meet the desires many had for real structural change and possibilities for socioeconomic resistance.

The issues that mobilized most of the efforts at the Free Skool were those around anti-gentrification, anti-poverty, cop watches and police violence, anti-racist action, and immigration defense and anti-border campaigns. These are all issues that have a connecting thread of class inequality. While these were, and remain, crucial issues, particularly as economic inequality and disparities in wealth grow under regimes of neoliberal austerity, globalization, and deindustrialization (at least in North America), there were noticeable significant gaps in perspective and practice related to Free Skool activities. Issues that were never given enough attention or commitment included feminism, gender diversity, sexual identity, and colonialism.

By the second decade of the twenty-first century these issues have become key components of anarchist organizing, in terms of practice and in terms of perspective (a too long overdue development). This has been driven by the experiences of participants from marginalized groups and identities as they have come up against the ongoing limits of anarchist practice within their own collective efforts and as more people from marginalized backgrounds enter anarchist circles and take part in anarchist projects as the movement has grown and expanded. This has also been spurred by the efforts of self-education and personal and political development—learning through everyday practice—of anarchists over time reflecting on the strengths and limitations of their own work and play. While classes on genderfucking, polysexuality, sexual health, or dis/abilities would have been atypical twenty years ago at venues like the Anarchist Free Skool, they have formed significant parts of anarchist work in the 2010s at anarchist spaces like the New Space in Vancouver (unceded Coast Salish territories) where I have been active more recently.

The shifting priorities and concerns within anarchism and anarchist spaces have contributed to an altering of organizational practices and preferences. Spaces like the Free Skool tended to host inclusive events geared toward anarchists of all tendencies as well as non-anarchists who might be interested in learning about anarchism. At current spaces, such as the New Space, events are often particularistic, identity or culture based, driven by and for specific self-identified groups who have too often been excluded or marginalized even within anarchist spaces and movements. In other cases, intersections of oppression are identified as bases for solidarity in rethinking anarchist and alternative projects. Thus an event like the SB! Festival, organized out of a free space and around anarchist pedagogical projects, was described as:

> An anarcha-feminist, queer, radical, anti-capitalist DIY music festival for anyone who wants it or thinks they might want it. A celebration in smashing patriarchy, showcasing artists who are underrepresented. This festival is for everyone who is disaffected or disgusted by the current independent music culture, dominated by straight, white males. (ShoutBack!, 2014, n.p.)

Spaces developed in the last decades of the twentieth century tended to draw people and organize on the basis that participants were anarchists first and foremost. Contemporary spaces often involve participation on the basis of personal identity, in which anarchists and non-anarchists organize around a primary identity, say queer, trans, and APOC, rather than as anarchists first and foremost. Even where affinity is based on a sense that participants are anarchist, there will more often be altergroupings or caucuses in which participants of particular identifications or backgrounds self-organize within current spaces. Thus a space may have, in addition to an overall space collective, an APOC caucus, a queer caucus, a women's caucus, a trans caucus, and more, depending on the needs and interests or challenges of participants in specific organizing or social contexts. The caucuses will generally have representation of issues and concerns to the larger collective at broader collective meetings.

In some ways the contemporary anarchist spaces are reminiscent of the awareness and consciousness-raising groups of the 1970s and 1980s, geared toward meetings of "affected groups" (discussion circles for women or queers, for example). Such groups and spaces are envisioned as "safe spaces" in which people who self identify as being of specific groups can meet is a respectful and supportive environment to talk without concern of harassment.

Classes at the Free Skool drew largely on anarchist classics. More contemporary classes tend to draw heavily from other traditions, such as postcolonial theory, critical race theory, whiteness studies, and queer theory. Indeed the whole notion of the Free Skool and classes that mirror academic courses (with a course reading list, weekly outline, facilitator, discussion, etc.) has been eclipsed be the issue-based singular approach preferred in the current spaces. In the current spaces there are often single meetings around an issue rather than ongoing classes. This may include a book launch or movie showing in which discussion, often around contributing to an active campaign, occurs rather than the set course format that runs over months.

Class Issues

Class struggle anarchism, while the most significant trend globally and historically in anarchist movements has always been challenged by more identity based and culture-centric expressions. This antagonism has been driven by a number of factors. These include the general antipathy to class analysis in North American politics more broadly (including within radical politics). It also reflects the middle strata background of many anarchist activists and projects in North America (in which an honest critique of class privilege would turn attention to the privilege of some anarchists themselves) and a lack of understanding of, at least, blue-collar working-class issues. It also reflects the inroads made by new social movement (NSM) theories and cultural politics within the academic milieux from which many anarchist activists have been drawn over the last two decades.

At the same time, and more positively, it reflects the growing cultural (ethnic, social, sexual, etc.) diversity of participants in anarchist movements in North America. And the growing assertiveness and confidence, individual and collective, of previously marginalized or silenced groups. This includes increased activity around issues of gender, sexuality, identity, and queerness. Other shifts include anarchist responses to ableism. It also reflects the gaps between anarchist sensitivity to, and actions to address, these specific but interlocking forms of domination and inferiorization (Adam, 1978).

Contemporary anarchist pedagogies must be attentive and responsive to the lived experiences, realities, and biases of a diversity of participants and their communities. This means openly questioning and challenging both the composition of anarchist movements (predominantly young white males, for example) and the analytical frameworks of anarchism (the predominance of economism and/or gaps in understanding gender domination, heteronormativity, and colonialism, etc.). To the extent that anarchist collective practices and pedagogical approaches in free schools and other shared projects face these issues honestly and concretely, they show significant and necessary growth and development.

At the same time, this does not mean losing or abandoning the important insights of strategic and tactical approaches that do not directly speak to issues of participants' experiences, such as analyses of the wage labor relationship and exploitation under capitalism. So contemporary anarchists must recognize that class (exploitation) matters (as many subculturists overlook or dismiss) while also understanding that the working class has never been monolithic or uniform. It has always been racialized, multiply gendered, sexualized, etc.

More recently a more substantial proportion of anarchists have come to understand the settler colonial character of capitalism on Turtle Island (named North America by colonialists). European capitalism was in key ways underwritten and bolstered by settler colonialism. At the New Space, an explicit commitment is made to anti-colonial perspectives and to supporting indigenous groups engaged in struggles.

Necessary Infrastructures

Like many synthesist anarchist projects, which bring together anarchists with diverse perspectives and differing views of strategy and tactics, free schools and their projects are often ephemeral. Economic pressures, like land speculation, commercialization, development, and gentrification contribute to the collapse of spaces lacking basic means such as the capacity to pay rent. Political pressures, such as arrests of organizers or selective city bylaw enforcement can speed up closures. Evictions by nervous or speculative landlords, or police in the case of squatted buildings, can shut things down directly. At the same time, anarchist free spaces show the rhizomatic character of many anarchist organizing projects, giving rise to new, but related, manifestations in other areas.

The Toronto free school projects of the last two decades have generally been semi-durable experiments lasting for a few years in one form before morphing into new projects. There is continuity as some of the people involved in earlier projects carry over their participation to help initiate, develop, and maintain successive projects. At the same time, the successive projects show the crucial need for what I term infrastructures of resistance as the life span of the specific school projects is often determined largely (or solely) by the availability of physical space (and associated resources such as books) to host the schools and root them in the broader community (Shantz, 2010).

Participants at the various Toronto free school projects are in agreement on the need for physical space in which organizing can occur on a more sustained basis. Kalin Stacey, a participant in the Anarchist Free University reflects on the need for physical space as a key feature of free schools that survive over time. For Stacey:

> One of the things that's really critical for a freeschool is that it's both a decentralized and learning project, but also a community building project.
>
> The best scenario for an established freeschool that sticks around is to have a radical community centre/social space, autonomous space that also is sustainable and can provide a meeting place. That's something the anarchist free school that happened in the late '90s [and beyond] in Kensington had that made it really effective. And, when they lost the space, they lost the school. (quoted in Kinch, 2013, p. 41)

This speaks to the pressing need, felt by participants, for infrastructures of resistance in anarchist organizing projects. It also speaks to the need, also understood by participants, to bring community struggles together with educational efforts. This is the key part played by infrastructures of resistance. Not only do they provide reliable resources necessary for ongoing organizing work (meeting space, phone lines, food preparation, etc.) They also provide venues in which people involved in diverse and seemingly disparate struggles can come into contact with one another, see commonalities and seek common ground, and strategize around the best ways to act in solidarity to develop their struggles mutually. Such infrastructures of resistance allow for a certain "collaborative advantage" such that limited resources in labor or materials might have a greater impact when deployed in conjunction with united (if not unified) struggles through shared projects and perspectives.

The experiences of the Toronto free schools would seem to confirm Paolo Friere's (1970) argument that for liberation education to be successful, and contribute to meaningful social change, it must be linked to a broader project of human life more generally. Free schools have played important parts in the development of anarchist movements in urban centers like Toronto and Vancouver from the middle 1990s to the present. At the same time, those schools have thrived most when involved in broader community organizing efforts, in which they had direct and vital interactions with political organizing and mobilization in their neighborhoods.

The challenges faced by free schools, in starting up, sustaining themselves, and in rising from the ruins are those faced by the movements themselves. Infrastructures of resistance are necessary to provide more durable bases for movements to continue and develop and to prevent the dissipation of efforts as struggles wax and wane. As Kinch (2013) reflects:

> Organically connected with the anti-authoritarian organizing scenes in the city, liberation education has risen and fallen with the tide of militancy in the city. Wresting physical and organization space from capitalism for the projects we need is a difficult task, but it's one that has to be done as we move forward.
>
> We can't always fight the system head on. We also have to build the systems that sustain ourselves and our struggles as we move out of the margins to really challenge capitalism and the state. (p. 42)

And to build alternatives in the here and now of everyday life. Infrastructures of resistance provide the necessary sustenance of struggles. They are the foundations of the new world in the shell of the old.

Such projects are highly labor intensive and require a great deal of day-to-day maintenance to keep them running effectively. This reality often runs up against anti-work attitudes and the preferences for play and "hanging out" that are perhaps too prevalent in anarchist subcultural scenes. While many anarchists express a healthy rejection and criticism of imposed capitalist work and work discipline they often fail to distinguish between self-valorizing sustenance work (required to keep people and communities thriving) and the capital valorizing tasks associated with the job form (and the sale of labor power to an owner of property).

Conclusion: Context Matters

For anarchists free schools are crucial resources within broader processes of contesting the domestication of dissent and building authentic forms of rebellion and resistance. They offer means by which people can keep the animal from being kicked out of us, to return to Halley's notion noted earlier. As one anarchist critic argues:

> The industrial system has found in the education model a rational way to domesticate the exploited, thus allowing for easier recuperation of resistance by redirecting it into institutional channels, like union negotiation or political reformism. The rebels who have interiorized the values transmitted by school try to retouch the repressive machine, rather than destroy it, and a domesticated child is one who only expresses themselves in the moment that the teacher (the state) allows them.
>
> Authentic rebellion starts in the streets and then builds alternatives both to corporatized universities and to the dominant society. (Anonymous, 2013, p. 27)

The post-Seattle and post-9/11 period has seen anarchism grow dramatically in terms of influence (both in the streets and in the academy) and in terms of legitimacy (many now at least have some sense of what anarchism is as compared with twenty years ago). In addition, anarchism has developed as perhaps *the* most significant idea system or perspective within radical social movements in North America, supplanting Marxism and its various Leninist and Maoist variants.

Free schools, as incubators of anarchist thought and action, are both products of and producers of their specific social contexts, local concerns, and issues. They are representative of the struggles that animate (and are animated by) them. Thus, in Toronto, where issues of housing, homelessness, and cuts to social welfare for poor people, along with deindustrialization and unemployment, and policies designed to criminalize poor and homeless people, were pressing political concerns, the AFS oriented itself toward defense of homeless people in a neighborhood undergoing, gentrification. Many anarchists at the Free Skool had experienced poverty and homelessness first hand. In Vancouver, where issues of resource extraction and extreme energy and pipelines are major areas of intense local struggles, and environmental politics are often entry points for politicization and/or radicalization, members have devoted time and resources to defending the land and supporting indigenous communities facing the perils of extractive industries and capitalist land development.

References

Adam, B.D. (1978). *The survival of domination: Inferiorization and everyday life.* New York, NY: Elsevier.

Anonymous. (2013). What do we learn in school that couldn't be learned elsewhere? *Fifth Estate, 47*(3), 25–27.

Bowles, S., & Gintis, H. (1977). *Schooling in capitalist America: Educational reform and the contradictions of economic life*. New York, NY: Basic Books.

Fifth Estate. (2013). Kicking the animal out of you. *Fifth Estate, 47*(3), 26.

Foucault, M. (1975). *Discipline and punish: The birth of the prison*. New York, NY: Random House.

Kinch, M. (2013). Toronto's free school: It takes a community. *Fifth Estate, 47*(3), 41–42.

Matthews, M. (1980). *The Marxist theory of schooling: A study of epistemology and education*. Brighton, UK: Harvester Press.

Quinn, D. (2008). Schooling: The hidden agenda. In N. van Gestel & J. Hunt, (Eds.), *The unschooling unmanual* (pp. 41–54). Ucluelet, BC: Natural Child.

Shantz, J. (2010). *Constructive anarchy: Building infrastructures of resistance*. Farnham, UK: Ashgate.

CONTRIBUTORS

Joanna Adamiak currently lives in Toronto, where she participates in organizing the anarchist bookfair, does prisoner support work, and serves as the treasurer of Freedonia, a BC and Ontario-based fund for cooperative projects. She is currently writing a dissertation about anarchist rural intentional communities and how they relate to colonization.

Sarah Amsler is a sociologist, critical theorist, and reader in education at the University of Lincoln (UK). She is also a member of the Social Science Centre, an autonomous higher education cooperative (http://socialsciencecentre. org.uk). Her work involves the politics of knowledge, education, political economy, and cultural practice. She uses critical theory and research to understand how these shape the formation of individual and collective subjectivities, the consolidation of and resistance to political-economic and cultural domination, and the material and symbolic organization of both everyday life and political possibility. Sarah is an editor and fellow at Heathwood and helps guide and review research in relation to the Critical Pedagogy and Alternative Education research cluster.

David Backer is an assistant professor in the College of Education and Social Work at West Chester University. He is an activist, writer, and researcher interested in the relationship between politics, economy, and education. Trained in social and political philosophy but working in multiple disciplines such as sociology, history, and literature, he focuses on the ways schools determine and are determined by social structures. Backer's first project focused on the relationship between classroom discussion and political economy, drawing a connection between closed patterns of interaction like recitation and large-scale systems like neoliberalism. He is currently researching the politics, legality, and economics of cooperative schools that are owned and governed by students, teachers, parents, and other user-members.

Matthew Bissen is an architect who is currently working to complete his PhD in earth and environmental science at the Graduate Center, CUNY. His research focuses on urban social and environmental activism. He is also a part-time faculty member at Parsons the New School for Design, teaching courses focused on the design of space in relationship to social, environmental, and learning dynamics.

Erin Dyke is an assistant professor of curriculum studies in the School for Teaching and Curriculum Leadership at Oklahoma State University. Her research focuses on pedagogies of social movement spaces; social justice, abolitionist, and decolonial movements in education; and gender/sexuality and education.

John M. Elmore is professor and chairperson in the Department of Professional & Secondary Education at West Chester University in Pennsylvania, where he teaches courses in critical pedagogy, politics of education, history of education, and philosophy of education. His research and publications have focused primarily on education for social justice, democracy, atheism, and anti-authoritarianism.

Rhiannon Firth completed her PhD research in the Department of Politics and International Relations at the University of Nottingham, published as *Utopian Politics: Citizenship and Practice* (Routledge, 2011). Her research interests include utopian political theory, prefigurative spatial politics, alternative epistemologies, autonomous communities, pedagogy, and consensus decision-making. She is involved in grassroots politics, DIY culture, and radical education groups. She is currently postdoctoral research fellow with the Cass School of Education and Communities at the University of East London.

David Gabbard is a professor in the Department of Curriculum, Instruction, and Foundational Studies at Boise State University in Idaho. His current work revolves around the development of a philosophy of collective learning that he hopes will displace the philosophy of education.

Robert H. Haworth is an assistant professor in the Department of Professional and Secondary Education at West Chester University, Pennsylvania. He teaches courses focusing on the social foundations of education and critical action research. He has published and presented internationally on anarchism, youth culture, informal learning spaces, and critical social studies education. Robert is the editor of *Anarchist Pedagogies: Collective Actions, Theories, and Critical Reflections on Education*, published by PM Press. Additionally, the music of Haworth's band Second Letter has been released through Lowatt Recordings.

Petar Jandrić is tenured senior lecturer in e-Learning at the Polytechnic of Zagreb and visiting associate professor at the University of Zagreb, Faculty of Humanities and Social Science. His research interests focus on the intersections between critical pedagogy and information and communication technologies. His chosen research methodologies are inter-, trans-, and anti-disciplinarity. Petar's previous academic affiliations include the Croatian Academic and Research Network, the National e-Science Centre at the University of Edinburgh, the Glasgow School of Art, and the Cass School of Education at the University of East London. He writes, edits, and reviews books, articles, course modules, and study guides, serves in editorial boards of scholarly journals and conferences, participates in diverse projects in Croatia and in the United Kingdom, regularly publishes popular science, and talks in front of diverse audiences.

Sandra Jeppesen is an activist, researcher, and educator. She researches autonomous media and anti-authoritarian social movements from a queer, trans, feminist, anti-racist, anti-capitalist, and anti-colonial perspective. A member of the former Collectif de Recherche sur l'Autonomie Collective (CRAC), she is co-founder of the Media Action Research Group (MARG, media-actionresearch.org), and associate professor in interdisciplinary studies at Lakehead University Orillia, Canada.

Ana Kuzmanić is an associate professor in visual arts at the University of Split, School of Architecture. She graduated with distinction from the University of Edinburgh with a master of fine arts, which is a terminal degree in the field. She has over fifty solo and group exhibitions in Great Britain, Croatia, Italy, Egypt, the Netherlands, USA, Lithuania, and Slovenia. Based in the conceptual framework of transdisciplinarity, her artistic praxis is embodied through research and expression in various media at the fringes between reality and virtuality. She is a founding member of the international arts collective Eastern Surf. Her artwork is inherently collaborative, and her recent projects are focused to the relationships between human beings and information technologies.

Eli Meyerhoff is an instructor with the Program in Education at Duke University. He has a PhD in political science from the University of Minnesota.

His academic work intersects education politics, geography, environmental studies, and political theory. He is in the editorial collective for *Abolition: A Journal of Insurgent Politics*, an open access journal.

Andre Pusey completed his PhD in the School of Geography, University of Leeds. His research utilizes a form of "militant ethnography" through the co-founding of the Really Open University, and his thesis evaluates the way in which the activism of the group created new radical values that attempt an exodus from the university-machine. He has published on radical education activism, autonomous social centers and the commons. He is currently a senior lecturer at Leeds Beckett University.

Andrew Robinson is author of more than twenty articles on aspects of critical theory and everyday life. He is coauthor of *Power, Resistance and Conflict in the Contemporary World* and has previously written on Deleuze, Gramsci, Sartre, Žižek, Laclau, Spivak, and Virilio.

Farhang Rouhani, associate professor of geography at University of Mary Washington, holds a BA in geography and English literature from the University of California, Berkeley (1993) and a PhD in geography from the University of Arizona (2001). He is a cultural and political geographer who has researched and written about globalization, state formation, and new media politics in Iran; diasporic Iranian and Muslim queer politics; and anarchist theories and practices.

Jeff Shantz has extensive experience as an anarchist community organizer. His publications include numerous articles in movement publications including *Anarchy, Social Anarchism, Green Anarchy, Earth First! Journal, Northeastern Anarchist, Industrial Worker, Anarcho-Syndicalist Review, Onward, Arsenal*, and *Processed World*. In addition, he has published in such academic journals as *Feminist Review, Critical Sociology, Critique of Anthropology, Capital and Class, Feminist Media Studies*, and *Environmental Politics*. His book *Constructive Anarchy: Building Infrastructures of Resistance* is a groundbreaking analysis of contemporary anarchist movements. He received his PhD in sociology from York University in Toronto and is currently a professor at Kwantlen Polytechnic University in Vancouver, teaching courses on critical theory, elite deviance, community advocacy, and human rights.

Dana Williams is an anarchist-sociologist currently living and working in Northern California at Chico State University. Current teaching and research include social movements, social inequalities, and altruism, and recent scholarship has appeared in *Comparative Sociology, Critical Sociology*, and *Teaching*

Sociology. Williams is the co-author (with Jeffrey Shantz) of *Anarchy & Society: Reflections on Anarchist-Sociology* (Brill).

Jason Thomas Wozniak is a PhD candidate in philosophy and education at Teachers College, Columbia University. He is also a co-founder of the Latin American Philosophy of Education Society. In addition, Jason has worked on popular education projects in Brazil, Argentina, and the United States.

INDEX

"Passim" (literally "scattered") indicates intermittent discussion of a topic over a cluster of pages.

Abraham, Itty, 87
absolutism, 21, 23, 25, 26, 31, 32
abstract labor, 127, 128, 136
Academia Comunitaria, Twin Cities, 183–91 passim
"Active Routine Learners" (ARLs) (Golay), 41–42
Adbusters, 195–96
admissions policy. See college and university admissions policy
Adorno, Theodor, 21, 22, 23
adult learning, 7
affinity groups, 144, 167, 168, 237, 238
African Americans, 59, 76
Agamben, Giorgio, 59
Al-Abbood, Noor, 91, 101
Algeria, 90
alienation, overcoming of. See dis-alienation, 59–69
Allen, Pamela, 67
Altemeyer, Bob, 23–24
alternative colleges and universities, 174–94, 227, 229–31, 248–52 passim
Amabile, Teresa, 38
ambiguity, toleration of, 38, 40. See also fear of ambiguity and uncertainty

American Indians. See Native Americans
Anarchist Anthropology (ExCo course), 178
Anarchist Free Skool, Toronto, 250–55 passim, 259
Anarchist Free University (AFU), Toronto, 227, 229–31, 248–52 passim
anarchists and anarchism, 4, 9–10, 70, 74–85 passim, 139–72 passim, 245–47; book fairs, 143–44, 243–44n3; feminism, 240; free schools, 245–60; primitivists, 88; Social Science Centre and, 111–13 passim; teaching by modeling, 153–72; Twin Cities, 185, 186, 190. See also North American Anarchist Studies Network (NAASN)
anarchist spaces, 249–59 passim
anarcho-syndicalism, 156, 157
Anderson, Warwick, 96, 100
anger, 68, 69, 141, 247
anticipatory reason, 120
anti-hierarchical approaches, 75, 78–79
Arendt, Jonathan, 58
Armaline, William T., 78

Arnold, June, 67
Arnstine, Donald, 27-28
Au, Wayne, 5
authoritarianism and authoritarian
    personality, 20-28, 31, 32, 40
The Authoritarian Personality (Adorno,
    Frenkel-Brunswik, Levinson, and
    Sanford), 21
authority, 45, 47, 49, 154-58 passim,
    163, 166, 232, 235; "Active Routine
    Learners" and, 41; age and, 241;
    authoritarianism and, 20, 21, 32;
    Bakunin on, 172n9; classroom
    decentering of, 161, 169, 226, 232;
    disobeying, 107; fear of, 247;
    unquestioning acceptance of, 38,
    39, 246
autonomous social centers (UK). *See*
    social centers movement (UK)

Baird, Karen, 213, 222n18
Ball, Stephen J., 58
Baltimore activist conference, 2012. *See*
    Mobilizing and Organizing from
    Below Conference (MOBCONF),
    Baltimore, 2012
"banking model" (education), 19-20, 24,
    57, 157
Beauvoir, Simone de, 120
Benscoter, Diane, 26
Bhabha, Homi, 97
"big Other" (Lacan), 36-47 passim
bisexuals, gay men, lesbians, and
    transgender people. *See* LGBTQ
    people
Black, Marc, 65
black Americans. *See* African
    Americans
black bloc, 236-37
Blackwell, Adrian, 228-29
Bloch, Ernst, 107, 120-21; *Principle of
    Hope*, 117
Boehnke, David, 178, 179, 184
Bowles, Samuel, 3, 24
Brand, Russell, 49
Brazil, 214-15
Brecht, Bertolt: *Lasager*, 47
Brigham Young University-Idaho, 51
Britain. *See* United Kingdom

Brookfield, Stephen, 7

Canada, 139-52 passim, 225-39 passim,
    248-59 passim
Castree, Noel, 77
Catholic Worker, 158
change, resistance to, 40
Chatterton, Paul, 12
childcare, 181, 190
child development, 37, 60
China, 86
Choi, Sujin, 65
choice, illusion of. *See* free choice, illu-
    sion of
Chomsky, Noam, 19, 46
Choudry, Aziz, 6-7
classrooms, 76-80 passim, 107, 212, 213,
    226, 228; anarchist models, 157-68
    passim; reactions against, 136;
    seating, 228-29
class struggle, 253, 255
Clover, Darlene E., 12
Colectivo Situaciones, 240
college and university admissions
    policy, 174, 177
college and university clerical workers,
    175, 178, 179
college and university credit, 184, 185,
    186, 194n13, 213
college and university faculty salaries.
    See salaries, faculty
college and university rankings, 174
college and university "undercom-
    mons," 126
colleges and universities, alterna-
    tive. *See* alternative colleges and
    universities
colleges and universities, for-profit. *See*
    for-profit college and universities
colonization and colonialism, digital.
    See digital colonialism and
    postcolonialism
commands and commanding 22, 23
commodification of education and
    schooling, 93, 95, 96, 122, 126
Common Core Standards, 5
communications technologies, 86-104
community colleges, 144, 148

community partnership and community-based learning, 80, 81, 142, 180–81, 228

compulsory schooling, 3, 16, 47–52 passim, 58, 247

Concordia University (Montreal), 227–28

conformity and conformism, 7, 25, 27, 38, 39

Connolly, Billy, 49

consciousness development, 28–31

consciousness-raising (CR), 66–70

consensus decision-making, 153, 156, 160, 163, 166, 168, 238

"consultas," 237, 239, 240

cooperative reason, 119, 120

cooperatives, 113. See also higher education cooperatives

corporate control, 48

Coté, Mark, 12

course structure, anarchist models of, 153–69 passim

CrabGrass (software), 159, 168

Crack Capitalism (Holloway), 127–28

creativity, hostility toward, 38, 39, 40

credits. See college and university credit

criminal justice, 24

criminology, 150–51

"critical consciousness" (Freire), 31

Critical Criminology Working Group (CCWG), 139–52

critical pedagogy, 17, 58, 63, 75–80 passim, 87, 98, 106–7, 114

Crowther, Jim, 12

curricula, 4–9 passim, 172n15, 198; "core," 20; Nomadic University, 196; Social Science Centre, 113, 117; Space Project, 133; standardized, 4, 5, 8; vocational, 139

Dantley, Michael E., 59

Dawkins, Richard, 26

Dawson, V.L., 38

Day, Dorothy, 158

Day, Richard, 12

Dean, John, 25

debt, 133, 135, 221n9. See also student debt

decision-making, 109, 153, 159–60, 162, 229–30. See also consensus decision-making

De Cleyre, Voltairine, 4

decolonization, 59, 62, 65, 66, 87–101 passim, 240, 245

Deleuze, Gilles, 10, 11, 58, 64–65, 67, 129, 136; schizoanalysis, 56, 64

Del Gandio, Jason, 237

democracy, 25, 43, 44, 49, 108–22 passim. See also direct democracy

demonstrations as learning sites. See protests and demonstrations as learning sites

dependency, desire for, 22

De Peuter, Greig, 12

Derrida, Jacques, 212

Deschooling Society (Illich), 36, 46

despotism. See authoritarianism and authoritarian personality

Detroit Geographical Expedition and Institute (DGEI), 76

Dewey, John, 58, 110, 117

dictators and dictatorship, 18, 21

diffusion of innovations (Rogers), 94

digital colonialism and postcolonialism, 86–104

digital divide, 92

Dillehay, Ronald, 23

direct democracy, 156, 159–60, 167, 196, 197, 238, 239

dis-alienation, 59–69 passim

Discourses of Dissent (Concordia University course), 227–28

"dislocation pedagogy" (Godlewska), 80–81

"Disorientation Gathering," University of Minnesota, 185

distance education. See e-learning

dogma and dogmatism, 18, 21, 23, 25, 31, 129

doublespeak, 24

Duque de Caxias, Brazil, 214–15

During, Simon, 98

Dyke, Erin, 175, 176, 187, 192n4

Eccedi Sottrai Crea (ESC), Rome, Italy, 184, 194n13

ego, 62–65 passim, 70

egoism and egocentrism, 32, 61–62
e-learning, 94, 95
Engels, Friedrich, 17, 19
England, 106–25 passim
Engleman, Melissa, 41
"epistemologies of space," 231
Esteves, Ana Margarida, 116, 121
experiential learning, 154, 157, 236–37
Experimental College (ExCo), Oberlin
    College, 174
Experimental Community Education of
    the Twin Cities (ExCo), 174–94
experts and expertise, 189, 223, 235,
    239–41 passim

failure, 82–83, 174–82 passim, 186, 188
"fanatical consciousness" (Freire), 25,
    30, 32
Fanon, Frantz, 88–97 passim, 101
fascism, 21, 23
fear-driven education, 27
fear of ambiguity and uncertainty, 25,
    26, 27, 40
fear of freedom, 21, 24, 29
Feenberg, Andrew, 95
feminist consciousness-raising. See
    consciousness-raising (CR)
Ferguson, Kathy, 10
Ferrer, Francisco, 155, 228
Fifth Estate, 246
films, 131, 132, 251
first-name basis, student-teacher, 161
food services, on-campus, 151
Forer, Anne, 66
for-profit college and universities, 2
Foster, John Bellamy, 3–4
Fotopolous, Takis, 39
Foucault, Michel, 44, 58, 246, 247
Frankfurt School, 89
free choice, illusion of, 19, 47
freedom, fear of. See fear of freedom
free schools and "free skools," 8–10
    passim, 112, 130, 156, 228; anarchist,
    127, 185–86, 190–91, 194n21, 245–60;
    Twin Cities, 174–94
Free Trade Area of the Americas (FTAA)
    protest, Quebec City, 2001, 237, 239
Freire, Paulo, 28–32 passim, 58, 77, 89,
    99, 117, 120, 258; "banking model"

(education), 19–20, 24, 57, 157; "nec-
    rophilic" disposition, 22; Pedagogy
    of the Oppressed, 36, 89, 220n1;
    "radical love," 7; We Make the Road by
    Walking, 206
Frenkel-Brunswik, Else, 21
Fromm, Erich, 17, 21, 22, 29
Frymier, Jack R., 40

Gabbard, David, 35–36, 51; Silencing Ivan
    Illich, 45
gay men, lesbians, bisexuals, and
    transgender people. See LGBTQ
    people
G8 protests, 234, 237, 251–52
geography, 74–85 passim
Ghanimi, Ali, 122
Gintis, Herbert, 3, 24
Giroux, Henry, 2, 58
global North and global South. See
    North-South relations
Godlewska, Anne, 80–81
Godwin, William, 19, 155
Golay, Keith: Learning Patterns and
    Temperament Styles, 41
Goldman, Emma, 4–5, 10, 249
Goodman, Paul, 155
Google, 86
government funding: Canada, 149
grades and grading, 82–83, 160, 162, 165,
    166, 213
graduate student unionization, 175
Graeber, David, 5–6, 204, 210
Gramsci, Antonio, 18–19
Great Britain. See United Kingdom
The Great Transformation (Polanyi),
    42–43
G20 demonstration, Toronto, 2010,
    233–37 passim
Guattari, Félix, 10, 11, 129, 136; schizo-
    analysis, 56; Three Ecologies, 221n1

Hagen, Everett E., 40
Haiven, Max, 6
Hall, Budd L., 12
Halley, Pat, 246
Hamilton, Ontario, 251
Haraway, Donna, 88, 92
Harris, Sam, 25–26

Harvie, David, 133, 134
Haworth, Robert H., 1–2, 78
Hegel, G.W.F., 60
hegemony (Gramsci), 18–19
Heyman, Rich, 76
hierarchy-countering approaches. *See*
   anti-hierarchical approaches
higher education cooperatives, 108–22
   passim
Holloway, John, 10, 132, 136; *Crack
   Capitalism*, 127–28
Holst, John, 7
homosexuality, 226
hooks, bell: "radical openness," 7, 8–9
Horton, Myles: *We Make the Road by
   Walking*, 206
Horvath, Roland, 91
hospitality, 212
How to Read Lacan (Žižek), 45, 46
Humanetrics: Jung Typology Test, 41
humility, 78, 83
hunger strikes, 178
hybridity and hybridization, 88, 92, 97,
   98, 99

"idiots" and "morons" (Žižek). *See*
   "morons" and "idiots" (Žižek)
Illich, Ivan, 45, 155; *Deschooling Society*,
   36, 46; *Tools for Conviviality*, 89, 93
Illogik (rapper), 248–49
incarceration, 2, 24, 246
incentives and rewards, 41, 60, 82, 94
Indians, American. *See* Native
   Americans
individualism, 39, 40, 44–45, 118, 120,
   166, 167
indoctrination, 17–18, 24–25
information technologies, 86–104
infoshops, 250–51
innovations, diffusion of. *See* diffusion
   of innovations (Rogers)
international law, 93
International Monetary Fund (IMF)
   protest, Washington, DC, 2000,
   237–38
internet, 51, 90, 96
intolerance, 23, 26, 27
"ivory tower syndrome," 77, 81

jingoism. *See* patriotism and jingoism
job training, education as. *See* vocational education
Jung Typology Test (Humanetrics), 41

Katz, Michael, 3
Kellner, Douglas, 58
Kim, Kyung Hee, 39
Kinch, Megan, 248, 250–51, 258
Kirscht, John P., 23
Kitchens, John, 9, 77
Koch, Andrew M., 61, 63–64
Kohan, Walter O., 197
Kompridis, Nikolas, 111, 117, 118
Kropotkin, Peter, 77, 79, 113, 119–20, 159
Kwantlen Center for Anarchist Studies
   (KCAS), 143
Kwantlen First Nation, 146, 148
Kwantlen Polytechnic University (KPU),
   139–52 passim

labor, abstract. *See* abstract labor
labor market training. *See* vocational
   education
labor unions. *See* unions
Lacan, Jacques, 45; "big Other," 36–47
   passim
Landstreicher, Wolfi, 63
Langellier, Kristin M., 67
language and languages: "big Other"
   and, 36; digital colonialism, 86;
   Stirner view, 61; Surrey, 146; as
   Trojan horse (Lacan), 45, 46. *See also*
   Spanish language
Larson, Miriam, 177, 180
Lasager (Brecht), 47
Latif, Ashar, 227, 230
Latin@s, 175, 181, 183, 187, 190
Latour, Bruno, 193n6
Lavia, Jennifer, 95, 97
law, international. *See* international law
Law, John, 193n6
leafleting, 151
*Learning Patterns and Temperament
   Styles* (Golay), 41
lectures, 132, 133, 134, 157, 159
Leeds, UK, 126–38
Leeds International Film Festival (LIFF),
   131, 132

lesbians, gay men, bisexuals, and transgender people. *See* LGBT people
Less Than Nothing (Žižek), 35, 36
Levin, Carl, 197
Levinson, Daniel, 21
LGBT people, 226, 227
Linguard, Bob, 97
Lithuania Free University, 178
Los Angeles, 83
Luddites, "diehards," "laggards," etc., 94, 97

Macalester College, 174–80 passim, 186–87
Macedo, Donaldo, 90
MacKinnon, Catherine, 66, 69
"magical consciousness" (Freire), 25, 29–30
Makarenko, Anton, 18
Mann, Horace, 3
mapping projects, 76
marketization of society, 42–43. *See also* commodification of education and schooling
Martin, Brian, 155
Martin, Peter, 58
Marx, Karl, 17, 18, 60, 117
Marxists and Marxism, 50, 58, 98, 100, 113, 194n13, 246, 259
masochism, 22
mass media, 8, 16, 58, 235
maturation, 60, 63–64
Maurin, Peter, 158
McLaren, Peter, 98
Means, Alexander, 121
media, mass. *See* mass media
memes, 26
Merrett, Christopher D., 77
Mignolo, Walter, 176, 188
military, 2, 24, 35, 43, 155
Mill, John Stuart, 10
Minneapolis, 185–86, 190
Mobilizing and Organizing from Below Conference (MOBCONF), Baltimore, 2012, 232–33
"Model for Public Space" (Blackwell), 228–29
Modern School movement, 156

moral education and regulation, 57, 58, 247
moralism, 23, 58
"morons" and "idiots" (Žižek), 35, 36–38, 42, 50
Motta, Sara C., 116, 121
moulding (pedagogy), 20, 56–70 passim, 150
mutual aid, 10, 113, 119–20, 155, 205
Myers, R.E., 40

"naive consciousness" (Freire), 29, 30
Nash, Paul, 25
nationalism, 21, 48, 57, 246
A Nation at Risk, 5
nation-state, 39, 43–44, 155
Native Americans, 146, 148
networked learning. *See* e-learning
Newman, Saul, 65
New Space, Vancouver, 254, 256
New York City, 4, 10. *See also* Occupy Wall Street (OWS)
No Child Left Behind, 8
Noddings, Nel, 58
Nomadic University, 196–97, 203
nonviolence and violence. *See* violence and nonviolence
North American Anarchist Studies Network (NAASN), 143, 223–25 passim, 232, 235, 239, 240
North-South relations, 92

Oberlin College, 174
occupation of buildings, 194n13. *See also* squatted spaces
Occupy Free School, Toronto, 248–53 passim
Occupy movement, 19, 79, 112, 135, 147
Occupy Toronto, 250, 251, 252
Occupy University (OccU), 195, 196, 198, 217, 219, 222n18
Occupy Wall Street, 195–222 passim
O'Connor, Alan, 231
orders (commands). *See* commands and commanding
Orwellian conditions, 24, 47

Pain, Rachel, 81–83, 84

parental responsibility. *See* responsibility, parental

parenting, authoritarian, 21

passivity, 57, 159, 167, 247; in authoritarians, 22. *See also* submissiveness

patriarchy, 66–69 passim, 177, 190

patriotism and jingoism, 21, 24, 48, 57, 155

Pawlowski, Lucia, 179

Pedagogy of the Oppressed (Freire), 36, 89, 220n1

People's Guide to Los Angeles (PGTLA), 83

Persinger, Michael, 32

personal responsibility. *See* responsibility, personal

Polanyi, Karl: *Great Transformation*, 42–43

police, 21, 151, 163, 234–40 passim, 253; training of, 140, 150, 152

polytechnic universities: Canada, 139–52 passim

popular education, 106, 113–14, 116

pornography, 51

postcolonialism, 74, 75, 86–101 passim

The Principle of Hope (Bloch), 117

privatization, 2, 5, 126

property "modification" and destruction, 236–37, 238

protests and demonstrations as learning sites, 233–40

Proudhon, Pierre-Joseph, 31

public education, 3–5 passim, 20, 46–47

punishment, 23–24, 60, 94

punk movement, 1–2, 9, 249–50

Purchase College. *See* State University of New York at Purchase

quantification of learning, 4–5

Quebec City anti-FTAA protest. *See* Free Trade Area of the Americas (FTAA) protest, Quebec City, 2001

Queer Theory (York University course), 225–28 passim

racism, 21, 59, 78–79

Radical Criminology, 142–43

Rancière, Jacques, 212

Rancourt, Denis, 172n16

Randolph, Bonnie Moore, 68

Ravitch, Diane, 5

Really Open University (ROU), Leeds, UK, 127–37 passim

reason, cooperative. *See* cooperative reason

Recknagel, Callie, 177–78

Reger, Jo, 68–69

religion, 24, 25, 26

resistance to colonization, 97–100

responsibility, parental, 58

responsibility, personal, 22, 39, 41, 94, 156, 157

rewards. *See* incentives and rewards

right-wing authoritarianism (RWA), 23–24

Rizvi, Fazal, 97

Rogers, Everett, 94

Romanish, Bruce, 24, 26–27

Rome, Italy, 184, 194n13

Rorty, Richard, 58

Ross-Valiere, Clydene, 68

Rostock, Germany, G8 protest, 2007, 234–35

routine learners. *See* "Active Routine Learners" (ARLs) (Golay), 41–42

Rush, Benjamin, 48–49

salaries, faculty, 149, 228

Sanford, R. Nevitt, 21

Santos, Boaventura de Sousa, 107, 110, 116, 118, 121–22

Saunders, Gary, 122

Scandrett, Eurig, 12

schizoanalysis (Deleuze and Guattari), 56, 64

school and state, 46–50 passim

school boards, 48

schools, free. *See* free schools and "free skools"

schools, pastoral imaginary order of, 45–52 passim

seating arrangements, 156, 162, 228–29, 232

sectarianism, 26, 31, 32, 144

self-actualization, 60–66 passim

self-grading, 165

self-management, 127–32 passim, 136, 154, 155

self-transformation, 59, 62, 63, 68
self-valorization, 56, 61, 65, 67, 258
service learning, 153, 158, 180, 184
Seth, Suman, 87
sexism, 67, 69
sex workers, 225, 236–37
Shor, Ira, 11, 162
Shout Back! Festival, Vancouver, 252
"Siberia Effect" (classroom seating), 162
Silencing Ivan Illich (Gabbard), 45
Simola, Hannu, 57
skill sharing, 9, 145, 155, 241, 243, 251
Smith, Adam, 3, 7–8
social centers movement (UK), 111–12,
    127, 130, 131
socialization, 16, 28, 48, 57, 58, 166, 248
Social Science Centre, Lincoln, UK,
    108–22 passim, 135
sociology, 113, 150–54 passim, 168, 169
Sociology of Anarchism (college
    course), 153–72
Sodexo, 151
Southall, Aidan, 92
South-North relations. *See* North-South
    relations
South Side Free Skool (SSFS),
    Minneapolis, 186, 190
Soviet Union, 18
space, epistemologies of. *See* "episte-
    mologies of space"
Space Project, Leeds, UK, 126–38
spaces, anarchist. *See* anarchist spaces
spaces, squatted. *See* squatted spaces
Spanish language, 175, 181, 190, 191
"special purpose teaching universities"
    (Canada), 148–49
spokescouncils, 234, 237–38
Spring, Joel, 3, 57
Springer, Simon, 79
squatted spaces, 127, 131, 257
Stacey, Kalin, 257
Stalinism, 18, 22
Stallman, Richard, 88, 89
standardization, 4, 5, 8, 20, 24, 77, 80, 83
Starr, Amory, 237–38
state, 43–50 passim, 62
State University of New York at
    Purchase, 213, 222n18
Stirner, Max, 19, 30, 56–70 passim

strikes, 132, 175, 178, 179
student debt, 2, 126, 196
student fees and tuition, 126, 129, 228
student involvement in course design,
    153–69 passim
student self-grading. *See* self-grading
student syndicalism, 156, 157
study groups, 131, 155
Stovall, David, 2
submissiveness and submission, 21,
    22–23, 24, 27, 39, 247
Suissa, Judith, 9–10
SUNY Purchase. *See* State University of
    New York at Purchase
Surrey, British Columbia, 139–52 passim
surveillance, 93, 247, 248
syllabi, 160, 166
syndicalism, student. *See* student
    syndicalism

Taylor, Joseph S., 4
"teaching universities" (Canada). *See*
    "special purpose teaching universi-
    ties" (Canada)
teach-ins, 142, 155, 232
techno-education, 97–101
technology, 92; acceptance curve, 94.
    See also digital colonialism and
    postcolonialism
Teixeira, Rob, 229
tests and testing, 5, 8, 20
Thorne, Niki, 249
Three Ecologies (Guattari), 221n1
Tolstoy College, 156
Tools for Conviviality (Illich), 89, 93
Toronto, 225–37 passim, 248–55 passim,
    259
Toronto Anarchist Bookfair, 243–44n3
Toronto Community Mobilization
    Network (TCMN), 234–35
Toronto Free School (ca. 2010–11),
    251–52
totalitarianism, 20, 24, 25, 26
transgender people, gay men, lesbians,
    and bisexuals. *See* LGBT people
truth, 29, 32, 36
typology, 41

uncertainty, toleration of, 38, 40.
    See also fear of ambiguity and
    uncertainty
unions, 175
United Kingdom, 106–38 passim
universities, for-profit. *See* for-profit
    college and universities
universities, polytechnic. *See* polytech-
    nic universities
universities and colleges, alterna-
    tive. *See* alternative colleges and
    universities
University Act (Canada), 149
university admissions. *See* college and
    university admissions policy
university clerical workers. *See* college
    and university clerical workers
university credit. *See* college and uni-
    versity credit
university faculty salaries. *See* salaries,
    faculty
University of Leeds, 129, 132
University of Minnesota (U of M),
    175–80 passim, 184–91
University of Phoenix, 2
University of Southern California, 83
university rankings. *See* college and
    university rankings
university "undercommons."
    See college and university
    "undercommons"
Uprising Books, Toronto, 230, 249, 250
Urick, Ronald, 40
user interfaces, 93
US News and World Report, 174
USSR. *See* Soviet Union
utopia, 9, 10, 88, 89, 120, 166, 175; dualis-
    tic views, 95, 97

Vancouver, British Columbia, 142, 251,
    254, 258, 259
Vandenberghe, Frédéric, 7
violence and nonviolence, 238, 239
vocational education, 139, 140, 148–52
    passim, 247
voting, Russell Brand view of, 49

We Make the Road by Walking (Horton
    and Freire), 206

Westby, Erik, 38
Who's Emma? (infoshop), 250
Wittkower, D.E., 92–93
women's consciousness-raising. *See*
    consciousness-raising (CR)
workplace learning, 6–7
workshops, 117, 225, 238, 241, 243–44n3,
    250; feminist, 113; MOBCONF, 232,
    233, 235; NAASN, 223–24, 240; peda-
    gogical, 195, 197–98; ROU, 129, 133
World Social Forum, 110, 116

York University, 225–27

"zero generation," 2
Zhao, Yong, 20
zines, 2, 178
Žižek, Slavoj, 50; *How to Read Lacan*, 45,
    46; *Less Than Nothing*, 35, 36

ABOUT PM PRESS

PM Press was founded at the end of 2007 by a small
collection of folks with decades of publishing, media, and
organizing experience. PM Press co-conspirators have
published and distributed hundreds of books, pamphlets,
CDs, and DVDs. Members of PM have founded enduring
book fairs, spearheaded victorious tenant organizing campaigns, and worked
closely with bookstores, academic conferences, and even rock bands to deliver
political and challenging ideas to all walks of life. We're old enough to know what
we're doing and young enough to know what's at stake.

We seek to create radical and stimulating fiction and non-fiction books, pamphlets,
T-shirts, visual and audio materials to entertain, educate, and inspire you. We
aim to distribute these through every available channel with every available
technology—whether that means you are seeing anarchist classics at our bookfair
stalls, reading our latest vegan cookbook at the café, downloading geeky fiction
e-books, or digging new music and timely videos from our website.

PM Press is always on the lookout for talented and skilled volunteers, artists,
activists, and writers to work with. If you have a great idea for a project or can
contribute in some way, please get in touch.

PM Press
PO Box 23912
Oakland, CA 94623
www.pmpress.org

FRIENDS OF PM PRESS

These are indisputably momentous times—the financial system is melting down globally and the Empire is stumbling. Now more than ever there is a vital need for radical ideas.

In the years since its founding—and on a mere shoestring—PM Press has risen to the formidable challenge of publishing and distributing knowledge and entertainment for the struggles ahead. With over 300 releases to date, we have published an impressive and stimulating array of literature, art, music, politics, and culture. Using every available medium, we've succeeded in connecting those hungry for ideas and information to those putting them into practice.

Friends of PM allows you to directly help impact, amplify, and revitalize the discourse and actions of radical writers, filmmakers, and artists. It provides us with a stable foundation from which we can build upon our early successes and provides a much-needed subsidy for the materials that can't necessarily pay their own way. You can help make that happen—and receive every new title automatically delivered to your door once a month—by joining as a Friend of PM Press. And, we'll throw in a free T-shirt when you sign up.

Here are your options:

- **$30 a month** Get all books and pamphlets plus 50% discount on all webstore purchases

- **$40 a month** Get all PM Press releases (including CDs and DVDs) plus 50% discount on all webstore purchases

- **$100 a month** Superstar—Everything plus PM merchandise, free downloads, and 50% discount on all webstore purchases

For those who can't afford $30 or more a month, we have **Sustainer Rates** at $15, $10 and $5. Sustainers get a free PM Press T-shirt and a 50% discount on all purchases from our website.

Your Visa or Mastercard will be billed once a month, until you tell us to stop. Or until our efforts succeed in bringing the revolution around. Or the financial meltdown of Capital makes plastic redundant. Whichever comes first.

Anarchist Pedagogies: Collective Actions, Theories, and Critical Reflections on Education

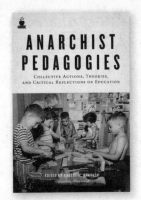

Edited by Robert H. Haworth
with an afterword by Allan Antliff

ISBN: 978-1-60486-484-7
$24.95   352 pages

Education is a challenging subject for anarchists.
Many are critical about working within a state-run
education system that is embedded in hierarchical, standardized, and authoritarian
structures. Numerous individuals and collectives envision the creation of
counterpublics or alternative educational sites as possible forms of resistance,
while other anarchists see themselves as "saboteurs" within the public arena—
believing that there is a need to contest dominant forms of power and educational
practices from multiple fronts. Of course, if anarchists agree that there are no
blueprints for education, the question remains, in what dynamic and creative
ways can we construct nonhierarchical, anti-authoritarian, mutual, and voluntary
educational spaces?

Contributors to this edited volume engage readers in important and challenging
issues in the area of anarchism and education. From Francisco Ferrer's modern
schools in Spain and the Work People's College in the United States, to
contemporary actions in developing "free skools" in the U.K. and Canada, to
direct-action education such as learning to work as a "street medic" in the
protests against neoliberalism, the contributors illustrate the importance of
developing complex connections between educational theories and collective
actions. Anarchists, activists, and critical educators should take these educational
experiences seriously as they offer invaluable examples for potential teaching and
learning environments outside of authoritarian and capitalist structures. Major
themes in the volume include: learning from historical anarchist experiments
in education, ways that contemporary anarchists create dynamic and situated
learning spaces, and finally, critically reflecting on theoretical frameworks and
educational practices. Contributors include: David Gabbard, Jeffery Shantz,
Isabelle Fremeaux & John Jordan, Abraham P. DeLeon, Elsa Noterman, Andre
Pusey, Matthew Weinstein, Alex Khasnabish, and many others.

"*Pedagogy is a central concern in anarchist writing and the free skool has played
a central part in movement activism. By bringing together an important group of
writers with specialist knowledge and experience, Robert Haworth's volume makes an
invaluable contribution to the discussion of these topics. His exciting collection provides
a guide to historical experiences and current experiments and also reflects on anarchist
theory, extending our understanding and appreciation of pedagogy in anarchist
practice.*"
—Dr. Ruth Kinna, Senior Lecturer in Politics, Loughborough University, author of
Anarchism: A Beginners Guide and coeditor of *Anarchism and Utopianism*

Anarchism and Education: A Philosophical Perspective

Judith Suissa

ISBN: 978-1-60486-114-3
$19.95   184 pages

While there have been historical accounts of the anarchist school movement, there has been no systematic work on the philosophical underpinnings of anarchist educational ideas—until now.

Anarchism and Education offers a philosophical account of the neglected tradition of anarchist thought on education. Although few anarchist thinkers wrote systematically on education, this analysis is based largely on a reconstruction of the educational thought of anarchist thinkers gleaned from their various ethical, philosophical, and popular writings. Primarily drawing on the work of the nineteenth-century anarchist theorists such as Bakunin, Kropotkin, and Proudhon, the book also covers twentieth-century anarchist thinkers such as Noam Chomsky, Paul Goodman, Daniel Guérin, and Colin Ward.

This original work will interest philosophers of education and educationalist thinkers as well as those with a general interest in anarchism.

"This is an excellent book that deals with important issues through the lens of anarchist theories and practices of education… The book tackles a number of issues that are relevant to anybody who is trying to come to terms with the philosophy of education."
—*Higher Education Review*

The Paul Goodman Reader

Edited by Taylor Stoehr

ISBN: 978-1-60486-058-0
$28.95   500 pages

A one-man think-tank for the New Left, Paul Goodman wrote over thirty books, most of them before his decade of fame as a social critic in the Sixties. A Paul Goodman Reader that does him justice must be a compendious volume, with excerpts not only from best-sellers like *Growing Up Absurd*, but also from his landmark books on education, community planning, anarchism, psychotherapy, language theory, and poetics. Samples as well from *The Empire City*, a comic novel reviewers compared to *Don Quixote*, prize-winning short stories, and scores of poems that led America's most respected poetry reviewer, Hayden Carruth, to exclaim, "Not one dull page. It's almost unbelievable."

Goodman called himself as an old-fashioned man of letters, which meant that all these various disciplines and occasions added up to a single abiding concern for the human plight in perilous times, and for human promise and achieved grandeur, love and hope.

"It was that voice of his that seduced me—that direct, cranky, egotistical, generous American voice… Paul Goodman's voice touched everything he wrote about with intensity, interest, and his own terribly appealing sureness and awkwardness… It was his voice, that is to say, his intelligence and the poetry of his intelligence incarnated, which kept me a loyal and passionate fan."
—Susan Sontag, novelist and public intellectual

"Goodman, like all real novelists, is, at bottom, a moralist. What really interests him are the various ways in which human beings living in a modern metropolis gain, keep or lose their integrity and sense of selfhood."
—W. H. Auden, poet

"Any page by Paul Goodman will give you not only originality and brilliance but wisdom, that is, something to think about. He is our peculiar, urban, twentieth-century Thoreau, the quintessential American mind of our time."
— Hayden Carruth, poet and essayist

"No one writing now in America makes better sense of literary subjects. His ability to combine linguistic criticism, politics, a version of the nature of man, anthropology, the history of philosophy, and autobiographical testament with literary analysis, and to make a closely woven fabric of argument, seems magical."
—Robert Meredith, *The Nation*

Romantic Rationalist: A William Godwin Reader

Edited by Peter Marshall
with a Foreword by John P. Clark

ISBN: 978-1-62963-228-5
$17.95   192 pages

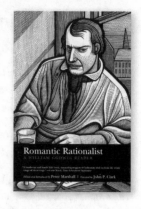

William Godwin (1756–1836) was one of the first exponents of utilitarianism and the first modern proponent of anarchism. He was not only a radical philosopher but a pioneer in libertarian education, a founder of communist economics, and an acute and powerful novelist whose literary family included his partner, pioneering feminist writer Mary Wollstonecraft, and his daughter Mary Godwin (later Mary Shelley), who would go on to write *Frankenstein* and marry the poet Percy Bysshe Shelley.

His long life straddled two centuries. Not only did he live at the center of radical and intellectual London during the French Revolution, he also commented on some of the most significant changes in modern history. Shaped by the Enlightenment, he became a key figure in English Romanticism.

This work offers for the first time a handy collection of Godwin's key writings in a clear and concise form, together with an assessment of his influence, a biographical sketch, and an analysis of his contribution to anarchist theory and practice. The selections are taken from all of Godwin's writings including his groundbreaking work during the French Revolution, *An Enquiry Concerning Political Justice*, and arranged by editor Peter Marshall to give a coherent account of his thought for the general reader.

Godwin's work will be of interest to all those who believe that rationality, truth, happiness, individuality, equality, and freedom are central concerns of human enquiry and endeavor.

"Peter Marshall has produced the most useful modern account of Godwin's life and now the most useful modern anthology of his writings. Marshall's selection is sensible and valuable, bringing out the important points. . . . His introduction is a good summary of Godwin's life and work. . . . Marshall is right to see him as 'the most profound exponent of philosophical anarchism.'"
—Nicolas Walter, *New Statesman*

"A handsome and handy little book, excavating nuggets of Godwinian wisdom from the whole range of his writings."
—Colin Ward, *Times Educational Supplement*

William Godwin: Philosopher, Novelist, Revolutionary

Peter Marshall
with a Foreword by John P. Clark

ISBN: 978-1-62963-386-2
$29.95   544 pages

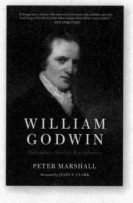

William Godwin has long been known for his literary connections as the husband of Mary Wollstonecraft, the father of Mary Shelley, the friend of Coleridge, Lamb, and Hazlitt, the mentor of the young Wordsworth, Southey, and Shelley, and the opponent of Malthus. Godwin has been recently recognized, however, as the most capable exponent of philosophical anarchism, an original moral thinker, a pioneer in socialist economics and progressive education, and a novelist of great skill.

His long life straddled two centuries. Not only did he live at the center of radical and intellectual London during the French Revolution, he also commented on some of the most significant changes in British history. Shaped by the Enlightenment, he became a key figure in English Romanticism.

Basing his work on extensive published and unpublished materials, Peter Marshall has written a comprehensive study of this flamboyant and fascinating figure. Marshall places Godwin firmly in his social, political, and historical context; he traces chronologically the origin and development of Godwin's ideas and themes; and he offers a critical estimate of his works, recognizing the equal value of his philosophy and literature and their mutual illumination.

The picture of Godwin that emerges is one of a complex man and a subtle and revolutionary thinker, one whose influence was far greater than is usually assumed. In the final analysis, Godwin stands forth not only as a rare example of a man who excelled in both philosophy and literature but as one of the great humanists in the Western tradition.

"The most comprehensive and richly detailed work yet to appear on Godwin as thinker, writer, and person."
—John P. Clark, *The Tragedy of Common Sense*

"An ambitious study that offers a thorough exploration of Godwin's life and complex times."
—*Library Journal*

"Marshall steers his course . . . with unfailing sensitivity and skill. It is hard to see how the task could have been better done."
—Michael Foot, *The Observer*

Breaking the Spell: A History of Anarchist Filmmakers, Videotape Guerrillas, and Digital Ninjas

Chris Robé

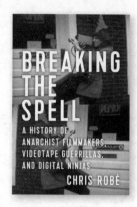

ISBN: 978-1-62963-233-9
$26.95   480 pages

Breaking the Spell offers the first full-length study that charts the historical trajectory of anarchist-inflected video activism from the late 1960s to the present. Two predominant trends emerge from this social movement-based video activism: 1) anarchist-inflected processes increasingly structure its production, distribution, and exhibition practices; and 2) video does not simply represent collective actions and events, but also serves as a form of activist practice in and of itself from the moment of recording to its later distribution and exhibition. Video plays an increasingly important role among activists in the growing global resistance against neoliberal capitalism. As various radical theorists have pointed out, subjectivity itself becomes a key terrain of struggle as capitalism increasingly structures and mines it through social media sites, cell phone technology, and new "flexible" work and living patterns. As a result, alternative media production becomes a central location where new collective forms of subjectivity can be created to challenge aspects of neoliberalism.

Chris Robé's book fills in historical gaps by bringing to light unexplored video activist groups like the Cascadia Forest Defenders, eco-video activists from Eugene, Oregon; Mobile Voices, Latino day laborers harnessing cell phone technology to combat racism and police harassment in Los Angeles; and Outta Your Backpack Media, indigenous youth from the Southwest who use video to celebrate their culture and fight against marginalization. This groundbreaking study also deepens our understanding of more well-researched movements like AIDS video activism, Paper Tiger Television, and Indymedia by situating them within a longer history and wider context of radical video activism.

"*Christopher Robé's meticulously researched* Breaking the Spell *traces the roots of contemporary, anarchist-inflected video and Internet activism and clearly demonstrates the affinities between the anti-authoritarian ethos and aesthetic of collectives from the '60s and '70s—such as Newsreel and the Videofreex—and their contemporary descendants. Robé's nuanced perspective enables him to both celebrate and critique anarchist forays into guerrilla media.* Breaking the Spell *is an invaluable guide to the contemporary anarchist media landscape that will prove useful for activists as well as scholars.*"
—Richard Porton, author of *Film and the Anarchist Imagination*

Revolutionary Mothering: Love on the Front Lines

Edited by Alexis Pauline Gumbs, China Martens, and Mai'a Williams with a preface by Loretta J. Ross

ISBN: 978-1-62963-110-3
$17.95   272 pages

Inspired by the legacy of radical and queer black feminists of the 1970s and '80s, *Revolutionary Mothering* places marginalized mothers of color at the center of a world of necessary transformation. The challenges we face as movements working for racial, economic, reproductive, gender, and food justice, as well as anti-violence, anti-imperialist, and queer liberation are the same challenges that many mothers face every day. Oppressed mothers create a generous space for life in the face of life-threatening limits, activate a powerful vision of the future while navigating tangible concerns in the present, move beyond individual narratives of choice toward collective solutions, live for more than ourselves, and remain accountable to a future that we cannot always see. *Revolutionary Mothering* is a movement-shifting anthology committed to birthing new worlds, full of faith and hope for what we can raise up together.

Contributors include June Jordan, Malkia A. Cyril, Esteli Juarez, Cynthia Dewi Oka, Fabiola Sandoval, Sumayyah Talibah, Victoria Law, Tara Villalba, Lola Mondragón, Christy NaMee Eriksen, Norma Angelica Marrun, Vivian Chin, Rachel Broadwater, Autumn Brown, Layne Russell, Noemi Martinez, Katie Kaput, alba onofrio, Gabriela Sandoval, Cheryl Boyce Taylor, Ariel Gore, Claire Barrera, Lisa Factora-Borchers, Fabielle Georges, H. Bindy K. Kang, Terri Nilliasca, Irene Lara, Panquetzani, Mamas of Color Rising, tk karakashian tunchez, Arielle Julia Brown, Lindsey Campbell, Micaela Cadena, and Karen Su.

"This collection is a treat for anyone that sees class and that needs to learn more about the experiences of women of color (and who doesn't?!). There is no dogma here, just fresh ideas and women of color taking on capitalism, anti-racist, anti-sexist theory-building that is rooted in the most primal of human connections, the making of two people from the body of one: mothering."
—Barbara Jensen, author of *Reading Classes: On Culture and Classism in America*

"For women of color, mothering—the art of mothering—has been framed by the most virulent systems, historically: enslavement, colonialism, capitalism, imperialism. We have had few opportunities to define mothering not only as an aspect of individual lives and choices, but as the processes of love and as a way of structuring community. *Revolutionary Mothering* arrives as a needed balm."
—Alexis De Veaux, author of *Warrior Poet: A Biography of Audre Lorde*

Rad Families: A Celebration

Edited by Tomas Moniz
with a Foreword by Ariel Gore

ISBN: 978-1-62963-230-8
$19.95   296 pages

Rad Families: A Celebration honors the messy, the painful,
the playful, the beautiful, the myriad ways we create
families. This is not an anthology of experts, or how-to
articles on perfect parenting; it often doesn't even try to
provide answers. Instead, the writers strive to be honest
and vulnerable in sharing their stories and experiences, their failures and their
regrets.

Gathering parents and writers from diverse communities, it explores the process
of getting pregnant from trans birth to adoption, grapples with issues of racism
and police brutality, probes raising feminists and feminist parenting. It plumbs the
depths of empty nesting and letting go.

Some contributors are recognizable authors and activists but most are everyday
parents working and loving and trying to build a better world one diaper change
at a time. It's a book that reminds us all that we are not alone, that community
can help us get through the difficulties, can, in fact, make us better people. It's a
celebration, join us!

Contributors include Jonas Cannon, Ian MacKaye, Burke Stansbury, Danny Goot,
Simon Knaphus, Artnoose, Welch Canavan, Daniel Muro LaMere, Jennifer Lewis,
Zach Ellis, Alicia Dornadic, Jesse Palmer, Mindi J., Carla Bergman, Tasnim Nathoo,
Rachel Galindo, Robert Liu-Trujillo, Dawn Caprice, Shawn Taylor, D.A. Begay,
Philana Dollin, Airial Clark, Allison Wolfe, Roger Porter, cubbie rowland-storm,
Annakai & Rob Geshlider, Jeremy Adam Smith, Frances Hardinge, Jonathan Shipley,
Bronwyn Davies Glover, Amy Abugo Ongiri, Mike Araujo, Craig Elliott, Eleanor
Wohlfeiler, Scott Hoshida, Plinio Hernandez, Madison Young, Nathan Torp, Sasha
Vodnik, Jessie Susannah, Krista Lee Hanson, Carvell Wallace, Dani Burlison, Brian
Whitman, scott winn, Kermit Playfoot, Chris Crass, and Zora Moniz.

"*Rad dads, rad families, rad children. These stories show us that we are not alone. That
we don't have all the answers. That we are all learning.*"
—Nikki McClure, illustrator, author, parent

"Rad Families *is the collection for all families.*"
—Innosanto Nagara, author/illustrator of *A Is for Activist*

"*This collection takes the anaesthetized myth of parenting and reminds us what intimacy
looks like. . . . The contributors describe the contours of family in a way that resonates.*"
—Virgie Tovar, editor of *Hot & Heavy: Fierce Fat Girls on Life, Love & Fashion*